EARLY CHRISTIANITY
AND
HELLENISTIC JUDAISM

EARLY CHRISTIANITY
AND
HELLENISTIC JUDAISM

Peder Borgen

T&T CLARK
EDINBURGH

T&T CLARK LTD
59 GEORGE STREET
EDINBURGH EH2 2LQ
SCOTLAND

First published 1996

ISBN 0 567 08501 5

British Library Cataloguing-in-Publication Data
A catalogue record for this book is available from the British Library

Printed in Great Britain by Page Bros, Norwich
Bound in Great Britain by Hunter & Foulis, Edinburgh

To my wife Inger

Contents

Preface

As the title suggests, the studies in this volume arose from a concern to understand better the interrelationship of Early Christianity and Judaism and the interaction between both and the wider Graeco-Roman world.

The following essays have previously been published:

"Catalogues of Vices, the Apostolic Decree, and the Jerusalem Meeting." Reprinted by permission from *The Social World of Formative Christianity and Judaism*, 126–41, edited by J. Neusner, P. Borgen, E. S. Frerichs, and R. Horsley, copyright 1988 Fortress Press, Philadelphia.

"John and the Synoptics." Reprinted by permission from *The Interrelations of the Gospels*, BETL XCV, 408–37, edited by D. L. Dungan, copyright 1990 Peeters Publishers, Leuven.

"John and the Synoptics. Response to P. Borgen," by F. Neirynck. Reprinted by permission from *The Interrelations of the Gospels*, BETL XCV, 438–50, edited by D. L. Dungan, copyright 1990 Peeters Publishers, Leuven.

"John and the Synoptics. A Reply," by P. Borgen. Reprinted by permission from *The Interrelations of the Gospels*, BETL XCV, 451–58, edited by D. L. Dungan, copyright 1990 Peeters Publishers, Leuven.

"The Sabbath Controversy in John 5:1–18 and Analogous Controversy Reflected in Philo's Writings." Reprinted by permission from *Heirs of the Septuagint. The Studia Philonica Annual*, BJS 230, 209–21, edited by D. Runia et alii, copyright 1991 Scholars Press, Atlanta.

"Judaism in Egypt." Reprinted by permission from *The Anchor Bible Dictionary*, 3, 1061–72, edited by D. N. Freedman, copyright 1992 Doubleday, a division of Bantam Doubleday Dell Publishing Group, Inc., New York.

"The Independence of the Gospel of John. Some Observations." Reprinted by permission from *The Four Gospels*, BETL C, 1815–34, edited by F. Van Segbroeck et alii, copyright 1992 Peeters Publishers, Leuven.

"John 6: Tradition, Interpretation and Composition." Reprinted by permission from *From Jesus to John*, 268–91, edited by M. C. de Boer, copyright 1993 Sheffield Academic Press, Sheffield.

"Polemic in the Book of Revelation." Reprinted by permission from *Anti-Semitism and Early Christianity*, 199–211, edited by C. A. Evans and D. A. Hagner, copyright 1993 Augsburg Fortress, Minneapolis.

"Jesus Christ, the Reception of the Spirit and a Cross-National Community." Reprinted by permission from *Jesus of Nazareth, Lord and Christ*, 220–36, edited by J. B. Green and M. Turner, copyright 1994 Wm. B. Eerdmans Publishing Co., Grand Rapids.

""Yes", "No", "How Far"?: The Participation of Jews and Christians in Pagan Cults." Reprinted by permission from *Paul in his Hellenistic Context*, 30–59, edited by T. Engberg-Pedersen, copyright 1994 T.&T. Clark, Edinburgh.

The remaining essays are published in this volume for the first time.

Biblical quotations in English are taken from *The Holy Bible Containing the Old and New Testament*, Revised Standard Version (New York: Nelson & Sons, 1952), and quotations in English from Philo's writings are taken from *Philo with an English Translation* by F. H. Colson,

1–10, Loeb Classical Library (Cambridge, Mass.: Harvard University Press, 1929–62), and from *Philo, Supplements*, 1–2, translated from Ancient Armenian Version of the Original Greek by R. Marcus, Loeb Classical Library (Cambridge, Mass.: Harvard University Press, 1953).

In some cases modifications of these translations have been made on the basis of the Greek text.

The preparation of this book was made possible thanks to a grant from The Norwegian Research Council. The Norwegian Research Council, the Joint Committee of the Nordic Research Councils for the Humanities (NOS-H), and the University of Trondheim with its Department of Religious Studies have over the years given me support and encouragement in my research. The civil engineer Olaf Torske has skilfully assisted me with his expert knowledge of computer science.

Trondheim, January 1996

Peder Borgen

Introduction

As can be seen from the table of contents, the essays have been organized in such a way that the first section contains rather general studies on Judaism and Early Christianity, on attitudes to participation in pagan cults, to militant and peaceful proselytism, and to the history of the Jews of Egypt. In the next section studies on the Gospel of John have been collected, such as a comparison between John and Philo on Sabbath observance, two studies on John, the Synoptics and gospel material in Paul's First Letter to the Corinthians, and an essay on tradition, interpretation and composition in John 6. In this section an interchange between F. Neirynck and the present author on John and the Synoptics has been included.

The study of Paul's letters is pursued further in the third section, making use of passages in the Acts of the Apostles and material from elsewhere inside and outside the New Testament. The discussion deals with catalogues of vices and the so-called Apostolic Decree, and on different views on the role of the reception of the Spirit by Christian converts. The fourth and final section concentrates on themes related to the Book of Revelation, such as the Christians' claim of being the true Jews against those who call themselves Jews but are not, and the theme of illegitimate 'invasions' and claims of philosophical, political, mythological and personal nature over against the true and legitimate ascents. In the last essay the reports by Philo and John the Seer on their own heavenly visionary ascents are compared.

1

These essays centre around related themes. The framework of communities is seen as central and formative. The essays deal with crossings of the borderline between communities, distinctions to be drawn between entry into and remaining in the community, aspects of community activities and community claims, and the self-understanding and the role of community within the larger perspective of historical events. All the time the focus is placed on the dimension of scriptural exposition and religious ideas and convictions as they are related to such aspects of community life and its foundation.

The general point of departure is the circumstance that research on Judaism has gradually moved away from regarding the traditional distinction between Palestinian (normative) Judaism and Hellenistic Judaism as of basic importance. One should pay more attention to the complexity of Judaism both within Palestine and in the Diaspora, as well as looking at the variety of tendencies which existed within Christianity as it emerged within Judaism and spread out into other nations. Although the present studies concentrate on data from the Diaspora, the assumption is that to some degree corresponding differences also existed in Palestine.

I. Jews and Christians in the Graeco-Roman World

The two first chapters deal with burning issues connected with crossing the boundary line between the Jewish communities and other peoples and communities. The essay "'Yes', 'No', 'How Far?'" analyses the problems which Jews and Christians had to face in the pluralistic towns and cities of the Roman world: how far should they integrate into pagan society at large? Could they participate in pagan cults? In daily life, where was the line to be drawn? In the examination of this question the problem of finding adequate and relevant sources has to be faced. In addition to Philo and Josephus and other literary documents, archaeological material is utilized. In the discussion of Early Christianity, some emphasis is given to Paul, especially to 1 Cor 8 and 10. Other sections of the New Testament, such as some passages in the Book of Revelation, contain other important data. Some of the scriptural expositions and ideas behind the various forms of behaviour are presented.

As one would expect, the data occurs in a variety of forms, and different tendencies and attitudes are expressed, and different historical situations are reflected. Nevertheless, the picture of Judaism and Christianity that may be gained in this way seems more adequate than the picture that was drawn when the material was selected and categorized on the basis of the distinction between Palestinian (normative) Judaism and Hellenistic Judaism, and correspondingly, between the Palestinian Church and the Hellenistic Church.

While the focus of this initial chapter is on the crossing of the boundary by Jews and Christians into the pagan world at large, the subsequent essay "Militant and Peaceful Proselytism and Christian Mission" examines the opposite movement: the recruitments of non-Jews for Judaism and Christianity. The scholarly debate on this issue has largely centred around similarities and differences between (Jewish) proselytism and (Christian) mission and evangelization. This formulation of the problem is found in the recent book by Scot McKnight where the following conclusion is drawn: ". . . although they [the Jews] anticipated that Day when hordes of Gentiles would convert, there is almost no evidence that Jews were involved in evangelizing Gentiles and aggressively drawing Gentiles into their religion." This view is examined and challenged on the basis of historical sources. In the present study it will be maintained that it is more historically correct and more fruitful to distinguish between two approaches to proselytism: on the one hand militant forms and on the other hand peaceful ways of recruiting non-Jews to Judaism. Both the public collective and political realm as well as the private and personal realms must be included in the analysis. The Christian mission is then seen as an eschatological and Christological form of recruitment which uses peaceful means, but combined with militant ideas of conquest.

Such boundary issues may be seen together with other aspects within a broader historical perspective. The broader history of the largest and most important Diaspora community in Antiquity, that of Alexandria and Egypt, is surveyed and examined in the study on "Judaism in Egypt". The quite extensive historical sources preserved make it possible to analyse its role both politically, culturally and religiously within the Ptolemaic and Roman contexts. Among the aspects discussed are the change from Hebrew to Greek language, the increasing role played by the Jews as a military and political force in Ptolemaic Egypt, ideas and attitudes expressed in Jewish literature, with the Greek translation of the Old Testament, the Septuagint, and the expository writings of Philo as the high points, and the active religious life connected with Onias' temple and found in the many synagogal communities.

The transfer from the Ptolemaic to the Roman period marks itself off as a central event. The Romans used the Greeks in their administration and gave them privileges. Nevertheless, in many respects the Roman period meant discontinuity with the Ptolemaic past: Alexandria became a provincial town; the Roman legions replaced the multi-ethnic Ptolemaic army, and from now on the resources of Egypt and Alexandria had to serve the needs and aims of the new rulers and their home base, Rome. Within this context the judicial, social and military situation of the Jews is investigated. The fact that during the period between 30 B.C. and A.D. 117 three armed Jewish uprisings and revolts took place demonstrates that the conditions of the Egyptian Jews were deteriorating and moving towards their extermination. The causes and circumstances for these tragic events are analysed.

Within this context the attitudes of non-Jews towards the Jews and the attitudes of the Jews towards non-Jewish surroundings can be traced by investigating on the one hand the writings of the Egyptian priest Manetho and on the other hand Alexandrian Jewish literature. Tensions are seen, as well as positive interaction at times. The tension led to a tragic pogrom in Alexandria in A.D. 38 and to the subsequent Jewish uprisings in 41, 66 and 115–17.

II. The Gospel of John

Tension and conflict within a community may lead to separation, persecution and exclusion. Within a Jewish context Sabbath controversies belong to this problem area, as exemplified by "The Sabbath Controversy in John 5:1–18 and Analogous Controversy Reflected in Philo's Writings". The parallel material in Philo's writings makes evident that the controversy on Sabbath observance reflected in John 5:1–18 is to be seen as a specifically Christian version of a conflict which also existed in the Jewish community in Alexandria, and which probably existed in most Jewish communities. In a distinct way John in 5:1–18 bases his reasoning for (modifying or) abrogating Sabbath observance on Christology. Nevertheless, in John, just as in Philo, exegetical interpretations of Gen 2:2–3 about God resting or not resting on the seventh day play a central role in the controversy. In John this conflict contributed to the way in which a "high Christology" was formulated.

Since the Sabbath question was part of the received Jesus-tradition, the healing story of the paralytic, John 5:1–18, makes possible a comparison with stories in the other gospels. Thus the study of John 5:1–18 provides insights into the transmission of gospel traditions in Christian communities, especially since such an analysis must include a comparison with material in the other gospels.

The problem of John's relationship to the Synoptic Gospels is yet to be solved in New Testament research. In the chapter "John and the Synoptics" an attempt is made to broaden the discussion of this problem by also bringing gospel material from Paul into the analysis: The areas of agreement between John 2:13–22; 5:1–18; 6:51–58 and the Synoptics are analysed against the background of the agreements which exist between the two mutually independent eucharistic traditions recorded in 1 Cor 10:3–4, 16, 17, 21; 11:23–34 and Mark 14:22–25. The question asked is: Are the agreements between John 2:13–22; 6:51–58 and the Synoptics closer or more striking than those between the above mentioned Pauline passages and Mark? They are not, and in the case of John 5:1–18 there are less agreements with the Synoptics. Does the analysis support the hypothesis that John and the Synoptics are mutually independent or the hypothesis that John is dependent on one or more of the Synoptics? Are written documents or oral tradition the primary sources?

Professor Neirynck comments on my study in the "Appendix. Interchange with F. Neirynck. A. Response to P. Borgen", followed by my "Reply". Neirynck defends the understanding that the Gospel of John is dependent on the Synoptic Gospels, while I argue in favour of John's independence. In order to do justice to Neirynck's various points no further presentation of the views expressed is given here, and the reader is referred to Neirynck's own formulations. The dialogue with F. Neirynck is continued in the essay "The Independence of the Gospel of John. Some Observations". A startingpoint for the study are two points made by Neirynck: 1) He does not "exclude

John's use of oral-tradition or source material; . . . direct dependence on the Synoptic Gospels does not preclude the possibility of supplementary information"; 2) "If the fourth evangelist was a teacher and preacher in his community who knew the earlier gospels, conflation and harmonization may have been quite natural to him".

These points made by Neirynck call for further analysis of methods and forms used by teachers or preachers in the transmission and interpretation of the oral and written sources. They also point to the relevance of examining the degree of agreement and differences which may exist between mutually independent versions of the same units of tradition. Since the teacher's or preacher's activities take place within the context of a community, influence from the needs and functions of the community should be brought into the discussion. Moreover, various stages and layers in the community's use of the gospel traditions may be reflected in the mateerial.

In this essay an attempt is made to bring the comparison with First Corinthians one step further by including in the analysis the sayings of Jesus in 1 Cor 7:10ff. and in 1 Cor 9:14. The conclusion reached by the present author is as follows: 1) The similarities between Paul's way of transmitting and interpreting Jesus-logia in the fifties A.D. and the transmission and exposition of tradition in John, strengthen the probability that the Fourth Gospel draws on a stream of traditions which was transmitted and elaborated upon in the history of the Johannine community, independently of the gospels of Matthew, Mark and Luke. 2) Insofar as some of the passages of John reflect their setting in the life of the community, the probability is strengthened that these sections are independent of the Synoptic Gospels.

The use of traditions in the Johannine community is further illuminated in the essay "John 6: Tradition, Interpretation and Composition." In the book *Bread from Heaven* (1965) I concentrated on the analysis of a section of John 6, the verses 31–58, understood as an exposition of the scriptural quotation in v. 31b, "bread from heaven he gave them to eat". In the present essay I look more closely at chapter 6 as a whole.

Some of the *aporiae* in the chapter are discussed, such as the different collective designations of people (crowd, men, Jews, etc.), the seemingly different meanings of the term "sign", and the relation of the eucharistic formulations in vv. 51ff. to the context. The Johannine interpretation of the two traditional stories about the feeding of the multitude and the crossing of the sea in John 6:1–21 are analysed and related to the biblical story of the manna miracle and the expectation of a prophet-king like Moses, and the various reactions of the crowd, Jesus and the disciples are discussed.

The reference to the Son of Man, verse 27, the new request for a sign and the discourse on the bread of life, verses 30–58, can be understood on the basis of John's high Christology. The Son of Man (and not the prophet-like-Moses) gives the bread which endures for eternal life. And Jesus himself is this (higher) manna miracle.

As for composition and structure, the seemingly confused verses 22–24 are seen as an expository elaboration of fragments from the preceding stories. The dialogue structure of verses 28–58(59) and the homiletic exposition of the Old Testament quotation about bread from heaven are not seen as representing just informal speech forms, but as reflecting the use of question and answer and dialogue forms in the discourses and exegetical activity in the Synagogue. Finally the section about the divided reaction among the disciples, verses 60–71 is examined as well as the connection between chapter 6 and chapter 5.

III. Acts of the Apostles and Paul's Letters

Tensions within the Jewish context and within Early Christianity at the borderline between Jews and gentiles are in focus in the two essays on themes from the Acts of the Apostles and the Pauline letters.

The chapter on "Catalogues of Vices, The Apostolic Decree, and the Jerusalem Meeting" takes up a much debated topic among New Testament scholars. In general the so-called Apostolic Decree in Acts 15:20, 29 and 21:25 is understood to be a *decree* that, according to the author of the Acts, was impressed upon the gentile Christians to make possible full social intercourse between Gentiles and Jews in the churches, but in a way in conflict with the views and attitudes of Paul. If so, its setting was primarily within the churches rather than being part of the entry requirement itself.

In the essay the so-called Apostolic Decree is seen within the context of catalogues of vices and virtues and their use in the teaching of proselytes when entering the Jewish nation. The suggestion is made that the catalogue mentioned in Acts 15 in the report from the Jerusalem Meeting was not a decree of which the primary aim was to regulate church life, but it was a sample catalogue of such catalogues of vices as those which, together with the requirement of circumcision, were presented to proselytes. Those present at the Jerusalem meeting agreed to remove the requirement of circumcision, and thus the "Christian proselytes" were not required to become Jews and citizens of the Jewish nation.

The large number of variant readings of the catalogue in Acts 15:20, 21 and 21:25 is puzzling if it was a decree. If the sample catalogue presented at the Jerusalem meeting was not understood to be a decree, however, then the existence of many versions creates no such problem. In the essay the two main versions are discussed further: the Alexandrian version, with emphasis on ritual observance, and the Western version, which focuses upon ethical vices and virtues. These observations are then seen in relationship to the catalogues against pagan vices found in Gal 5:(13f.,) 19–21, and 1 Cor 6:9–11. Moreover, it is maintained that the catalogue of vices in Acts 15:20, 29 and 21:25 as such is not in contradiction to Paul's report on the Jerusalem meeting in Gal 2:1–10.

As explanation of the many variant readings the suggestion is made that the sample catalogue brought to Antioch, Syria, and Cilicia (Acts 15:20–35) was in some circles actualized along the lines of Leviticus 17–18 so as to specify dietary matters as in the Alexandrian version. Both the men from James (Gal 2:11ff.) and the persons in Corinth who advocated strict observance (1 Cor 8) were among those who in particular activated the elements of dietary observances in the Jewish proselyte traditions. The Western version of Acts 15:20, etc., listing three vices and the Golden Rule, is akin to the Pauline version built into Gal 5:13–21 which consists of an extensive list of ethical vices and the love command and also includes a proselyte catalogue of virtues (5:22–23).

Also in this chapter, transmission and applications of traditions in the life of the community have been illustrated.

The chapter "Jesus Christ, the Reception of the Spirit and a Cross-National Community" deals with requirements and experiences related to the entry of Gentiles into the Galatian churches as they had to face further Jewish admission requirements. As shown in previous studies, there were different practices within Judaism.

Some Jews did not seem to regard physical circumcision as an entry requirement in the strict sense of the word, but understood it to be one of the commandments which the convert had to obey after having become a proselyte. Against this background the present author maintains that this view seems to be held by the Jewish Christian intruders into the Galatian churches. In their view the Galatian converts, who had heard the preaching of Christ and received the Spirit, needed a completion by obeying this commandment, cf. Gal 3:3. They compelled the Galatian converts to take circumcision if they wished to remain within the people of God.

In the essay new light is thrown on the understanding of the reception of the Spirit. Since Paul places emphasis on the Galatian converts' reception of the Spirit, Gal 3:2–5, it is relevant to point to the view that Abraham, as the model for new life as a member of the Jewish people, had received and had an indwelling of the Spirit, as seen from Philo, *Virt.* 212–19. Thus Paul's opponents could have meant this experience to be the initial stage which needed circumcision as supplement. Paul then emphatically counters that the Galatian converts received the Spirit not by accepting the Law of Moses, but by accepting (through faith) the preaching of Jesus Christ crucified. On this basis they should also *remain* members of the people of God without adding the observance of circumcision. Circumcision would have made them become members of the Jewish people under the Law of Moses as a national law.

The problem area of the relationship of Paul's letters and the Acts of the Apostles is brought into the discussion, and also some of the difficult questions within the Acts of the Apostles itself, and some new observations are made. The similarities between Paul's conversion account from Galatia and the account of Cornelius' conversion in Caesarea support the view that Luke's use of the Cornelius story in Acts 15:7–11 exemplifies a type of argument which was used not merely at the Jerusalem meeting but also more widely both before and after. By the same token it is probable that cases like the Cornelius incident or the Galatian episode were referred to at the Jerusalem meeting, regardless of whether or not the Cornelius episode was itself specifically included. Luke, it would appear, had good historical and theological basis for using one such tradition (as it happened, the story about Cornelius), and for building it into his overall scheme of the Acts of the Apostles.

IV. The Revelation to John

In the essay "Polemic in the Book of Revelation" the attempt is made to identify the various tensions and conflicts present in the *ekklesiai* to which the book is addressed, in particular the conflict with the synagogal communities. The view is defended that this conflict was an intramural conflict within a Jewish context in which Christians thought themselves to be the true Jews over against those who say that they are Jews but are not, as it is explicitly stated in Rev 2:9 and 3:9.

Two main observations are seen as providing support of this understanding:

1. The Book of Revelation draws on and interprets a Biblical and traditional Jewish geographical outlook and thus claims the Jewish heritage for the Christians. The Biblical idea of Israel being the priestly people of God is transferred to the Christian churches that have been brought into being by the redemptive death of Jesus Christ, Rev 1:5–6.

2. The thinking in the Book of Revelation resembles the self-understanding of the Qumran community that they were the true Israel within Judaism. The Qumran community, as well as John, understand their adversaries to represent demonic powers. The Christian Israel in the Book of Revelation has a cross-national structure that is lacking in the Qumran community, however.

The question is raised how far the Book of Revelation reflects common Jewish community features and social "markers" which could be recognized by people from the outside. One such feature was the fact that both the Synagogue and the *ekklesia* were organized groups who rejected the pagan polytheistic gods and worship. Insofar as there was tension within the groups with regard to separation from or integration into the pagan surroundings, they had this struggle in common. Moreover, John the Seer and some (other) Jews had in common that they opposed the Roman ideology and government.

Thus each group, the *ekklesia* and the Synagogue, claimed to be the true Israel, with the effect that they mutually denied the right of the other group to carry the name.

In the struggle between the Jewish and Christian communities on the one hand and on the other hand between them and the surrounding peoples and communities, the thought category of illegitimate claims and actions over against legitimate understandings, attitudes and actions expresses at times their outlooks, evaluations and identities. In various ways the distinction may be seen as the difference between an illegitimate and a legitimate entering into the divine realm.

The struggle may take place in the area of philosophy, of biblical interpretations, of mythology and of religio-political encounters in historical situations. A combination of some of these elements may be the case.

In the essay "Illegitimate Invasion and Proper Ascent" it is shown that material found in Philo's writings and in the Book of Revelation fits into this thought-category of illegitimate invasion and proper ascent. A passage from the Gospel of John is also included. A common ground between Philo and John the Seer is the challenge they had to face in their encounter with Roman emperor worship. Both regarded the Roman emperors' claim to divinity as illegitimate over against the legitimate and proper divinity of Moses and Jesus respectively. Both Philo and John the Seer interpret Scripture and the situation of the people of God relative to this challenge. Thus, Philo's expository writings, as well as the historical treatises *In Flaccum* and *De Legatione ad Gaium*, throw light on the Book of Revelation in the New Testament. One point of similarity is Philo's picture of Moses as a historical and cosmic figure and John the Seer's picture of the historical and cosmic Christ. Although John the Seer and Philo both place the people under God's heavenly "viceregent", Jesus, the Lamb, and Moses respectively, their identification of this people differed. John saw this people in the cross-national *ecclesiai* of Christ, while Philo belonged to the synagogal community.

This essay is meant to prepare the ground for further studies on the interpretations of Moses, Jesus and aspects of Roman imperial ideology and practice in specific historical situations.

The final chapter has been given the title "Autobiographical Ascent Reports: Philo and John the Seer." The following three points motivated the present author to write this essay: 1) From 1:10 to the end the Book of Revelation takes the form of a report of John the Seer's own visionary experiences. Since the author does not use pseudonymity like authors of other apocalyptic books, exegetes have thought that John the Seer, as a Christian prophet, was unique in this respect. This view needs be subject to further testing. 2) There has in recent scholarship been an increasing awareness of the fact that apocalyptic literature was not necessarily centred on eschatology. Mystical visions, ascents and revelatory knowledge of the heavenly world played an important part. Thus apocalyptic and mystical texts overlap. 3) Interpretation of Scriptures and of traditions were often done under the influence of visionary experiences and inspiration. Therefore, here there might be some common ground between Philo and John the Seer.

Against this background it is relevant to use Philonic passages on heavenly ascents as comparative material to the Revelation of John, in particular his report on his own ascents. Philo did not only tell about the ascents of Biblical persons. In *On the Special Laws* 3:1–6 he reports on his own ascents. Although he draws on Greek astrological and philosophical terminology in his report, the report on ascents in the midst of his continuous struggles due to troublesome civil cares suggests that his ascent experiences were autobiographical. Moreover, the function of these ascents in his interpretations of Scriptures and his various allusions to the historical situation also justify a comparison with the ascent report of John the Seer.

In conclusion: since Philo gives a first hand report on his own ascent, John the Seer is not unique when he states his own name and gives an autobiographical report on his own ascents and visionary experiences.

I

JEWS AND CHRISTIANS IN THE GRAECO-ROMAN WORLD

1

"Yes", "No", "How Far?": The Participation of Jews and Christians in Pagan Cults

Introduction

Research on Judaism has gradually moved away from regarding the traditional distinction between Palestinian (normative) Judaism and Hellenistic Judaism as of basic importance. By extension, the distinction between the Palestinian Jewish church and the Hellenistic church does not provide us with a satisfactory basis for categorization.[1] Thus, although the differences between Palestine and the Diaspora are not to be ignored, one should pay more attention to the complexity of Judaism both within Palestine and in the Diaspora, as well as looking at the variety of tendencies which existed within Christianity as it emerged within Judaism and spread out into other nations. Although the present study concentrates on data from the Diaspora, the assumption is that to some degree corresponding differences existed in Palestine as well.

The complexity of Judaism and Early Christianity may be studied from different angles. In this essay, the focus is on the attitudes to pagan cults which emerge in encounters with the non-Jewish and non-Christian world. Some of the ideas behind the various forms of behaviour will be presented. The purpose is to *exemplify*

---

[1] The champion of "normative" Judaism is Moore (1927–30); correspondingly, Goodenough (1953–68) 3–58, stresses the distinctiveness of Hellenistic Judaism. Among the scholars who argue against this sharp distinction, see especially Meyer (1937); Hengel (1969); Delling (1974) 133–76. See also Borgen (1965); Marshall (1973) 271–75; Borgen (1987C) 207–32; Hengel (1989); Kasher (1990); Kasher, Rappaport and Fuks (1990).

these different attitudes rather than to study all aspects of the situation in one particular place. Thus the data utilized will come from Asia Minor, Greece, Alexandria and Egypt and will cover a span of some centuries, with an emphasis on the first century A.D.

In studying Judaism, Josephus and Philo are important sources. In addition other literary documents will be used, as well as archaeological material. Some of the sources, especially the archaeological data, give information about specific cases, while other sources reflect attitudes in the form of polemic, apologetics, or advice. In the discussion of Early Christianity, some emphasis will be given to Paul, especially the problems discussed by him in 1 Cor 8 and 10. Both chapters will be examined on the basis of the understanding that they are parts of the same letter.[2] Other sections of the New Testament, such as some passages in the Book of Revelation, contain other important data. Only occasionally will Christian and Gnostic sources from the second century A.D. and onwards be drawn into the discussion. As one would expect, the data does not only occur in a variety of forms, but different tendencies are expressed and different historical situations are reflected. Nevertheless, the picture of Judaism and Christianity that may be gained in this way seems more adequate than the picture that was drawn when the material was selected and categorized on the basis of the distinction between Palestinian (normative) Judaism and Hellenistic Judaism and, correspondingly, between the Palestinian church and the Hellenistic church. In the analysis some consideration will be given to the various types of sources.

The Problem

Within Judaism there exists a long tradition of polemic against pagan cults. This polemic was taken over by Christianity, at first as it existed within the context of Judaism, and then also when it grew into the Graeco-Roman world with an identity of its own. Accordingly, for Gentiles to join Judaism and Christianity meant to leave the worship of the many gods and turn to the One God and worship Him. Thus, according to Philo, *Virt.* 102–04, the proselytes have abandoned the images of their gods, and the tributes and honours

---

[2] See various introductions such as Conzelmann (1969) 13–15.

paid to them, and have turned away from idle fables to the clear vision of truth and the worship of the one and truly existing God. Similarily, in Gal 4:8–9 Paul tells us that the Galatians formerly were in bondage to beings that by nature are no gods and now have come to know God. And according to 1 Thess 1:9 the Thessalonians have turned to God from idols.

In the pluralistic towns and cities of the Roman world it was difficult to separate the worship of the One God from the worship of the many gods. Thus the attitudes both among Jews and Christians varied along a wide scale, from different forms of participation to strict isolation. The question of "how far one might go" was a pressing one in the daily life of many.

Paul's letters reflect this problem and the boundary question is discussed in some detail in his First Letter to the Corinthians.[3] C. K. Barrett's essay "Things Sacrificed to Idols" offers a convenient point of departure for our discussion. His conclusion is: ". . . in the matter of εἰδωλόθυτα . . . Paul was not a practising Jew." "Paul is nowhere more un-Jewish than in this μηδὲν ἀνακρίνοντες" (1 Cor 10:25).[4] An alternative understanding will be proposed in this essay: Since on the level of daily life there was a variety of behavioural patterns among Jews relative to pagan cult, there were Jews and

---

[3] Besides 1 Cor, see Romans 14; Gal 5:13–21; cf. 1 Thess 4:1–8; 2 Cor 6:14–18, etc.

[4] Barrett (1965) 138–53. The quotation is taken from pp. 146–47. Barrett's view is shared by other scholars. Cf. Conzelmann (1969) 208 n. 14. On p. 149 Barrett states that "in permitting the eating of εἰδωλόθυτα, Paul allows what elsewhere in the New Testament was strictly forbidden. In particular, he contradicts the requirements of the Apostolic Decree." According to Barrett, Paul's attitude with regard to εἰδωλόθυτα brought him into uncomfortable controversy with the Cephas group, p. 150. Barrett has developed further the suggestion made by T. W. Manson, that the question about sacrificial food was raised at Corinth by Peter. Manson (1962) 190–224. Other scholars, such as Conzelmann (1969) 163, n. 9, rightly states that there is no basis for connecting the Cephas group with the Apostolic Decree. H. Conzelmann may also be right in his view that the Apostolic Decree was not known in Corinth, pp. 163–64. They were however familiar with lists of vices, which stated that participation in idolatry was forbidden, 1 Cor 6:9. In Borgen (1988) 126–41 (the essay is reprinted below) another approach to the problem is suggested. In the New Testament the catalogues of vices, including the catalogue referred to as the Apostolic Decree, list vices in a summary fashion. Thus, they had to be further specified and applied to specific situations and cases, such as illustrated by the problems in the Corinthian congregation.

Christians who followed a practice similar to that of Paul, and some even went further than he did.[5] Paul's First Letter to the Corinthians demonstrates that there was tension among persons who followed different applications of the rule that one should not take part in pagan worship.

"Yes"

The task then is to sketch some of the different practices of the Jews with regard to pagan cults and to discuss some of the data in the New Testament against this background.

Some years ago, W.C. van Unnik demonstrated that Josephus' version in *Ant.* 4:126–58 of the story in Num 25:1–16 about the seduction of the Hebrew youth by the Midianite women reflects the pressures which Jews felt from society at large. Josephus reads into the biblical story arguments used by Jewish apostates in his own time.[6] This passage and other sources reflect aspects of polemical exchanges between Jews and non-Jews due to problems of separation and integration.

Although Num 25:1–16 does not say anything about a counsel of Balaam, Josephus follows a broad Jewish tradition when he interprets this passage on the basis of Num 31:16: "Behold, these (the women of Midian) caused the people of Israel, by the counsel of Balaam, to act treacherously against the Lord." Balaam's counsel to the pagan king Balak was that the Midianites should send their comeliest girls to the Israelite boys in order to seduce them and make them renounce the laws of their fathers and the true God and worship the gods of the Midianites and Moabites (*Ant.* 4:129–30).

Some of the Jewish men then accepted the belief in a plurality of gods and sacrificed to them in accordance with the established

---

[5] Cf. the way in which A. F. Segal assumes that there was a variety of attitudes and practices among ordinary Jews with regard to the food laws: "Although Jewish commensality was frequently noted by Roman and Greek writers, we do not know how ordinary Jews, as opposed to strict Pharisees, observed the dietary laws in the first century. Since there was no explicit law forbidding Jews and gentiles from eating together, we must assume that some, possibly many, ate with gentiles, despite qualms. There was obviously a range of practice that we cannot precisely reconstruct . . .", Segal (1990) 231.

[6] Unnik (1974) 241–61.

rites of the people of the country. They revolted against Moses and his decrees (*Ant.* 4:131, 139, 145–49). Josephus interprets the revolt in Greek terms, as a fight for freedom against tyranny. The leader of the revolt, Zambrias, wants self-determination and freedom from the tyrant Moses:

> But *me* thou [Moses] shalt not get to follow thy tyrannical orders; for thou hast done nought else until now save by wicked artifice, under the pretext of 'laws' and 'God', to contrive servitude for us and sovereignty for thyself, robbing us of life's sweets and of that life of self-determination, which belongs to free men who own no master (δεσπότης) ... not to live as under a tyranny, hanging all my hopes for my whole life upon one. And woe be to any man who declares himself to have more mastery over my actions than my own will (*Ant.* 4:146 and 149).

To be free, ἐλεύθερος, was a cherished Greek ideal and it is here defined as being αὐτεξούσιος, having "self-determination" in the sense of the power to make an independent decision without being forced.[7]

Although Josephus disagrees with this charge made by Zambrias, he formulates it in such an appealing way that he probably draws on points of criticism that had been levelled by non-Jews and apostates against the nation of the Law of Moses. In *Ap.* 2:173–74 Josephus even characterizes Moses and his legislation in a way which makes Zambrias' polemic quite understandable, logical and to the point: Moses is praised because he ordered the life of his people from its earliest youth and left nothing to the self-determination (οὐδὲν ... αὐτεξούσιον) of the individual. Moses made the Law the standard and rule, that the Jews might live under it as under a father and despot (δεσπότης).[8]

Views held by non-Jews in Josephus' own time also find their expression in the words of the girls:

> Seeing then ... that ye have customs and a mode of life wholly

---

[7] Unnik (1974) 255–57. See Epictetus, *Diss.* 4:1:62 and 68. On "freedom", see Schlier (1960) 2:484ff. See further MacMullen (1967) 9–13.

[8] Unnik (1974) 256–57.

alien to all mankind . . . it behoves you, if ye would live with us, also to revere our gods . . . (ἡμῖν συνοικεῖν καὶ θεοὺς ἡμετέρους σέβειν). Nor can any man reproach you for venerating the special gods of the country whereto ye are come, above all when our gods are common to all mankind, while yours have no other worshipper. They must therefore either fall in with the beliefs of all men or look for another world, where they could live alone in accordance with their peculiar laws . . . (*Ant.* 4:137–38).

Similar opinions are also voiced by non-biblical persons mentioned in Josephus' writings. Thus, according to Josephus, when Agrippa, the son in law of Augustus, visited the East during the years of 16–13 B.C., the Ionians made a petition to him claiming that ". . . if the Jews were to be their fellows, they should worship their (the Ionians') gods . . ." (εἰ συγγενεῖς εἰσιν αὐτοῖς ᾿Ιουδαῖοι, σέβεσθαι τοὺς αὐτῶν θεούς, *Ant.* 12:125–26; cf. 16:58–59). A corresponding idea is communicated by Apion in *Ap.* 2:66: ". . . why then, if they are citizens, do they not worship the same gods as the Alexandrians?" (. . . *quomodo ergo . . . si sunt ciues, eosdem deos quos Alexandrini non colunt?*) Also in *Mek. Exod.* 15:2 in an exposition of Songs of Songs 5:9 a similar point is made by pagan polytheists: ". . . come and mingle with us."[9] The general separation of the Jews from others is further documented in non-Jewish sources, such as by the historian Diodorus Siculus, *Bibliotheca Historica*, Fragments of Book 34:1: the Jews "alone of all nations avoided dealings with any other people and looked upon all men as their enemies".

The main points of Josephus' interpretation of Num 25:1–16 are in this way confirmed by parallel viewpoints found in other sources. It is then obvious that his exegesis reflects the problem of apostasy in his own time. Such Jews who apostasized, followed the example of the biblical Zambrias, said "Yes" to participation in pagan cults and left Judaism.

These ideological exchanges of a polemical nature presuppose the experience of separation and apostasy/integration, but they do not report in any direct way on specific cases in empirical life. Archaeology can at times give more direct empirical evidences, although they may be difficult to interpret with certainty. Some

---

[9] See Baer (1961) 82.

inscriptions suggest that individual Jews compromised with polytheism and with society at large. It is difficult to decide, however, whether they still remained members of the Jewish community or had left it. The examples which follow illustrate how certain Jews integrated extensively and said "yes" to pagan society, though probably without renouncing Judaism.

From Cyrene we know that in the year 60 A.D. the Jew Eleazar son of Jason had a prominent administrative position as a guardian of the laws (νομοφύλαξ) in the city, and his name is found together with those of two high-priests of Apollon on an inscription in honour of a pagan deity. Eleazar probably had not renounced Judaism, since he did not follow a common fashion of exchanging his Jewish name for a Greek one.[10]

From an inscription dated about 150 B.C. and found in Iasos in Asia Minor we learn about a Jerusalemite, Nicetas, who as a resident alien (μέτοικος) made a donation of 100 drachmas to the festival of Dionysos. Since he came from Jerusalem, he was probably a Jew.[11] In Acmonia in inland Asia Minor the family of the Tyrronii produced an "Archisynagogos", Tyrronius Cladus, and a High Priest of the imperial Cult, Tyrronius Rapon.[12] It is obvious that the Synagogue leader was a member of the Jewish community. It is impossible, however, to decide whether Nicetas and Tyrronius Rapon actually were members of the Jewish community and identified themselves as Jews. It should not, however, be taken for granted that they had left the Jewish community.

As for early Christianity, we only have literary sources from the first century A.D. Some of these literary sources exemplify how some Christians integrated extensively and said "yes" to pagan society, but nevertheless remained within the Christian congregation. Thus in spite of the polemic levelled in the Revelation to John against Christians who participate in polytheistic cults, these passages give evidence for assuming that this kind of compromise with the pagan community existed in the Christian congregations in Pergamum and Thyatira. Thus the *ekklesia* in Pergamum was divided on the

---

[10] The inscription of the *nomophylakes* of Cyrene is published in QAL 4 (1961) p. 16, n. 2. See Applebaum (1979) 178 and 186, and Delling (1987) 60.

[11] Frey (1952) 15, n. 749; See Kittel (1944) col. 15, Trebilco (1991) 182.

[12] Calder (1939) n. 264 and n. 265; Sheppard (1979) 170–80.

question of how to relate to the polytheistic community at large. Some adhered to the teaching that Christians were to be integrated with society and thus could take part in pagan cults. Here it should be added that in Pergamum as in other cities it was difficult to function without joining in with or being involved in polytheistic cults, since such cults were woven together with most aspects of the life of the city.[13]

John labelled the teaching of these members of the congregation as the teaching of Balaam. J. Roloff considers it unlikely that this phrase "the teaching of Balaam" was coined by John himself. Rather it was used by the criticized persons themselves. If so, they regarded Balaam positively as a prototype of Gnostic prophets.[14] A more satisfactory context is the one provided above where the Ionians claimed that if the Jews were to be their fellows, they should worship the Ionian gods. As seen already the same point is made by Josephus in his interpretation of the Balaam story. To John, therefore, to yield to such pressures from the gentile surroundings would mean to "hold the teaching of Balaam who taught Balak to put a stumbling block before the sons of Israel . . ." (Rev 2:14). To John they said "Yes" and were apostates. In their own eyes, however, although they said "yes" they functioned within the pagan community without leaving the Christian congregation.

The inducement to worship the gods of the many might come from within the Jewish and Christian communities themselves. Thus, in his paraphrase of Deut 13:1–11 Philo presupposes that there were Jews who, on the basis of inspired prophetic oracles, were encouraged to worship the gods recognized in the different cities. Philo also refers to family members or friends who might urge Jews to fraternize with the multitude, frequent their temples, and join them in their libations and sacrifices (*Spec.* 1:315–16).[15]

---

[13] See Ohlemutz (1940); Hansen (1971) 434–70; Radt (1978) 3–20; Radt (1988) esp. 179–285.

[14] Roloff (1984) 54–55.

[15] Deut 13:7b (LXX): ". . . worship foreign gods . . ." (λατρεύσωμεν θεοῖς ἑτέροις), and Philo, *Spec.* 1:316: ". . . fraternize with the many (συνασμενίζειν τοῖς πολλοῖς) and resort to the same temples and join in their libations and sacrifices . . ." Deut 13:10 (LXX) implies that the seducer is to be reported to the authorities, while Philo, *Spec.* 1:316, rephrases this to mean that the report on the seducers is to be sent to all lovers of piety. See Seland (1995) 63–80, 98–107, 123–37. It should be added

Similarily, in Thyatira Jezebel claimed to be a prophetess while also teaching the people in the *ekklesia* to participate in pagan cults:"But I have this against you that you tolerate the woman Jezebel, who calls herself a prophetess and is teaching and beguiling my servants to practise immorality and to eat food sacrificed to idols" (Rev 2:20).

Neither John in the edict to Thyatira, nor Philo in his paraphrase of Deut 13:1–11 elaborates upon the exact content of the prophetic messages favouring participation in the polytheistic cults of the many. Philo mentions the ("inspired") oracles and pronouncements (λόγια καὶ χρησμοί) of the false prophet, *Spec.* 1:315, and John refers to (false) prophetic teaching (διδαχή), Rev 2:24, cf. 2:20.

Having discussed apostasy and identified a form of integration which is meant to stop short of leaving Judaism and Christianity respectively, we shall make a further comment on the attitudes held and actions suggested against them by those who regarded both groups as renegades. First the attitudes of Jews such as Philo and Josephus are to be presented. In Numbers 25 the punishment of the Jewish apostates was death. Philo follows this view in his use of the Phinehas story in *Spec.* 1:54–56. If needed, their execution was to be effected on the spot.[16] Josephus (*Ant.* 4:141–44) tells a somewhat different story: Moses did not order the trespassers to be killed, but tried to win them back by way of conversion (μετάνοια). When this failed, Phinehas and other zealous Jews killed many of the transgressors.[17] Correspondingly, in Rev 2:16 Jesus Christ gives the congregation in Pergamum the alternative of repentance or the sword, where the latter is understood by John as being the sword of his mouth.

By these examples from Jewish and Christian sources we have illustrated how some Jews said "Yes" to participation in pagan cults to such an extent that they became apostates or were treated as apostates by some. Moreover, we have seen that there also were Jews (see Philo, *Spec.* 1:315–16) and Christians (Rev 2:14 and 20)

---

that in another passage Philo tells of how Jews felt the attraction of pagan cults with their poetry and music, beautiful sculptures and paintings, *Spec.* 1:28–29. A broader discussion of Philonic material is given by Sandelin (1991) 109–50.

[16] See the detailed discussion in Seland (1995) esp. 123–25, etc.

[17] In another context Philo (*Praem.* 162–64) also offers apostates the possibility of conversion.

who attempted to remain Jews and Christians and at the same time compromised to a large extent with the pagan surroundings. They said "yes", some in a limited way, but others went as far as participating in pagan worship.

"No" and "How Far?"

With this background in mind, how is the controversy among the Christians in Corinth to be understood, and what is Paul's own view and attitude? To judge from Paul's First Letter to the Corinthians, he himself and some others with him reasoned up to a certain point along a line similar to that followed by the false prophet in Deut 13:1–11 and *Spec.* 1:315–16 and by the prophetess Jezebel in Rev 2:20: Paul correspondingly referred to revealed insight, *gnosis*, and both he and some other Christians in Corinth practised limited integration with society at large, but were more restrictive in their practice than those in Thyatira and Pergamum who followed the false prophess, Jezebel and the teachings of Bileam. According to Paul, he himself and the others reasoned on the basis of accepted insights:

> "We know that 'all of us possess knowledge'."
> οἴδαμεν ὅτι πάντες γνῶσις ἔχομεν (1 Cor 8:1).
> "We know that 'an idol is nothing in the world',
> and that 'there is no God but one'."
> οἴδαμεν ὅτι οὐδέν εἴδωλον ἐν κόσμῳ,
> καὶ ὅτι οὐδεὶς θεὸς εἰ μὴ εἷς (1 Cor 8:4).

These two statements taken together meant that the *gnosis* consisted of insights drawn from the view that no idols had any existence. From this view, which is also documented in Jewish sources,[18] "we" (1 Cor 8:1 and 4) drew the conclusion that they could eat sacrificial meat. Paul did not regard paganism as an *adiaphoron*, however, since he warns the Corinthians against participating in the sacrificial act in pagan worship. These warnings are given by Paul in 1 Cor 10:1–22. The warning in 10:7 refers back to the incident of the golden

---

[18] For the view that idols are non-beings or demons, see Deut 32:17; Ps 95:5; *Enoch* 10:1; 99:7; *Jub.* 1:1; *'Abod. Zar.* 2:3. Cf. Justin *Apol.* 5:1, 2; 12:5; 19:1; 21:6.

calf: "Do not be idolaters as some of them were; as it is written, 'The people sat down to eat and to drink and rose up to dance'" (Exod 32:6). In 1 Cor 10:8, moreover, he refers to Num 25:1–18, the seduction of the Hebrew youth by Midianite women, and reports that twenty-three thousand Israelites fell on a single day. In 1 Cor 10:14–22 Paul gives further warnings against actual participation in idolatrous worship.

Philo, Josephus, Paul and John of Patmos say "no" to participation in pagan cults. In everyday life, the negative attitude of refusal led to the question of "how far?", meaning "where is the boundary line to be drawn?". For example, Philo's "no" did not prevent him from praising the pagan *gymnasium*. He indicates that Jews sent their children to it for their education. He says that the parents benefit the children physically by means of the *gymnasium* and the training given there, and they have given them mental training by means of letters, arithmetic, geometry, music, and philosophy (*Spec.* 2:230). Philo's writings even betray such an expert knowledge of Greek sports that he himself probably was active in athletics during his youth.[19] He also says that he watched boxing, wrestling and horse-racing (*Prob.* 26 and *Prov.* 58). In the *gymnasia* there were numerous statues of deities, and the games in which the students participated were religious festivals. In Cyrene there is even found an inscription from 3–4 A.D. dedicated to Hermes and Heracles with a list of ephebes in which five of the names are obviously Jewish.[20]

Although Philo refers to the triennial festivals of wrestling, boxing, and so forth, he does not comply: he states that a Jew should try to avoid taking part, but if compelled to do so, should not hesitate to be defeated (*Agr.* 110–21). Correspondingly, R. Simeon ben Lakish is said to have once been a professional gladiator, which he justified on the ground of grim necessity (*b. Git.* 47a).[21]

Jews also frequented the theatres, in spite of the fact that the performances included pagan cultic activity. For example, in the

---

[19] Harris (1976) 90–91; Mendelson (1982) 26; Feldman (1968) 224–26; Chambers (1980) 129–44; Hengel (1974) 1:70–74.

[20] The inscription is published in *QAL* 4 (1961) p. 20 n. 7. See Applebaum (1979) 177 and 219.

[21] Borgen (1984) 253 and n. 103. There was disagreement among rabbis on the question of whether a Jew might watch gladiator fights or not, *t. 'Abod. Zar.* 2:7.

theatre in Priene in Asia Minor there was an altar in the middle
of the front row, the horse-shoe shaped row with the seats of honour.
The altar was dedicated to the god Dionysos.[22] Philo frequented
the theatre in Alexandria, and in Miletus in Asia Minor an inscription
in the theatre read "Place of the Jews, who also are godfearing."
The inscription was written sometime between 100 B.C. and 200
A.D.[23] According to the rabbinic material the attendance at theatres
was generally prohibited because of the idolatrous activities which
took place. A Jew might go to an amphitheatre, however, if the state
required him to do so.[24] There were both strict and more lenient
views among the rabbis as to whether or not Jews could attend pagan
wedding parties.[25] Among those Jews who said "no" to participating
in pagan cults, Philo and others drew the boundary line in such
a way as to enable them to participate extensively in the areas of
sports and cultural activities.

The question of food and meals was another difficult issue both
for Jews and Christians in relationship to pagan cultic life. In most
of the cases mentioned above where Jews participated in pagan
sacrifice, they would also have shared in pagan sacrificial meals.
A quotation from *t. Hull.* 2:13 implies that some Jews in Caesarea
Maritima joined in pagan rituals and sprinkled blood from a
slaughtered animal for idolatrous purposes in addition to offering
its fat parts for idolatrous purposes:

> If one slaughters an animal in order to sprinkle its blood for
> idolatrous purposes or to offer its fat parts for idolatrous purposes,
> such meat is considered as sacrifices of the dead. If it had already
> been slaughtered, and one sprinkled its blood for idolatrous
> purposes and offered its fat parts for idolatrous purposes . . .
> This happened in Caesarea.[26]

---

[22] Akurgal (1978) 196–98.

[23] Frey (1952) 14–15, n. 748. See Hommel (1975) 167–95. Feldman (1968) 226–27.

[24] Feldman (1968) 226, with reference to *b. 'Abod. Zar.* 18b ; Porton (1988) 250,
with references to *t. 'Abod. Zar.* 2:5–7.

[25] See Blaufuss (1909) 37–38.

[26] Translation from Levine (1975) 45.

Sacrificial food is only one part of the much larger spectrum of eating traditions which serve as a boundary line between the Jews and others. This general separation might also be touched upon here since it pertains to our topic. As already noted the historian Diodorus Siculus stated that the Jews "alone of all nations avoided dealings with any other people and looked upon all men as their enemies". He adds that the Jews had introduced their laws in order to "share table (τραπέζης κοινωνεῖν) with no other nation". The same attitude towards separation is also seen in several other places, such as in *Jub.* 22:16 ("do not eat with them") and 3 Macc 3:4. However, this general impression needs to be specified further and in some cases to be modified. Although Joseph in *Joseph and Aseneth* 7:1 had a table of his own and did not eat with the Egyptians, he nevertheless had a meal in the house of Pentephres, the Egyptian priest of Heliopolis. Similarly, although the *Letter of Aristeas* records that the Jewish delegates dined with the pagan king Ptolemy II Philadelphus, here it is explicitly stated that the food was chosen and served in accordance with the habits of the Jews, and that no pagan acts of worship took place, *Ep. Arist.* 181–86.

Philo indicates another solution to the problem in *Jos.* 202: Joseph held a banquet for Egyptians and Jews together by entertaining each group in accordance with their different ancestral practices. Philo himself probably adopted this practice of a selective eating. He tells that he had taken part in ill-regulated meals at which he had to fight by means of *logos* (as learned from the Laws of Moses) in order to win the noble victory of self-mastery (*Leg. all.* 3:156). Since the purpose of the dietary Laws of Moses, according to Philo, is to control the unruly (pagan-like) desires and to get rid of extravagance (*Spec.* 4:100–31),[27] such "ill-regulated (ἀδιάγωγος) and extravagant meals" as mentioned in *Leg. all.* 3:156, probably meant that forbidden food was served, possibly also in a pagan cultic setting.

In rabbinic writings there are numerous warnings against Jews eating with Gentiles,[28] including the *Baraita 'Abod. Zar.* 8a: "If a gentile held a banquet for his son and invited all the Jews in his town, notwithstanding that they eat their own food and drink their

---

[27] Concerning ethical interpretation of the dietary laws see Stein (1957) 146–48.

[28] See Str-B 4:1, 374–78.

own wine, the scripture charges them, as if they had eaten of the sacrifices of the dead." Such a casuistic formulation seems to presuppose, however, that some Jews used to accept such invitations and bring their own food with them. Moreover, there are passages, such as *m. 'Abod. Zar.* 5:5 and *m. Ber.* 7:1, which deal with questions arising from gentile guests sharing tables in the home of Jews.

A specific historical case is reported by Paul in Gal 2:11–14. Although details are not given, Paul makes it clear that "some who came from James" stressed separation during the meals so that Jews could follow their own customs. Since Paul at the meeting in Jerusalem had reached a general agreement on circumcision and a division in the allocation of work areas between himself and Peter, Gal 2:1–10, "some who came from James" might have advocated that Jews and Gentiles were to have different meals, but in the same room, in accordance with Philo's picture of the banquet arranged by Joseph, *Jos.* 202.[29]

Returning to the problem area of pagan cults, some further comments should be made on the participation in meals in pagan settings and the use of sacrificial food in general. Philo tells about some pagans who, when sacrificing to the Emperor Gaius, poured the blood upon the altar and took the flesh home and feasted themselves on it (*Legat.* 356). Although Philo mentions pagan temples and worship in several places, his information about sacrifice and things connected with it are difficult to analyse because he largely interprets them in ethical thought-categories. Thus pagan sacrifice represents vices while the sacrifice as prescribed in the Laws of Moses, symbolizes virtues (cf. *Spec.* 1:192–93).

In *Ebr.* 14–15, 20–29 and 95 some specifics can be traced, however.[30] The Scriptural reference is Deut 1:18–21 concerning a disobedient

---

[29] Betz (1979) 108, comes close to this understanding: "If Cephas' shift of position resulted in 'separation', this must have been the demand made by the 'men from James'. If they made this demand, it was made because of their understanding of the Jerusalem agreement (cf. 2:7–9). The separation of the mission to the Jews from that to the Gentiles would imply that Peter would retain his Jewish way of life, and this included first of all the dietary and purity laws. As a result, cultic separation would have to be observed also during table fellowship with Gentile Christians."

[30] See Borgen (1987C) 227–28; concerning club life in Alexandria, see Borgen (1965) 124–25, with reference to Heinemann (1962) 431.

son who does not listen to his father and mother (*Ebr.* 14). The accusations brought against the son are listed as "disobedience, contentiousness, paying of contributions and drunkenness", *Ebr.* 15. The "paying of contributions" (συμβολῶν εἰσφορά) means that the person joined a social association or club. Religious activities always played a role at such gatherings. On the whole Philo sharply criticizes people who joined such clubs as well as the practices of the clubs, implying that some Jews did join. He argues that the lifestyle in the club is characterized by gluttony and indulgence, so that by paying their contributions they are actually mulcting themselves in money, body and soul (*Ebr.* 20–22). The disobedient son made a god of the body, worshipping the vanity most honoured by the Egyptians, Apis, whose symbol is the golden bull of Exod 32.

Round it the frenzied worshippers make their dances and raise and join in the song, but that song was not the sweet wine-song of merry revellers as in a feast or banquet, but a veritable dirge, their own funeral chant, a chant as of men maddened by wine, who have loosened and destroyed the tone and vigour which nerved their souls (*Ebr.* 95).

The disobedient one learns from others, joins "the many" and also consents to initiate evil himself, *Ebr.* 23–26.

From this it is seen that Philo ties the excessive indulgence in food and the pagan god together as a worship of the body as god. He calls this a lifestyle of "irregularity" (ἐκδιαίτησις). Philo uses this term and the corresponding verb to mean acting against the Laws of Moses and subverting the Jewish customs and abandoning the old Jewish ways of communal life, *Somn.* 2:123; *Jos.* 254; *Mos.* 1:31; 241; 278; 298; *Mos.* 2:167; 270; *Spec.* 3:126; *Praem.* 98; *Flac.* 14 and 50. To Philo participation in the religious meals in an association was both a breaking of the Jewish dietary laws and also at the same time eating forbidden and idolatrous food.

Philo seems here to exclude the possibility that Jews could enter the social clubs of the non-Jews. He does not exclude this possibility completely, however, since in *Ebr.* 20 he says: "As for contributions and club subscriptions, when the object is to share the best of possessions, prudence, such payments are praiseworthy and profitable." To Philo prudence, φρόνησις, means wisdom which guides and regulates human life in accordance with the divine Laws of Moses, *Praem.* 79–81 (see also *Mos.* 1:25; 2:189, 216; *Spec.* 1:191–93; 277; 2:18, 62, 257–59; *Virt.* 180). So Philo is of the opinion that Jews might join non-Jewish social clubs and be permitted to keep their own customs and standards of behaviour. He does not specify how this could be done, however. As to the problem of the cultic aspects (sacrifices, etc.) in club activities, Philo does not specify how a Jew should behave in order to avoid taking part in idolatrous worship. Such specification is also lacking when he reports on experiences he has had when attending performances in the theatre and the hippodrome, *Prob.* 26 and *Prov.* 58.

Before returning to New Testament material, some points should be made on the (later) rabbinic sources. It would lead too far to survey all the relevant material, and it would be nearly impossible to date the various traditions. G. G. Porton, who has studied the interrelations between Jews and Gentiles in Mishnah-Tosefta concludes that the rabbis were not quite as strict as one might think. He writes:

> Mishnah-Tosefta display a rather practical attitude toward the gentiles as idolators. On the one hand, Israelites must avoid any direct or indirect contact with gentile religious rites . . . the texts support the view that unless it is clear that the gentile is engaging in religious activity, the Jews need not be concerned with inter-acting with non-Jews . . . Furthermore, the authors of Mishnah-Tosefta seem to have assumed that the individual Jews could determine when the gentile was an idolator, so that much of the concern with idolatry was internalized . . . The goal was to avoid idolatry, while at the same time existing and flourishing in an environment which necessitated daily contact with idols and their worshippers . . ."[31]

It is even possible that some rabbis limited the definition of idolatry to direct participation in idolatrous worship. *m. Sanh.* 7:6 may be understood in this way:"The idolator [is culpable] no matter whether he worships or sacrifices or burns incense or pours out a libation

---

[31] Porton (1988) 258.

or bows himself down to it or accepts it as his god or says to it, Thou art my god."[32]

As for the attitude taken by Jews towards pagan deities, it should be mentioned that some individuals, in contrast to Paul and the majority of Jews in general, had a positive understanding of them and even thought that Moses had founded polytheistic worship. Thus Artapanus claimed that Moses established the Egyptian cults: Moses "divided the state into 36 nomes and appointed for each of the nomes the god to be worshipped, and for the priests the sacred letters, and that they should be cats and dogs" (*Eusebius Praep. Evangel.* 9:27, 4).[33] Moreover, as mentioned above, Jews in Cyrene had their names written on an inscription dedicated to Hermes and Heracles.[34] An inscription from Upper Egypt demonstrates that a Jew worshipped a god in the temple of Pan.[35]

As already shown, Paul sided with the predominant Jewish traditions, in saying an emphatic "no" to idolatry, 1 Cor 10:7 and 14–22. Idolatry is a central term in catalogues of vices from which the (Christian) proselytes should abstain, 1 Cor 6:9; Gal 5:20; 1 Pet 4:3; Col 3:5; Eph 5:5; Rev 22:15; Rev 9:20. The practical problem remained, however, how to decide exactly where the boundary line was to be drawn. Therefore in many cases there would be disagreements and differing solutions. It is fortunate that 1 Cor 8 and 10 gives us an insight into the diversity of views and approaches present in some such cases.

In Paul's report on the congregation in Corinth, it is evident that there were persons who were strict in their drawing of the boundary line, and others who on the basis of their spiritual *gnosis* were more lenient and drew the line at actually taking part in the sacrificial ceremony itself. The stricter ones had a comprehensive definition of the sacrificial act:

Some, through their familiarity (τῇ συνηθείᾳ) up to the present with idols, eat the food as something sacrificed to an idol (ὡς

---

[32] Baer (1961) 82–89. *m. Sanh.* 7:6 is cited on p. 89; Borgen (1987C) 227.

[33] Charlesworth (1985) 899.

[34] See n. 20, above.

[35] Frey (1952) 1537–38; Delling (1987) 86 n. 584.

εἰδωλόθυτον); and their conscience (ἡ συνείδησις), being weak, is defiled (1 Cor 8:7).

The adjective εἰδωλόθυτος, means "sacrificed to idols", and the corresponding noun in the neuter "meat offered to idols". The proselyte catalogue in Acts 15:20, 29 and 21:25 (with two main versions in the manuscripts and several variations) in referring to idolatry stresses the aspect of sacrificial food by using the terms τὰ εἰδωλόθυτα (15:29); τὸ εἰδωλόθυτον (21:25) and τά ἀλισγήματα τῶν εἰδώλων (15:20: "the pollutions of idols").[36] Elements of such lists, namely eating things sacrificed to idols and adultery, are also found in Rev 2:14 and 20. Although these Greek terms isolate a certain aspect of idolatry, namely food, they might, nevertheless, have had various applications for practice in daily life. Those who applied the terms broadly, then, understood a meal consisting of food from sacrifices, either in an idol's temple (1 Cor 8:7, 10) or at home (10.28), to be an integral part of idolatrous worship.

Thus we have seen that in everyday life, the attitude of "no" led to the question of "how far?", meaning "where is the boundary line to be drawn?". Various Jews and various Christians drew the boundary differently with regard to sports, cultural activities, meals and with regard to being present where idols were placed and polytheistic worship was performed. Paul refers to guidance on these matters from gnosis, and he also refers to the concept of conscience, συνείδησις. The role of this concept is then to be analysed.

Syneidesis in 1 Corinthians 8 and 10

The concept of "conscience", συνείδησις, is used by Paul in 1 Cor 8:7, 10, 12 and 10:25, 27, 28, 29. The word was not a philosophical term in Stoicism, but rather has its roots in the common language of daily life.[37] The word meant basically "knowing together" with someone else or with oneself, and may have various shades of meaning. P. J. Tomson refers to the study by H.-J. Eckstein, who discerns the following potential meanings: "Mitwissen, Bewusstsein, Gewissen,

---

[36] For the understanding of the so-called Apostolic Decree as being a proselyte catalogue of vices, see Borgen (1988) 126–41, and ch. 8 below.

[37] Eckstein (1983) 65–66.

Inneres". Tomson states that "especially in view of the correlation with one's outward actions, the last word is more effectively rendered 'intention'."[38] Tomson associates this meaning of *syneidesis* with the conscious intention which is a decisive halakhic factor, especially in the area of laws concerning idolatry. R. Eliezer, for example, followed a strict rule about a Jew who slaughters for a non-Jew: "The unspecified intention . . . of a gentile is towards idolatry" (*m. Hul. 2.7*).

How then is 1 Cor 8:7–12 to be understood?

However, not all possess this *gnosis*. But some, through being hitherto accustomed to idols, eat food as really offered to an idol; and their *syneidesis*, being weak, is defiled. 8 . . . 9 Only take care lest this liberty of yours somehow become a stumbling block to the weak. 10 For if anyone sees you, a man of *gnosis* at table in an idol's temple, might he not be "edified", if his conscience is weak, to eat food offered to idols? 11 . . . 12 Thus, sinning against your brethren and wounding their *syneidesis* when it is weak, you sin against Christ.

Tomson maintains that the concept of halakhic intention illuminates the meaning of the first, essential sentence:

The minds of the neophytes are still dominated by their awe of pagan deities . . . Thus when eating pagan food which they know may well have been consecrated to the gods, the 'delicate', whose consciousness is still dominated by idolatry, eat it ὡς εἰδωλόθυτον, 'as idol food' . . . To these delicate, and these alone, Paul is ready to apply R. Eliezer's principle: 'The unspecified intention of gentiles is towards idolatry.' The consciousness of the delicate is 'defiled', i.e. it is not yet pure and directed towards the Creator. By inconsiderate behaviour, the 'knowing' can 'edify' the 'delicate consciousness' towards idolatry, and 'wound' its relation to Christ.[39]

---

[38] Tomson (1990) 211, especially n. 110.
[39] Tomson (1990) 215–16.

Tomson's interpretation is generally convincing. There are some weak points, however. First, he translates ἀσθενής as "delicate" instead of "weak". By doing this he fails to discuss the term adequately in its Hellenistic context as well as from its Jewish aspect. In his essay "Determinism and Free Will in Paul", A. J. Malherbe shows how, according to the Stoic theory of cognition, it is because of a person's weakness that he gives his assent to false judgments. Thus, "weak" does not just mean that a person is sensitive. "Paul associates weakness with cognition; and he recognizes the importance of habituation for their condition."[40] The "weak" did not possess "gnosis", 1 Cor 8:7.

Second, the translation of *syneidesis* as intention does not adequately express that the term as used by Paul in 1 Cor 8 and 10 implies a consciousness based on certain sets of criteria and standards. Thus, Paul's use can be more precisely be understood on the basis of the general characterization of the word given by H.-J. Eckstein with reference to its Greek usage from the 1st century B.C. onwards: "Das Bewusstsein, das rational oder affektiv die eigenen Taten moralisch oder unabhängig von sittlichen Kriterien verurteilt oder gutheisst."[41] In connection with food and sacrifice the meaning can then be formulated in this way: the conscious and existential classification of food on the basis of a person's experiences and of criteria held by him. 1 Cor 8:7 may then be paraphrased in this way: due to their experiences from participation in pagan sacrifice and the criteria gained from this, the conscious and existential classification of the food made by the recent converts was that it was sacrificial food offered to idols. In this way the act of eating became a sacrificial act and the persons partook of the table of demons (1 Cor 10:21). The conscious and existential engagement of the converts was defiled, according to Paul, because it was drawn into pagan worship.

In 1 Cor 8:10–11 the specific case is recorded of a man of *gnosis* reclining in a temple of idols. The person who has *gnosis* does not classify this meal as an idolatrous meal, but the conscious and existential understanding of the meal on the part of the recent converts

---

[40] See Malherbe (1994) 234. Malherbe refers to *SVF* 1:67; 3:177; Plutarch *adv. Colot.* 1122C; Cicero, *Tusc. Disp.* 4:15.

[41] Eckstein (1983) 56.

will, by seeing the person of *gnosis* in this situation, be "built up" to classify it as a case of eating food sacrificed to idols. Paul here seems to assume that the recent convert will interpret this positively and see it as approval for participation in polytheistic sacrificial meals. This may lead him to attempt a syncretistic fusion of Christianity and polytheistic worship. According to Paul, the convert is in this way destroyed. This Pauline passage might be compared with Philo, *Ebr.* 14–15, 20–29 and 95. Philo addresses the problem of whether a Jew might join pagan associations and clubs, similar to the case described by Paul where a Christian participates in a meal in an idol's temple. Philo is even more negative with respect to this than Paul. He thinks that in general the Jew would in such a case join in with the others and worship pagan gods, while Paul restricts himself to the actual meal and thinks that the weak convert is the one who in this setting is drawn into idolatrous worship by eating food offered to idols. Philo does not completely exclude the possibility of Jews joining, however, if they want to share the virtue of prudence.

This passage in Philo supports Tomson's general thesis, that Paul draws on Jewish ideas about the importance of the attitude, intention and criteria held by a person when one is judging whether food is sacrificial or not. Tomson's analysis needs, however, to be supplemented by further examination of the Hellenistic ideas which have also influenced Paul.

Paul gives instruction for two more cases in 1 Cor 10:25–29: Verses 25–26 present a rule based on Scripture:

<u>Πᾶν τὸ</u> ἐν μακέλλῳ πωλούμενον <u>ἐσθίετε</u>
<u>μηδὲν ἀνακρίνοντες διὰ τὴν συνείδησιν.</u>
τοῦ κυρίου γὰρ ... (Ps 24:1 is cited).

In v. 27 the rule is then applied to the normal case in which the unbelievers invite to dinner:

εἴ τις καλεῖ ὑμᾶς τῶν ἀπίστων καὶ θέλετε πορεύεσθαι <u>πᾶν τὸ</u>
παρατιθέμενον ὑμῖν <u>ἐσθίετε</u>
<u>μηδὲν ἀνακρίνοντες διὰ τὴν συνείδησιν.</u>

There is an exception to this application of the rule, however, when a person explicitly says that it is sacrificial meat (v. 28):

ἐὰν δέ τις ὑμίν εἴπῃ, Τοῦτο ἱερόθυτόν ἐστιν, μὴ ἐσθίετε δι' ἐκεῖνον τὸν μηνύσαντα καὶ τὴν συνείδησιν.

It is difficult to decide whether the person who says "This is sacrificial food" (Τοῦτο ἱερόθυτόν ἐστιν, v. 28) is himself a pagan polytheist, or one of the Christian "weak" persons. He is probably meant to be a pagan, since the word ἱερόθυτον is the common form used by polytheists themselves, while Paul in 1 Cor 8:7 uses the Jewish pejorative form, εἰδωλόθυτον.[42]

What then is the meaning of "because of the one who has declared and the consciousness (Author's trans. of τὴν συνείδησιν)", 10:28? In verse 29 Paul makes it clear that he here refers to the consciousness of the other person, probably the one who made the declaration. If so, the person has made the meal an act of pagan worship, and for that reason the Christians are to abstain from eating. There is here a conflict between two sets of criteria and two classifications of the meal: 1) the Christian in his freedom: he takes part in the meal with thankfulness and gives thanks. The scriptural basis is Ps 24:1: "the earth is the Lord's, and everything in it" (1 Cor 10:25–27 and 30). 2) the polytheist draws his criteria from the polytheistic sacrificial practice and "theology". His conscious and existential classification (συνείδησις) is that it is sacrificial food, which he understands to be part of polytheistic sacrificial ritual.

The problem arises when Christians and polytheists take part in a meal and both claims are made. One can then assume that to the polytheist it will not be problematic to include the Christian person and his God in a sacrificial act to one or more of his gods. If so, the pagan person's understanding and spoken claim that "This is sacrificial meat" will draw the Christian into acts of syncretistic worship. When the meal and the food in this way function as being part of a sacrifice, then the principle of freedom does not apply any more. Paul says that the Christian must in that case abstain from eating (1 Cor 10:28–29).

---

[42] A pagan: Lietzmann and Kümmel (1949) 51–52; Barrett (1971) 241–42; Conzelmann (1969) 210; Tomson (1990) 216. A "weak" Christian: Maurer (1964) 914.

The interpretation of 1 Cor 10:30 is still somewhat problematic: "If I partake with thankfulness, why am I denounced because of that for which I give thanks." The partaking mentioned here seems to contradict the advice given in verse 29 that the Christian should not eat. One might then relate verse 30 to the whole section of vv. 25–29 which deals with the question of a Christian partaking in a meal with unbelieving gentiles. Another possibility is that verse 30 presupposes selective eating by a Christian: When he is partaking in the meal, he is to abstain from eating that which is claimed to be pagan sacrificial meat, but he is not to be denounced for partaking and eating that upon which he has said his prayer of thanksgiving. In support of this interpretation one might refer to the emphasis on πᾶν, "all, everything, whatever" in verses 25 and 27. This seems to imply that the claim "This is sacrificial meat (food)" does not refer to all the various kinds of food which are thought to be served at the meal. Paul's description of the cases here is so brief that it is impossible to reach a certain conclusion as to which of these two alternatives is the correct one.

On the basis of this interpretation of 1 Cor 10:25–30, the interpretation of the formulaic phrase μηδὲν ἀνακρίνοντες διὰ τὴν συνείδησιν in vv. 25 and 27 (cf. v. 28 and Rom 13:5) may be paraphrased in this way: Other person's conscious and existential classifications of food on various sets of criteria do not as such call for any questioning by the Christians, for God is the Creator so that they can for that reason eat whatever is served. When someone explicitly states that the food is sacrificial, then the situation is different and the rule does not apply.

Tomson has rightly related 1 Cor 10:25 and 27 to rabbinic ideas and practice: In contrast to R. Eliezer some of the Sages held the same view as Paul, that there were gentiles whom one knew they did not worship idols. "According to the latter opinion, in questions of 'implicit intention' it was unnecessary to 'inquire further' and have the gentile make his intention explicit."[43]

To summarize, the term *syneidesis* as used by Paul in 1 Cor 8 and 10 implies a consciousness based on certain sets of criteria and standards. In connection with food and sacrifice the meaning can then be formulated in this way: the conscious and existential

---

[43] Tomson (1990) 219.

classification of food on the basis of a person's experiences and of criteria held by him. 1 Cor 8:7 may then be paraphrased in this way: due to their experiences from participation in pagan sacrifice and the criteria gained from this, the conscious and existential classification of the food made by the recent converts was that it was sacrificial food offered to idols. In this way the act of eating became a sacrificial act and the persons partook of the table of demons (1 Cor 10:21). The conscious and existential engagement of the converts was defiled, according to Paul, because it was drawn into pagan worship.

As for the meaning of "because of the one who has declared and the consciousness (τὴν συνείδησιν)"in 1 Cor 10:28, Paul makes it clear in verse 29 that he is referring to the consciousness of the other person, probably the one who made the declaration. If so, the person has drawn the meal into the sphere of pagan worship, and for that reason the Christians are to abstain from eating.

Other Guiding Concepts

As already shown above, on the basis of the Jewish belief that God was the only God, Paul stated that food from sacrifices was not really idolatrous, since the gods had no existence, 1 Cor 8:4 and 8. And from the conviction that Israel's God was the Creator, as stated in Ps 24:1, "the earth is the Lord's, and everything in it", he drew the conclusion that Christians might eat whatever is sold in the meat market, 1 Cor 10:25. This meant that neither Jewish dietary laws nor the objections to eating pagan sacrificial meat were to be followed. The same reasoning is found in the *Letter of Aristeas* in a question asked of the Jewish high priest Eleazar: ". . . why, since there is one creation only, some things are considered unclean for eating?" (*Ep. Arist.* 129). In his answer Eleazar did not draw the conclusion that the Jewish dietary laws were to be abandoned (*Ep. Arist.* 130–71), while Paul did, on the basis of a reasoning similar to that indicated in *Ep. Arist.* 129.

It is worth noticing that Paul cites phrases which are akin to those found in Zambrias' speech according to Josephus in *Ant.* 4:145–49. Zambrias championed freedom (ἐλευθερία) and self-determination (τὸ αὐτεξούσιον) against the Laws of Moses, and Paul expresses a similar idea when he quotes "everything is permissible to me", πάντα μοι ἔξεστιν, 1 Cor 6:12 (with a minor variation in 1 Cor 10:23) and also refers to freedom, ἐλευθερία, 1 Cor 10:29. Moreover, the issues are similar: illicit marriage with a pagan woman in *Ant.* 148 and intercourse with a prostitute in 1 Cor 6:12–20; participation in pagan sacrifice in *Ant.* 149, and the eating of sacrificial food in 1 Cor 10:28. In contrast to Zambrias Paul modifies the idea of freedom on the basis of the Old Testament tenet that God is the Creator, 1 Cor 6:16; 8:4–6 and 10:26. He also draws on Christology and other motifs, and in this way he interprets the principle of freedom in such a way as to exclude sexual immorality and participation in pagan sacrifice.

The Jewish ephebes in Cyrene who took part in the activities in the gymnasia and whose names were included on an inscription in honour of Hermes and Heracles, the Jew who in Upper Egypt worshipped a god in a temple of Pan,[44] and Christians who followed the teachings of Balaam in Pergamum (Rev 2:14) and of the prophetess Jezebel (Rev 2:20), did not abstain from what took place in an idol's temple. Did Paul allow Christians to dine in an idol's temple (εἰδωλεῖον)? According to 1 Cor 8:10 he was open to this possibility: " For if any one sees you, a man who has *gnosis*, at table in an idol's temple . . ." Some scholars take this statement at face value, while others regard it as a rhetorical example. Grammatically, the conditional formulation implies that such a situation may occur. It seems too easy to say that Paul's example was an impossible one. Accordingly, he must have considered it possible for *a man who has gnosis* to join in a meal in a dining room in a pagan temple, without taking part in the cult ceremonies. Again it is a question of where to draw the line.[45] Although he did not prohibit the eating of sacrificial food as such, those who took part in the sacrificial ritual offered the

---

[44] Cf. Philo's warnings against Jewish "prophets" who would lead Jews to mingle with the many, *Spec.* 1:315–16.

[45] Tomson (1990) 196–97 agrees with Hurd (1965) that Paul's question in 1 Cor 8:10 is clearly rhetorical. P. J. Tomson thinks that the fact that σέ is left out in P46 and some other manuscript witnesses, may be read as reflecting the impossibility of Paul's rhetorical example (196 n. 45). Against Tomson it must be said that P46 shows that the scribe wished to weaken the fact that the formulation in 1 Cor 8:10 allows for Paul's example to be possible. See Mosbeck (1951) 107; Barrett (1965) 148–49; Barrett (1968) 188 n. 1, and 195–96; and Conzelmann (1969) 176–77 and 205–06 are among those who regard 1 Cor 8:10 to refer to a real possibility.

sacrificial meat to demons and not to God (1 Cor 10:19–22). Thus he applied a functional interpretation of εἰδωλόθυτον: when persons offered the meat as sacrifice, it implied a demonic context, while outside of this direct context, it was ordinary food even when the setting for the meal was the dining-room in a temple.[46]

In this way Paul in 1 Cor 8 and 10 drew the boundary line just at the pagan altar-table when sacrifices were performed. Apart from this, the belief in the One God, the Creator, allowed the possibility of eating sacrificial food either in an idol's temple or at home. Paul may here illustrate how Philo could accept that Jews joined pagan clubs and still followed Jewish principles, *Ebr.* 20.[47]

In conclusion, on the basis of different sources it has been demonstrated that on the level of daily life there was a variety of behavioural patterns among Jews relative to pagan cults. Thus, there were Jews and Christians who followed a practice similar to that of Paul, and some who went even further than he did. Tension between different views and practices existed, as is also seen in Paul's First Letter to the Corinthians chapters 8 and 10.

Appendix:
Religious Complexity in the Pagan World

It may be of interest to note that parallel variations in attitudes were also held by non-Jews. For example, only Greeks might be initiated into the Eleusian mysteries, and foreigners were barred access to the temple of Hera at Argos.[48] In some temples slaves were

---

[46] As for entering a pagan temple as such, Josephus tells that Jewish envoys together with many Jews in Rome met before the council gathered by Caesar (Augustus) in the temple of the Palatine Apollo (*J.W.* 2:80ff. and *Ant.* 17:301ff.).

[47] It would be beyond the scope of the present paper to discuss Christian and (anti-) Gnostic material in the time after the New Testament. The survey given above makes clear, however, that there is no need for looking at material on Gnosticism in order to explain the various attitudes towards pagan sacrifice and sacrificial food in Paul's letters and in the Book of Revelation. The variety of attitudes reflected in Jewish sources give us sufficient background for understanding the struggle in Early Christianity in the New Testament period. For a survey of the post-New Testament material, see Brunt (1985) 113–24.

[48] Wächter (1910) 118–22; Eitrem (1915) 217. Concerning intolerance among non-Jews, see Josephus, *Ag. Ap.* 2:259–70.

not admitted to take part in the worship.[49] In some temples men were excluded and in others women, and so forth.[50] On the other hand some cults were inclusive and open, among them the worship of the Ephesian Artemis with its great festivals to which pilgrims came from near and far. In an inscription from Ephesus the following lines are found: "Since the goddess Artemis, leader of our city, is honoured . . . among Greeks and also barbarians . . ."[51] In a similar way several cults were civic in nature and their celebrations were events for all the inhabitants of a city or a province, sometimes also including pilgrims who came from afar to take part. For example, the imperial cult in Asia Minor was celebrated both in sanctuaries and elsewhere, such as in the central square, in the council house, in the theatres, sports arenas, and so on. The involvement of the whole community meant that householders performed sacrifice on altars outside their houses when the processions passed by. Non-citizens and foreigners were occasionally included in invitations to the feasts. Banqueting played an important role in the celebrations. It is worth pointing out that the veneration of the emperor went together with the worship of various gods.[52]

In some cults the rules for admission stressed ethical virtues. Of particular interest in this connection is a syncretistic cult group in Philadelphia (Alasehir) in Lydia. An inscription gives us a valuable insight into this cult of the late second or early first century B.C. The ordinances were given by divine revelation to a person by the name of Dionysios in his sleep. Dionysios allows entry into this cultic association to those who qualify on ethical grounds without debarring anyone based on sex or class:

When coming into this *oikos* let men and women, free people and slaves, swear by all the gods neither to know nor make use

---

[49] Wächter (1910) 123–25.

[50] Wächter (1910) 125–34.

[51] The inscription is published in Newton (1890) 142–45, n. 482 (and addendum on p. 294). See Oster (1987) 75. The phrase "both Greeks and barbarians" is also used by Apollonios of Tyana, *Ep.* 97 regarding the various peoples who were admitted to the temple of Artemis. The same wording is used by Paul in Rom 1:14, as well as by Philo, *Mos.* 2:12, 18, etc.

[52] Price (1984) 109–14; 229–33.

wittingly of any deceit against a man or a woman, neither poison harmful to men nor harmful spells ... Apart from his own wife, a man is not to have any sexual relation with another married woman, whether free or slave, nor with a boy nor a virgin girl ... A free woman is to be chaste ...[53]

Thus religous pluralism was characterized by diversity and complexity. In addition the dining arrangements varied. At some temples the dining rooms were adjacent to the sanctuary itself. This was the case in the Asclepeion-Lerna complex north of the forum of Corinth. The temple of Asclepius is located on the higher level to the east, and on the lower level to the west there was a peristyle court, with access to three dining rooms with 11 couches in each. These rooms were attached to the foundation area of the temple, and a ramp led from the temple on the upper level to the courtyard and the dining rooms on the lower level. The rooms were in use from the fourth century B.C. to the fourth century A.D.[54] Inside the holy *temenos* of the Heraion at Argos there was a separate banquet hall.[55] Similarily, the banquet hall at Perachora north of Corinth was located in the vicinity of the sanctuary.[56] In such dining rooms it seems that parties might possibly have had their meals according to their own liking, if they so wished, since the rooms were not part of the sanctuary proper where the altar was located, and at least some of them did not have sufficient space for a permanent altar in addition to the couches and transportable tables.

In some places the banquet hall had the altar in the centre, however, and the dining was by necessity an integral part of the sacrificial ceremony. The so-called "Podium Hall" (24x10 m.) in Pergamum exemplifies such a hall for sacred meals. The hall received its name by the excavators because a podium, ca. 1 m. high and 2 m. deep, runs along the walls of the structure. The participants lay on the podium with their heads toward the centre of the room. In the middle section of the room the entrance was through the door on the one side and on the opposite side there was a niche with an altar before

---

[53] Barton (1981) 7–41, esp. p. 9; Weinreich (1919) 1–68.

[54] See Roebuck (1951) 51–55.

[55] Gruben (1976) 106–07.

[56] Tomlinson (1969) 164–72; Vicker (no date) 2–3.

it. There might be room for 70 cult participants in the hall. Reclining together they took their sacred meals. The food was placed on a marble slab which ran along the front edge of the podium. The hall was dedicated to the god Dionysos and probably belonged to a cultic association.[57] In such a cultic dining room it would have been impossible not to be drawn into the sacrificial act itself.[58]

---

[57] Radt (1988) 224–28; cf. Radt (1978) 20–21, where Radt had preliminarily suggested that it was the hall of an oriental cult.

[58] The Deputy Director of the Department of Culture and Tourism, Ankara, Ms Nimet Berkok, and the Director of the Ephesus Museum, Selahattin Erdemgil, have given me very helpful professional assistance in the study of ancient archaeological sites in Turkey. The insights thus gained have contributed to the perspective followed and to some of the specifics mentioned in this essay.

2

Militant and Peaceful Proselytism and Christian Mission

Introduction

In his book *A Light Among the Gentiles. Jewish Missionary Activity in the Second Temple Period* Scot McKnight distinguishes between proselytism and mission:

> ... although there is clearly an almost universally positive attitude toward proselytes and proselytism, a positive attitude toward, and an acceptance of, proselytes is to be methodically distinguished from aggressive missionary activity among the Gentiles. In other words, although Jews clearly admitted proselytes, and although they clearly encouraged Gentiles to convert, and although they anticipated that Day when hordes of Gentiles would convert, there is almost no evidence that Jews were involved in evangelizing Gentiles and aggressively drawing Gentiles into their religion.[1]

McKnight discusses eight methods of proselytizing: 1. God's intervention; 2. Jewish missionaries through evangelism; 3. Distributing literature; 4. The Synagogue as an institution for proselytizing; 5. Education; 6. Good deeds; 7. Various means, such as marriage, adoption, political and economic advantage, etc.; 8. Force.[2]

The data which McKnight himself presents call for a more differentiated conclusion to be drawn, as indicated by his own

---

[1] McKnight (1991) 48.

[2] McKnight (1991) 50–68.

formulations: "... there is *almost* no evidence that Jews were involved in evangelizing Gentiles . . ."[3] (the italics are mine). In his final conclusion he goes further when he states: "Although there is *some evidence* for conversion *through literature and missionaries,* the predominant means of conversion appears to have been the life of individual Jewish citizens."[4] (The italics are mine.) Moreover, in his survey of the methods of proselytizing, McKnight includes conversions caused through the use of force.[5] One must then raise the question of why he did not classify this method as the Jews "aggressively drawing Gentiles into their religion"?[6] Thus a more precise conclusion seems to be: among the Jews there were different ideas, attitudes and activities at work with regard to receiving or bringing non-Jews into the Jewish religion.

In this study two different approaches to proselytism will be discussed, on the one hand militant forms and on the other peaceful ways of recruiting non-Jews into Judaism. Some cases show kinship with both methods. The Christian mission can be seen as an eschatological/christological form of recruitment which belongs to this mixed category, but with emphasis on the peaceful aspect.

A. Militant Proselytism[7]

1. Military Conquest

One of the aggressive methods was military conquest. This might be called "sword-mission". This method of making recruits to a religion has been used by peoples within the Muslim religion as well as by peoples within Christendom.[8] In historical research it is both necessary and correct to examine how the Jewish nation has, at times, conquered others, politically and religiously, by military means.

---

[3] McKnight (1991) 48.

[4] McKnight (1991) 117.

[5] McKnight (1991) 68.

[6] McKnight (1991) 48.

[7] For the following, see Borgen (1995) 9–18.

[8] Rosenbloom (1978) 109; Seligson (1965) 92.

In 129 B.C. Antiochus VII died in the war against the Parthian nation. His successor to the throne, Demetrius II, was a weak king and was soon drawn into internal conflicts. This situation gave John Hyrcanus (135/4–104 B.C.) the opportunity to expand his kingdom. He marched southwards and conquered the Idumaean towns Adora (today: Dura), situated west-south-west of Hebron, and Marisa, located between Hebron and Ashdod.

Hyrcanus also captured the Idumaean cities of Adora and Marisa, and after subduing all the Idumaeans, permitted them to remain in their country so long as they had themselves circumcised and were willing to observe the laws of the Jews. And so, out of attachment to the land of their fathers, they submitted to circumcision and to making their manner of life conform in all other respects to that of the Jews. And from that time on they have continued to be Jews (*Ant.* 13:257–58).

In *Ant.* 15:254 Josephus gives the following characterization of Hyrcanus' policy towards the Idumaeans:

Hyrcanus had altered their political system into the customs and the laws of the Jews.

Hyrcanus wanted in this way to "Judaize" the Idumaeans and integrate them into his kingdom.[9] This fusion of religion and politics was logical, since Hyrcanus was not only political and military leader, but also the religious leader, as high priest (*Ant.* 13:230).[10] According to Josephus, the Idumaeans chose to become Jewish proselytes in order to avoid being exiled away from the land of their fathers (*Ant.* 13:258).

In the same way Aristobulus (104–103 B.C.) proselytized by means of military conquest. Josephus writes: Aristobulus "made war on the Ituraeans and acquired a good part of their territory for Judaea, and compelled the inhabitants, if they wished to remain in their country, to be circumcised and to live in accordance with the laws of the Jews" (*Ant.* 13:318). Josephus cites Strabo, who, referring

---

[9] Schürer (1973) 207; Rosenbloom (1978) 95. See also Avi-Jona (1977) 74.

[10] See Mendels (1992) 44–45; 60–62.

to the historian Timagenes (first cent. B.C.) wrote: "... he acquired
additional territory for them [the Jews], and brought over to them
a portion of the Ituraean nation, whom he joined to them by the
bond of circumcision" (... δεσμῷ συνάψας τῇ τῶν αἰδοίων περιτομῇ),
Ant. 13:319.[11] These literary sources make evident that the Ituraeans
were forced to become Jewish proselytes. Thus there is no basis
for A. Kasher's view that the Idumaeans and Ituraeans became
proselytes voluntarily, i.e. without force.[12]

The punishment for refusing to be Judaized in this manner was
not always just emigration. Alexander Jannaeus' (103–76 B.C.) men
demolished Pella "because the inhabitants would not take upon
themselves the ancestral customs of the Jews" (οὐχ ὑποσχομένων
τῶν ἐνοικούντων ἐς τὰ πάτρια τῶν ᾿Ιουδαίων ἔθη μεταβαλεῖσθαι),
Ant. 13:397. Several other towns were destroyed, probably for the
same reason. Josephus reports that towns which had been destroyed
were rebuilt under Pompeius and Gabinus and that inhabitants
who had been exiled were allowed to return (*Ant.* 14:75–76; 88;
J.W. 1:155–57; 165–66).[13]

What was the lasting effect of this compulsory proselytizing?
We lack information on this matter from the Ituraeans, but Josephus
gives us glimpses from the history of the Idumaeans. As already
written above, he tells that since the time when they were conquered
by John Hyrcanus they have been Jews (*Ant.* 13:258).[14] In his work
on the great Jewish war against the Romans, he tells how the Idumaeans
actively entered the war claiming that they were Jews. During the
siege of Jerusalem by the Romans the Idumaeans wanted to enter
the city and participate in its defence (*J.W.* 4:233–353).[15] In the city
there was a fierce conflict between the Jewish authorities and the

---

[11] Iturea was located in the highlands of Lebanon. At the time of Aristobulus
it probably reached south to Galilee. See Schürer (1973) 217–18; 561–73.

[12] Kasher (1988) 46–77; 79–85. See also Kasher (1990) 121–23; 156–59; 175–78.
For criticism of Kasher's views, see Feldman (1993) 325–26.

[13] Schürer (1973) 228.

[14] Cohen (1989) 29, maintains that from the Jewish point of view the proselytes
were not called Jews, although they were members of the Jewish communities.
This view of Cohen needs be modified, however, since Josephus calls the Idumaean
proselytes "Jews", *Ant.* 13:258.

[15] Schürer (1973) 497–98.

zealots. The high priests Ananus and Jesus and their men learned that the Idumaeans worked together with the zealots, and they shut the city gates against them (J.W. 4:236). According to Josephus the high priest Jesus addressed them from a tower on the city wall, and the Idumaean military leader, the officer Simon, son of Caathas, gave a reply. In these speeches the Idumaeans are called a nation, ἔθνος (J.W. 4:243, 272). They were simultaniously Jewish family members, οἱ οἰκεῖοι, kinsmen, οἱ συγγενεῖς, and fellow-tribesmen, οἱόμόφυλοι, as distinct from members of other tribes (foreigners), οἱ ἀλλόφυλοι (J.W. 4:274–77).[16] Jerusalem was their metropol, and they wanted to defend the House of God and their common fatherland, ἡ κοινὴ πατρίς (J.W. 4:274, 279, 281).[17]

Correspondingly, Josephus writes that Herod was of Jewish descent (Ant. 20:173) and that his father, Antipater, included himself among the Jews when he negotiated with the Egyptian Jews (Ant. 14:131). There were at times tensions between the traditional Jews and the Idumaean Jews, however. In his conflict with Herod, Antigonus held it against him that he was an Idumaean, that is, a half Jew, ἡμιιουδαῖος (Ant. 14:403). The Idumaean Costobarus, whom Herod had appointed governor of Idumaea and Gaza, did not think it proper for the Idumaeans to adopt the customs of the Jews (Ant. 15:255).[18]

Joseph R. Rosenbloom correctly writes that after the end of the independent Hasmonean reign the Jews were not in the position of power necessary for using military means to force a people to convert.[19] As a much later example, this time from Southern Arabia, Rosenbloom mentions the king of Himyar, Dhu Nuwas. He became a devoted Jew and attacked the Christian city Najran. He besieged the city, giving its inhabitants the choice of accepting Judaism or being killed. This event took place between A.D. 520 and 530.[20]

[16] Cf. Zeitlin (1935) 329–31.
[17] See further Kasher (1988) 224–39.
[18] See further Kasher (1988) 214–23.
[19] Rosenbloom (1978) 96.
[20] Rosenbloom (1978) 102; Seligson (1965) 78.

2. Proselytes from Fear

National independence was the presupposition for the conquests and subsequent gaining of proselytes by force under John Hyrcanus, Aristobulus and Alexander Jannaeus. Many Jews lived, however, in the Diaspora away from their home country. Also in this context, dreams and ideas about recruiting proselytes by military force might be entertained, although the actual execution of the ideas in reality might not be possible under the circumstances. The Book of Esther has its life setting in just such a context.

The Book is a historical romance about Jewish persons who are pictured as having lived in the Persian court. The Book was probably written during the Maccabean period, possibly when John Hyrcanus reigned in Palestine.[21] In the book it is related that the Persian king, Ahasuerus/Xerxes (LXX: Artaxerxes), banished his queen, Vashti, from his presence because she refused to put on her finest clothes and appear before the guests at a lavish stag-party in the courtyard of the palace. From among the virgins in the country the king selected Esther, a Jewish girl, to be the queen. Esther was the niece and adopted daughter of the Jew Mordecai. Mordecai learned of a palace plot to assassinate the king. He told Esther, who in turn informed the king and saved his life.

Mordecai refused to prostrate himself before Haman, the king's first man. Haman obtained permission from the king to destroy all Jews in the kingdom on the 13th day of the month of Adar. Esther approached the king and told him that this decision would mean the destruction of her and her people. She persuaded him to make a new edict permitting the Jews to take vengeance on their enemies. Haman was hanged, the Jews annihilated their enemies and Mordecai was appointed Haman's successor.

This book has been and is very popular among the Jews and has been subject to many modifications and expansions. Thus there are six extended sections in the Greek text of the Septuagint. Josephus renders the Book of Esther in *Ant.* 11:184–296. He relies on the version of the Septuagint, including its expansions.[22]

---

[21] See Moore (1992) 626–33 and Moore (1992A) 633–43.

[22] *ibid.*

Of special importance in our connection is the permission given to the Jews to kill their enemies by military force (Esth 8:7–14 and Josephus, *Ant.* 11:271–83). Against this background many pagans became Jewish proselytes from fear: Then "there was gladness and joy among the Jews, a feast and a holiday. And many from the peoples of the country declared themselves Jews, for the fear of the Jews had fallen upon them" (Esth 8:17).

Shaye J. D. Cohen maintains that the verb מתיהדים does not mean "became Jews", but "pretended to be Jews" or "played the Jews".[23] The word, which only occurs here in the Old Testament, means "to confess that one belongs to Judaism".[24] This meaning of the word makes the understanding suggested by Zeitlin and Cohen less probable.[25] Moreover, both the Septuagint and Josephus understood the word to mean that the pagans became proselytes. In the Septuagint it is explicitly described how they became Jews, that is, by being circumcised: "... and many of the peoples [the Gentiles] were circumcised (περιετέμοντο), and became Jews ('Ιουδάιζον), for fear of the Jews". Josephus also gives the same specification: "... so that many of the other nations also, for fear of the Jews, had themselves circumcised (περιτεμνόμενα)..." (*Ant.* 11:285).[26] This understanding is also supported by the Targum Esther on Esth 8:17, where it is said that they became proselytes.[27]

There are other examples of persons who became proselytes out of fear. In the Book of Judith it is related that Achior the Ammonite, when he saw the head of Holofernes, believed in God, accepted circumcision and was adopted into the household of Israel (Jdt 14:5–10). Of special importance is the historical report that, when the Jews massacred some Roman soldiers, the Roman officer Metilius alone saved his life by entreaties and promises to become a Jew and be circumcised (Josephus, *J.W.* 2:454).

The Book of Esther is the scroll of the festival of Purim. Besides the book itself, the first evidence for the celebration of Purim occurs

---

[23] Cohen (1989) 29, n. 54; see also Zeitlin (1965) 873.

[24] Gesenius (1949) 289: "sich zum Judentum bekennen."

[25] See Feldman (1993) 554, n. 5.

[26] See Feldman (1993) 289; 337.

[27] Sperber (1968) ad loc.

in 2 Macc 15:36. Here it is called Mordecai's Day. Josephus tells that Mordecai wrote to all Jews who lived in the kingdom of Artaxerxes telling them to observe the festival of Purim. The festival should be observed for all time and never be forgotten (*Ant.* 11:293–95).

In the *Babylonian Talmud Yebamot* 24b the proselytes in the Book of Esther are criticized for becoming proselytes for the doubtful reason of fear. Therefore they were not true proselytes. Down through the centuries the festival of Purim has been observed, however. Thereby, traditions have been kept alive which tell about persons becoming proselytes because of military actions which created fear.[28]

B. Militant and Peaceful Proselytism

1. Religio-political Proselytism

The country of Adiabene was located half-way between Antioch and the Caspian Sea. Queen Helena and one of her sons, Izates, became converts to Judaism. Izates grew up in the land of Charakene, close to the Persian Gulf, so that he could be safe from the envy and hatred of his half-brothers. Here a Jewish merchant, Ananias, visited the wives of the king of the country and taught them to worship God after the manner of the Jewish tradition. Through them he came into contact with Izates, whom he won over to Judaism. When Izates returned to Adiabene to take over the kingdom, Ananias accompanied him. Queen Helena had in the meantime received instruction from another Jew and had been persuaded to accept the Laws of Moses. Thus both became Jewish proselytes and consequently established close contact with Jerusalem and Palestinian Jews. King Izates received also instruction from another Jew, Eleazar, who came from Galilee. The two Jews, the merchant Ananias and the Galilean Eleazar, had different views on the necessity of circumcision. In the precarious situation of the king, Ananias made the judgment that the king should abstain from taking circumcision:

> The king could, he said, worship God even without being circumcised if indeed he strived after following the ancestral laws of the Jews. This counted more than taking circumcision.

---

[28] See Fishman (1973) 70–110.

He told him, furthermore, that God Himself would pardon him if, constrained thus by necessity and by fear of his subjects, he failed to perform this rite (*Ant.* 20:41–42).

It is evident that Ananias was of the opinion that King Izates had the status of being a Jewish proselyte, even without being circumcised. He did not regard King Izates just as a sympathizer. Thus Ananias did not only say that the king was to worship God and follow certain aspects of the ancestral laws of the Jews (τὰ πάτρια τῶν ᾿Ιουδαίων), but stated that he should zealously follow the Jewish ancestral laws (*Ant.* 20:41). Ananias even tells the king that "this counted more than taking circumcision" (τοῦτ' εἶναι κυριώτερον τοῦ περιτέμνεσθαι) (*Ant.* 20:41). This formulation cannot mean that to worship the Jewish God as a sympathizer counted more than taking circumcision. Thus, in Ananias' judgment the king was a Jewish proselyte who, due to the circumstances, broke one commandment, circumcision, and would receive forgiveness by God for this.

Eleazar, "who had a reputation for being extremely strict concerning the ancestral laws (περὶ τὰ πάτρια) . . ." (*Ant.* 20:43), disagreed with Ananias and regarded the sin of not taking circumcision to be a most severe one: "In your ignorance, O King, you are guilty of the greatest (τὰ μέγιστα) offence against the laws and thereby against God" (*Ant.* 20:44). According to Eleazar, the king had to make his conversion complete by being circumcised. If not, the king was guilty of the greatest offence against the Jewish laws to which he, as a proselyte, had committed himself. Thus Eleazar said to the king: "How long will you continue to be uncircumcised?" (*Ant.* 20:45).

Scholars have maintained that since Izates was a monarch his case was a very special one, and that Ananias advised the king not to take circumcision due to caution, not because of religious belief.[29] King Izates' situation was hardly unique, however, since Jewish proselytes elsewhere might also face severe dangers from the pagan surroundings. Thus Philo (*Spec.* 4:178) writes: "For the proselyte, because he has turned his kinsfolk . . . into irreconcilable enemies . . ." In any case the passage in Josephus gives proof of different viewpoints on circumcision as applied to the case of a Jewish proselyte.

---

[29] See Nolland (1981) 192–94, and Feldman (1969) 410–11.

Ananias placed less emphasis on the commandment of circumcision than did Eleazar.[30]

Izates governed at the time when Claudius was Roman emperor.[31] In spite of a very turbulent political period, he managed to stay in power for 24 years until his death at 55 years of age. When his brother Monobazus and other relatives saw that Izates had won the admiration of all men due to his piety, they also abandoned their ancestral religion and adopted the Jewish religion and way of life (*Ant.* 20:75). The high nobles in Adiabene reacted negatively to their conversion to Judaism, and made political and military moves to have them removed, but in vain. The nobles were executed by King Izates (*Ant.* 20:76–80). During the Jewish war against Rome relatives of Monobazus fought on the side of the Jews against the Romans (*J.W.* 2:520; 6:357).

Ananias, Eleazar and other Jews were active in recruiting Queen Helena and her son Izates for Judaism. Their method was that of teaching and advice.[32] Correspondingly, Jews were active in gaining proselytes in Rome to such an extent that they were exiled from the city by Cornelius Scipio Hispanus (ca. 139 B.C.) and later by the emperor Tiberius in A.D. 19.[33]

According to Josephus King Izates was a proselyte by conviction. It is, nevertheless, probable that religio-political factors also were of importance in a situation in which Adiabene sought to keep as much independence as possible under pressure from the Parthians, Armenians, and the Romans.[34]

The religio-political motifs were even more evident when conversions to Judaism were caused by marriages arranged between leading political families. The Arabian Syllaeus wanted to marry Salome, Herod's sister: "This connection, he said, would not be unprofitable to Herod through his association with the government of Arabia, which was even now virtually in [Syllaeus'] hands and by rights should be more so" (*Ant.* 16:224). Herod and the other

---

[30] McEleney (1974) 328: "Obviously, Ananias thought the precept was dispensable in necessity."

[31] Schürer (1986) 163.

[32] McKnight (1991) 56 and 59–60.

[33] McKnight (1991) 72–73.

[34] See Neusner (1964) 60–66.

Jews agreed on the condition that Syllaeus became a Jewish proselyte before the wedding took place. Syllaeus would not submit to this, however, saying that if he did, he would be stoned to death by the Arabs (*Ant.* 16:225).

Agrippa I had promised his daughter Drusilla to King Antiochus Epiphanes of Commagene after the king had contracted with Agrippa to convert to Judaism. When the agreement was to be implemented, Antiochus Epiphanes rejected the marriage since he was not willing to convert after all (*Ant.* 20:139). Drusilla was then given to King Azizus of Emesa who had consented to be circumcised (*Ant.* 20:139). Later Drusilla's marriage to Azizus was dissolved, and she then married Felix (*Ant.* 20:143; cf. Acts 24:24). Another daughter of Agrippa I, Berenice, persuaded King Polemo of Cilicia to be circumcised and to take her in marriage. Polemo was willing chiefly on account of her wealth (*Ant.* 20:145–46). The marriage had not lasted long before Berenice deserted him. Polemo was granted a divorce, and the agreement that he should live as a Jew was anulled (*Ant.* 20:146). Berenice was together with Agrippa II when Paul appeared before him (Acts 25:13 – 26:32).

2. Proselytes by Militant Force or by Free Choice

When John Hyrcanus made the Idumaeans Jewish proselytes and Aristobulus did the same with the Ituraeans, the ethnic groups, as collectives, were Judaized.[35] Collective groups are predominant also in the Book of Esther, with the Jewish people on one side and other peoples on the other. However, the many who, according to the story, became proselytes from fear, became Jews as individuals. And the Ammonite Achior and the Roman Metilius exemplify cases in which individuals became Jewish proselytes.

In Josephus, *Life* 112–13 and 149–54 two individuals are put under pressure to be circumcised and become proselytes. Josephus tells of two pagan nobles who had fled from the region of Trachonitis to take refuge among the Jews. They found that the conflicting views of the Jewish masses and those of Josephus himself created tension among the Jews.

---

[35] Concerning collective conversions to Judaism, see Rosenbloom (1978) 93–117 ("Group Conversion to Judaism").

a) The view championed by the Jewish people:
They demanded that the two men had to be circumcised: "When the Jews would compel them to be circumcised if they would reside among them . . ." (τούτους περιτέμνεσθαι τῶν 'Ιουδαίων ἀναγκαζόντων, εἰ θέλουσιν εἶναι παρ' αὐτοῖς . . . (*Life* 113)). According to *Life* 149 some asserted that the men "ought not to live if they refused to conform to the customs of those (οὐκ ὀφείλειν ζῆν . . ., μὴ μεταβῆναι θέλοντας εἰς τὰ παρ' αὐτοῖς ἔθη . . .) with whom they had sought refuge."

b) Josephus' view, as formulated by himself:
". . . every one should worship God in accordance with the dictates of his own conscience, and not under constraint . . ." (δεῖν ἕκαστον κατὰ τὴν ἑαυτοῦ προαίρεσιν τὸν θεὸν εὐσεβεῖν, ἀλλὰ μὴ μετὰ βιάς (*Life* 113)).

As for the methods used, Josephus mentions formulated demands addressed to himself by the crowd (*Life* 113). They were instigated by "some" (*Life* 149). The two foreigners were accused of being sorcerers who made it impossible to defeat the Romans (*Life* 149). The people demanded that they should not be allowed to live if they refused to be circumcised, and on one occasion made an armed assault on their house in Tarichaeae, intending to kill them (*Life* 149–51). Josephus then felt himself forced to arrange for the escape of the two men, who fled to the district of Hippo, east of the Lake of Gennesaret (*Life* 152–54).

3. General Characterization of Proselytism

A comprehensive body of material in Philo of Alexandria's writings deals with proselytes, who become Jews. In most of these passages the focus is on individual persons. According to Philo the conversion of gentiles to Judaism has three aspects:[36]
  1. Religious conversion: The central theme is the change from worshipping many gods to the worship of the One True God. On the whole the conversion passages do not specify the various gods, but refer to them in a general way.

---

[36] See Borgen (1980).

In *Virt.* 102–04 Philo tells how the proselytes have abandoned the images of their gods, and the tributes and honours paid to them, and thus turned away from idle fables to the clear vision of truth and the worship of the one and truly existing God within the context of the Jewish Law.[37]

2. Ethical conversion: Another theme is the change from a pagan way of life to the Jewish virtuous life, which has the worship of the One God as a source. For example, *Virt.* 181–82 reads:

> For it is excellent and profitable to desert without backward glance to the ranks of virtue and abandon vice that malignant mistress; and where honour is rendered to the God who is, the whole company of the other virtues must follow in its train as surely as in the sunshine the shadow follows the body. The proselytes become at once temperate, continent, modest, gentle, kind, humane, serious, just, high-minded, truth-lovers, superior to the desire for money and pleasure . . .

3. Social conversion: In *Virt.* 102–04 Philo says that the proselytes have left their family, their country, their customs. Abraham is the prototype of the proselyte who leaves his home in this way (*Virt.* 214). The proselytes thus have made their kinsfolk into mortal enemies (*Spec.* 4:178). According to Philo, proselytes have entered the Jewish nation, *politeia*, a term which means "rights of a citizen, body of citizens, government, constitution of a state, commonwealth". The proselytes have entered a "new and godly commonwealth, *politeia*" (*Spec.* 1:51); in *Virt.* 180 it is explicitly stated that the proselytes enter "the government of the best law", that is, the Laws of Moses. Thus they join "a commonwealth, *politeia*, full of true life and vitality" (*Virt.* 219).

Although these passages on proselytes deal primarily with individuals, it is pertinent to ask if this concept also can be applied to collectives, such as ethnic groups and nations.

In the same section where Philo tells about the announcement of the Laws of Moses to the Greek half of the world, and reports on the Septuagint festival celebrated annually on Pharos, he also

---

[37] See also *Joseph and Asenath* 13:11–12.

expresses the hope that all nations will accept these Laws and become proselytes:

> Thus the Laws are shown to be desirable and precious in the eyes of all, ordinary citizens and rulers alike, and that too though our nation has not prospered for a long time . . . But if a fresh start should be made to brighter prospects, how great a change for the better might we expect to see! I believe that they would abandon their peculiar ways, and throwing overboard their ancestral customs, turn to honouring these (i.e. our) laws alone. For, when the brightness of their shining is accompanied by national prosperity, it will darken the light of the others as the risen sun darkens the stars (*Mos.* 2:43–44).

When Philo looks forward to a new period of prosperous times for the Jews, he may be referring to his philosophy of history, according to which kingdoms come and go and their fortunes change so that one kingdom succeeds another (*Immut.* 174).[38] Or maybe he is looking forward to prosperity for the Jewish nation in the eschatological time. It is to be noticed that prosperity in its broadest sense is seen as one aspect of the eschatological blessing in *Praem.* 98ff. and 168, as well as in other Jewish writings, such as in *Sib. Or.* 3:741–59.

The universal acceptance of the Laws of Moses is also the future hope expressed in *Sib. Or.* 3:702–30. When the peoples see how well God guards and cares for His Elect, then they will say: "Come, let us all fall on the ground and entreat the immortal king, the great eternal God. Let us send to the Temple, since he alone is sovereign and let us all ponder the Law of the Most High God . . ." (*Sib. Or.* 3:716–19)[39]. Such parallel ideas support the understanding that Philo in *Mos.* 2:43–44 envisions the time when all nations will become Jewish proselytes by abandoning their own laws and accepting the Laws of Moses.

As for methods used, according to *Virt.* 177 Moses actively reached out to the gentiles. He invites polytheists and offers them instruction, exhorting them to turn away from the many gods to God, the Creator

---

[38] Cf. Philo's description of the glorious fortunes of the Roman empire at the time when Gaius Caligula began his reign as emperor (*Legat.* 8–13).

[39] Charlesworth (1983) 378, cf. 741–59; cf. Volz (1934) 172 and 390.

and Father of all. Correspondingly, Philo encourages those whose actions serve the common weal to "use freedom of speech and walk in daylight through the midst of the *agora*, ready to converse with crowded gatherings . . . and . . . feast on the fresh sweet draught of words which are wont to gladden the minds of such as are not wholly averse to learning" (*Spec.* 1:321). ". . . we [the Jews] should follow her [nature's] intentions and display in public (προτιθέναι) all that is profitable and necessary for the benefit of those who are worthy to use it" (1:323).[40]

In these characterizations of proselytism by Philo, there is no mention of military force. He does not exclude military force being used in the future, however, should enemies attack the Israelites. Then ". . . there shall come forth a man, says the oracle (Lev 26:5 (LXX)), and leading his army and doing battle, he will subdue great and populous nations . . ." (*Praem.* 93).[41]

C. Militant Proselytism, Using Peaceful Means

1. The Confession to Christ, Proselytism and Mission

In the New Testament the military motif of conquest serves as a background for the missionary outreach, but the motif has been transformed by the methods of recruitment by peaceful means.

Some of the points of agreement between Christian mission and Jewish conquest are as follows:

1. The active and conscious reaching out to the nations. Several passages within the Pauline corpus as well as elsewhere in the New Testament testify to this point. As examples one might mention Paul's call as apostle to the gentiles, Gal 1:16: ". . . [he] was pleased to reveal his Son in me, in order that I might preach him among the nations . . ." Another outstanding example is Matt 28:19: "Go . . . make disciples of all nations . . .". A militaristic reaching out to the nations is pictured in Num 24:7–8 (LXX): ". . . he shall rule over many nations . . . he shall consume the nations . . ." With variations, the Septuagint version of this passage is also found in

---

[40] McKnight (1991) 55. Cf. Josephus, *Ant.* 9:208–14.
[41] See Borgen (1992) 341–61.

the Targums,[42] in Josephus *Ant.* 4:7, cf. 10:208–10 and in Philo *Mos.* 1:290–91 and *Praem.* 95–97. In *Mos.* 1:290–91 the following phrases may be quoted: ". . . he shall rule over many nations, and his kingdom spreading every day . . . it [the people] shall eat up many nations . . .".

2. The basis for this mission to the nations is a Jewish sovereign who has a universal claim on the nations. As examples from the New Testament Rom 1:3–5 and Matt 28:18–19 might be cited. Rom 1:4–5: ". . . his Son, who was a descendant from David . . . who was appointed Son of God in power . . . by his resurrection from the dead, Jesus Christ our Lord, through whom we have received grace and apostleship . . . among the nations . . ." Matt 28:18–19: "All authority in heaven and earth has been given to me. Go therefore . . . all nations".[43]

This conquest scene about the cosmic authority of Jesus corresponds to the installation of Moses as universal king in *Mos.* 1:155–57. And this God-given charge to Moses will be brought to its fulfilment by "the Man" who shall rule over many nations, again as seen in Num 24:7 (LXX), as rendered by Philo in *Mos.* 1:290–91 and *Praem.* 95–97.

3. Other features from Jewish military conquest traditions are also traceable:[44] According to 1 Cor 15:24f. at the future eschaton the final victory over all authorities will be won:[45] "Then comes the end when he [Christ] delivers the kingdom to God the Father after destroying every rule and every authority and power. For he must reign until he has put all his enemies under his feet." Although no combat is pictured in Phil 2:10–11,[46] the passage is to be mentioned here, since the scene is the *proskynesis* of Jesus Christ as Lord, that is, as the cosmic and universal ruler: ". . . that at the name of Jesus every knee should bow, in heaven and on earth and under the earth, and every tongue confess that Jesus Christ is Lord, to the glory of God the Father".

---

[42] Vermes (1961) 159ff.

[43] Windisch (1909) 61.

[44] Windisch (1909); Leivestad (1954).

[45] Leivestad (1954) 133–34.

[46] Leivestad (1954) 113–14.

Within military thought-categories the crucifixion is interpreted as a triumph over the principalities and powers:[47] "He [God] disarmed the principalities and powers and made a public example of them, triumphing over them in Him" (Col 2:15). The most elaborate use of ideas from militant messianism is found in the Book of Revelation.[48] The Roman emperor represents antichrist and together with the pagan nations he attacks the saints. Christ is depicted as a victorious conqueror. Here also the decisive victory is paradoxically understood to be won by Jesus in his sacrificial death on the cross. On that basis he was exalted as King of kings and Lord of lords to rule the nations with an iron rod.

Accordingly, Paul and the other missionaries were soldiers (Phil 2:25; Phlm 2) who fought an ideological war:[49] "For though we live in the world we are not carrying on a worldly war, for the weapons of our warfare are not worldly but have divine power to destroy strongholds. We destroy arguments and every proud obstacle to the knowledge of God, and take every thought captive to obey Christ" (2 Cor 10:3-5). Commenting on this passage H. Windisch[50] wrote: ". . . die Vorstellung von dem in kriegerischem Kampf die Welt erobernden jüdischen Messias ist auf das sonst so friedsame Werk der Ap. übertragen."

Although the apostles and missionaries experience suffering and persecution, their work can be seen as victorious and triumphant:[51] 1 Cor 2:14: "But thanks be to God, who in Christ always leads us in triumph . . .". R. Leivestad renders the meaning of this verse as follows: "What makes Paul praise God is that God leads us everywhere, so that the knowledge of Christ is spread all over the world, a knowledge which certainly implies death to those who are perishing, but abundant life to those who are saved."[52] As seen from this survey, in the New Testament the Jewish motif of conquest is central, but not as a conquest by military means, but one by peaceful

---

[47] Yabro Collins (1976); Leivestad (1954) 100-04.

[48] Leivestad (1954) 246-48.

[49] Leivestad (1954) 146-47.

[50] Windisch (1924) 296.

[51] Leivestad (1954) 140-45; 147-48.

[52] Leivestad (1954) 148.

methods of persuasion and in this way making proselytes of all nations. The inauguration of the eschatological era by the appearance of Jesus as the Messiah, meant that now the Jewish (cosmic and universal) thoughts of the conquest of all nations was to take place.

2. Proselyte Ideas, but Transformed

As a background to missionary ideas and practices in Early Christianity, Philo's ideas about proselytes are strikingly parallel with the threefold understanding of conversion. Thus, in Christian mission, conversion also consisted of these three aspects:

1. Religious conversion which meant a change from many gods to the one God: Gal 4:8–9 and 1 Thess 1:9 may illustrate the theme "from many gods to one God": "Formerly, when you did not know God, you were in bondage to beings that by nature are no god; but you have come to know God . . ." (Gal 4:8–9); ". . . how you turned to God from idols, to serve a living and true God . . ." (1 Thess 1:9–10). A corresponding formulation in Philo is found in *Virt.* 102–04: "the proselytes . . . abandoning . . . the temples and images of their gods . . . to the worship of the one and truly existing God . . .".

The eschatological setting is explicitly stated by Paul. In Gal 1:3–4 Paul talks of liberation from the present evil age. As a statement in the prescript of the Letter it makes clear that the whole Letter is to be understood from this point of view. Another central idea in the Letter is that the promise to Abraham is put in effect in Jesus Christ: all nations shall now receive the blessing. The eschatological and Christian adaptation of such Jewish proselyte-tradition is also evident in 1 Thess 1:9–10, by the fact that reference to the resurrection and the *parousia* of Jesus and the wrath to come is added (my italics): ". . . how you turned to God from idols, to serve a living and true God, *and to wait for his Son from heaven, whom he raised from the dead, Jesus who delivers us from the wrath to come*".[53] The christological identification of this deliverer from the wrath to come is a unique feature in Paul's rendering of this conversion-tradition. The christological aspect is specified as being Jesus, whom God raised from the dead.

---

[53] Bussman (1971) 52–53.

2. Ethical conversion from pagan immorality to Jewish/Christian morality. The transition from pagan immorality to a moral way of life is pictured in Christian sources in a way similar to ideas found in Philo: The lists of vices in 1 Cor 6:9–10 and Gal 5:19–21 have points in common with Philo's descriptions of pagan life. For example, without using the form of a catalogue, Philo, in *On the Contemplative Life*, describes the life of the gentiles, as does Paul, as a life of idolatry, immorality and excessive banqueting.

In 1 Cor 6:11 and Gal 5:22–23 the new life of the converts is seen in contrast to the gentile life of vices. In Gal 5:22–23 Paul even renders a list of virtues similar to the list given by Philo in *Virt.* 182. Paul writes: "But the fruit of the Spirit is love, joy, peace, patience, kindness, goodness, faithfulness, gentleness, self-control."

Both in 1 Cor 6:10–11 and in Gal 5:19–23 the eschatological perspective is explicitly stated. Immoral life will lead to exclusion from the kingdom of God.

3. Social conversion from other peoples to one people (=Jewish proselytism), and to one community among many peoples (=Christian mission).

Christian sources draw on Jewish traditions in their characterization of how the Christian "proselytes" form a cross-national community, a people among many peoples. The best example is found in Eph 2:11–22. In accordance with the proselyte pattern of contrast, the present is described against the pagan background, when they were uncircumcised gentiles, alienated from the commonwealth of Israel, ἡ πολιτεία τοῦ ᾽Ισραήλ. In the present they are not strangers or foreigners, but fellow-citizens, συμπολῖται, and members of the household of God. In Eph 2:12 the term πολιτεία was used, the very term which also is central to the Jewish people/nation in Philo's passages on proselytes. The conclusion of this analysis of Eph 2:11–22 seems then at first to be that Christian mission and Jewish proselytism are identical entities. The passage seems to tell how the gentile converts were brought into the commonwealth of Israel, i.e. to be members and citizens of the Jewish nation, within the limits set by the political circumstances.

In spite of this use of legal and technical terminology from the realm of state and ethnic communities, the passage in Eph 2:11–22 breaks away from this context. According to Eph 2:11–22 the Christian proselytes are not to make an ethnic and judicial break away from their families, country and nation. Thus the gentile converts are not to become citizens of the Jewish nation of the Torah. The law of commandments is abolished. In this way the Jewish idea of the people of God has been reshaped to mean the church of Christ into which both gentiles and Jews are to enter. The atonement in Christ has made this new inclusive community possible.

While Jewish proselytism brought gentile converts into the Jewish nation, Christian mission brought them into a cross-national community of Jews and gentiles, "built upon the foundation of the apostles and prophets, Christ himself being the chief cornerstone in whom the whole structure is joined together and grows into a holy temple in the Lord" (Eph 2:20–21).

Nevertheless, the agreements between these Christian sources on the one hand and Philo's description on the other hand are close. Christian missionary preaching and teaching here clearly use Jewish traditions about the conversion of proselytes. At several points, then, Christian mission and Jewish proselytism have the same content and have the same view on the change from polytheism to the true God and from a gentile lifestyle to a Jewish/Christian ethical lifestyle.

3. Forced to be Regular Jewish Proselytes?

At the time when King Izates of Adiabene became a Jewish proselyte, and Agrippa II, Drusilla and Berenice were engaged in religio-political proselytizing by dynastic marriages there were controversies within Early Christianity which had, among other places, spread to Antioch, Syria, Cilicia and Galatia. Jewish Christians in Judaea and Jerusalem were directly drawn into these controversies, as seen from Acts 15 and Paul's Letter to the Galatians. There was a conflict between an eschatological and cross-national recasting of Jewish proselytism and some Jewish Christians who wanted to bring the Christian gentile converts into the Jewish nation by means of circumcision, as normally was the case with proselytes.

In this controversy widespread formula-like phrases are used: One formula is: ἀναγκάζειν τινὰ περιτέμνεσθαι:

Gal 2:3: "... not even Titus who was with me and who was a Greek was compelled to be circumcised."
οὐδὲ ... ἠναγκάσθη περιτμηθῆναι ...

Gal 6:12: "they compel you to be circumcised"
οὗτοι ἀναγκάζουσιν ὑμᾶς περιτέμνεσθαι

Ant. 13:318: "... he ... compelled the inhabitants ... to be circumcised, and to live according to the Jewish laws."
ἀναγκάσας τε τοὺς ἐνοικοῦντας ... περιτέμνεσθαι
καὶ κατὰ τοὺς ' Ιουδαίων νόμους ζῆν

Life 113: "When the Jews would have compelled them to be circumcised if they wanted to be with them, I did not allow any compulsion to be put upon them ..."
τούτους περιτέμνεσθαι τῶν ' Ιουδαίων
ἀναγκαζόντων, εἰ θέλουσιν εἶναι παρ' αὐτοῖς ...

Ptolemeus: "The Idumaeans ... having been subjugated by the Jews and having been compelled to undergo circumcision ..."[54]
ἀναγκασθέντες περιτέμνεσθαι

Compare also phrases about yielding to force:

Ant. 13:258: "... they submitted to circumcision ..."
(Gal 5:1: "... do not submit again to a yoke of slavery.")

Although these parallels occur in different contexts, all demonstrate that it was widespread to regard circumcision as a basic identity marker for a Jew and that, when necessary, gentiles were forcefully circumcised. By this marker they were brought into a life within the context of the Law of Moses.

Hyrcanus and Aristobulus used military force, a method not used by the intruders into the congregations in Galatia. Thus, this situation was more akin to that experienced by Josephus when he was put under severe pressure by the people after two gentiles from the region of Trachonitis had fled to the Jews for refuge. The Jewish crowd wished to compel the two gentiles to be circumcised as a condition of residence among them. When both the two gentiles and Josephus were in danger of being killed, Josephus finally had to help them to flee so that they could escape death or forcible

---

[54] Stern (1976) § 146.

circumcision (*Life* 112–13; 149–54). This incident illustrates the kind of pressure and persecution which Paul's opponents feared might be applied to them. This fear motivated them to compel the Galatian Christians to be circumcised (Gal 6:12).

Paul refuses to make circumcision a condition for the Galatian converts to remain in the people of God. According to him, there is a christological basis for the transition. Instead of binding the change to physical circumcision, Paul ties it to the death of Christ Jesus: "And those who belong to Christ Jesus have crucified the flesh with its passion and desires" (Gal 5:24). In 1 Cor 6:11 the transition is marked by baptism and by being justified in the name of Jesus Christ and in the Spirit of our God.

For the Jewish proselytes the new life, characterized by lists of virtues, is a life in accordance with the Laws of Moses. It is to be lived in the new context of the Jewish nation, as it was organized at the various places in the Roman empire, for example in the form of a *politeuma*. According to the Christian mission, as understood by Paul, the gentile converts are not under the Law of Moses (Gal 5:18). They are not members of the Jewish *politeuma*. But their new life outside of the Jewish nation is in accordance with the Laws of Moses, as Paul says in connection with the list of virtues, in Gal 5:22–23: ". . . against such things there is no Law" (Gal 5:23b).

In another type of phrase a conditional clause is followed by a main clause:

Acts 15:1: "Unless you are circumcised according to the custom of Moses, you cannot be saved."
ἐὰν μὴ περιτμηθῆτε τῷ ἔθει τῷ Μωυσέως, οὐ δύνασθε σωθῆναι

Ant. 13:257: "Hyrcanus . . . permitted them to remain in their country, if they had themselves circumcised and and were willing to observe the laws of the Jews."
ἐπέτρεψεν αὐτοῖς ἐν χώρᾳ, εἰ περιτέμνοιντο τὰ αἰδοῖα καὶ τοῖς Ἰουδαίων νόμοις χρῆσθαι θέλοιεν

These statements have in common that they state that circumcision is a basic condition. The people referred to were to become Jews. The contents of the main clauses differ, however. Hyrcanus made circumcision the condition upon which the Idumaeans were allowed to remain in their own country. In the controversy among the Christians in Antioch, some saw circumcision as the condition for experiencing the eschatological salvation. Gentiles were to become Jews to be saved. Circumcision led a person into a life as a Jewish proselyte committed to the Laws of Moses:

Acts 15:5: "It is necessary to circumcise them, and to charge them to keep the law of Moses."
δεῖ περιτέμνειν αὐτοὺς παραγγέλλειν τε τηρεῖν τὸν νόμον Μωυσέως.

Gal 5:3: "I testify again to every man who receives circumcision that he is bound to keep the whole law."
μαρτύρομαι δὲ πάλιν παντὶ ἀνθρώπῳ περιτεμνομένῳ ὅτι ὀφειλέτης ἐστὶν ὅλον τὸν νόμον ποιῆσαι

Ant. 13:257: "Hyrcanus . . . permitted them to remain in their country, if they had themselves circumcised and and were willing to observe the laws of the Jews."
ἐπέτρεψεν αὐτοῖς ἐν χώρᾳ, εἰ περιτέμνοιντο τὰ αἰδοῖα καὶ τοῖς Ἰουδαίων νόμοις χρῆσθαι θέλοιεν

Ant. 13:258: ". . . they submitted to use circumcision and the way of life of the Jews in other respects."
τὴν περιτομὴν καὶ τὴν ἄλλην τοῦ βίου δίαιταν ὑπέμειναν τὴν αὐτὴν Ἰουδαίοις ποιήσασθαι

Thus circumcision was the marker at entry into the Jewish community as an integrated member under the Laws of Moses. Gal 5:3 renders such a traditional phrase, as seen from the quotations listed above. The question is how the word πάλιν, "again", is to be understood. Many scholars do not think that the word here carries its distinctive meaning "again". Thus it does not refer to a statement made by Paul to the Galatians at an earlier occasion.[55] Since Paul here draws on a traditional standard phrase which is used in connection

---

[55] Schlier (1971) 231; Betz (1979); Oepke and Rohde (1973) 156; Dunn (1993) 265.

with proselytes, it seems more probable that Paul has used this or similar formulations during his missionary stay among the Galatians in order to make evident the consequences of being circumcised. Against such a background it is understandable that the intruders might interpret such words in their own way and claim that Paul had preached circumcision (Gal 5:11).[56] Paul had replaced circumcision by the cross of Christ, and on this basis it was possible for gentiles to become the children of Abraham without becoming Jews, Rom 4 and Gal 3. Such a distinction had not been drawn by the intruders, however.

When Paul and the other participants at the meeting in Jerusalem, with the exception of the "false brethren" (Gal 2:4), rejected the traditional form of proselytism, what then was their alternative?

First one should be reminded of the case of King Izates. As shown above, the two Jews, Ananias and Eleazar, gave different advice with regard to circumcision. Thus, in given situations, there were some Jews who deliberately would regard a convert as a proselyte without the commandment of circumcision being observed.

Those who proclaimed that the eschatological era had dawned in Jesus Christ, formulated the alternative in an even more radical way. For example, to Paul faith in Jesus Christ was such a basic foundation that he could relativize the question of uncircumcision or circumcision. Instead of working for integrating gentile converts into the Jewish state religion and national religion under the Laws of Moses, proselytes who confessed Christ were integrated into a cross-national community of Jews and gentiles. Along this line it is said by Paul in Rom 4:11–12 that Abraham is the father of those who believe, of both those uncircumcised and those circumcised.

Conclusion

1. In the period from John Hyrcanus to the Jewish war against the Romans there is evidence for a variety of methods and motifs for recruiting converts from the gentiles into Judaism and the Jewish nation. In the writings of Josephus and in non-Jewish writings there are sources which tell of active and even very aggressive methods

[56] Borgen (1982) 37–46; also in Borgen (1983) 33–46. See further Borgen (1987C) 255–59.

of conquering peoples and making them Jewish proselytes. Such methods were logical, since the Jewish religion was a state religion in which politics and religion were merged into one.

In the aetiological story of the Purim festival, the Book of Esther, and in the apocryphal Book of Judith one reads about gentiles who became proselytes out of fear for their lives. Josephus testifies to the fact of persons becoming proselytes from fear. It should be added that non-Jewish sources relate that Jews in Rome at times were very active in recruiting proselytes.

In the *Babylonian Talmud Yebamot* 24b, it is stated that a conversion for the sake of marriage, fear or love is not valid. Thus, according to the rabbis, such a person is not a proselyte. From the material presented in this study it is evident that a statement like this one is to be understood as criticism against times when such motifs for becoming a proselyte were accepted as legitimate.[57]

2. For Paul and other Christians, faith in Jesus Christ was so basic that both uncircumcision and circumcision were made to be relative and actually irrelevant. Instead of understanding proselytism to mean that a gentile convert was being integrated into a national state and religion under the Laws of Moses, the "proselytes" who confessed Christ were integrated without circumcision into a cross-national people that included both Jews and gentiles.

From Gal 1:15–16 and from the Acts of the Apostles we learn that Paul was called an apostle to the gentiles. His conquest of the nations shows in this way kinship both with the conscious foreign policy and military conquest of the Hasmonean kings and with the religio-political foreign policy and proselytizing activity of the Herodian dynasty. Paul's missionary conquest was not made by means of military arms or foreign policy, but by the proclamation of the gospel and by powerful deeds to bring Jews and gentiles to belief in Christ and thereby into a cross-national and cross-ethnic fellowship.

---

[57] A similar understanding is found in Feldman (1993) 337.

3

Judaism in Egypt

The connection of the Jews with Egypt goes back into the distant past of the second century B.C. The memory of the captivity and the Exodus has been central to the Jews throughout the centuries and has contributed much to the identity of the people. Evidence of Jewish settlement in Egypt comes from a later time, however.[1] Emigration took place around 600 B.C., increased by the capture of Jerusalem and the destruction of the first temple by the Babylonians in 587. Documentation for this emigration is found in Jer 44:11: "The word came to Jeremiah concerning all the Jews that dwelt in the land of Egypt, at Migdol, at Tah'panhes, at Memphis, and in the land of Pathros . . ."

A. Preludes

A series of Aramaic papyri of the 5th century found at Elephantine Island, opposite Assuan in Southern Egypt, has revealed that there was a military colony of Jews on the island.[2] They had a temple with pillars of stone and five stone gateways. There was an altar for sacrifices to their god Yahu. In addition there were other gods, such as Anath and Bethel. Thus, the religion of these Jews tended to be syncretistic, such as presupposed by Jeremiah in the word

---

[1] Davies and Finkelstein (1986) 375–76.

[2] *ibid.*, 376–400; Sachau (1911); Porten (1968).

of God addressed against the Egyptian Jews: "Why do you provoke me to anger with the works of your hands, turning incense to other gods in the land of Egypt" (44:8). The temple at Elephantine existed before the Persian king Cambyses invaded Egypt in 525 B.C.

An order issued by the authority of Darius II in 419 B.C. instructs the colony to celebrate the Feast of Unleavened Bread and probably the Passover. There are also probably references on the ostraca found to the Day of Preparation and the Sabbath. The relations between these Jews and their neighbours worsened, and in the year 410 B.C. the priest of the Egyptian god Khnum, the patron god of Elephantine, with the aid of the local Persian commander, Waidrang, stirred up the Egyptians to attack the Jews, destroy their temple and stop all sacrifice. The Jews wrote to Bagohi, the Persian governor of Judea, and to others, such as the high priest in Jerusalem, Johanan. Another copy went to the Samarian governor's two sons, Delaiah and Shelemiah. In these letters they tried to enlist support for the restoration of the temple. The authorization was given that the "altar-house of the God of Heaven" should be rebuilt so that "the meal-offering and incense" may again be offered. Thus no permission of animal sacrifices was given.

In 404 B.C. Egypt revolted against the Persians, and won independence. A letter reporting the accession of the Egyptian king Nepherites, written in 399 B.C., is the latest dated document. The earliest dated document was written in 495 B.C. Thus these papyri give direct information about a century of the life of this Jewish community, which was founded at an even earlier date.

The Jews were organized as a combined temple community and a sociomilitary community. As members of the military garrison the Jews served together with non-Jews in the same detachment, but the leaders were non-Jews, Persian and other nationals. The governor and the garrison commander exercised both civil-judicial and military functions. These seem to have been Persians, and so also the police. A person with a Hebrew name was "Anani the Scribe (and) chancellor at the court of satrap Arsames in Memphis". Although the leaders at Elephantine seem to have been non-Jews, the garrison as such must have been predominantly Jewish, since it was known as "the Jewish force". The Jews had their own priests and other leaders who represented them. One of the leaders, who had the name of Jedaniah, was in charge of the communal archives and the temple treasures. Intermarriage with non-Jews is documented, and also on the other hand the participation in Jewish observance on the Sabbath by non-Jews who either had become proselytes or were active symphathizers.

The existence of the Jewish temple at Elephantine in Egypt, as well as the Samaritan temple on Mount Gerizim, the temple at Araq el-Emir in Transjordan, and Onias' temple at Leontopolis in Egypt show that the Deuteronomic programme of centralized and exclusive worship in the Jerusalem temple was not put into effect among Jews everywhere. The temple and the Jewish military colony at Elephantine testify to a rich variety within Jewish religion and life at the time of Ezra and Nehemiah. Its origin has been connected with the statement in the *Letter of Aristeas* that Jews went as auxiliaries to fight in the army of the Egyptian king Psammetichus against the king of the Ethiopians. The ruler referred to is probably Psammetichus I, who largely relied on foreign mercenaries in his fight for uniting Egypt as an independent kingdom. Some of the Jews who took part in the campaign against the Ethiopians might then have been stationed at Elephantine.

No corresponding line can be drawn of the history of the Elephantine Jewish community after the latest datable document from 399 B.C. No traceable evidence for its continued existence has been found. The community might have been removed from the island. In any case, it disappears from the scene of history.

B. The Hellenistic Period

1. From Alexander to Ptolemy VI (332–181 B.C.)

The history of the Jews under Macedonian/Ptolemaic rule falls into two sub-periods, the reign of Ptolemy VI Philometor serving as a dividing line. During the period before the reign of Ptolemy VI Philometor (181–145 B.C.) the Jews settled in towns and in the country and gradually grew in sufficient number to form communities of their own within the general structure of the Ptolemaic society. The period from the beginning of Ptolemy VI Philometor until the

Roman conquest (181–30 B.C.) was the time in which the Jews in Egypt fully flourished.[3]

As background the general political context needs be sketched. Alexander the Great conquered Egypt in 332 B.C. and after his death in 323 B.C. his senior generals, the Diadochs, formed a collective group of rulers. One of the generals, Ptolemy, was satrap of Egypt. When the collective leadership broke up, the empire was divided into three main parts, the kingdom of Antigonid Macedonia, the Seleucid kingdom in Western Asia and the Ptolemaic kingdom in Egypt.

Ptolemy I, called Soter, managed to defend his position in Egypt and founded the Ptolemaic dynasty. Egypt became an independent "Macedonian" kingdom, engaged in hard struggle for maintaining its independence and for playing a leading role in the affairs of the Hellenistic world. Alexandria, the city founded by Alexander, became the capital, and from this northern centre of Egypt, in close approximity to the other centres of Greek civilization, the Ptolemies ruled over the long and narrow country created by the river Nile. Since the native Egyptians regarded the Ptolemies as an alien government – in spite of all the Egyptian traditions taken over by these rulers – the Ptolemies employed Macedonians, Greeks and people from other non-Egyptian nations in their administration and army. Moreover, many prisoners of war from various nations were brought to Egypt as slaves.[4]

In the Seleucid realm, a decentralized administrative system prevailed, built on a reorganization of the old Persian satrapies. The government of Ptolemaic Egypt, on the other hand, became a highly centralized and more ruthlessly efficient version of the ancient Pharaonic system. This reorganization took mainly place during the reigns of Ptolemy I Soter ([323]304–284 B.C.) and Ptolemy II Philadelphus (284–246 B.C.). The whole land was the personal possession, the "house", of the king. The first man in the state beside the king was the *dioketes*, who bore responsibility for the entire possessions and income of the king. Egypt had of old been divided into *nomes*, and these into *toparchies*. The local administrative unit was the village. The chief officials were the military *strategos*, and

---

[3] Tcherikover (1957) 189.

[4] Rostovtzeff (1941) 1–43, 255–422.

the *oikonomos* for economic matters. The leading officials were usually Greeks and Macedonians.[5]

The encounter of the Jews with Hellenistic Egypt, therefore, took place within the framework of the Ptolemies' military and economic expansions. According to Josephus (*J.W.* 2:487; *Ag. Ap.* 2:35) Alexander the Great gave the Jews permission to settle in Alexandria on a basis of equal rights with the Greeks. They received this favour from Alexander in return for their loyalty to him. Josephus' reports on this do not appear to be credible. They have a clear apologetic motive, and seem to be composed with the aim of ascribing the privileges accorded the Jews of Alexandria to Alexander the Great himself. Josephus' statement about the equal rights of Jews and the Greek full citizens of Alexandria is very much debated in recent research.[6]

Josephus has more reliable information on the immigration of Jews from Palestine to Egypt during the interim period of Alexander's successors, the Diadochs (323–301 B.C.). Ptolemy I Soter conquered Palestine for the first time in 320 B.C.; he conquered it again in 312 B.C., 302 B.C., and finally in 301 B.C. It is probable that in the course of these wars numerous Jewish prisoners were taken into Egypt, as also is told in the *Letter of Aristeas* 12–14. According to *Aristeas* (12–27, 37), 100,000 Jewish captives were brought to Egypt, of whom 30,000 were placed in fortresses, and the rest, i.e. old men and children, Ptolemy gave to his soldiers as slaves. Ptolemy II Philadelphus (284–246 B.C.) gave amnesty and freedom to the slaves.

Some Jews seemed to follow Ptolemy I voluntarily, as exemplified by the High Priest Hezekiah and some of his friends who followed him. Josephus, drawing on material from Hecataeus of Abdera, tells that Hezekiah and the other Jews following the battle of Gaza, 312 B.C., received in writing the conditions attaching to their settlement and political status, and emigrated (*Ag. Ap.* 1:186–89). The historical value of Josephus' report is disputed among scholars. Recent research has shown, however, that the sections in Josephus, *Ag. Ap.* 1:183–204, do not render material from a Jewish forger, but information derived from the work of the authentic Hecataeus, who was a contemporary of Alexander and Ptolemy I.[7] In another passage Josephus (*Ag. Ap.*

---

[5] Hengel (1974) 18–19.

[6] Tcherikover (1966) 272; Kasher (1985) 2; Tcherikover (1957) 1–3.

[7] Kasher (1985) 2–3; Tcherikover (1966) 272–73 and 426–27.

1:194) reports that after Alexander's death myriads of Jews migrated to Egypt and Phoenicia in consequence of the disturbed condition of Syria.

The Jews settled all over Egypt, in the towns and in the country. Although living in Egypt, their ties with Jerusalem and Palestine remained strong and communication was made the easier by the fact that for about 100 years (301-198 B.C.) Palestine was one of the Ptolemies' foreign possessions.

Some places, such as Migdol, Tahpanhes, Noph/Memphis and the land of Pathros (i.e. the southern country) were inhabited by Jews already from the time of the prophet Jeremiah (Jer 44:1). The settlement in various places in Lower Egypt is attested by inscriptions, some of which come from the third century. Numerous papyri from the middle of the third century and later give evidence of Jewish population in the villages and towns of the Fayûm.[8] The evidence for Jewish presence in Upper Egypt during the third century is meagre. The existence of a Jewish community at Elephantine in Upper Egypt until about 400 B.C., Jeremiah's reference to the land of Pathros, and the attestation of ostraca of Jewish settlements in the second century B.C. indicate that some Jews lived also in that part of the country during the third century B.C. This conclusion is supported by evidence for the existence of a Synagogue in upper Egypt already in the third century B.C.[9]

Besides this Synagogue at an unknown place in Upper Egypt, third-century Synagogues are known to have existed in Schedia, Crocodilopolis-Arsinoe, and Alexandrou-Nesos. Since the Synagogues were centres of Jewish religious, political and cultural life, the reference to a Synagogue indicates that there was an organized Jewish community at that place.

The inscription at Schedia (Kafr ed Dauwar, 20 kilometres southeast of Alexandria) contains the dedication of a Synagogue: "in honour of King Ptolemy and Queen Berenice his sister and wife and their children, the Jews built the *proseuche*." A similar inscription has been found in Crocodilopolis-Arsinoe, the main city, the metropolis, of the Fayûm district (about 100 kilometres south of Cairo): "in honour of King Ptolemy, son of Ptolemy and Queen Berenice, his

---

[8] Tcherikover (1957) 3.

[9] Tcherikover (1957) 3–4, 8.

wife and sister and their children, the Jews in Crocodilopolis (dedicated) the *proseuche*." In Alexandrou-Nesos, another town in the Fayûm district, a juridical papyri dated 218 B.C. contains a petition of an unnamed woman, complaining that a local Jew, Dorotheos, had stolen her cloak. She reports that Dorotheos fled to the Synagogue holding the cloak. By the intervention of a person by the name of Lezelmis the cloak was deposited with the Synagogue verger, Nikomachos, to keep till the case was tried.[10]

What was the nature of these communities? The dedication of the Synagogues to the king show that the Jewish communities recognized the king and were recognized by him. The dedications are on behalf of the reigning sovereign in the same way as are the pagan dedications, but direct ruler worship was avoided by the Jews.[11] The recognition of the Synagogue by the king implied that he had given the Jews a legal status as a community, most probably in the form of a *politeuma*.

The settlers from various ethnic groups were in many places organized as such *politeumata*. Such communities in Egypt were the *politeumata* of Idumaeans, Phrygians, Cretans, Lycians, Cilicians, and Boeotians. The legal status of such a *politeuma* has not been clarified at every point, but basically it was the confirmation by the king that an ethnic community was permitted – within limits – to live in accordance with its ancestral laws. In the case of the Jews, this meant the right to live according to the Laws of Moses.[12] It is probable that the High Priest Hezekiah, who joined Ptolemy in 312 B.C., received the charter of such a *politeuma*, an event which Josephus cited Hecataeus as relating: that Ptolemy I gathered Jews who were prepared to follow him to Egypt and read them from a document: "For he possessed (the conditions) of their settlement and their political constitution (drawn up) in writing" (*Ag. Ap.* 1:189). A variant of the formula "to live according to their ancestral laws" was also used by the Seleucid King Antiochus III on the occasion

---

[10] Tcherikover (1957) 8 and 239–41; 3:141, 164; Kasher (1985) 138, 144–46.

[11] Fraser (1972) 226–27, 282–83, 298–99, cf. Philo, *Legat.* 137–38, 141–42, 356–57; Josephus, *Ant.* 12:67; Kasher (1985) 30 and 257, n. 92.

[12] Tcherikover (1957) 6–8; Tcherikover (1966) 299–301; Kasher (1985) 30, 41.

of his conquest of Jerusalem in 198 B.C.[13] Moreover, in the *Letter of Aristeas* 310 the Jewish community of Alexandria is called *politeuma*. The largest Jewish community in Egypt was this one in Alexandria. The first authentic evidence of the presence of Jews in Alexandria is given by Aramaic and Greek inscriptions from the necropolis of Ibrahamiya in the environs of the town, probably of the reign of Ptolemy I or II.[14] The Alexandrian literature, especially the translation of the Bible into Greek, testifies to the strength and vitality of the Jewish community of Alexandria already from the third century B.C.

The main occupation for the Jews in Egypt were military service and agriculture. Although the Ptolemies identified themselves with Pharaonic and other Egyptian traditions, they were aliens among the native Egyptians. As noted earlier, they depended therefore upon Macedonian and other non-Egyptian military personnel for their power. Accordingly numerous Jews served in the army as soldiers on duty or as soldiers of the reserves. To lessen the cost of maintaining an army, and to make the military forces identify themselves with the government, the Ptolemies adopted the policy of settling large number of soldiers in special military colonies, where in return for a plot of farm land they were obliged to return to active service upon call. This plot of land was liable to be withdrawn and restored to the king's possession, yet, in the process of time, it became gradually a permanent possession and could as such be inherited by the leaseholder's (the *cleruch's*) children. The terms used to designate such a military colony was *katoikiai* or *cleruchies*.[15]

There is no evidence for self-contained Jewish military units in the third century B.C. Josephus (*J.W.* 2:487ff.) reports that Alexandrian Jews were permitted to take the title of Macedonians, which probably meant that some Jews served in the Macedonian unit. The possibility should not be excluded, however, that there were separate Jewish units or sub-units at places where the Jews were numerous enough to form fairly large communities, such as in the Fayûm.[16] Some Jews served as officers, such as Eleazar, son

[13] Tcherikover (1957) 7 and n. 19; *Ant.* 12:142.

[14] Tcherikover (1957) 3, n. 8 and Tcherikover (1964) 138–39.

[15] Tcherikover (1957) 11–15.

[16] Kasher (1985) 40–48.

of Nicolaus, who, according to an inscription at the Fayûm, served as *hegemon*. This term generally designated a high officer next in the rank to the *strategos*.[17]

The other main area of occupation of the Jews in the third century B.C. was agriculture. Having received allotments by the king, many soldiers were at the same time farmers. Other Jews were lease-holders, "king's peasants," field hands, vine-dressers, shepherds, and so on. Jews also held positions in the police and in the governmental administration. A renegade Jew, Dositheos, son of Drimylos, served as one of the two heads of the royal secretariate; later he was called to the highest priestly office in Egypt – that of being priest in the ruler-cult as the eponymous priest of Alexander and the deified Ptolemies. He served during the reigns of Ptolemy III Euergetes I (246–221 B.C.) and Ptolemy IV Philopator (221–204 B.C.).[18]

As the Jews penetrated into Ptolemaic Egypt, Hebrew and Aramaic gradually ceased to serve as spoken and literary languages, especially in Alexandria, but also increasingly in other parts of Egypt, as seen from inscriptions and papyri written in Greek. Since the Jewish communities within limits were permitted to follow the ancestral laws, the knowledge of the Laws of Moses was a fundamental need for the Jews themselves, and to a varying degree also for their sovereigns and employers, the different levels of the Ptolemaic administration.[19]

The Greek translation of the Hebrew Bible, the Septuagint (the Translation of the Seventy), probably was initiated during the reign of Ptolemy II Philadelphus (284–246 B.C.) and was (with the exception of the Book of Daniel) completed towards the mid-second century B.C. The Greek spoken and written by the Jews reflected their background. The Septuagint (LXX) contains many Hebraisms; and a learned Greek, Cleomedes, gibes at the rude folk dialect used in the Synagogues. The translators to some extent modified the Hebrew text, at times drawing on some of the current exegetical traditions.[20] As for the legendary story about the translation as recorded in the *Letter of Aristeas*, it will be discussed below.

---

[17] Tcherikover (1964) 163; Kasher (1985) 46.

[18] Tcherikover (1957) 230–36; Kasher (1985) 60.

[19] Cf. Kasher (1985) 5; Tcherikover (1957) 31; Tcherikover (1966) 348.

[20] Tcherikover (1957) 30–32; Tcherikover (1966) 348; Fraser (1972) 689–90.

The Septuagint served as basis for the Jewish Alexandrian literature. The pieces preserved of this literature from the third century are largely found in Eusebius, *Praeparatio Evangelica*. Eusebius has five fragments of Demetrius, and Clement of Alexandria preserves still another fragment. Demetrius wrote in the third century B.C. under Ptolemy IV Philopator (221–204 B.C.), probably in Alexandria. His work was apparently called *On the Kings of Judaea*. The fragments mainly concerned the patriarchal history of the Septuagint Pentateuch and were probably part of the preface to an account of the Judaean monarchy. He formulates the biblical history in the form of Greek chronological historiography, corresponding to the chronological presentation of Egyptian history by the Egyptian priest Manetho, who also lived in the third century B.C. The goal which Demetrius and Manetho had in common was to demonstrate the considerable age of the respective national traditions.[21] Demetrius is also an exegete. He builds his book on the Septuagint and raises exegetical problems and gives answers (cf. the exegetical form of *quaestiones et solutiones*).

Eusebius has also preserved parts of the drama *The Exodus* written in Greek iambic trimeter by one Ezekiel, otherwise unknown. The tragedy covered most of the life of Moses in a version which for the most part followed the Septuagint translation quite closely, from Moses' birth and to the Exodus with the crossing of the Red Sea, the destruction of the Egyptians, and closing with a description of the oasis Elim. A remarkable departure from the Septuagint text is found in a dialogue between Moses and his father-in-law, in which Moses describes a dream. In his dream Moses is conveyed to Sinai's peak, where he sees a gigantic throne and upon it, God himself in human semblance. God bids him approach the throne, gives him the sceptre, seats him on the throne and crowns him. From the throne, Moses beholds the whole universe. According to the interpretation, Moses will cause a great throne to arise, and he himself will rule over mortals. Moreover, he will see all things in the present, past and future.

The fragments place emphasis on the Passover, and they express a cosmic understanding of Jewish existence. Moses' cosmic kingship implies a claim by the Jewish nation to be the ruler of the world.

---

[21] Hengel (1974): 69: Fraser (1972) 690–94; Attridge (1984) 246–97; Doran (1987) 248–51.

Accordingly, the opposing Egyptians, who fought against the Jews, were destroyed. The tragedy shows how an Egyptian Jew employs Greek literary form to interpret Jewish self-understanding. The tragedy was written during the second half of the third century or the first half of the second century B.C.[22]

The Egyptian priest Manetho counselled Ptolemy I Soter on native religion, and in his history of Egypt he also interpreted the Exodus of the Hebrew people. He represented them as mixed up with a crowd of Egyptian lepers and others, who for various maladies were condemned to banishment from Egypt. Manetho's work reflects the hostility of Egyptians to foreigners, and especially to Jews.[23] At the same time his polemic against the Jews testifies to the fact that they represented an important factor in Egyptian society already.

2. From Ptolemy VI (181–145 B.C.) to the Roman Conquest (30 B.C.)

The Jews of Egypt not only consolidated their positions during the period from Ptolemy VI Philometor (181–145 B.C.) to the Roman conquest in 30 B.C., but they became a considerable military and political force. The background was the weakening of the Ptolemaic government since the mismanagement of the Egyptian economy by Ptolemy IV Philopator (221–204 B.C.) and Ptolemy V Epiphanes (204–181 B.C.). The Ptolemaic relationship to the native Egyptians deteriorated, fomenting local revolts. Moreover, the foreign policy of the Seleucids in Antioch grew more aggressive, and they consistently were at the attack militarily. Family quarrels and court intrigues drained the strength of the Ptolemaic dynasty from the inside. When the Ptolemaic kings called for assistance from Rome, the new power in the West, Egypt became almost a client of Rome. In 198 B.C. Antiochus III (222–187 B.C.) conquered Palestine, and in 170 B.C. Antiochus IV Epiphanes (175–164 B.C.) invaded Egypt, but had to withdraw upon the ultimatum given him by the Roman envoy Popilius Laenas.[24]

---

[22] Nickelsburg (1984) 25–30; Fraser (1972) 707–08; Cf. Borgen (1984) 267–68.

[23] *Ag. Ap.* 1:229; 2:1–15; Aziza (1987) 41–52; Fraser (1972) 508–09.

[24] Tcherikover (1966) 73–89; Rostovtzeff (1941): 705 and 871; Wilson (1962) 55–56; Fraser (1972) 119–20.

When the relation between Jerusalem and the Seleucid occupants grew tense, pro-Ptolemaic sympathies developed in the city, and shortly before the Maccabean revolt, which started against the Seleucid government in 167, many Jews emigrated to Egypt. Of special importance is the emigration of Onias of the high priestly family in Jerusalem.

According to Josephus (*J.W.* 1:33 and 7:423), the high priest of Jerusalem, Onias III, fled to Egypt during the persecution by Antiochus IV Epiphanes (175–164 B.C.) in 175 B.C. Conversely, Josephus presents another version (*Ant.* 13:62 ff. and 12:387) in which he connected the emigration to Egypt with the appointment of Alcimus to the high priesthood in Jerusalem, about 162–160 B.C. When Onias IV realized that the Seleucid authorities had managed to abolish his family's claim to the high priesthood, he left for Egypt. In Egypt he found an ally in Ptolemy VI Philometor (181–145 B.C.). V. Tcherikover, after having analysed the passages in detail, reaches the conclusion that the account in Josephus' *Antiquities* is the more reliable one.[25]

Onias IV and his sons Helkias and Hananiah had a remarkable career in Egypt. Onias was priest and warrior and was given an important role to play in Ptolemy VI's counter-move against the threatening power of the Seleucids. Onias and his Jewish followers formed a military force of some size, and they were settled in the Leontopolis district about 190 kilometres south east of Alexandria. The settlement is today identified as Tell el-Yehoudieh 3 kilometres south of present-day Shibin el Qanatir. Onias built a temple, and the area along the eastern branches of the Nile Delta was called "the Land of Onias". The settlement and the temple were probably built some years after Onias and his followers had emigrated to Egypt, that is, when Onias had gained a reputation as a good general and had organized around him a Jewish force of military value. V. A. Tcherikover suggests that the date of the founding of the military settlement (*katoikia*) might have been some time before the death of Ptolemy VI Philometor in 145 B.C.[26] The location of this military centre was strategically important, and the fact that the Jews were assigned the defence of such a sensitive area for about a hundred

---

[25] Tcherikover (1966) 228–31; 276–77; Kasher (1985) 7.

[26] Tcherikover (1966) 277–80; Tcherikover (1957) 2 and 19–21.

years indicates their strong position in Ptolemaic politics.[27] Their alliance with the Ptolemaic rulers also proved that they favoured a centralized government and wanted to mark themselves off from the native Egyptians.

The many intrigues and conflicts within the weakened Ptolemaic dynasty caused problems, however. In the conflict between Ptolemy VI Philometor and his younger brother, Ptolemy VII Euergetes II (Physcon), the power of the population increased, and for a century the populace, especially in Alexandria, played a decisive and disastrous part in Egyptian politics. The death of Ptolemy VI Philometor in 145 left queen Cleopatra II and her son faced with Ptolemy VII who ruled Cyrene. Onias, his friend Dositheus and the Jewish soldiers were the leading force in support of Cleopatra. The Queen could not withstand Ptolemy VII Euergetes II, however, and she was forced to marry him. He then ruled as king from 145 to 116 B.C. Ptolemy VII turned against the supporters of the late Philometor. Accordingly he persecuted the Jews. Josephus tells that when preparing to attack Onias, he decided to exterminate the Jews of the country and ordered that they should be thrown naked and fettered at the feet of drunken elephants. The elephants, however, left the Jews untouched and attacked the king's men and killed many of them. When the king saw that the Jews were not hurt, he repented of his evil intent. The Jews instituted a festival in memory of this day of salvation (*Ag. Ap.* 2:53–55). The story, although legendary, is probably based on a version of some actual danger.[28]

The relationship between Ptolemy VII and the Jews was normalized, as is seen by the fact that Synagogues were dedicated to him. Such a move from the king might have been furthered by the native Egyptians' numerous revolts, and unrest in the Greek population of Alexandria.

When Ptolemy VII died, his niece-wife, Cleopatra III reigned from 116 to 101 B.C. Cleopatra chose her younger son Ptolemy X Alexander I to be co-regent. The Alexandrians compelled her to depose him and allow the older son, Ptolemy IX Lathyrus, to share her throne. In the subsequent tension, and conflicts among the Queen, her sons and the population, the Queen's control of the capital and

---

[27] Kasher (1985) 7–8.

[28] Fraser (1972) 1 and 121; Tcherikover (1966) 282; Tcherikover (1957) 21–22.

the country was largely built on the loyal support of the Jews. The sons of Onias IV, Helkias and Hananiah, were appointed high officers in the Queen's army. Josephus tells that Cleopatra appointed the two Jewish generals "at the head of the whole army". Although probably an exaggeration, the statement testifies to their leading position in the army also beyond the Jewish units (*Ant.* 13:349). When Ptolemy Lathyrus, having fled to Cyprus, conducted a campaign against his mother with Seleucid help, Cleopatra entered into an alliance with the Hasmonean king Alexander Jannaeus.[29]

The Jewish leaders were not only military supporters of the Queen, they also influenced her in her political decisions. When Cleopatra in the years 104–102 B.C. went to Palestine against the Seleucids and Ptolemy IX Lathyrus, some of her advisers recommended her to betray her ally, King Jannaeus, and seize the country for herself. Hananiah said: "I would have you know, that this wrong to the king will turn all the Jews who dwell in your kingdom into your foes" (*Ant.* 13:354). Moreover, this incident shows that Hananiah, although of high priestly family from Jerusalem, recognized the Hasmonean government and did not try to return to Jerusalem and its temple. Hananiah's brother, Helkias, had been killed in one of the battles fought in Palestine.[30]

Cleopatra's younger son, Ptolemy X Alexander I had been recalled to Alexandria in 107 B.C. and was her co-regent, untill he murdered her in 101 B.C. Ptolemy X Alexander I was expelled in 89 B.C. by a combination of the Alexandrian populace, the army, and the older brother, Ptolemy IX Lathyrus, known as Soter II, who gained the support of the Alexandrians due to the popularity of his wife, Berenice IV. In 88 B.C. there seems to have been a persecution of the Jews in Alexandria, but further details are not known.[31]

During the half of the century from Ptolemy IX Lathyrus' (Soter II) death in 80 B.C. to the death of Cleopatra VII in 30 B.C. the conflicts between the Alexandrians and the Ptolemies continued almost without interruption. Josephus tells of two incidents in which the Jews were directly involved. The first took place during the turbulent reign

---

[29] Tcherikover (1957) 23 and Tcherikover (1964) 141–42; Tcherikover (1966) 283.

[30] Tcherikover (1966) 283–84; Kasher (1985) 11.

[31] Kasher (1985) 12; Fraser (1972) 123–24.

of the Roman "puppet", Ptolemy XI Auletes. In 58 B.C. he was forced
to leave the city, and in 55 B.C. the Roman proconsul of Syria, Gabinus,
whose cavalry was commanded by Mark Antony, marched to Egypt
to restore Ptolemy XI Auletes to the throne. The guarding of Pelusium
in North Eastern Egypt was in Jewish hands, and through the
interference of Rome's friend Antipater, the strong man in Jerusalem,
the Jews allowed the Romans pass through Pelusium without any
hindrance and to enter Egypt.[32]

In a similar way the Jewish garrison at Pelusium yielded to pressure
from Jerusalem in 48 B.C., when Julius Caesar was at Alexandria
in a very unfavourable situation. When king Mithridates of Pergamum
went with auxiliary troops to extricate him, he at first met opposition
from the Jewish garrison at Pelusium. Antipater showed the Jews
a letter from the High Priest, Hyrcanus II, and persuaded them
to change their allegiance, and even to provide Mithridates with
supplies needed for the journey.[33]

Although the Egyptian Queen Cleopatra VII had outstanding
leadership abilities, the reign of the Ptolemaic dynasty was approaching
its end. The Roman Antony and the Egyptian Queen were defeated
by Octavian in the battle at Actium in 31 B.C., and Antony and
Cleopatra ended their lives subsequently. The Romans annexed
Egypt in 30 B.C. and made it into a province. A new era had begun.

In this most glorious period of the Egyptian Jews as far as political
history is concerned, what is known about their religious and cultural
life?

The Synagogues referred to in inscriptions from this period are:[34]

a) Two Synagogues in Alexandria are referred to in inscriptions,
one from Hadra, dated to the second century B.C. ("to God, the
Highest . . . the sacred precinct and the *proseuche* and its
appurtenances"), and one from the Gabbary quarter south west
of Alexandria, dated to 37 B.C. ("In honour of the queen and the
king, to the great God who listens to prayer, Alypos made the *proseuche*
in the 15th year, Mecheir . . .").

b) Two inscriptions in Athribis in the southern part of the Delta
are probably to be dated to the second century B.C. ("In honour

[32] Tcherikover (1966) 284; Kasher (1985) 12–13.

[33] Tcherikover (1966) 284; Smallwood (1976) 37–38.

[34] Tcherikover (1957) 139–40; Schürer (1986) 47–50.

of King Ptolemy and Queen Cleopatra, Ptolemaios son of Epikydes chief of police and the Jews in Athribis (dedicated) the *proseuche* to the supreme God", and "In honour of King Ptolemy and Queen Cleopatra and their children, Hermeas and his wife Philotera and their children (gave) this place for sitting for the *proseuche*").

c) Two inscriptions attest the presence of Synagogues in the western Delta, both dated between 143 and 117 B.C. One is in Xenephyris ("In honour of King Ptolemy and Queen Cleopatra his sister and Queen Cleopatra his wife, the Jews of Xenephyris (built) the gateway of the *proseuche* when Theodoros and Achillion were *prostatai*), the other is in Nitriai ("In honour of King Ptolemy and Queen Cleopatra his sister and Queen Cleopatra his wife, the benefactors, the Jews in Nitriai (dedicated) the *proseuche* and its appurtenances").

d) As for upper Egypt, a large number of ostraca have been found in the vicinity of Thebes with Hebrew names inscribed on them. Most of these ostraca refer to the reigns of Ptolemy VI Philometor (181–145 B.C.) and Ptolemy Euergetes II (145–116 B.C.).[35]

Thus the Jewish population was spread out over all of Egypt. Usually the Synagogues served as the community centres. An exception of special interest is Onias' temple and the Land of Onias. At Leontopolis (Tell el-Yehoudieh) in the nome of Heliopolis, an extensive number of Jewish epitaphs has been found. The remains of Onias' temple are thought to have been identified in the same Tell. Originally it was probably meant to compete with the Jerusalem Temple, and to express rejection of its high priest. Later this claim seems to have been modified, so that the Jewish garrison at Pelusium in 48 B.C. complied to the letter from the High Priest in Jerusalem, Hyrcanus II, and let the army of Mithridates pass through the town.[36] For Egyptian Jews in general, there is no evidence that Onias' temple became a serious alternative to the Temple in Jerusalem.[37]

Josephus tells that Onias asked Ptolemy to build a temple to make it possible for him to worship God after the manner of his fathers. The temple was built on the pattern of the Temple in Jerusalem. Thus Onias' temple shows that those who belonged to it stressed

---

[35] Tcherikover (1957) 194–226.

[36] *J.W.* 1:33; 7:436. Schürer (1986) 145–47; Tcherikover (1966) 275–84; Kasher (1985) 119–35; Tcherikover (1964) 145–63.

[37] Tcherikover (1957) 45.

the continuity with the traditions from Jerusalem.[38] Josephus likewise conveys their need for legitimation for having a temple in Egypt. They based it on a prediction by the prophet Isaiah, as stated in a letter purported by Josephus to have been written by Onias: "For this is indeed what the prophet Isaiah foretold, 'There shall be an altar in Egypt to the Lord God', and many other such things did he prophesy concerning this place". The reference is to Isa 19:18–19. Onias was both high priest and warrior, and the Jewish community in the Land of Onias was a military settlement. They had a temple and a fortress, and they received help from God in their military activity (*Ant*. 13:65 and 68).

The main Jewish community in Egypt, the one in Alexandria, continued to express their religious convictions in literary forms. *Aristobulus*, the *Letter of Aristeas* and the *Sibylline Oracles* 3, belong to this period. Aristobulus came from a high-priestly family and lived at the time of Ptolemy VI Philometor (181–145). His work has the form of an exegetical dialogue, where he answers questions raised by the Ptolemaic king.[39]

The author of the *Letter of Aristeas*, addressed to Aristeas' brother Philocrates, presents himself as a Greek courtier of Ptolemy II Philadelphus (284–246 B.C.). He tells about a series of events connected with the Greek translation of the Torah. According to *Ep. Arist.* the translation took place during the early part of the reign of Ptolemy II Philadelphus, and was done by seventy Jewish scholars sent from the High Priest in Jerusalem upon request from King Ptolemy. The date when the Letter was written is uncertain, but it presupposes the existence of the Septuagint translation. A date in the middle or second half of the second century B.C. is probable, and in spite of its own claim to have been written by a non-Jew, a Jew must have been the real author.[40] The *Sibylline Oracles* also use a pagan figure as medium, the prophetess named Sibyl. *Sib. Or.* 3 in the standard collection is Jewish. Its main corpus has been dated to the time of Ptolemy VI Philometor (181–145 B.C.).[41]

---

[38] *J.W.* 1:33; *Ant.* 12:389, in contradiction with *J.W.* 7:425–32. Kasher (1985) 132–35; Hayward (1982) 429–43.

[39] Borgen (1984) 274–79; Borgen (1987) 8–9.

[40] Walter (1987) 83–85; Fraser (1972) 698–704; Kasher (1985) 208–11.

[41] Collins (1984) 365–71.

These books have several features in common. They all express a positive attitude to the Ptolemaic rulers: *Aristobulus* has an exegetical dialogue with King Ptolemy. *Aristeas* tells how King Ptolemy II Philadelphus wants copies of Jewish books for his Library, and how he entertains the Jewish scholars. In *Sib. Or.* 3 a Ptolemaic king, probably Ptolemy VI Philometor or his anticipated successor, is endorsed as a virtual Messiah (3:162–95, 652–56; Collins (1984) 366–67).

All three books place emphasis on what Jews and Gentiles have in common. Both Aristobulus and Aristeas agree that when the Greek poets and philosophers speak of "Zeus", they mean the true God, whom the Jews worship. Similarily, in two Jewish inscriptions from Ptolemaic times, found in Upper Egypt, Pan, as the universal god, seems to be identified with the God of the Jews.[42] The Sibyl (*Sib. Or.* 3:97–161), draws on myths and legends which were familiar to the Gentiles. At the same time, all three books exalt the Jews, their philosophy and religion and express a feeling of Jewish superiority. Aristobulus states that Jewish philosophy, found in the Laws of Moses, has many points of agreement with the Greeks, whose philosophers and legislators learned from Moses. The pagan Aristeas makes king Ptolemy to express admiration of the Jewish Temple, worship, wisdom and Laws; the Jewish sages exceed the philosophers in their wisdom; the Sibyl appeals to the Greeks to refrain from idolatry and adultery, and prophesies that people from all countries will send gifts and worship in the Temple in Jerusalem. The Jews carry the moral leadership of the human race.

Ep. Arist. and especially the *Sibylline Oracles* level criticism against idolatry. *Ep. Arist.* contrasts the one God, the Creator, with the idols and idolatry of the Egyptians. The Sibyl offers very sharp criticism of Romans and Greeks for their idolatry and adultery. Also in the fragments of *Aristobulus* there is a similar statement: Orpheus and Aretus, in quotations given, had no holy concepts of God since they used polytheistic names of the One God. Both *Ep. Arist.* and *Sib. Or.* 3 present the views of Jewish communities for whom Jerusalem and its Temple were the centre. Aristeas describes the Temple and its cult, the city and the country, and tells about the gifts to the Temple from King Ptolemy. *Sib. Or.* 3 shows great interest in the Jerusalem

---

[42] Hengel (1974) 264.

Temple. The Greeks can avoid disaster by sending sacrifices to the Jewish Temple. The people from all countries will come confessing their sins and acknowledge the God who is worshipped in the Jerusalem Temple.

Both *Ep. Arist.* and *Sib. Or.* 3 deal with politics. Aristeas pictures the ideal kingship and the ideals of his rule. The Sibyl idealizes Ptolemy VI Philometor, and has throughout the book an emphasis on warfare. The Jews play a role in some of the military actions, although the hope is expressed of a life of peace round the Temple in Jerusalem.

In different ways the writings take up a position on two fronts. On the one hand they go against Jewish isolationists, and on the other hand they avoid assimilation and apostasy by stressing allegiance to some distinctive marks of Judaism, such as the Temple of Jerusalem and Jewish standards. Moreover, Aristeas defends Jewish observances, such as the dietary laws; Aristobulus glorifies the Sabbath, and has a section on the celebration of the Passover.

Another book from this period, the historian Artapanus' *On the Jews*, is more syncretistic.[43] Artapanus probably wrote his book in Alexandria in the second century B.C. The fragments preserved by Eusebius and Clement tell about Abraham, Joseph and Moses. His concern is similar to that of Aristobulus, Aristeas, and the Sibyl: he weaves Jewish and non-Jewish elements together, so as to glorify the Jewish people. He reflects an Egyptian environment outside the Hellenistic circles connected with the Ptolemaic administration. Artapanus pictures Moses as the father of Egyptian civilization including the political organization of the country. Moses is even seen as father of Egyptian polytheistic religion, and the Egyptian priests bestow on him semi-divine honours. He is called Hermes (=Thoth) because he has interpreted the sacred letters of the hieroglyphic script. Moses is moreover pictured as a successful warrior against the Ethiopians, in command of a peasant army. Even in this role he ends up being loved by the Ethiopians so that they submit to circumcision, as also do some of the priests.

Artapanus shows kinship with Ezekiel the Tragedian in giving Moses divine attributes, but he does it in a syncretistic way. In his glorification of Moses and in his version of the salvation of the Jews

---

[43] Fraser (1972) 704–06; Attridge (1984) 166–68.

in the Exodus, Artapanus is in direct opposition to the anti-Jewish account of Moses given by the Egyptian priest Manetho.

Thus, the literature from the period between Ptolemy VI Philometor (181–145 B.C.) and the Roman conquest reflects the tension within the Jewish communities with a wide range of attitudes from assimilation to separation. Typical for the literature is the attempt to combine distinctive Jewish observances with a fusion of Jewish and Greek ideas or Jewish and Egyptian ideas. The superiority of the Jewish religion is stressed, and in the end time the Jewish nation will play an exalted role among the nations.

C. The Roman Period

In many respects the transfer into Roman rule meant discontinuity with the Ptolemaic past.[44] The Ptolemaic capital had become a provincial city in the Roman Empire. The Roman prefect in the *praetorium* replaced the Ptolemy and his court in the palace. The Roman legions replaced the multi-ethnic Ptolemaic army. From now on, the resources of Egypt and Alexandria had to serve the needs and aims of the new rulers and their home base, Rome. Nevertheless, the victory of Augustus had brought to an end the Ptolemaic dynasty which had proved itself unable to rule effectively. At first, therefore, the Roman conquest meant fresh life into a decaying administration. The result was economic progress. Apart from the appointment of the prefect, Augustus and his early successors only changed so much as was necessary to control the bureaucracy and make it more efficient.

Philo tells that Augustus confirmed the rights of the Jewish community to live in accordance with their ancestral laws.[45] Nevertheless, they entered into a new situation in important areas. They were eliminated as a military factor together with the Ptolemaic army as a whole, even though their realization of being dependent on the central government had caused them to changed their allegiance from the Ptolemaic dynasty to the Romans. Nevertheless it was the Greeks that the Romans used in their administration and whom they gave privileges. The problem was how to distinguish Greek

---

[44] Tcherikover (1957) 55–65; Tcherikover (1963) 1–8; Kasher (1985) 18–20.

[45] *Flac.* 50 and *Legat.* 152–58.

from non-Greek among the rather mixed population of Egypt. In 4–5 B.C. it was decided that the criterion was to be *gymnasium* education.

A few Jews continued the tradition of Dositheus, Onias, Helkias and Hananiah and had high posts in the government of the country, now in the Roman administration. The most prominent examples were Philo's brother Alexander and his son Tiberius Alexander. Alexander was *alabarch*, which probably meant that he was custom superintendent on the Eastern side of the Nile. He was also steward of the property of Antonia, mother of the emperor Claudius. Tiberius Alexander attained the high offices of procurator of Palestine, prefect of Egypt, highest ranking officer in Titus' army in the Jewish war and probably prefect of the Guard in Rome. Alexander remained faithful to Judaism, and donated the gold plating of the nine gates of the Temple court in Jerusalem. His son, Tiberius Alexander, left his ancestral religion, just as did Dositheus, son of Drimylos, in the third century B.C.[46]

On the whole it proved more difficult for Jews to meet the requirements for entering governmental posts, although Philo indicates that it still was possible, since he admonishes Jews who pursue education with no motive higher than from desire of an office under the rulers.[47]

During the period between 30 B.C. and A.D. 117 three armed uprisings and revolts demonstrate that the situation of the Egyptian Jews was deteriorating and moved towards their extermination: the armed uprising at the death of emperor Gaius Caligula in A.D. 41; the impact of the Jewish war in Palestine on the tensions in Egypt, A.D. 66 and 70–73; and the suicidal Messianic revolution of Jews in Cyrene and Egypt in the years A.D. 115–17.

What were the causes and circumstances for these tragic events to take place? The main reason for the crisis in A.D. 38–41 was the growing conflict between the Jews and the Greeks, and Gaius Caligula's

---

[46] Tcherikover (1957) 49, n. 4; Tcherikover (1960) 188–90; Smallwood (1976) 257–59; Kasher (1985) 347.

[47] Tcherikover (1963) 14–15; Borgen (1965) 122–29; Mendelson (1982) 44–46; Borgen (1984) 254–56; Borgen (1984A) 115–17.

enforcement of the emperor worship.[48] The Greeks wanted a ruling from the prefect Flaccus on the constitutional question of Jewish status in the city, and they succeeded in getting Flaccus to issue an edict making the Jews to be "foreigners and aliens". They were now aliens without the right of domicile, and without the right to have an administration of their own under the leadership of the council of elders.

Flaccus issued this edict after the anti-Jewish forces exploited the visit of the Jewish king Agrippa by setting up a lunatic named Carabas in royal robes in the *gymnasium*, saluting him as king in a mocking scene. Then the crowd claimoured for the installation of images of the emperor in the Synagogues. A cruel pogrom followed. The Jews were driven together into a ghetto, and members of the Jewish council of elders were arrested and tortured so severely that some died. An embassy of five persons, headed by Philo, was sent to Rome for the purpose of explaining to Gaius Caligula the traditional rights of the Jewish community.

The Greeks sent a counter-embassy, headed by the anti-Jewish writer Apion. Philo's mission was a complete failure.

Suddenly the situation changed. In A.D. 41, Gaius Caligula was assassinated and Claudius succeeded him. The Alexandrian Jews started an armed uprising against the Greeks, and they received help by Jews from Egypt and from Palestine. Roman intervention put an end to the conflict, and Claudius issued an edict giving back to the Jews the rights held before the pogrom started, reinstating the *politeuma* and protecting the Synagogues. The struggle before the emperor continued. Finally he settled the questions in a letter.[49] He confirms the rights of the Jews, chastises both ethnic groups for their share in the disturbances in Alexandria, and forbade Jews to participate in the activities in the *gymnasium* and to take *gymnasium* education. Claudius stated explicitly that the Jews lived "in a city not their own".

In A.D. 66 the Alexandrian Greek *polis* wanted the emperor Nero to cancel the Jews' rights in the city. In the same year Nero decided to recognize the exclusive sovereignty of the Greek *polis* in Caesarea

---

[48] Philo, *To Flaccus* and *On the Embassy to Gaius*; Bell (1926) 14–30; Smallwood (1976) 237–50; Tcherikover (1957) 65–74; Barraclough(1984) 429–36.

[49] Tcherikover (1960) 36–55; Bell (1924) 1–37.

Maritima over all residents in the city, thereby cancelling the rights of the Jewish community. According to Josephus a number of Jews entered the amphitheatre in Alexandria where the members of the *polis* were deliberating on the subject of an embassy to be sent to Nero. The Greeks tried to capture the Jews, got hold of three of them, and took them away to be burned alive. This aroused the whole Jewish community who attempted to set fire to the amphitheatre. The Roman Prefect, Philo's nephew Tiberius Alexander, crushed the Jewish revolt. The soldiers killed the Jews, burned and plundered their houses. The Jews tried to oppose the Roman troops with arms, but they were totally routed. According to Josephus 50,000 Jews were killed.[50]

The Jewish community structure was not abolished, however. The council of elders as institution remained intact. In A.D. 73 some Jewish guerrilla-fighters, the Sicarii, fled from Palestine to Egypt, and instigated the Egyptian Jews to revolt under the slogan "No lord but God". After the Sicarii had killed some of the moderate Jews of rank, the leaders of the council of elders in Alexandria called a general assembly and charged the Sicarii for causing dangerous trouble. The assembly seized 600 Sicarii on the spot. The Sicarii who escaped farther into Egypt were arrested and brought back to Alexandria. All were put to death by the Romans. Moreover, the Romans, fearing that the Jews might again join together in revolutionary actions, demolished Onias' temple. This indicates that this temple was still a centre of militant Judaism.[51]

The suicidal revolution in A.D. 115 to 117 involved the Jews in Alexandria and Egypt, in Cyrene and on Cyprus.[52] The Jews "as if shaken by a strong rebellious spirit", attacked their Greek and Egyptian neighbours. At first the Jews were victorious, but then began to suffer defeats, and when it developed into a war with the Romans they were crushed. All who participated in the war fought to exterminate the enemy.

The Jewish revolt was Messianic in character. Its aim was to destroy pagans and their polytheistic temples, and to establish Jewish control

---

[50] Tcherikover (1957) 78–79.

[51] *J.W.* 7:409–20 and 433–36.

[52] Tcherikover (1957) 89–90; Tcherikover (1963) 28–32; Hengel (1983) 655–86; Smallwood (1976) 397.

of the whole area, and probably also with the final aim of delivering Judaea and Jerusalem from Roman occupation. The aim was the liquidation of the Roman regime and the setting up of a new Jewish commonwealth, whose task was to inaugurate the Messianic era. In Cyrene a Jewish Messiah appeared, King Loukuas-Andreas.[53]

The revolution was crushed by the Roman legions. In many places the Jewish population was almost totally annihilated. The great Synagogue as well as other Synagogues and buildings in Alexandria and in all of Egypt were demolished. Some Jews, mainly in Alexandria it seems, survived, but the strength of Egyptian Jewry had been broken for ever. In this way the more than 700 years of Jewish settlement and history in Egypt had virtually come to an end, and it took more than a century for Jewish life in Egypt to reawaken.

D. Status of the Jews

After this historical survey some further comments should be made with regard to the status of the Jewish communities.

Philo declares that there were a million Jews resident in Alexandria and the country from the slope into Libya to the boundaries of Ethiopia (*Flac.* 43). They worked in many professions.[54] In Alexandria there were many Synagogues scattered all over the city. One of the Synagogues was larger and more beautiful than the others.[55] Of the five quarters of Alexandria, two were called Jewish because most of the Jews inhabited them. In the other sections of the city there were many Jews scattered about (*Flac.* 55). Papyri, ostraca and inscriptions also testify to the Jewish habitation all over Egypt in the later Ptolemaic and early Roman periods.[56]

The organization of the Jewish communities varied in different places. In Alexandria there was a united corporation of the large Jewish community. According to the *Letter of Aristeas* the Jewish community formed a *politeuma* at whose head stood elders and leaders. From the time of Strabo (about 63 B.C. to some time after

---

[53] Hengel (1983) 655–86.
[54] Tcherikover (1957) 48–55.
[55] *Legat.* 134–35; cf. *t. Sukk.* 4:6; *b. Sukk.* 516; *y. Sukk.* 5:55a; Kasher (1985) 349–51.
[56] Tcherikover (1964) 197–209.

A.D. 21) there was an *ethnarch* at the head. Strabo defines his function: He "governs the people and adjudicates suits and supervises contracts and ordinances just as if he were head (*archon*) of a sovereign state".[57] According to Philo (*Flac.* 74), a *genarch*, who was presumably identical with the *ethnarch*, died when Magius Maximus was to become prefect of Egypt for the second time in A.D. 11–12. At that time Augustus reintroduced a council of elders, the *gerusia*, who assumed the leadership, although the office of *ethnarch* does not seem to have been abolished. The degree of autonomy of Alexandrian Jewry may have been made possible by the fact that Alexandria from Augustus had no city council.[58]

Similar forms of organization probably existed in the places of Egypt where the Jewish communities were of sufficient size. Thus, the Jewish *politarch* at Leontopolis may have been the equivalent of the *ethnarch* in Alexandria.[59] Of course, the priestly military leadership of the Land of Onias gave this community a distinction of its own during the time of Onias IV and his sons.

Both in the Ptolemaic period and the Roman period the rights of the Jews of Egypt were generally, as already shown, based on the formula that they were permitted to live and have government according to their ancestral laws and customs. The implications and applications of this formula depended, however, on the interplay among the Jewish communities, the political authorities and the other groups in the country.

Certain rights were commonly recognized: The right to worship their God; to own and gather in Synagogues as community property; to keep the Sabbath and celebrate the feasts of the New Moon, of Passover/Unleavened Bread, of the Weeks, the Day of Atonement, the feast of Tabernacles, etc.;[60] the celebration of the other feasts, such as the celebration of the Septuagint at Pharos (*Mos.* 2:41–42) and the celebration of the feast in memory of their deliverance when

---

[57] Stern (1976) 278.

[58] Stern (1976) 280; Kasher (1985) 254–55.

[59] Kasher (1985) 127.

[60] *Spec.* 2:39–222; cf. *Legat.* 116–18.

Ptolemy VII Euergetes II (Physcon) wished to have them killed by elephants.[61]

Tensions existed at some of these points, however. Philo refers to a Roman prefect who attempted to compel Jews to do service to him on the Sabbath and in this way do away with the law of the seventh day and other laws (*Somn.* 2:123–32). On the other hand there were Jews who internalized the meaning of the observances to such a degree that they did not comply with external customs and regulations.[62]

One specific point in their laws which the Romans permitted them to follow was the right to pay the tax to be transmitted to the Temple in Jerusalem.[63] Strabo, the Talmud, and a papyrus testify to the existence of Jewish legal institutions in Egypt, based on the office of *ethnarch* and/or the council of elders. According to Strabo, the *ethnarch* presided over the courts and supervised contracts. The supervision of contracts is indirectly confirmed by the papyrus recording the registration of a loan-contract between two Jews of Alexandria in 13 B.C. at the Jewish records office.[64] Finally, the *ethnarch* supervised the implementation of the edicts of the Roman authorities.[65]

Against this background it is a problem that according to papyri found at Abusir el-Meleq (approximately 130 kilometres south east of Alexandria) the Jews to a large extent resorted to non-Jewish tribunals both in Ptolemaic and Roman times. The reason seems to be that the jurisdiction of the Jewish court was not compulsory, at least not in cases of a general nature. Moreover, legal documents from Fayûm in the third and second centuries B.C. show that the Jews freely used the Hellenistic laws of Ptolemaic Egypt. M. Stern supposes that Jewish organization and law were not yet established in those military settlements at that time.[66]

---

[61] Schürer (1986) 145.

[62] *Migr.* 89–93; Borgen (1984) 260–61.

[63] *Legat.* 311–17; *Ant.* 14:216 and 16:160–66; Rajak (1985) 23.

[64] Stern (1976) 280–82; *t. Pea* 4:6; *t. Ketubot* 3:1; Tcherikover (1960) 8–10.

[65] Applebaum (1984) 474.

[66] Tcherikover (1957) 32–36; Tcherikover (1960) 1–24; Stern (1976) 280–82.

In some respects the Jews had a more favourable or equal status to that of the "Greek" citizens of Alexandria. The Jews were permitted to have their own council of elders, while the Greek citizens were denied a corresponding council.[67] In case of corporal punishment, the Jews were punished with the same kind of flogging as the Greek citizens (*Flac.* 78–80).

In other areas the situation of the Jews was less favourable. Augustus introduced a capitation tax, the *laographia*, payable by the male population of Egypt between the ages of fourteen and sixty or sixty-two.[68] The Greek citizens of Alexandria were exempted, while the Greek members of the capitals, the *metropoleis* of the *nomes* paid a reduced rate. The criterion for this concession was the Greek education, and from A.D. 4/5 the "members of the *gymnasium*" were recognized as a class. The Jews in Egypt in general were classified as non-Greeks and made liable for the tax. Those who could prove that they met the criterion for Greek citizenship were treated as the Greeks. This increased the tension between the Greeks and the Jews, and was one of the causes of the conflict in Alexandria in A.D. 38.

After the destruction of the Temple of Jerusalem in A.D. 70 and the victory of the Romans in the Jewish war, the Jewish tax, *fiscus Judaicus*, was founded. The Jews had to pay the tax previously paid to the Temple of Jerusalem to the Temple of Jupiter Capitolinus. This tax was an additional burden beyond the other taxes levied on the Jews in Egypt.[69] All through the Ptolemaic and Roman periods a delicate balance existed between the Jews' refusal to recognize divine attributes of the political heads of state, and their expression of loyal acceptance of their rule. The dedication of the Synagogues to the political head of state is documented by archaeological findings for members of the Ptolemaic dynasty, but not for the Roman emperors, as far as Egypt is concerned. Philo, in *Legat.* 133, tells, however, that honorific inscriptions and emblems in honour of the emperors were placed in the Synagogues.[70] Upon the accession of Gaius Caligula, the Jewish community of Alexandria expressed their loyalty by

---

[67] Lewis (1985) 29.

[68] Tcherikover (1957) 59–65; Smallwood (1976) 231–34.

[69] Tcherikover (1957) 80–82.

[70] Cf. *Flac.* 48–49; Smallwood (1970) 220–21.

passing a resolution in Gaius' honour. Flaccus did not forward this resolution to Gaius Caligula, however (*Flac.* 97–103). Philo praises Augustus that he ordered sacrifices of whole burnt offerings to be carried out daily at his expense in the Temple of Jerusalem as a tribute to the most high God (*Legat.* 157–317). This delicate balance between the political authority of the emperors and the exclusive claim of the monotheistic worship of the Jewish nation was upset when Gaius Caligula demanded that images of the emperor be placed in the Synagogues and in the Temple of Jerusalem (*Flac.* 41–50; *Legat.* 134–35, 188, 203, 346, etc.).

During the late Ptolemaic and the early Roman periods the literary output of Egyptian Jews reached its height. In addition to the monumental works of Philo, the Wisdom of Solomon, the *Third Book of Maccabees* and *Sib. Or.* 5 seem to belong to these two hundred years.

The Wisdom of Solomon was probably written sometime between 200 B.C. and A.D. 50, most probably during the first century B.C.[71] The central theme is the view that God's cosmic Wisdom is sought and made known to the King of Israel, Solomon, and is seen to be at work in the history of Israel and its worship of the One God. God's deliverance of the righteous and his warfare against the ungodly is the subject of the first part (Wis 1:1 – 6:11). This "book of eschatology" is framed by exhortations addressed to rulers, kings and judges. In the second part, "the book of wisdom" (Wis 6:12 – 9:18) the king, writing in the first person, directs the attention of his royal colleagues to his own example, as seeker of God's wisdom. In the third part, Wisdom of Solomon 10–19, the blessings of godliness and the curse of ungodliness is seen in the different fates of the Israelites and the Egyptians in the biblical story. A lengthy and sharp attack on idolatry occurs in Wis 13–15.

The book Wisdom of Solomon outlines the cosmic significance of Jewish existence; interprets the universal role of Israel, represented here by the king, presumably Solomon; and attacks Egyptian idolatry on the basis of Israel's monotheism. Some Greek philosophical concepts have been "conquered" and made to serve Jewish self-understanding and Jewish imperial ideology.

---

[71] Schürer (1986) 568–79; Nickelsburg (1982) 175–85.

The *Third Book of Maccabees* is an aetiological romance probably written at the beginning of the Roman period to explain an already existing festival, and to provide the Jews of Alexandria with ammunition in their struggle against the resident Greeks.[72] The main basis for the book seems to have been an older aetiological legend, recorded by Josephus in *Ag. Ap.* 2:5. As already stated earlier, according to this legend Ptolemy VII Physcon (145–116 B.C.) cast the Jews, who supported Cleopatra, before drunken elephants. These turned instead against the king's friends, and the king changed his plans.

In 3 Macc this story seems to have been transferred back to the time of Ptolemy IV Philopator (222–204 B.C.) and woven together with the problems the Jews faced when that king wanted the Jews and others to worship Dionysos as condition for giving them full citizenship. The book offers support to the view that the Jews had an intermediate status higher than the native Egyptians, but lower than the full citizens of Alexandria. The King removed the privileges of the Jews and degraded them to the rank of natives. Their previous state was that of an ethnic *politeuma* in exile "worshipping God, and living according to His law they held themselves apart in the matter of food". They had the Jerusalem Temple as their religious centre. On the condition that they entered into the royal cult of Dionysos they could obtain full citizenship. The end result was that the King issued a letter of protection for the Jews to all the governors in the provinces and permitted the Jews to put to death apostates among their own people.

Philo's numerous works bring together many of the elements found in earlier literature:[73]

1. The positive evaluation of the Ptolemaic rulers, found in the *Letter of Aristeas*, in *Aristobulus* and the *Sibylline Oracles* 3, is also expressed by Philo in his praise of King Ptolemy II Philadelphus (*Mos.* 2:28–31) and his positive evaluation of the Ptolemaic kings in *Legat.* 138–39. He extends this positive view to the Roman rulers Augustus and Tiberius (*Legat.* 141–61). This positive attitude is conditioned upon their recognition of the rights of the Jews to live

---

[72] Schürer (1986) 537–42 with criticism of Kasher (1985) on pp. 211–32; Nickelsburg (1982) 169–72.

[73] Borgen (1984) 233–82 and Borgen (1984A) 98–154.

in accordance with the laws of their ancestors and to worship the One God. Accordingly, Gaius Caligula and the prefect Flaccus are under the judgment of God for their removal of the privileges of the Jews and their attempt to force them to worship the emperor.[74]

2. Philo continues the approach seen especially in the *Letter of Aristeas*, in *Aristobulus* and the Wisdom of Solomon to interpret the Laws of Moses and Jewish existence in general by means of Greek ideas and religious traditions. According to Philo, the authentic philosophy is formulated by Moses, and Greek philosophy contains elements of this true philosophy and is at some points derived from the teachings of Moses.

3. The sharp polemic against polytheistic cults expressed in writings such as *Sibylline Oracles* 3, Wisdom of Solomon and 3 Macc is also found in Philo's writings. Philo even advocates the death penalty for renegades to be executed on the spot, corresponding to the killing of Jewish apostates according to 3 Macc.[75]

4. The universal role of the Jewish people is a central theme in Jewish literature in Egypt. According to Philo, Moses was appointed king of a nation destined to offer prayer for ever on behalf of the human race (*Mos.* 1:149; cf. *Spec.* 1:97; *Legat.* 3–4). The translation of the Laws of Moses into Greek made God's cosmic Laws known to the Greek-speaking world. Other peoples have begun to honour these laws, and Philo expresses the wish and hope that the time will come when all nations will cast aside their ancestral customs and honour the Laws of Moses alone (*Mos.* 2:43–44).

The quality of the life of the Jewish nation when they adhere to the cosmic principles given them in the Laws of Moses, will bring victory over their enemies, and the Jewish nation will be the head of all nations (*Praem.* 79–172). Philo favours the achievement of this aim by peaceful means, but he does not exclude the possibility of military warfare (*Virt.* 22–50; *Praem.* 93–95). He even draws on the expectation of an eschatological warrior-king, who will be a Jewish world emperor (*Praem.* 95 and *Mos.* 1:290, based on Num 24:7 (LXX)). Moreover, the diaspora Jews will return to their home land (*Praem.* 164–65). Philo himself oscillates between military and spiritual warfare, but he testifies to the existence of a militant

---

[74] Stemberger (1983) 43–48; Borgen (1987C) 275–76.

[75] *Spec.* 1:54–55 and 315–16; Alon (1977) 112–24.

eschatology in the Jewish community, ideas which probably inspired the Jews to take up arms at the death of Gaius Caligula in A.D. 41, and in the revolts of A.D. 66 and A.D. 115–17.

5. Philo continues the tendency found in the earlier writings to stress the superiority of the Jewish nation. Philo's emphasis of the God-given role of the Jewish nation suggests that he did not only fight for equal rights for the Jews, but claimed that the call of the Jews was to be the head nation with other nations as their vassals.[76]

6. Philo testifies to the continuation of ideological attacks of the Jews from the non-Jews. His treatises *De confusione linguarum* and *De mutatione nominum* defend the Laws of Moses and Jewish institutions against apostates who are inclined to mock. And in *Apologia pro Iudaeis* he defends the Jews against attacks and criticism akin to the negative interpretation of Moses by the Egyptian historian Manetho and others. Thus, Philo tells that there were people who abused Moses as an impostor and prating mountebank (*Apol.* 6:2).

In this connection it should be mentioned that Josephus, *Against Apion*, the anti-Jewish *Acts of the Alexandrian Martyrs*, and Gnostic writings prove that there was a broad stream of anti-Semitic traditions, attitudes and literature in Egypt. The Jewish polemic against aspects of pagan culture and against some of the other ethnic groups, such as the Egyptians, was at times as pointed. Thus, the *Sib. Or.* 5, written towards the end of the first century A.D., is openly hostile to the Gentiles in Egypt and Rome.[77] An eschatological saviour will appear, and the adversaries will be destroyed and a glorious Jerusalem will appear.

The Jewish expansion by ideological and peaceful means was defeated by the persecution of Alexandrian Jews in A.D. 38 and the subsequent edict by Claudius: the Jews were to be content with their established privileges in a city which was not their own.[78]

Accordingly, the God-given universal calling of the Jewish nation could not be fulfilled by peaceful means. The militaristic eschatology was the alternative, and the fierce revolution in A.D. 115 was a

---

[76] Borgen (1984A) 109–11.

[77] Schürer (1986) 595–608; Kasher (1985) 327–45; Pearson (1984) 340–41; Collins (1987) 436–38; Tcherikover (1963) 1–32; Hengel (1983) 655–85.

[78] Tcherikover (1957) 69–74; Tcherikover (1960) 36–55; Smallwood (1976) 246–50.

logical result. The establishment of a Jewish empire by military means failed, however, and led instead to disastrous destruction in A.D. 117 rather than to a new age with the Jewish nation as the head.

II

THE GOSPEL OF JOHN

4

The Sabbath Controversy in John 5:1–18 and Analogous Controversy Reflected in Philo's Writings

Philo and John

Scholars refer, of course, to Philo in their discussion of the ὁ λόγος in the Prologue of John.[1] Also at several other points scholars have utilized Philonic material in their interpretation of John, such as in their analysis of terms such as "light", "darkness", "water" and "bread", often emphasizing their symbolic use.[2] Philo's exegetical method and some of his exegetical ideas/traditions have been used to illuminate John's interpretation of the Old Testament, for example in the analysis of the Discourse on bread from heaven in John 6:31–58, and also in the analysis of John 5:17 where Jewish exegetical debates on Gen 2:2–3 are reflected.[3] The present study will demonstrate that Philo's exegesis of Gen 2:2–3 is of special interest also because it plays a role in a controversy about Sabbath observance within the Jewish community in Alexandria. This controversy, moreover, provides an important parallel to the situation of the Johannine community reflected in John 5:1–18.

Before we compare John and Philo in this way it is necessary to investigate how John uses traditional material and how it reflects a controversy about the Sabbath question in which the Johannine community was involved. Among the texts of relevance in Philo's

---

[1] See Dodd (1953) 65–73; 276–81; Bultmann (1941) 9; Brown (1966) 519–20; Barrett (1978) 153–54; Lindars (1972) 39–40; 82–83; Borgen (1987C) 77, 84.

[2] See especially Dodd (1953) 54–73.

[3] See for example Borgen (1965); Lindars (1972) 218–19; Barrett (1978) 255–56; Borgen (1987C) 12, 70, 85.

writings *Migr.* 89–93 is central for such a comparison. Moreover, the insights gained into the situation reflected in John 5:1–18 contribute to the scholarly discussion of the history of the Johannine community.

The Use of Tradition

In his book *Historical Tradition in the Fourth Gospel* C. H. Dodd demonstrates that John 5:1–9, the healing of the paralytic at Bethsatha, follows the same general pattern as that of several healing stories in the Synoptic Gospels.[4] The structure was seen in the following points:

The scene:
Vv. 1–3: . . . there was a feast of the Jews, and Jesus went up to Jerusalem. Now there is in Jerusalem by the Sheep Gate a pool, in Hebrew called Bethsatha, which has five porticoes. In these lay a multitude of invalids, blind, lame, paralysed.

The patient and his condition:
V. 5: One man was there, who had been ill for thirty-eight years.

Intervention by Jesus, leading up to word of healing:
Vv. 6–8: When Jesus saw him and knew that he had been lying there a long time, he said to him, 'Do you want to be healed?' The sick man answered him, 'Sir, I have no man to put me into the pool when the water is troubled, and while I am going another steps down before me'. Jesus said to him, 'Rise, take up your pallet, and walk'.

Recovery of the patient:
V. 9: And at once the man was healed, and he took up his pallet and walked.

---

[4] Dodd (1963) 174–80.

Like some of the healing stories in the Synoptics so also this story in John is dated to a Sabbath day, "Now that day was the Sabbath" (John 5:9).[5]

According to Dodd the subsequent controversial dialogue, vv. 10ff., is connected somewhat artificially with the miracle through the reference to the Sabbath in v. 9.[6] In this way vv. 10–18 serve as the transition from the narrative of the healing at Bethsatha to the discourse which follows in vv. 19ff.[7]

This discussion by Dodd of vv. 10–18 is sketchy and needs to be brought further. Dodd refers to Luke 13:10–17, the healing of the crippled woman on the Sabbath, as a story parallel to John 5:1–18. He mentions that in both places a controversy follows upon the story of healing. We can then classify Luke 13:10–17 and John 5:1–18 as case stories (John 5:1–9/Luke 13:10–13) followed by halakhic exchanges (John 5:10–18/Luke 13:14–17). The same form of a case-incident followed by a halakhic controversy dialogue/action occurs in Matt 12:1–18/Mark 2:23–28, the plucking corn on the Sabbath. In John 9:1–41, the healing of the blind on the Sabbath, vv. 1–7 (the case story), the controversy dialogue/action, vv. 8–41, is developed into a lengthy judicial hearing. A fragment of a controversy dialogue is found in John 7:21–23, based on the same healing story as the one in John 5:1–9.

The objections by the critics and Jesus' answer can be listed in this way:

The objections raised:
John 5:10:
So the Jews said to the man who was cured, 'It is the Sabbath, it is not permitted for you to carry your pallet'.
John 5:15–16:
The man went away and told the Jews that it was Jesus who had healed him. And this was why the Jews persecuted Jesus, because he did this on the Sabbath.

---

[5] See Mark 3:1–6; Luke 13:10–17.

[6] Dodd (1963) 118.

[7] See Dodd (1953) 320. So also Lindars (1972) 52 ("a transitional dialogue").

John 9:16, 24:

V. 16. Some of the Pharisees said, 'This man is not from God, for he does not keep the Sabbath'.

V. 24. So for the second time they called the man who had been blind, and said to him, 'Give God the praise; we know that this man is a sinner'.

Luke 13:14:

But the ruler of the Synagogue, indignant because Jesus had healed on the Sabbath, said to the people, 'There are six days on which work ought to be done; come on those days and be healed, and not on the Sabbath day'.

Matt 12:2 (cf. Mark 2:24):

But when the Pharisees saw it, they said to him, 'Look, your disciples are doing what is not permitted on the Sabbath'.

Jesus' answer:

John 5:17:

But Jesus answered them, 'My Father is working still, and I am working'.

John 7:21–23:

Jesus answered them, 'I did one deed, and you marvelled at it. Moses gave you circumcision ... and you circumcise a man upon the Sabbath. If on the Sabbath a man receives circumcision, so that the law of Moses may not be broken, are you angry with me because on the Sabbath I made a whole man well?'

John 9:25:

(He [the man] answered, 'Whether he is a sinner, I do not know; one thing I know, that though I was blind, now I see'.)

Luke 13:15–16:

Then the Lord answered him, 'You hypocrites! Does not each of you on the Sabbath untie his ox or his ass from the manger, and lead it away to water it? And ought not this woman, a daughter of Abraham whom Satan bound for eighteen years, be loosed from this bond on the Sabbath day?'

Matt 12:3–6:

He said to them, 'Have you not read what David did, when he was hungry, and those who were with him: how he entered the house of God and ate the bread of the Presence, which it was not permitted for him to eat nor for those who were with him, but only for the priests? Or have you not read in the law how on the Sabbath the priests in the temple profane the Sabbath and are guiltless? I tell you, something greater than the temple is here'.

As one should expect, these controversy sections refer back to the case stories both in a more general way as well as by repeating some of the words in the stories. In Matt 12:2–6 the words "Sabbath" and "the disciples" from the case story are repeated, and the actual objectionable action of plucking corn on the Sabbath is referred to in an implicit way: "Look your disciples are doing what is not permitted on the Sabbath" (12:2). In Luke 13:14–17 the "crime" of healing on the Sabbath is referred back to in a general way as the healing, and the word "Sabbath" is repeated. Also other words are repeated with some variations: "the ruler of the Synagogue", v. 14 refers back to "in the Synagogues" in v. 10, and "eighteen years" occurs both in v. 10 and in v. 16. The words "free/loose from" (v. 12 ἀπολέλυσαι and v. 16 λυθῆναι) also belong together.

This method of repeating words from the case story in the controversy dialogue/actions is much developed in John 5:10–18, and it has a systematic outline. In vv. 10–13 the sentence ἆρον τὸν κράβατόν σου καὶ περιπάτει from v. 8 (also in v. 9) is repeated and paraphrased. In vv. 14–16 the phrase ὑγιὴς γένεσθαι – ἐγένετο ὑγιής (vv. 6 and 9) is repeated and paraphrased. (The word ὑγιής was referred to in passing already in v. 11). The term σάββατον from v. 9 is repeated in each section, in v. 10 and v. 16 respectively. This word also occurs in the final section, vv. 17–18, where the speaking and acting person in the case story, Jesus himself, is in the centre.

Thus in vv. 10–16 there is a mechanical and systematic use of phrases from the case story, vv. 1–9. This fact indicates that the case story is the more stable and authoritative element in the tradition, while the subsequent controversy dialogue/action is the more flexible part of tradition. In this way the controversy section in John 5:10–18 has the nature of an expository commentary to the case story, vv. 1–9.[8] It is in accordance with this understanding of the controversy section as a more flexible expository commentary that John 7:21–23 has a halakhic answer different from the one in 5:17–18. In v. 21

---

[8] Borgen (1987B) 80–94.

the sentence "I did one deed and you all marvelled at it" presents in summary fashion the case story of the healing told in 5:1–9. Although the verb "marvel" (θαυμάζω) has a somewhat negative sound here, it is important to notice that in the Synoptics this word often characterizes the impression a miracle has made, Matt 8:27; 9:33; 15:31; 21:20; Luke 8:25; 11:18; cf. Acts 2:7.[9]

Then John 7:22–23 follow a halakhic reasoning parallel to those used in Matt 12:1–8 and Luke 13:10–17. In all three passages the argument moves from the lesser to the greater. In Matt 12:3–5 the incident in 1 Sam 21:1–6 (David ate the bread of the Presence in the Temple) and the lawful breaking of the Sabbath laws by the priests in the Temple (cf. Num 28:9–10) are the lesser cases which tell about modifications of the Laws of Moses. In Jesus' situation there is even more reason for freedom of observance: "I tell you, something greater than the temple is here" (Matt 12:6). In Luke 13:15 the lesser case is the work done on the Sabbath in order to tend to the needs of animals. The greater case is Jesus' healing of "a daughter of Abraham" (Luke 13:16). Similarily, in John 7:22–23 the lesser case is the performing of circumcision, i.e. on one member of the body, on the Sabbath, and the greater is Jesus' healing of the whole man.[10] Thus there is a similar method of arguing from the Scriptures and practice in John 7:21–23 and in Matt 12:1–8 and Luke 13:10–17.

In John 7:22–23 Jesus' defence of the healing on the Sabbath is different from the one given in 5:17 ("My Father is working still, and I am working"). Nevertheless, in both places there is a direct usage of halakhic exposition documented in Jewish sources. The parallel to John 7:22–23 is found in rabbinic sources, such as in *t. Sabb.* 15:16: "He supersedes the Sabbath for one of his members, and shall he not supersede the Sabbath for his whole self?"[11]

Also in John 5:17 Jewish exegesis is utilized. When it is said in v. 17 that God works up to now, that is, including the Sabbath, a widespread exegetical debate on Gen 2:2–3 is presupposed and

---

[9] See Bultmann (1931) 241.

[10] See Pancaro (1975) 158–68, and commentaries.

[11] See also *b. Yoma* 85b. Further discussion in commentaries on the Gospel of John, such as in Barrett (1978) 134–35.

used.[12] The problem was the conviction that God cannot stop working. Consequently, the notion of the Sabbath rest of God, as stated in Gen 2:2–3, stands in tension with this working. Evidence for such exegetical debate of the Sabbath rest of God is found as early as the second century B.C., in Aristobulus,[13] and more material is found in Philo and in rabbinic writings.

According to rabbinic exegesis, the Sabbath commandment does not forbid one to carry something about in one's house on the Sabbath. God's homestead is the upper and lower worlds. He may thus be active within it without coming into conflict with the Sabbath (Gen. Rab. 30:6). Philo, relying on the Septuagint rendering, notices that Gen 2:2–3 reads κατέπαυσεν, not ἐπαύσατο. Thus the text means "caused to rest", not "rested", for He causes to rest that which, though actually not in operation, is apparently making, but He himself never ceases making (Leg. all. 1:5–6). Thus, the meaning of the Seventh Day to Philo is that God, who has no origin, is always active. "He is not a mere artificer, but also Father of the things that are coming into being" (Leg. all. 1:18). All created beings are dependent and really inactive in all their doings: ". . . the number seven . . . Its purpose is that creation, observing the inaction which it brings, should call to mind him who does all things invisible" (Her. 170).

An interpretation of Gen 2:2–3 similar to that of Philo, seems to be presupposed in John 5:1–18. The Son of God brings the Father's upholding and providential activity to bear upon the case of the healing of a person on the Sabbath. And the healed person is dependent and inactive, even in the carrying of the mat on the Sabbath, because the Son of God told him to do so.

According to John 5:1–18 God's providential activity was made manifest in the healing of the paralytic by the Son on the Sabbath. On the basis of God's/the Son's work on the Sabbath, the Sabbath observance could be abrogated. Thus John 5:1–18 both addresses itself to Christology and marks the end of Sabbath observance. It is of importance to notice that Gen 2:2–3 already in Philo's time was used as argument in favour of the abrogation of the Sabbath

---

[12] For the following, see Borgen (1987A) 89–92.

[13] Walter (1964) 170–71; Borgen (1984) 277; Borgen (1983A) 180, 184–85, and Borgen (1987C) 12.

observance.[14] In *Migr*. 89–93 Philo refers to some fellow Jews who search for the inner meaning of the laws to the extent that they were at the point of ignoring the external and specific observances. They are taught by the sacred word to let go nothing that is part of the customs fixed by divinely empowered men (89–90). Against this background Philo gives the following advice and warning against those who draw wrong conclusions from the circumstance that God is active on the Seventh day, as stated in Gen 2:2–3 according to Jewish exegesis:

> It is quite true that the Seventh day is meant to teach the power of the Unorginate and the non-action of created beings (cf. Gen 2:2–3). But let us not for this reason abrogate (λύομεν) the enactments laid down for its observance, and light fires or till the ground or carry loads or demand the restoration of deposits or recover loans, or do all else that we are permitted to do as well on days that are not festival seasons.

> Why, we shall be ignoring the sanctity of the Temple and a thousand other things, if we are going to pay heed to nothing except what is shown us by the inner meaning of things. Nay, we should look on all these outward observances as resembling the body, and their inner meaning as resembling the soul, so we must pay heed to the letter of the Laws. If we keep and observe these, we shall gain a clearer conception of those things of which these are the symbols; and besides that we shall not incur the censure of the many and the charges they are sure to bring against us.

Here we find a conflict between two ways of reasoning, both relying upon the Laws of Moses. Philo's view might be characterized in this way: the universal principles and activity of the Creator are tied to the external observances of a particular people, the Jewish nation. On this basis this particular nation has a universal function. The view which Philo criticizes seems to be: The Laws of Moses and the specific observances give witness to the universal principles and activity of the Creator. The universal principles can then be followed apart from the particular external laws and observances

---

[14] See Borgen (1983A) 87–88; Borgen (1987C) and Borgen (1987A) 90–91.

of the Jewish nation. Consequently, God's activity and universal principles can be present also when one works on the Sabbath just as one does on other days.

Migr. 91 has striking points of similarities with John 5:1–18. Both places deal with the Sabbath. In both places the exegesis of Gen 2:2–3 is presupposed and utilized, although this Old Testament passage is not quoted and therefore not interpreted in an explicit way. And in both places the understanding that God is always active is witnessed to by the Sabbath in such a way as to give freedom from the specific observances, such as the prohibition against carrying a load. In John 5:10ff. the load is the mat carried by the one healed. Also the criticism of Jesus' healing on the Sabbath is in accordance with *Migr.* 91, when Philo prohibits such actions which as well could be done on other days as on the festival seasons. The same rule serves as basis for the criticism of Jesus' healing of the crippled woman on the Sabbath, Luke 13:10–17: 'There are six days on which work ought to be done; come on those days and be healed, and not on the Sabbath day' (v. 14). Philo warns that those who held the views he criticized will be subject to censure by the community which will bring charges against them. Correspondingly, John 5:16 and 18 tell that Jesus' fellow-Jews persecuted and sought to kill him. Thus John 5:1–18 has interpreted the Jesus tradition under the influence of Jewish controversies on Sabbath observance such as the conflicting views and practices documented in Philo, *Migr.* 86–91.

There is a basic difference, however, between the spiritualizing Jews whom Philo criticizes, and the views expressed in John. According to John, the activity of the Creator is the basis of the activity of the Son on the Sabbath, and the Son is the historical person Jesus of Nazareth. This view leads to the conclusion that the Sabbath observance is to be abrogated. The spiritualists in Alexandria, on the other hand, referred to an abstract doctrine of God's providential activity in defence of their freedom from Sabbath observances.

Interpretation

The preceding analysis of the use of tradition in John 5:1–18 has at the same time dealt with aspects of content and interpretation.

Further discussion is needed, however, both on the life-setting of the passage, and John's interpretation of it within his Gospel.

Within the Gospel the discussion about the Sabbath observances, John 5:1–18, 7:21–24 and 9:13–16 are but the starting point for debates on Christology.[15] John 5:1–18 and 7:21–24 in themselves keep closely together the themes of Sabbath and of Christology. In John 7:21–24 the christological aspect is not made explicit, just as also is the case in the stories about Sabbath observances in the Synoptic Gospels. In John 5:17–18 Jesus is explicitly identified as the Son of God, and this claim causes the controversy together with the conflict about Sabbath observance. Both aspects of the controversy are based on Jewish exegesis of Gen 2:2–3, however, and tie in with corresponding controversy already present in Judaism. The conclusion is: John 5:1–18 and 7:21–24 have their life-setting in the situation of the Johannine community in the period prior to the time of the writing of the Gospel. On the basis of the Jesus-tradition the community freed itself of Sabbath observance by referring to the authority and the Sabbath work of Jesus. In this controversy the Johannine Christians drew on exegetical and halakhic debates on Sabbath observance in contemporary Judaism and applied the Jesus-tradition to these debates.

Two observations already made support this understanding. First, the form of a case-story followed by a controversy exchange has parallels in the Synoptics and has then a firm place in the gospel tradition. John has thus received such a unit and built it into his Gospel. Second, John 7:21–24 is best understood as a fragment of another version of the same unit, in which the same healing story, as the case, is followed by a controversy section which draws on other Jewish debating points on the question of Sabbath observance. The reference to the reaction of marvel to the healing miracle, 7:21, is, as has been shown, a traditional feature in the miracle stories, and indicates that a version of the healing story slightly different from the one in 5:1–9 is presupposed.

What was the function of John 5:1–18 in its life-setting? J. L. Martyn thinks that the passage reflects a certain historical incident in the life of the Johannine church: A member of John's church serves to make real in the life of a Jew the healing power of Jesus. At that,

---

[15] See Dahl (1962).

the Jewish authorities step in and question the man. Then the Christian finds the man and talks with him, but does not lead him to full Christian confession. He rather gives him a solemn warning: "See, you are well! Sin no more, that nothing worse befall you". The man represents the Jew who, though presumably thankful to be healed, nevertheless remains wholly loyal to the Synagogue, and even might become an informer against his healer.[16] In support of his interpretation Martyn points to the parallelism between John 5:15 and 11:46. John 5:15 reads: "the man went away and told the Jews that it was Jesus who had healed him". Correspondingly John 11:46 says: "But some of them went to the Pharisees and told them what Jesus had done."[17]

Against this understanding of Martyn it must be stressed that there is a basic difference between the two statements. In John 5:15 it is *the man healed* by Jesus (and not some spectators) who tells the Jewish authorities who healed him. In John 11:46 *the spectators* to Jesus' calling Lazarus back from the grave reported it to the Pharisees. Thus the healing story in John 5:1–18 is an initiation story which served as paradigm for the entry into the Johannine community. The healing then represents salvation as a whole, and the word in v. 14, "See you are well! Sin no more, that nothing worse befall you", does not mean that the illness was caused by sin.[18] The word is rather an admonition to a convert to live a new life. When the man went away and told the Jewish authorities that Jesus had healed him (John 5:15) he gave his witness to them about Jesus as his healer. This open information to the Jewish authorities about the healing incident is presupposed in John 7:21–24, and it is in general agreement with the point made in John 18:20 that Jesus said nothing secretly. The point in John 5:1–18 is then to offer guidelines to a convert: he is set free from the observance of the Sabbath laws (and from keeping the other Jewish feasts) on the basis of Jesus' divine authority, his non-conformity to the observance and his resulting death.

The Synoptic Gospels give evidence for the fact that the question of Sabbath observance was a controversial issue for the emerging church in its relationship to the synagogual communities, Matt 12:1–14 and parallels and Luke 13:10–17; 14:1–6, etc. Further evidence

---

[16] Martyn (1979) 70–71.

[17] Martyn (1986) 113.

[18] Cf. Barrett (1978) 255.

is seen in Gal 4:10–11 where Paul criticizes the Galatian Christians for accepting and conforming to the Jewish cultic calendar: "You observe days, and months, and seasons, and years! I am afraid I have laboured over you in vain". In Col 2:16 there is even an explicit reference to Sabbath observance: "Therefore, let no one pass judgment on you in questions of food and drink or with regard to a festival or a new moon or a Sabbath".

Although our analysis of John 5:1–18 together with 7:21–24 does not provide sufficient material for a reconstruction of the history of the Johannine community, it nevertheless contributes to such attempts. One such reconstruction is suggested by J. L. Martyn.[19] He distinguishes between I. The Early Period (before the Jewish war until the 80s); II. The Middle Period (the late 80s?), and III. The Late Period (the time when the Gospel was written).

Martyn's middle period is of primary interest for the present discussion. According to him, in this period some in the Synagogue demanded exegetical proof for what the Johannine Christians proclaimed about Jesus. This led to midrashic debates. The Synagogue authorities introduced the reworded *Birkat ha-Minim* (curse on the deviators) into the liturgical services in order to be able to identify and eject those who confessed Jesus as the Messiah (John 9:22). Our analysis is in agreement with Martyn's point that midrashic exegesis and debates became important in this middle period. In disagreement with Martyn there are reasons for distinguishing between the period indicated by John 5:1–18 and 7:21–24 and a later period suggested by John 9:22.

At the time of John 5:1–18 and 7:21–24 the Sabbath observance as such was a burning and controversial issue and Jewish halakhic exegesis and reasoning were utilized by the Johannine Christians. Since they referred to Jesus' authority in this controversy, the Sabbath issue contributed to the formulation of a "high Christology". Jesus was understood to have a higher authority than the written and practised Torah. Against the background that some Jews already had referred to God's activity on the Sabbath (Gen 2:2–3) as basis for abrogating the external observances of the Sabbath, Jesus' authority was interpreted correspondingly: as the Son of the Creator and

---

[19] Martyn (1977) 149–75.

Upholder he also works on the Sabbath and thereby puts an end to the external observances.

This conflict with(in) the synagogual community should be dated to the 50s and 60s, rather than to the late 80s as indicated by Martyn. Gal 4:10–11 and Col 2:16 support this dating, as also does Philo, *Migr.* 86–91. Philo shows that Gen 2:2–3 was used in the same way in Sabbath controversies even earlier than the 50s. Moreover, he states that those who do away with the external Sabbath observance will be censured by the community. In *Mos.* 2:209–20 he retells the story of the Sabbath breaker who suffered death penalty by stoning, in accordance with Exod 31:14 and 35:2. In this connection Philo also refers to the keeping of the Sabbath in his own days (2:216). Thus, it is in accordance with the Sabbath laws that the Jewish authorities sought to kill Jesus as a Sabbath breaker, John 5:15 and 18.

Our dating is in general agreement with Brown's reconstruction of the history of the Johannine community.[20] In what he calls phase one (mid 50s to late 80s) a high Christology developed, such as stated in John 5:18, which led to debates with Jews who thought the Johannine community was abandoning Jewish monotheism by making a second God out of Jesus. Our analysis suggests two changes in Brown's scheme. First, more stress should be placed on the controversies about the Sabbath observances, and how these controversies contributed to the formulation of a high Christology, as in John 5:1–18 seen against the background of Philo, *Migr.* 86–91. Second, a distinction should be drawn between the period of such Sabbath controversies and the subsequent period when traditions from this earlier period were just starting points for debates on Christology as such.

Many scholars maintain that the original healing story, John 5:1–9, had no reference to the Sabbath. This point was added by John in v. 9b as an afterthought, and not stated at the outset of the story as in the Synoptics. John similarily added the reference to

---

[20] Brown (1979), with a summary chart on pp. 166–67.

the Sabbath in 9:14, since the Sabbath is not mentioned in the healing story, vv. 1–7.[21]

Some observations speak against this view:

1. Synoptic material should be used as comparative material, but not to such an extent that it is a standard blueprint for details, such as whether a Sabbath reference must come at the outset or at the end of a story.

2. When the Johannine Christians saw the freedom from Sabbath observation to be so important that it entered into a controversy with the Jewish leaders for that reason, the most natural explanation is that such controversy was part of the authoritative Jesus tradition which they had received, and was not just a new idea added to this tradition.

3. The fact that both John 5:1–18 and 7:21–23 have formed this Sabbath controversy tradition in the encounter with current Jewish halakhic debates on the Sabbath, supports the view that John 5:1–18 presupposes a real encounter in the history of the Johannine community, an encounter caused by the Jesus-tradition in words and practice.

4. The form of a case followed by a subsequent halakhic exchange belonged to the forms handed on in the Jesus tradition, as can be seen from its ocurrences in all gospels. Thus, in John 5 the whole of vv. 1–18 is based on this traditional form, and the Sabbath motif was part of this form. Thus, the reference to the Sabbath in v. 9b is not an afterthought to the preceding traditional story of the healing. As a motif which already belonged to this tradition of case incident followed by a halakhic exchange, the reference to the Sabbath had been placed at the point where it could be made clear that it was the central issue for both parts of the form.

5. Also in John 7:21–23 the Sabbath question is stressed as the issue both of the healing story and the halakhic exchange. The incident is dated to the Sabbath: ". . . are you angry with me because on the Sabbath I made a whole man well?" As already stated, the halakhic exchange draws on arguments about Sabbath observance also found

---

[21] See Haenchen (1959) 46–50; (Haenchen seems to have modified his views in Haenchen (1984) 243–60); Bultmann (1971) 239, n. 2, and 242; Dodd (1963) 174–80; Fortna (1970) 48–54; Martyn (1979) 69; Pancaro (1975) 10–14; Lindars (1972) 215; Schnackenburg (1971) 117.

in rabbinic writings. As for John 9:14, the Sabbath reference probably comes from a tradition which had the form of a case-incident followed by a halakhic exchange. The chapter in its present form is then an expository elaboration of such a unit of tradition. In this elaboration the reference to the Sabbath serves as stepping stone for a more independent presentation of a christological debate.

Conclusion

The story of the healing of the paralytic as a controversial case followed by a subsequent halakhic exchange, is a traditional form, parallels of which are found in Matt 12:1–18/Mark 2:23–28 and Luke 13:10–17. The Sabbath question was part of the received Jesus-tradition. These and other similar traditions contributed to the conflicts between the Christians and the Jewish authorities on the question of Sabbath observance. In this conflict the tradition behind John 5:1–18 was adapted to the specific arguments employed in the conflict, here exegesis of Gen 2:2–3 about God working on the Sabbath. In this way the conflict contributed to the way in which a "high Christology" was formulated. In the present context of the Gospel of John the section of John 5:1–18 serves as point of departure for a general christological debate, 5:19ff.

The parallel material in Philo's writings makes evident that the Sabbath controversy reflected in John 5:1–18 is to be seen as a specifically Christian version of a conflict which also is documented to exist in the Jewish community in Alexandria, a tension and a conflict which probably existed in most of the Jewish communities: Some Jews interpreted the Laws of Moses in such a way that they could claim to be faithful to their basic tenets and at the same time ignore the external observances. In a distinct way John in 5:1–18 bases his reasoning for abrogating the Sabbath observance on Christology. Nevertheless, in John, just as in Philo, exegetical interpretations of Gen 2:2–3 play a central role in these controversies.

The present study has then shown that Philo does not only throw light upon ideas in John. Philo can even throw light upon John beyond the area of exegetical metods and exegetical traditions. Philo's writings illustrate how exegesis of the Laws of Moses played a central role in controversies in the Jewish community. Thus, he provides parallel and comparative material to the way in which exegesis of the Laws of Moses (*in casu* Gen 2:2–3) was a basic factor in the controversy between the Synagogue and the emerging Christian community.

5

John and the Synoptics

I. An Independent Oral and / or Written Tradition?

The relationship of John to the Synoptic Gospels is a problem yet
to be solved in New Testament research. Until World War II the
predominant view was that John used one, two or all Synoptic Gospels.
After the research done on this material by P. Gardner-Smith shortly
before the outbreak of the War, a trend away from that position
gained momentum. A new consensus seemed to emerge: John was
independent of the Synoptics.[1]

Many scholars who followed this trend assume that John utilizes
an ancient oral tradition independent of the other gospels. A major
work along this avenue of research was C. H. Dodd's book *Historical
Tradition in the Fourth Gospel* (Cambridge 1963, reprint 1965). Dodd
attempted to uncover the traditional material in John by comparing
it with what is most obviously related to the Synoptic Gospels, namely,
the passion narratives. He then proceeds with the analysis to the
materials where there are fewer and fewer apparent synoptic contacts:
the narratives of Jesus' ministry, those regarding John the Baptist
and the first disciples, and, finally, the discourse materials.

Among the scholars who more or less accept the theory that John
builds on oral tradition which is wholly, or mainly, independent
of the Synoptics are: R. Bultmann (1955, etc.); P. Borgen (1959);

---

[1] Cf. Smith (1980) 425–26; Neirynck (1977) 73ff.

D. M. Smith (1963, etc.); R. Schnackenburg (1965); C. H. Dodd (1965); A. Dauer (1972).[2]

In his survey of the writings of Dodd and others, R. Kysar makes the following observations: ". . . Dodd's proposal along with others like it raises anew the persistent questions about the nature of the early Christian traditions – questions which must be answered before proposals such as Dodd's can prove very helpful. For example, exactly how rich and creative was the pre-literary history of the gospel materials? . . . What is needed, it seems to me, is a more highly developed method of johannine form criticism; and until such methodology can be developed, our efforts in this regard may satisfy little more than the fancy. Dodd began our effort toward the development of a johannine form critical method but that method still remains essentially primitive and crude years after his initial endeavours."[3]

In recent years the view that John is dependent upon the Synoptic Gospels has gained new impetus. For example, F. Neirynck and M. Sabbe reject theories of "unknown" and "hypothetical" sources behind John, whether they are supposed to be written or oral.[4] Neirynck writes that ". . . not traditions lying behind the Synoptic Gospels but the Synoptic Gospels themselves are the sources of the Fourth Evangelist."[5] Similarly M. Sabbe concludes his study of John 18:1–11 in this way: "For better understanding of the relation between John and the Synoptic Gospels and for a more homogeneous explanation of John's text as a whole, the awareness of the redactional creativeness of John combined with a direct dependence upon the Synoptics, is more promising."[6]

A more complex hypothesis has been suggested by M.-É. Boismard.[7] In agreement with Neirynck, he believes that the author of the Fourth

---

[2] Bultmann (1955) 524; Borgen (1959) 246–59; Smith (1963/64) 336–51; Haenchen (1959) 19–54; Brown (1966), Brown (1970), see also Brown (1961) 143–60; Lindars (1969/1970) 318–29; Lindars (1972); Schnackenburg (1965), Schnackenburg (1971), Schnackenburg (1975); Dodd (1963); Dauer (1972).

[3] Kysar (1975) 66–67.

[4] Neirynck (1977) 103–06; Neirynck (1979); Sabbe (1977) 205–34.

[5] Neirynck (1977) 106.

[6] Sabbe (1977) 233.

[7] Boismard (1977). For surveys, cf. Neirynck (1977) 82–93; Smith (1982) 106–11.

Gospel knew all three Synoptic Gospels. While Neirynck explains the differences between John and the Synoptics as the work of the Evangelist himself, Boismard attributes these differences, as well as the similarities, to various types of sources. According to Boismard, the author of the Gospel of John, whom he calls John II-B (ca. A.D. 90–100), revised his own first recension of the Gospel which Boismard calls John II-A. The primary source behind John II-A is Document C (John I, ca. A.D. 50), which is also one of the sources behind the Synoptic Gospels. Finally, a later redactor (John III) worked over the finished Gospel, making some changes and additions.[8]

Against this background it seems pertinent to look afresh on Paul's letters in order to gain insight into pre-synoptic usage of gospel materials. In this way we may find evidence as to the form and the method employed in the transmission of tradition and thus make the hypothesis of oral tradition less hypothetical.

Among the passages containing traditional gospel material in Paul's letter, the passages on the Lord's supper in 1 Cor 10:3–4, 16, 17, 21 and 11:23–29 (34) stand out. Only here does Paul use a unit of gospel tradition of some length.[9] What can we learn from these passages about agreements with the Synoptics and about the nature of the pre-synoptic use of gospel materials?

1. A comparison between 1 Cor 10:3–4, 16, 17, 21; 11:23–29 and Mark 14:22–25 makes possible the following generalizations: Between mutually independent versions (units of oral/written tradition) there may be close verbal agreement in the form of sentences, word pairs and set-phrases, single words and/or corresponding variant terms.

The agreement between John 2:13–22; 6:51–58 and the Synoptics are not closer, nor more striking, than those between the above mentioned Pauline passages and Mark, and, in the case of John 5:1–18, the agreements with the Synoptics are even fewer.

Thus, our analysis of these three Johannine passages supports the hypothesis that John and the Synoptics are mutually independent.

---

[8] Cf. Neirynck (1979) 9–16.

[9] Concerning Paul and the gospel tradition in general, see the recent works by Dungan (1971); Fjärstedt (1974); Allison (1982) 1–32; Stuhlmacher (1983A) 240–50; Stuhlmacher (1983) 16–20, 157–82.

2. What is the nature of the tradition behind the gospels? The passages examined in 1 Cor 10 and 11 show that units of tradition were received and handed on and that they were used and activated in the Christian communities (1 Cor 11:23–25(26)). Some modifications took place in the process, but the formulations were quite stable even during decades of transmission (cf. 1 Cor 11:23–26 with Mark 14:22–25).

Interpretative activity is also evident. The expositions can have the form of a commentary attached to a cited unit of tradition. In this way 1 Cor 11:(26)27–34 is attached to the quoted institution of the Lord's Supper in vv. 23–25 (26), and John 5:10–18 is attached to the story in v. 19. In the same manner John 2:17–22 is attached as an exposition of the cleansing of the temple in vv. 13–16. The unit of tradition may also be presupposed, and not quoted, as is the case in the discussion of the Lord's Supper in 1 Cor 10:3–4, 16–17, 21 and John 6:51–58.

3. The expositions have largely the form of paraphrases of sentences, phrases, word sets, and words from the given tradition. Synonyms may be used, and expressions may be rephrased. In the expository paraphrase, words and fragments from the tradition may be moulded into traditional form.

4. The transmission and exposition of tradition can take both a written and oral form. The written form is found in written documents, as 1 Cor, John and the Synoptics. The oral form seems primary, however, for the following reasons: a) Paul states explicitly that 1 Cor 11:23ff. was brought orally to the church in Corinth. Thus, there is a basis for assuming that the tradition as recorded in the Gospels was also primarily transmitted orally. b) Paul gives his expositions of the gospel tradition in written form because he is not present himself and thus cannot interpret the tradition in person (i.e. orally). This evidence suggests that similar kinds of exposition in the four gospels primarily originated in oral settings. c) The material discussed in 1 Cor 10 and 11 and in the Gospels belong to identifiable pericopes. Among the passages discussed in John, John 2:13–22 and 5:1–18 are easily delimited from their contexts, while 6:51–58 is part of the more complex entity of John 6 understood as a whole. Both in 1 Cor 10 and 11 and in John 2:13–22; 5:1–18 and 6:51–58 the tradition is interpreted in order to meet the concerns and needs of the Christian communities. This observation also speaks in favour

of the view that the oral form is primary, although the written form also may be used.

Paul and Mark

Paul, in 1 Cor 11:23ff., and Luke 22:15–20 represent a version of the institution different from the one in Mark 14:22–25 and Matt 26:26–28.[10] A comparison between Paul and Mark–Matt is of importance, nevertheless, since we can see in this way what kind of agreement might exist between two mutually independent versions of the same unit of tradition.[11] Since there is hardly any specific agreement between Paul's eucharistic passages and Matt, the comparison will be limited to Mark.

The correspondences between eucharistic traditions in 1 Cor and Mark 14:22–25 are:

Sentences (almost verbatim agreement):

1 Cor 11:24: τοῦτό μού ἐστιν	Mark 14:22 τοῦτό ἐστιν τό
τὸ σῶμα . . .	σῶμά μου

Scattered parts of sentences (phrases):

1 Cor 11:25 τοῦτο . . . ἡ . . .	Mark 14:24 τοῦτο . . . τὸ αἷμά
διαθήκη . . . ἐν τῷ ἐμῷ	μου τῆς διαθήκης
αἵματι	
1 Cor 11:23 ἔλαβεν ἄρτον	Mark 14:22 λαβὼν ἄρτον
1 Cor 11:24 ἔκλασεν καὶ	Mark 14:22 ἔκλασεν . . . καὶ
εἶπεν	εἶπεν

Word sets:

1 Cor 11:26 ἐσθίητε τὸν ἄρτον . . . τὸ ποτήριον πίνητε
1 Cor 11:27 ἐσθίῃ τὸν ἄρτον . . . πίνῃ τὸ ποτήριον
 τοῦ σώματος . . . τοῦ αἵματος . . .
1 Cor 11:28 . . . τοῦ ἄρτου ἐσθιέτω . . . τοῦ ποτερίου πινέτω
1 Cor 11:29 . . . ἐσθίων . . . πίνων . . . ἐσθίει . . . πίνει . . .
 τὸ σῶμα

---

[10] Bornkamm (1959) 152; Schürmann (1955) 1: (Luke 22:19–20 is halfway between Mark/Matt and Paul).

[11] About Mark's independence of Paul, see Schürmann (1955) 8.

1 Cor 11:25 . . . τὸ ποτήριον   Mark 14:22–24 . . . ἐσθιόντων
. . . πίνητε   . . . ἄρτον . . . τὸ σῶμα . . .
1 Cor 10:3–4 . . . ἔφαγον . . .   ποτήριον . . . ἔπιον . . . τὸ
   ἔπιον . . .   αἷμα
1 Cor 10:16 τὸ ποτήριον . . . τοῦ αἵματος . . . τὸν ἄρτον κλῶμεν
   . . . τοῦ σώματος . . .
1 Cor 10:17 ἄρτος . . . σῶμα . . . ἄρτου
1 Cor 10:21 . . . ποτήριον . . . πίνειν . . . ποτήριον

Single words:
1 Cor 11:24 εὐχαριστήσας   Mark 14:23 εὐχαριστήσας
1 Cor 11:24 ὑπέρ   Mark 14:24 ὑπέρ
1 Cor 11:23 παρεδίδετο   Mark 14:21 παραδίδοται
1 Cor 10:16 εὐλογίας ὃ   Mark 14:22 εὐλογήσας
   εὐλογοῦμεν
1 Cor 10:17 οἱ πολλοί . . .   Mark 14:23–24 πάντες . . .
   πάντες   πολλῶν

Variant words (corresponding in meaning):
1 Cor 11:24 εὐχαριστήσας   Mark 14:22 εὐλογήσας
1 Cor 11:25 ἐμῷ   Mark 14:24 μου
1 Cor 11:23 ἐν τῇ νυκτί   Mark 14:17 ὀψίας
1 Cor 11:26 ἄχρι οὗ   Mark 14:25 ἕως τῆς ἡμέρας
                                         ἐκείνης ὅταν

There are 68 words in 1 Cor 11:23b–26. Of those, 25 words are
also used in Mark 14:22–25. Out of 49 words in 1 Cor 11:23b–25,
21 are found in Mark 14:22–25. Thus, a third to almost a half of the
number of words used here are the same coming from two mutually
independent versions of this unit of tradition.

This comparison makes possible the following generalization:
Between mutually independent versions of units of oral and/or
written traditions there may be close verbal agreements in the form
of sentences, word pairs and sets, single words, and corresponding
variant terms. At the same time there are differences which give
each version its distinctive character. There are no specific agreements
found in the contexts of the passages in Paul and the passage in
Mark, apart from the fact that Paul seems to presuppose a passion
narrative, corresponding to the passion narratives in the Gospels.

After having examined the agreements between the eucharistic traditions in 1 Cor and Mark, our analysis also raises the question: What insights can these passages in 1 Cor 10 and 11 give us into the nature of the pre-synoptic traditions?

Tradition Received and Handed On. 1 Cor 11:23–25(26)

It is commonly recognized that Paul in 1 Cor 11:23ff. cites the institution of the Lord's Supper as a unit of tradition. This is made clear by Paul's introductory sentence: "I have received (παρέλαβον) from the Lord that which I have given (παρέδωκα) to you." The two verbs are equivalents of two rabbinical technical terms for the transmitting of tradition, קבל מן and מסר ל.[12] 1 Cor 11:23 then indicates that the chain of tradition goes back to the words of Jesus, and that as the Lord, his institution of the Supper had juridical (binding) authority for the congregation in Corinth.[13]

Although Paul cites this given unit of tradition about the Lord's Supper, he at the same time brings interpretative elements into his rendering. This interpretative element is especially evident in v. 26. Paul here formulates a sentence parallel to v. 25b, so that at first Jesus seems to be still speaking:

25, ὁσάκις ἐὰν πίνητε . . .
26, ὁσάκις γὰρ ἐὰν ἐσθίητε . . . καὶ . . . πίνητε . . .

In spite of this similarity, v. 26 is Paul's own formulation of the traditional phrase, since in this sentence he refers to Jesus in the third person as the Lord: "For as often as you eat this bread and drink this cup, you proclaim the Lord's death until he comes." In this formulation Paul moreover draws on words about eschaton (ἄχρι οὗ ἔλθῃ), which in varied formulation also occur in the synoptic accounts.[14]

---

[12] Cf. Jeremias (1955) 128f.; Riesenfeld (1970) 15–18; Gerhardsson (1961) 288ff.; 305; 321f. Gerhardsson (1977) 27.

[13] Cf. Conzelmann (1969) 230–31; Gerhardsson (1961) 322; Stuhlmacher (1983) 19; Bornkamm (1959) 146–48; Käsemann (1964) 120–32.

[14] Conzelmann (1969) 237; cf. Jeremias (1955) 115; Käsemann (1964) 121; Bornkamm (1959) 148.

An Attached Paraphrasing Commentary

By this interpretative formulation in v. 26 Paul sets the theme, "to eat the bread and drink the cup," within the perspective of eschaton. This perspective dominates the subsequent verses.[15] Before analysing 1 Cor 11:27–34, we will first present the text:[16]

1 Cor 11:23–34:
"The text":
23 Ἐγὼ γὰρ παρέλαβον ἀπὸ τοῦ κυρίου, ὃ καὶ παρέδωκα ὑμῖν,
 ὅτι ὁ κύριος Ἰησοῦς ἐν τῇ νυκτὶ ᾗ παρεδίδοτο ἔλαβεν ἄρτον
24 καὶ εὐχαριστήσας ἔκλασεν καὶ εἶπεν, τοῦτό μού ἐστιν τὸ <u>σῶμα</u>
 τὸ ὑπὲρ ὑμῶν. τοῦτο ποιεῖτε εἰς τὴν ἐμὴν ἀνάμνησιν.
25 ὡσαύτως καὶ <u>τὸ ποτήριον</u> μετὰ τὸ δειπνῆσαι, λέγων, τοῦτο τὸ
 <u>ποτήριον</u> ἡ καινὴ διαθήκη ἐστὶν ἐν τῷ ἐμῷ αἵματι, τοῦτο ποιεῖτε,
 ὁσάκις ἐὰν <u>πίνητε</u>, εἰς τὴν ἐμὴν ἀνάμνησιν.

Theme:
26 ὁσάκις γὰρ ἐὰν ἐσθίητε <u>τὸν</u> <u>ἄρτον</u> τοῦτον καὶ ποτήριον <u>πίνητε</u>,
 τὸν θάνατον τοῦ κυρίου καταγγέλλετε, ἄχρι οὗ ἔλθῃ.

Commentary:
27 Ὥστε ὃς ἂν ἐσθίῃ <u>τὸν ἄρτον</u> ἢ <u>πίνῃ</u> <u>τὸ ποτήριον</u> τοῦ κυρίου
 <u>ἀναξίως</u>, <u>ἔνοχος</u> ἔσται <u>τοῦ σώματος</u> καὶ <u>τοῦ αἵματος</u> τοῦ κυρίου.
28 δοκιμαζέτω δὲ ἄνθρωπος ἑαυτόν, καὶ οὕτως ἐκ <u>τοῦ ἄρτου</u> ἐσθιέτω
 καὶ ἐκ <u>τοῦ ποτηρίου</u> πινέτω.
29 ὁ γὰρ ἐσθίων καὶ <u>πίνων</u> <u>κρίμα</u> ἑαυτῷ ἐσθίει καὶ πίνει μὴ <u>διακρίνων</u>
 τὸ <u>σῶμα</u>.
30 διὰ τοῦτο ἐν ὑμῖν πολλοὶ ἀσθενεῖς καὶ ἄρρωστοι καὶ κοιμῶνται
 ἱκανοί.
31 εἰ δὲ ἑαυτοὺς <u>διεκρίνομεν</u>, οὐκ ἂν <u>ἐκρινόμεθα</u>.
32 <u>κρινόμενοι</u> δὲ ὑπὸ τοῦ κυρίου παιδευόμεθα, ἵνα μὴ σὺν <u>τῷ κόσμῳ</u>
 <u>κατακριθῶμεν</u>.
33 Ὥστε, ἀδελφοί μου, συνερχόμενοι εἰς τὸ <u>φαγεῖν</u> ἀλλήλους
 ἐκδέχεσθε.

---

[15] Cf. Käsemann (1964) 121–32.

[16] See especially Käsemann (1954/55) 248ff.; Käsemann (1964) 122ff.; Bornkamm (1959) 168.

34 εἴ τις πεινᾷ, ἐν οἴκῳ ἐσθιέτω, ἵνα μὴ εἰς <u>κρίμα</u> συνέρχησθε.

1 Cor 10:16–17, 21:

16 <u>τὸ ποτήριον</u> τῆς εὐλογίας, ὃ εὐλογοῦμεν, οὐχὶ κοινωνία ἐστὶν
τοῦ <u>αἵματος</u> τοῦ χριστοῦ; <u>τὸν ἄρτον</u>, ὃν κλῶμεν, οὐχὶ κοινονία
τοῦ <u>σώματος</u> <u>τοῦ</u> χριστοῦ ἐστιν;

17 ὅτι εἷς <u>ἄρτος</u>, ἓν <u>σῶμα</u> οἱ πολλοί ἐσμεν, οἱ γὰρ πάντες ἐκ τοῦ
ἑνὸς <u>ἄρτου</u> μετέχομεν.

21 οὐ δύνασθε <u>ποτήριον</u> κυρίου <u>πίνειν</u> καὶ <u>ποτήριον</u> δαιμονίων.

By using technical terms for the transmission of tradition (παρέλαβον-
παρέδωκα) Paul introduces in 1 Cor 11:23 a quote of the Institution
of the Lord's Supper (11:23b–25).

In vv. 27ff. Paul gives a paraphrasing commentary on the quoted
unit of tradition. From this fact we see that (already) in the middle
of the fifties the Jesus-tradition was so fixed that it was quoted and
used as basis for an added exposition. As can be seen from the words
underscored with a single line in vv. 27ff., Paul utilizes fragments
– words and phrases – from the quoted tradition and builds them
into a paraphrasing exposition which applies it to a case-situation.
In Paul's exposition the genitive τοῦ κυρίου (v. 27) serves as a clarifying
addition to the fragments from the quoted tradition, . . . τὸ ποτήριον
and . . . τοῦ σώματος . . . As can be seen from the words underscored
by a double line, legal terms are woven together with these fragments
from the tradition of the Lord's Supper. Such legal terms are: ἀναξίως,
ἔνοχος ἔσται (v. 27); and κρίμα . . . διακρίνων . . . in v. 29. In vv.
30–32 Paul elaborates upon these legal terms, without drawing
on fragments from the eucharistic tradition. Finally, in vv. 33–34
he returns to the explicit discussion of the eucharistic meal. Here
he refers back to the institution of the Lord's Supper, vv. 23ff., and
even back to the situation in Corinth, pictured in vv. 17ff. In these
concluding verses, 33–34, we again, as in vv. 27–29, find terminology
from (the eucharistic) meal (τὸ φαγεῖν-ἐσθιέτω) woven together
with a legal term (κρίμα).

Although Paul writes the exposition himself and applies the
eucharistic tradition to a specific case, he nevertheless uses traditional

ethical/legal forms. The form of casuistic legal clauses is especially evident:[17]

27 ὃς ἂν ἐσθίῃ . . . ἔνοχος ἔσται . . .
29 ὁ γὰρ ἐσθίων . . . κρίμα ἑαυτῷ ἐθίει

The following sentences give rules for avoiding judgment:
31 εἰ δὲ ἑαυτοὺς διεκρίνομεν, οὐκ ἐκρινόμεθα.
("But if we judged ourselves truly, we should not be judged.")
32 κρινόμενοι . . . παιδευόμεθα, ἵνα μὴ . . .
("But when we are judged . . . we are chastened, so that we may not . . .")
34 εἴ τις πεινᾷ, ἐν οἴκῳ ἐσθιέτω, ἵνα μὴ . . .
("if any one is hungry, let him eat at home, so that you shall not . . .")

The form of v. 31 is similar to that of John 3:18 and Matt 6:14. All these sentences give the condition (in conditional clauses, 1 Cor 11:31 and Matt 6:14, or by a participle, John 3:18) for avoiding (1 Cor 11:31 and John 3:18) or gaining (Matt 6:14) what is stated in the main verb. To the sentences in 1 Cor 11:32 and 34 where the main verb is followed by ἵνα μή to show what is to be avoided, there are parallel forms in Matt 5:25; John 5:14; Luke 12:58 and Matt 7:1. The common parenetic imperative is used in 1 Cor 11:28 (δοκιμαζέτω) (cf. v.34), and in v. 33 (ἐκδέχεσθε). Finally, v. 30 has a descriptive sentence by which Paul explains phenomena which exist in the Corinthian church.

The exposition is in argumentative form. The case of eating unworthily is stated in v. 27, an exhortation then follows in v. 28, followed by the rationale in v. 29 (γὰρ). The negative effect which this has (διὰ τοῦτο) on the Corinthian church is narrated in v. 30. In vv. 31–32 the opposite alternative is presented, and then in v. 33ff. the conclusion is drawn.

---

[17] For such casuistic statements see Matt 5:21,22, etc. See examples from the Old Testament and from the Qumran writings in Nauck (1957) 29ff. Examples from rabbinic writings and Philo are given by Borgen (1965), esp. 88f.; see further Fiebig (1925) 3–20.

This analysis shows that Paul uses a variety of forms in his elaboration and that he changes style from third person singular to first and second person plural, and from indicative to imperative, etc. Paul's style is, moreover, argumentative. He draws logical conclusions. This analysis indicates that the help to be gained from an author's own particular style and other individual characteristics is limited. On the basis of such criteria one can hardly draw the conclusion that 1 Cor 11:27–29 is produced by Paul himself, since traditional style and terminology are used here. The section is, nevertheless, composed by Paul, and the following guide rule can be formulated: In the expository paraphrasing of gospel traditions, both words and phrases are fused together into traditional forms.[18]

Moreover, Paul does not indicate that he uses a novel approach when he comments on a given unit of tradition. From this one can assume that there were two activities running parallel in the church communities: a) gospel tradition was being received, preserved and handed on, exemplified by 1 Cor 11:23ff. and b) it was commented upon, paraphrased and applied to relevant concerns and situations, as exemplified by 1 Cor 11:27ff.

Fragments: Eucharist and Manna

After we have analysed 1 Cor 11:23–34, some remarks should be added on 1 Cor 10:3, 4, 16, 17 and 21. It is significant that Paul here uses an expository paraphrase of fragments from the eucharistic tradition without first quoting the tradition itself.[19]

16 τὸ ποτήριον τῆς εὐλογίας, ὃ εὐλογοῦμεν, οὐχὶ κοινωνία ἐστὶν τοῦ αἵματος τοῦ χριστοῦ; τὸν ἄρτον, ὃν κλῶμεν, οὐχὶ κοινωνία τοῦ σώματος τοῦ χριστοῦ ἐστιν;
17 ὅτι εἷς ἄρτος, ἓν σῶμα οἱ πολλοί ἐσμεν, οἱ γὰρ πάντες ἐκ τοῦ ἑνὸς ἄρτου μετέχομεν.

---

[18] Cf. Wright (1966) 110–11: "What the ancient writer was aware of was that he wrote within a particular tradition: it was this that largely decided the literary form to which we have given a name. He was a Deuteronomist, a priestly writer, a follower of the sages, an anthologist of the prophets, or the like." (Quotation from Vawter (1960) 33); Le Déaut (1971) 270: "The authors were conscious of writing in a tradition rather than in a certain literary form." Cf. also Borgen (1965) 59.

[19] Cf. Schürmann (1970), 86; Conzelmann (1969) 201f.; Jeremias (1955) 131.

21 οὐ δύνασθε <u>ποτήριον</u> κυρίου <u>πίνειν</u> καὶ <u>ποτήριον</u> δαιμονίων.

The words underscored by a single line are taken from the eucharistic tradition, as quoted in 1 Cor 11:23ff. The terms . . . τῆς εὐλογίας, ὃ εὐλογοῦμεν raise the question whether Paul also draws on other versions of the tradition,[20] since the corresponding term in 1 Cor 11:24 is εὐχαριστήσας, just as in Luke 22:17,19. On the other hand, Matt 26:26 and Mark 14:22 have εὐλογήσας.

In 1 Cor 10:16–17, 21 the fragments from the eucharistic tradition occur within the context of 1 Cor 10:14–22. The heading of the passage is Paul's paraenetic imperative in v. 14: "Flee from idolatry." The reference to the Lord's Supper (vv. 16–17, 21) and to the Law of Moses (Lev 7:6, 15; Deut 18:1–4) in v. 18 serves as argumentative basis for the warning against idolatry. The conclusion in vv. 21–22 has the form of a rule for mutually exclusive alternatives:

v. 21
οὐ δύνασθε <u>ποτήριον</u> κυρίου <u>πίνειν</u> καὶ <u>ποτήριον</u> δαιμονίων.
οὐ δύνασθε τραπέζης κυρίου μετέχειν καὶ τραπέζης δαιμονίων.

("You cannot drink the cup of the Lord and the cup of demons. You cannot partake of the table of the Lord and the table of demons".)

The same form is found in Matt 6:24 (Luke 16:13):

v. 24
οὐ δύνασθε θεῷ δουλεύειν καὶ μαμωνᾷ
("You cannot serve God and Mammon".)

Thus, in 1 Cor 10:21a Paul's paraphrase of a fragment from the eucharistic tradition has been given a traditional form, a form which also occurs in the Gospels in Matt 6:24 par.[21]

---

[20] Such a version of the eucharistic tradition would draw on the Jewish technical terms for the cup of wine over which the thanksgiving after the meal has been said, cf. Str-B 4:72; 628; 630f.; Conzelmann (1969) 202, Barrett (1968) 231.

[21] 21 Cf. Resch (1904) 53.

The passage from 1 Cor 10:14–22 reflects its oral nature. Paul exhorts the Corinthian church by means of a letter in lieu of appearing in person. The oral style is especially evident when Paul in v. 15 addresses the church as if he was speaking to them: "I speak (λέγω) as to sensible men; judge for yourselves what I say (ὅ φημι)." Formulations from the eucharistic tradition are also reflected in the haggadic reference to the manna and the well in the desert, 1 Cor 10:3–4, when it is said: ". . . they all ate the same spiritual food, and they all drank the same spiritual drink." In this passage Israel typifies the Christian people of God. In this way the events of the journey through sea and desert are applied to baptism (v. 2) and the Lord's Supper (vv. 3–4). The formulation in 1 Cor 10:3–4 seems even to reflect eucharistic phrases, as can be seen from the similarity to the wording in 1 Cor 11:26.

1 Cor   10:3: . . . τὸ αὐτὸ πνευματικὸν βρῶμα ἔφαγον . . .
         4: . . . τὸ αὐτὸ πνευματικὸν πόμα . . .
1 Cor 11:26: . . . ἐσθίητε τὸν ἄρτον . . .
         . . . τὸ ποτήριον πίνητε . . .

As can be seen from these observations, already in the mid-fifties the biblical stories about the manna and the well are being applied to the Lord's Supper.[22]

By comparing the eucharistic traditions recorded in 1 Cor 10 and 11 with Mark 14:22–25, we thus have shown that close agreement may exist between two mutually independent versions of the same unit of tradition. Furthermore, the analysis of 1 Cor 10 and 11 has given us insight both into the tradition received and handed on, and into the expository use of the tradition. Although the passages are part of a written document, its oral form seems to be primary.

Eucharistic Traditions in John, Paul and the Synoptics

Paul's usage of eucharistic gospel traditions in 1 Cor 10:3–4, 16–17, 21 and 11:23–34 can further our understanding of John's use of tradition. It can strengthen the hypothesis that John draws on oral traditions and is independent of the Synoptic Gospels. Such a theory

---

[22] Cf. Käsemann (1964) 114; Schürmann (1970) 173.

does more than just allude to unknown and hypothetical sources behind John. Paul makes it possible to provide dated evidence for analogous use of gospel tradition independent of the Synoptics.

The best starting point for the examination of the hypothesis is found in John 6:51b–58, since John here draws on eucharistic tradition in a way which comes very close to Paul's handling of it. John has closer agreements with Paul than with the Synoptics.

The agreements between John and Paul are:

John 6:51–58 and 1 Cor 10:3–4, 16–17, 21; 11:23–29

Word sets:

John	1 Cor
6:53 φάγητε τὴν σάρκα πίητε αὐτοῦ τὸ αἷμα	11:24–25 τὸ σῶμα . . . ἐν τῷ ἐμῷ αἵματι
6:54 ὁ τρώγων μου τὴν σάρκα καὶ πίνων μου τὸ αἷμα	11:27 τοῦ σώματος καὶ τοῦ αἵματος
6:55 ἡ . . . σάρξ μου καὶ τὸ αἷμά μου	10:16 τοῦ αἵματος . . . τοῦ σώματος
6:56 ὁ τρώγων μου τὴν σάρκα καὶ πίνων μου τὸ αἷμα	11:26 ἐσθίητε . . . πίνητε
6:57 ὁ τρώγων με	11:27 ἐσθίη . . . πίνη
6:52 τὴν σάρκα . . . φαγεῖν . . .	11:28 . . . ἐσθιέτω . . . πινέτω
6:58 ὁ τρώγων τοῦτον τὸν ἄρτον	11:29 ὁ . . . ἐσθίων . . . πίνων . . . ἐσθίει καὶ πίνει . . .
6:55 βρῶσις . . . πόσις	10:3–4 ἔφαγον . . . ἔπιον
	10:3–4 βρῶμα . . . πόμα

Sentences (in parts):

John 6:51b ὁ ἄρτος . . . ὃν ἐγὼ δώσω ἡ σάρξ μού ἐστιν ὑπέρ . . .	1 Cor 11:23–24 . . . ἄρτον . . . τοῦτό μού ἐστιν τὸ σῶμα τὸ ὑπέρ . . .
	Luke 22:19 . . . ἄρτον . . . ἔδωκεν . . . τοῦτό ἐστιν τὸ σῶμά μου τὸ ὑπέρ . . .

Subject matter, not words:

John	1 Cor
6:53 ... οὐκ ἔχετε ζωὴν ἐν ἑαυτοῖς	11:29 ... κρίμα ... 11:34 ... μὴ εἰς κρίμα
6:54 ... ἔχει ζωὴν αἰώνιον κἀγὼ ἀναστήσω αὐτὸν τῇ ἐσχάτῃ ἡμέρᾳ	11:32 ... μὴ σὺν τῷ κόσμῳ κατακριθῶμεν

M.-É. Boismard[23] emphasizes the agreements between John 6:51b and 1 Cor 11:24: John reflects a liturgical tradition here which is represented by Paul's version of the institution of the Lord's Supper. (Boismard thinks that Luke 22:19b is probably an addition by a scribe.) Moreover, Boismard suggests that John's term "my flesh" instead of "my body" in the synoptic and Pauline versions of the institution, translates Jesus' own words in Aramaic. Thus, John here renders a tradition which is independent of the Synoptics, in spite of the verbal similarities which exist. Boismard's view that John has stronger kinship with Paul than with the Synoptics, should be more thoroughly investigated.

1. John presupposes the institution of the Lord's Supper and paraphrases parts from it, without quoting the story of the institution itself. Similarly, Paul in 1 Cor 10:16–17, 21 selects words from the eucharistic tradition without quoting it. The story of the institution is presupposed as known, so that the commentary in 1 Cor 11:(26)27ff. is also a close parallel, although the institution is quoted in 11:23–25(26).

2. John and Paul use tradition in the same way. They make expository paraphrases of fragments. The fragments consist of word sets. The sets in John 6:51b–58 are ὁ ἄρτος/βρῶσις – ἡ σάρξ, πόσις – τὸ αἷμα, and φαγεῖν (τρώγειν) – πίνειν. Correspondingly, the Pauline word sets in 1 Cor 10:3–4, 16–17, 21 and 11:27–29 are: ὁ ἄρτος/βρῶμα – τὸ σῶμα, ποτήριον/πόμα – τὸ αἷμα, and ἐσθίειν/φαγεῖν – πίνειν.

3. There are similarities between John and Paul with regard to the form given to the expository paraphrases. In John 6:53 the eucharistic fragments are built into a sentence where a conditional clause (ἐάν) is followed by the main clause. Correspondingly, in 1 Cor 11:27 Paul paraphrases words from the tradition to a sentence where a conditional relative clause (ὃς ἄν) is followed by a main

---

23 Boismard (1977) 204–05.

clause. In John 6:54, 56, 57, 58 a participial phrase tied to the subject takes the place of the subordinate clause, as also is the case in 1 Cor 11:29 (ὁ . . . ἐσθίων καὶ πίνων). In both places there is variation of style between second and third person.

Moreover, both John and Paul use argumentative style. For example, negative and positive alternatives are presented to the readers (John 6:53–54; 1 Cor 11:27–28), and the rationale (γάρ) is given (John 6:55; 1 Cor 11:29). Then a conclusion is drawn (John 6:58; 1 Cor 11:33).

4. Both John and Paul apply the biblical story of the manna and the well to the eating and drinking in the Lord's Supper. In John 6:(31)51b–58 words from the eucharistic tradition are made part of the midrashic exposition of the Old Testament text on the manna, cited in v. 31. In 1 Cor 10:3–4 the Israelites' eating and drinking in the desert typify the Lord's Supper. Against this background, it is probable that John 6:55 ("For my flesh is food (βρῶσις) indeed, and my blood is drink (πόσις) indeed") refers to the manna and the well, just as do the corresponding terms (βρῶμα-πόμα) in 1 Cor 10:3–4.[24]

5. Moreover, both John 6:41, 43 and 1 Cor 10:10 refer to murmurs by the Israelites in the desert.

6. The formulation in John 6:51b ὁ ἄρτος δὲ ὃν ἐγὼ δώσω ἡ σάρξ μού ἐστιν ὑπὲρ τῆς τοῦ κόσμου ζωῆς, is similar to 1 Cor 11:24 τοῦτό μού ἐστιν τὸ σῶμα τὸ ὑπὲρ ὑμῶν and Luke 22:19 τοῦτό ἐστιν τὸ σῶμά μου τὸ ὑπὲρ ὑμῶν διδόμενον, and reflects wording in the presupposed institution story in the Johannine community.

The fact that the verb δίδωμι is used in John 6:51b–52 and Luke 22:19, but not in 1 Cor 11:23ff., cannot undermine the view that John 6:51b–58 is in closest agreement with 1 Cor 10:3–4, 16–17, 21; 11:23–34, especially since the term in John 6:51–52 is a repetition of the word ἔδωκεν from the Old Testament quotation in John 6:31.[25]

Finally the form of the larger passage from John 6:31–58 should be sketched out, and the discussion of oral tradition pursued further.

In my book *Bread from Heaven* I examined material exemplifying the midrashic character of John 6:31–58. The quotation from the Old Testament, "Bread from heaven he gave them to eat" (v. 31),

---

[24] Cf. Borgen (1965) 91–92, where reasons are given for the preference of the reading ἀληθῶς instead of ἀληθής.

[25] Borgen (1965) 86–90.

is paraphrased throughout vv. 32–58. The systematic structure of this paraphrasing method becomes evident from the fact that the quotation's final word "to eat" (φαγεῖν) does not occur in vv. 32–48. In verse 49, however, this word from the Old Testament quotation is introduced into the exposition, and in the remaining part of the discourse this term (and its synonym τρώγειν) has a central position.[26]

In each part of the exposition the interpretation presented is questioned by "the Jews." In the first part, vv. 32–48, objection is raised against the identification of Jesus with the "bread from heaven" (v. 31). The basis for this objection is the gospel tradition about Jesus as son of Joseph: "Is not this Jesus, the son of Joseph whose father and mother we know? How does he now say 'I have come down from heaven'?" (John 6:42).[27]

Correspondingly, in the second part, vv. 49–58, the use of the term "to eat" (v. 31) in connection with Jesus is questioned. This time gospel traditions about the eucharist are utilized: "How can this man give us his flesh to eat?" (vv. 52–58).[28]

What in our analysis indicates that John draws on oral tradition? First, the close agreement between John 6:51–58 and Paul in parts of 1 Cor 10 and 11, make it probable that John is not dependent upon the Synoptics. Neither can it be maintained that John is dependent upon Paul's letter in 1 Cor. Thus, Paul and John most probably draw on oral eucharistic traditions, combined with the biblical/haggadic stories about the manna and the well. Second, the common celebration of the eucharist supports the view that not only Paul, but also John, utilizes liturgical traditions. Third, 1 Cor 10:17, 21 shows that the story of the institution was already known in the mid-fifties to readers in the Corinthian church, and expository elaboration could therefore presuppose this story of institution. John 6:51–58 has the same usage of word sets, and so forth, from the institution of the Lord's Supper, the same form, argumentative style, and so forth. There are, therefore, strong arguments in favour of drawing the conclusion that John 6:51–58, just as 1 Cor 10:16–17, 21, presupposes the oral tradition about the Lord's Supper and develops expository paraphrase on parts of it.

---

[26] Borgen (1965) 33–35.

[27] Borgen (1965) 80–83.

[28] Borgen (1965) 87ff.

John's use of the term ἡ σάρξ, and not τὸ σῶμα which is found in the synoptic and Pauline versions, is consistent with this conclusion. The Johannine version of the institution is also documented by Ignatius' use of the term ἡ σάρξ, in *Ign. Rom.* 7:3; *Ign. Phld.* 4:1; *Ign. Smyrn.* 7:1, and also by Justin in *Apol.* 1:66:2, 29.[29]

This understanding agrees generally with Boismard's, when he suggests that John here reflects a liturgical and oral tradition which is also represented by Paul. Boismard fails to connect this conclusion to his analysis of other parts of the Gospel of John, where he rather employs literary source criticism. With reference to the background supplied by John 6:51–58 the following question is pertinent: Are there other passages in John which have a connection with the life of the Johannine community, its transmission and exposition of tradition?

II. "Text" and Commentary

In the preceding sections we discussed the expository use of fragments of the tradition in John 6:51b–58 where the unit of tradition was presupposed and not stated. Using 1 Cor 11:23–34 as a model we shall now examine some of the passages in John where a unit of tradition is followed by an expository commentary. Passages such as John 2:13–22; 5:1–18; 9:1–41 and 12:44–50 fall into this category. Here, John 5:1–18, and 2:13–22 will be in the centre of discussion. John 9:1–41 cannot be included since the analysis would then expand beyond the limit of this chapter. The author has, however, analysed John 12:44–50 in a recent publication.[30]

This kind of commentary is identified on the basis of the following criteria: 1. Words and phrases from the quoted tradition are repeated and paraphrased in the commentary. (This criterion is central for delimiting the commentary in John 5:1–18.) 2. The commentary may elaborate upon a theme not only by using words and phrases, but also by employing varied forms of repetition, such as the use of synonyms, metaphorical expressions, biblical phrases and quotations, and so forth, to comment upon the theme and words concerned.

---

[29] Brown (1966) 285. In *Apol.* 1:66:3 Justin has τὸ σῶμα.

[30] Borgen (1979) 18–35.

John 2:13–22 and 12:44–50 follow to some degree this more complex method in addition to repeating words and phrases in a direct way. Various gospel traditions may be worked into such commentaries.[31]

John 5:1–18

In John 5:1–18, vv. 1–9 quote a story about healing from the tradition, and the commentary then follows in vv. 10–18.

Dodd, and other scholars, have shown that the story about healing, vv. 1–9, has the same form as several stories about healing in the Synoptics. Dodd deals only with John 5:10–18 in a summary fashion without examining it.[32] In these verses phrases from the quoted unit of tradition (vv. 1–9) are repeated and paraphrased. This commentary has a systematic outline: In vv. 10–13 the sentence ἆρον τὸν κράβαττόν σου καὶ περιπάτει from v. 8 (also in v. 9) is repeated and paraphrased.

In vv. 14–16 the phrase ὑγιὴς γενέσθαι/ἐγένετο ὑγιής (vv. 6 and 9) is repeated and paraphrased. Finally in vv. 17–18, the speaking and acting person in the story of healing, Jesus himself becomes the explicit focal point of the commentary.

The term σάββατον in v. 9 is repeated in each of the three parts of the commentary – in v. 10, v. 16 and v. 18 respectively. These repetitions of words and phrases from the quoted story of healing end in v. 18, which thus marks the close of the combined quotation and commentary in 5:1–18. The Evangelist elaborated upon the christological theme of 5:1–18 in the discourse of 5:19ff. Up to this point John 5:1–18 is in accord with the model form of quoted tradition and attached commentary found in 1 Cor 11:23–34. Is the paraphrastic commentary in John 5:10–18, like the one in 1 Cor 11:27ff., put into traditional form?

There is little in common formally between John 5:10–18 and 1 Cor 11:27ff., apart from the expository paraphrase. In both cases, however, narrative stories are interpreted, viz. the act of healing (John) and the story of a meal (1 Cor). While the exposition in 1

---

[31] Such commentaries are also found in the Synoptics, as shown by J. Wanke in his study Wanke (1980) 208–33; cf. Stanton (1983) 273–87.

[32] Dodd (1953) 320, characterizes briefly vv. 10–18 as the transition from the narrative of the healing at Bethesda to the discourse which follows.

Cor 11:27ff. is a didactic monologue, the exposition in John 5:10–18 has the form of a dialogue, more precisely of a legal debate on a controversial action (miracle) performed on the Sabbath.

The differences between John and Paul should not be exaggerated, however. In 1 Cor 10:14–22 questions are also formulated (vv. 16 and 18), as well as questions and answers (vv. 19–20). Similarly, the exposition of the eucharist in John 6:51–58 includes the schema of question and answer (vv. 52ff.).

Nevertheless, concerning traditional forms there are closer agreements between John 5:1–18 and passages which state a case followed by a judicial exchange. Consequently, with regard to form, Matt 12:1–8 (plucking grain on the Sabbath), and Luke 13:10–17 (the healing of a crippled woman on the Sabbath), parallel in an interesting way John 5:1–18.[33] A synoptic presentation of these three passages makes the agreement of form evident. Since a comparison between Matt 12:1–8 and Mark 2:23–28 is also of interest for our discussion, the Markan version is included in the presentation. The agreement of form raises the question of John's dependence on (or independence of) the Synoptic Gospels, and therefore agreements of content are included in this survey.

John 5:1–18 *The case, vv. 1–9*	Matt 12:1–8 *The case, v. 1*
Μετὰ ταῦτα ἦν ἑορτὴ τῶν Ἰουδαίων, καὶ ἀνέβη Ἰησοῦς εἰς Ἱεροσόλυμα. 2 ἔστιν δὲ ἐν τοῖς Ἱεροσολύμοις ἐπὶ τῇ προβατικῇ κολυμβήθρα, ἡ ἐπιλεγομένη Ἑβραϊστὶ Βεθζαθά,	1 Ἐν ἐκείνῳ τῷ καιρῷ ἐπορεύθη ὁ Ἰησοῦς τοῖς σάββασιν διὰ τῶν σπορίμων. οἱ δὲ μαθηταὶ αὐτοῦ ἐπείνασαν, καὶ ἤρξαντο τίλλειν στάχυας καὶ ἐσθίειν.

---

[33] Rabbinic parallels might also have been included, e.g *m.Ter.* 8:1:
Case:
    "(If a priest) was standing and offering sacrifices at the altar, and it came known that he is the son of a divorcee or of a halusah . . ."
Debate:
    "R. Eliezer says, 'All sacrifices that he had (ever) offered on the altar are invalid.' But R. Joshua declares them valid. If it became known that he is blemished . . . his service is invalid."
Cf. also Peck (1981) 35–46.

πέντε στοὰς ἔχουσα. ἐν ταύταις κατέκειτο πλῆθος τῶν ἀσθενούντων, 3 τυφλῶν, χωλῶν, ξηρῶν. 5 ἦν δέ τις ἄνθρωπος ἐκεῖ τριάκοντα καὶ ὀκτὼ ἔτη ἔχων ἐν τῇ ἀσθενείᾳ αὐτοῦ. 6 τοῦτον ἰδὼν ὁ Ἰησοῦς κατακείμενον, καὶ γνοὺς ὅτι πολὺν ἤδη χρόνον ἔχει, λέγει αὐτῷ, Θέλεις ὑγιὴς γενέσθαι; 7 ἀπεκρίθη αὐτῷ ὁ ἀσθενῶν, Κύριε, ἄνθρωπον οὐκ ἔχω, ἵνα ὅταν ταραχθῇ τὸ ὕδωρ βάλῃ με εἰς τὴν κολυμβήθραν. ἐν ᾧ δὲ ἔρχομαι ἐγώ, ἄλλος πρὸ ἐμοῦ καταβαίνει. 8 λέγει αὐτῷ ὁ Ἰησοῦς, Ἔγειρε ἆρον τὸν κράβαττόν σου καὶ περιπάτει. 9 καὶ εὐθέως ἐγένετο ὑγιὴς ὁ ἄνθρωπος, καὶ ἦρεν τὸν κράβαττον αὐτοῦ καὶ περιπάτει. Ἦν δὲ σάββατον ἐν ἐκείνῃ τῇ ἡμέρᾳ.

Expository dialogue, vv. 10–18

10 ἔλεγον οὖν οἱ Ἰουδαῖοι τῷ τεθεραπευμένῳ, Σάββατόν ἐστιν, καὶ οὐκ ἔξεστίν σοι ἆραι τὸν κράβαττον. 11 ὁ δὲ ἀπεκρίθη αὐτοῖς, Ὁ ποιήσας με ὑγιῆ ἐκεῖνός μοι εἶπεν, Ἆρον τόν κράβαττόν σου καὶ περιπάτει. 12 ἠρώτησαν αὐτόν, Τίς ἐστιν ὁ ἄνθρωπος ὁ εἰπών σοι, Ἆρον καὶ περιπάτει; 13 ὁ δὲ ἰαθεὶς οὐκ ᾔδει τίς ἐστιν, ὁ γὰρ Ἰησοῦς ἐξένευσεν ὄχλου ὄντος ἐν τῷ τόπῳ. 14 μετὰ ταῦτα εὑρίσκει αὐτὸν ὁ Ἰησοῦς ἐν τῷ ἱερῷ καὶ

Expository dialogue, vv. 2–8

2 οἱ δὲ Φαρισαῖοι ἰδόντες εἶπαν αὐτῷ, Ἰδοὺ οἱ μαθηταί σου ποιοῦσιν ὃ οὐκ ἔξεστιν ποιεῖν ἐν σαββάτῳ. 3 ὁ δὲ εἶπεν αὐτοῖς, Οὐκ ἀνέγνωτε τί ἐποίησεν Δαυίδ ὅτε ἐπείνασεν καὶ οἱ μετ' αὐτοῦ; 4 πῶς εἰσῆλθεν εἰς τὸν οἶκον τοῦ θεοῦ καὶ τοὺς ἄρτους τῆς προθέσεως ἔφαγον, ὃ οὐκ ἐξὸν ἦν αὐτῷ φαγεῖν οὐδὲ τοῖς μετ' αὐτοῦ, εἰ μὴ τοῖς ἱερεῦσιν μόνοις; 5 ἢ οὐκ ἀνέγνωτε ἐν τῷ νόμῳ ὅτι τοῖς σάββασιν οἱ ἱερεῖς ἐν τῷ ἱερῷ τὸ σάββατον βεβηλοῦσιν

εἶπεν αὐτῷ, Ἴδε ὑγιὴς γέγονας. μηκέτι ἁμάρτανε, ἵνα μὴ χεῖρόν σοί τι γένηται. 15 ἀπῆλθεν ὁ ἄνθρωπος καὶ ἀνήγγειλεν τοῖς Ἰουδαίοις ὅτι Ἰησοῦς ἐστιν ὁ ποιήσας αὐτὸν ὑγιῆ. 16 καὶ διὰ τοῦτο ἐδίωκον οἱ Ἰουδαῖοι τὸν Ἰησοῦν, ὅτι ταῦτα ἐποίει ἐν σαββάτῳ. 17 ὁ δὲ Ἰησοῦς ἀπεκρίνατο αὐτοῖς, Ὁ πατήρ μου ἕως ἄρτι ἐργάζεται, κἀγὼ ἐργάζομαι. 18 διὰ τοῦτο οὖν μᾶλλον ἐζήτουν αὐτὸν οἱ Ἰουδαῖοι ἀποκτεῖναι, ὅτι οὐ μόνον ἔλυεν τὸ σάββατον, ἀλλὰ καὶ πατέρα ἴδιον ἔλεγεν τὸν θεόν, ἴσον ἑαυτὸν ποιῶν τῷ θεῷ.

καὶ ἀναίτιοί εἰσιν; 6 λέγω δὲ ὑμῖν ὅτι τοῦ ἱεροῦ μεῖζόν ἐστιν ὧδε. 7 εἰ δὲ ἐγνώκειτε τί ἐστιν. Ἔλεος θέλω καὶ οὐ θυσίαν, οὐκ ἂν κατεδικάσατε τοὺς ἀναιτίους. 8 κύριος γάρ ἐστιν τοῦ σαββάτου ὁ υἱὸς τοῦ ἀνθρώπου.

Mark 2:23–28 *The case, v. 23*	Luke 13:10–17 *The case, vv. 10–13*
23 καὶ ἐγένετο αὐτὸν ἐν τοῖς σάββασιν παραπορεύεσθαι διὰ τῶν σπορίμων, καὶ οἱ μαθηταὶ αὐτοῦ ἤρξαντο ὁδὸν ποιεῖν τίλλοντες τοὺς στάχυας.	10 Ἦν δὲ διδάσκων ἐν μιᾷ τῶν συναγωγῶν ἐν τοῖς σάββασιν. 11 καὶ ἰδοὺ γυνὴ πνεῦμα ἔχουσα ἀσθενείας ἔτη δέκα ὀκτώ, καὶ ἦν συγκύπτουσα καὶ μὴ δυναμένη ἀνακύψαι εἰς τὸ παντελές. 12 ἰδὼν δὲ αὐτὴν ὁ Ἰησοῦς προσεφώνησεν καὶ εἶπεν αὐτῇ, Γύναι, ἀπολέλυσαι τῆς ἀσθενείας σου, 13 καὶ ἐπέθηκεν αὐτῇ τὰς χεῖρας. καὶ παραχρῆμα ἀνωρθώθη, καὶ ἐδόξαζεν τὸν θεόν.

Expository dialogue, vv. 24–28	*Expository dialogue, vv. 14–17*
24 καὶ οἱ Φαρισαῖοι ἔλεγον αὐτῷ, Ἴδε τί ποιοῦσιν τοῖς σάββασιν	14 ἀποκριθεὶς δὲ ὁ ἀρχισυνάγωγος, ἀγανακτῶν ὅτι

ὃ οὐκ ἔξεστιν; 25 καὶ λέγει αὐτοῖς, Οὐδέποτε ἀνέγνωτε τί ἐποίησεν Δαυίδ, ὅτε χρείαν ἔσχεν καὶ ἐπείνασεν αὐτὸς καὶ οἱ μετ' αὐτοῦ; 26 πῶς εἰσῆλθεν εἰς τὸν οἶκον τοῦ θεοῦ ἐπὶ Ἀβιαθὰρ ἀρχιερέως καὶ τοὺς ἄρτους τῆς προθέσεως ἔφαγεν, οὓς οὐκ ἔξεστιν φαγεῖν εἰ μὴ τοὺς ἱερεῖς, καὶ ἔδωκεν καὶ τοῖς σὺν αὐτῷ οὖσιν; 27 καὶ ἔλεγεν αὐτοῖς, Τὸ σάββατον διὰ τὸν ἄνθρωπον ἐγένετο, καὶ οὐχ ὁ ἄνθρωπος διὰ τὸ σάββατον. 28 ὥστε κύριός ἐστιν ὁ υἱὸς τοῦ ἀνθρώπου καὶ τοῦ σαββάτου.

τῷ σαββάτῳ ἐθεράπευσεν ὁ Ἰησοῦς, ἔλεγεν τῷ ὄχλῳ ὅτι ῞Εξ ἡμέραι εἰσὶν ἐν αἷς δεῖ ἐργάζεσθαι. ἐν αὐταῖς οὖν ἐρχόμενοι θεραπεύεσθε καὶ μὴ τῇ ἡμέρᾳ τοῦ σαββάτου. 15 ἀπεκρίθη δὲ αὐτῷ ὁ κύριος καὶ εἶπεν, Ὑποκριταί, ἕκαστος ὑμῶν τῷ σαββάτῳ οὐ λύει τὸν βοῦν αὐτοῦ ἢ τὸν ὄνον ἀπὸ τῆς φάτνης καὶ ἀπαγαγὼν ποτίζει; 16 ταύτην δὲ θυγατέρα Ἀβραὰμ οὖσαν, ἣν ἔδησεν ὁ Σατανᾶς ἰδοὺ δέκα καὶ ὀκτὼ ἔτη, οὐκ ἔδει λυθῆναι ἀπὸ τοῦ δεσμοῦ τούτου τῇ ἡμέρᾳ τοῦ σαββάτου; 17 καὶ ταῦτα λέγοντος αὐτοῦ κατῃσχύνοντο πάντες οἱ ἀντικείμενοι αὐτῷ καὶ πᾶς ὁ ὄχλος ἔχαιρεν ἐπὶ πᾶσιν τοῖς ἐνδόξοις τοῖς γινομένοις ὑπ' αὐτοῦ.

John 5:1–18 and Synoptics

Sentences (almost verbatim agreement):
John 5:8 ἔγειρε ἆρον τὸν
  κράβαττόν σου καὶ
  περιπάτει
John 5:9 . . . εὐθέως . . . ἦρεν
  τὸν κράβαττον αὐτοῦ καὶ
  περιπάτει
John 5:10 ἆραι τὸν κράβαττον

John 5:11 ἆρον τὸν κράβαττόν
  σου καὶ περιπάτει
John 5:12 ἆρον καὶ περιπάτει
John 5:14 μηκέτι ἁμάρτανε

Mark 2:9 ἔγειρε καὶ ἆρον τὸν
  κράβαττόν σου καὶ
  περιπάτει
Mark 2:11 ἔγειρε ἆρον τὸν
  κράβαττόν σου καὶ
Mark 2:12 ἠγέρθη καὶ εὐθὺς
  ἄρας τὸν κράβαττον
(John 8:11 μηκέτι ἁμάρτανε)

Part of sentences:

John 5:10 σάββατόν . . . οὐκ
ἔξεστίν σοι (ἆραι)

Matt 12:2 (cf. Mark 2:24) ὃ
οὐκ ἔξεστιν (ποιεῖν) ἐν
σαββάτῳ

Words:

John 5:6 . . . ἰδὼν ὁ ᾿Ιησοῦς
. . . λέγει
John 5:10 . . . ἔλεγον . . . οἱ
(᾿Ιουδαῖοι) . . .
(John 5:3d παραλυτικῶν)

Mark 2:5 ἰδὼν ὁ ᾿Ιησοῦς . . .
λέγει
Mark 2:24 οἱ (Φαρισαῖοι)
ἔλεγον
Mark 2:3 παραλυτικόν

Subject matter, not words:

John 5:18 making himself equal
with God
John 5:14 Sin no more

Matt 2:7 It is blasphemy. Who
can forgive sins but God alone?

John 5:16 The Jews persecuted
Jesus
John 5:18 the Jews sought all the
more to kill him.

Mark 3:6 The Pharisees went out,
and immediately held council
with the Herodians against
him, how to destroy him.

John 5:17 My Father is working
still, and I am working.

Matt 12:8 (cf. Mark 2:27, Luke
6:5) For the Son of Man is lord
of the Sabbath.

As the basis for our analysis of these points of agreement between John and the Synoptics, the views of Boismard, Sabbe, Neirynck, Lindars and Brown should be given in outline.

Boismard finds three levels in John 5:1–18. The original part of John 5:1–18 ran like this: "After this there was a feast and Jesus went up to Jerusalem. And a certain man was there who had been ill. When Jesus saw him, he said to him: 'Rise, and take your pallet and walk'. And at once the man (rose) and took up his pallet and walked." This story was part of the first stage (John II-A) of the Gospel written by the Evangelist. In his final version (John II-B) he added all the rest of John 5:1–18, except for parts of v. 16 and all of vv. 17–18 which were added by the later Redactor (John III).

Boismard therefore thinks that John II-B changed the original story of healing into a controversy on the Sabbath.[34]

M. Sabbe is right when he objects to Boismard's reconstruction of the original story of healing, that it (John II-A as a whole) has no theological significance. This in itself makes one want to question just that very probability.[35]

In his comments on Boismard's analysis, Neirynck maintains that there is no need for distinguishing between stages John II-A and II-B. Since, according to Boismard, an expansion and reworking of the material have taken place in John II-B, why would not then John II-B also have extensively reworked the story of healing itself on the basis of Mark 2:1–12 (the healing of the paralytic) illuminated by the Sabbath controversy in Mark 3:1–6?[36]

An alternative hypothesis is suggested by Lindars.[37] According to him, the verbal similarities between John 5:8–9a and Mark 2:9, 11–12a are so close that it can scarcely be doubted that an almost identical source lies behind them both. It is also possible that John has taken the reference to the Sabbath (John 5:9b), from background material to Mark 2:1 – 3:6, since the Sabbath is discussed in Mark 2:23–28 and 3:1–6.

The agreements listed above should be discussed against this background. Do the agreements between John 5:1–18 on the one hand and Matt 12:1–8 and Luke 13:10–17 on the other hand indicate that John is dependent upon the Synoptic Gospels? An argument in favour of dependency must take cognizance of the fact that all three pericopes have the same structure: A case of Sabbath violation is followed by a legal dispute. In addition, it might be argued that Matt's interpretative expansion in Matt 12:1–8 of Mark 2:23–28, could suggest that John 5:1–18 is a product based on Markan material. G. Stanton's analysis of Matt 12:5–8 can be quoted here.[38] "While

---

[34] Boismard (1977) 156–65.

[35] Sabbe (1980) 125–30.

[36] Neirynck (1979) 177–80.

[37] Lindars (1972) 209.

[38] Stanton (1983) 275. It should be added here that in the judicial debates in John and Matt, Jesus refers to scriptural passages. Matt 12:3–7 refers to 1 Sam 21:1–6; Lev 24:5–9; Num 28:9–10 and Hos 6:6. The words of Jesus in John 5:17 draw on Jewish exegetical traditions tied to Gen 2:2f. and Exod 20:11. Cf. Brown (1966)

it is possible that verses 5–7 may all stem from the evangelist, verse 7 is almost certainly part of the evangelist's own addition to and interpretation of Mark 2:23–28. Matthew is stressing that God is merciful and that the Sabbath commandment should be considered in the light of his kindness. The Sabbath commandment is not abolished; it is subordinated to the kindness and mercy of God. In this way the conduct of the disciples is defended."

Matthew understood the exposition as enhancing the meaning of the received word of Jesus, and therefore as also having the form of a saying of Jesus. John has the same understanding of the expository elaborations of the Gospel tradition in the dialogue in John 5:10–18.

Finally, the strongest argument in favour of John's dependence is the verbatim agreement between John 5:8, etc. (ἔγειρε ἆρον τὸν κράβαττόν σου καὶ περιπάτει, etc.) and Mark 2:9 (ἔγειρε καὶ ἆρον τὸν κράβαττόν σου καὶ περιπάτει, etc.).

As for this phrase, "take up your mat and walk," etc. (John 5:8, etc. and Mark 2:9, etc.) it should be noted that another stereotyped phrase from the gospel tradition has also been worked into the paraphrase of the commentary, namely μηκέτι ἁμάρτανε (v. 14) which also occurs in the non-Johannine pericope of John 7:53 – 8:11.[39] By analogy, the use of this stereotyped phrase in these two mutually independent stories also supports the view that the expression "take up your pallet and walk" (John 5:8, etc., Mark 2:9, etc.) is a stereotyped phrase as well and could occur in various contexts in stories which are independent of each other.[40] Apart from this phrase the two stories of healing, John 5:1–9 and Mark 2:1–12, are very different with hardly any further verbal agreement. Thus, the stories are much more different than are the Pauline (1 Cor 11:23–26) and Markan (Mark 14:22–25) stories of the Lord's Supper, where there is close agreement between sentences, phrases and words, although they are mutually independent.

The other agreements listed in the survey also call for comment.

216–17; Borgen (1983A) 180, 184–85 and Borgen (1987A) 88–92.

[39] Lindars (1972) 312, seems to think that the phrase in John 8:11 is taken from 5:14. If so, it shows how a stereotyped phrase may be extracted from a story, leaving the rest of the story intact. Against Lindars it may be said that the phrase has a more natural place in the context of 8:11, while it is used rather abruptly in 5:14.

[40] Cf. Haenchen (1980) 269: "'wandernde' Einzelzuge."

The agreement between John 5:10 . . . οὐκ ἔξεστιν . . . and Matt 12:2 is due to the fact that a traditional form, corresponding to Paul's use of traditional (gospel) forms in 1 Cor 10:21 and 11:27ff., is used in John's paraphrase.

The references to the persecution of Jesus (John 5:16), and the seeking to kill him (v. 18), are all features which have a basis in the gospel tradition. The persecution of Jesus and the search to kill Jesus are elements which are central in John, as can be seen from 5:16, 18; 7:19–20, 25; 8:37 and 40; 11:53; 15:20. They are also central to the Johannine community since a direct correlation is made between the persecution of Jesus and attempts to kill him, and the persecution of the disciples the Christians and attempts to kill them, John 15:20; 16:2.[41] The passion narratives and the killing of Jesus show that these elements have a firm basis in the gospel tradition and in history.

John 5:16, 18 and Mark 3:6 par, connect this motif in the gospel tradition with Jesus' apparent violation of the Sabbath in different ways. There is no verbal agreement between Mark 3:6 and John 5:16, 18, and thus it seems arbitrary to draw the conclusion that John here is dependent on Mark as indicated by Neirynck. John's independence is supported by the observation that the expository commentary in John 5:10–18 is attached to the story (the case) just as in Matt 12:1–8 and Luke 13:10–17, while the corresponding discussion in Mark 3:1–6 precedes the story of healing.

The motif of blasphemy in John 5:18 ("making himself equal with God") has a distinctive use that is different from the corresponding use of this motif in Mark 2:7 par and 14:64 par. Thus, these parallels do not prove that John is dependent upon the Synoptics. Arguments based on form can also be advanced against John's dependency on the Synoptics. In spite of the similarity of form between, on the one hand John 5:1–18 and on the other Matt 12:1–8 and Luke 13:10–17, John has a distinctive use of this common form. The form can hardly be said to be taken from the synoptic passages: Only in John 5:10–18 does the legal debate have the function of changing the stage (vv. 10–13 the Jews and the person healed; vv. 14 Jesus and the healed person; vv. 15–18 the healed person, the Jews and Jesus). Moreover, only in John 5:10–18 phrases from the story (the case) are repeated

---

[41] Cf. Pancaro (1975) 45f.

quite mechanically in the subsequent legal debate. Only John has, therefore, an extensive paraphrase of parts of the story used as a "text".

The question still remains as to whether the passage comes from an oral tradition or whether it is based on a written document. Three points suggest that John 5:1–18 not only draws on oral tradition, but is itself an oral unit which has been written down.

1. The story of healing (John 5:1–9), has the same form as have the stories of healing in the Synoptics. Consequently, John here seems to reproduce transmitted tradition corresponding to Paul's rendering of the eucharistic tradition in 1 Cor 11:23–25(26). The expository commentary in John 5:10–18 corresponds to Paul's commentary in 1 Cor 11:(26)27ff. John 5:1–18, as a whole, is therefore a unit parallel to 1 Cor 11:23–34, and results from a corresponding expository activity in the Johannine community.

2. This hypothesis is supported by a consideration of the *Sitz im Leben* of John 5:1–18. The life setting of the passage concerns the controversy between the church and the Synagogue, in which Christology, the Sabbath and the Law of Moses were central issues. The importance of these questions for understanding the actual situation of the Johannine community is evident from John 9:1–41. The studies of J. L. Martyn and S. Pancaro have shown that the history of the Johannine community is reflected in these two passages.[42]

3. The evangelist has more interest in the christological aspect as such than in the Sabbath question. Accordingly, in the discourse which follows in John 5:19ff. phrases and terms about the Sabbath and the Sabbath controversy are not repeated any more, whereas the christological idea in John 5:17 ("My Father is at work even till now, and so I am at work too,"), *is* developed.[43]

---

[42] Martyn (1979); Pancaro (1975) 497–512.

[43] Additional note on John 5:9: Did the point about the Sabbath belong to the story of the healing in the oral transmission, or was it added to form a basis for the expository dialogue found in John 5:10–18? This question has been much debated, since the reference to the Sabbath in v. 9b seems to be an addition to the story about healing. R. E. Brown, in discussing E. Haenchen's view that the reference to the Sabbath and the Sabbath controversy in vv. 9b–13 constitutes a secondary addition to the healing narrative, says: "One almost needs the Sabbath motif to give this story significance." Brown (1966) 210.Two further observations support the view of Brown. The story of healing (John 5:1–9), is a tradition with legal authority (cf.

Our analysis has shown that John 5:1–18 follows a traditional structure in which a controversial state of affairs concerning the Sabbath is followed by judicial dialogue. Paul in 1 Cor 11:23–34 uses the same basic form of a story from the gospel tradition followed by an expository commentary of legal nature. Since the similarities between the two mutually independent traditions of 1 Cor 11:23–25(26) and Mark 14:22–25 are much more extensive and clearer than they are between John 5:1–18 and the Synoptics, the Johannine passage is certainly independent of the Synoptic Gospels.

John 5:1–18 is probably an oral unit transmitted and exposed through activity of the Johannine community. This view is supported by the parallel structure of "text" and "commentary" in 1 Cor 11:23–34 and by the life setting of John 5:1–18 where we find conflicts between church and Synagogue about the Sabbath and the Law of Moses in relation to Christology. By adding John 5:19ff. to the Sabbath controversy, the evangelist seems to want to develop the christological aspect more independently of the Sabbath controversy.[44]

John 2:13–22

Before we analyse the way in which gospel material has been used in John 2:13–22, the similarities to the Synoptic Gospels and Acts should be noted and discussed. The similarities are:

---

1 Cor 11:23–25(26) which legitimates the attitude of the Johannine community towards the Sabbath (the Law of Moses). Consequently the commentary given in vv. 10–18 presupposes that the story of the healing already was known to be connected with the Sabbath. The expositor therefore does not need to prove to his readers that the healing story raises the problem of Sabbath observance. Furthermore, the reference to the Sabbath in v. 9b at the end of the story of the healing corresponds to Paul's formulation of 1 Cor 11:26, where he extracts from the quoted tradition the theme to be dealt with in the commentary. Thus, the Sabbath motif is placed in John 5:9b as a topical heading for the succeeding commentary and it is based on the meaning of the healing story. This use of the Sabbath reference in v. 9b as a topical heading is in accordance with the scholarly form of commentary found in vv. 10–18, using repetition of phrases and alluding to midrashic exegesis.

[44] Cf. Barrett (1978) 257ff.

John 2:13–22 and the Synoptics

I. 2:13–17

A) Agreements with all the Synoptics:
Parts of sentences:

John 2:14 ἐν τῷ ἱερῷ τοὺς πωλοῦντας	Matt 21:12/Mark 11:15/Luke 19:45 εἰς τὸ ἱερόν . . . τοὺς πωλοῦντας

Words:

John 2:16 (μὴ) ποιεῖτε	Matt 21:13 ποιεῖτε Mark 11:17 πεποιήκατε Luke 19:46 ἐποιήσατε
John 2:16 τὸν οἶκον . . . οἶκον 17 τοῦ οἴκου	Matt 21:13/Mark 11:17/Luke 19:46 ὁ οἶκος . . .

B) Agreements with Matt and Mark:
Parts of sentences:

John 2:15 τὰς τραπέζας ἀνέστρεψεν	Matt 21:12/Mark 11:15 τὰς τραπέζας . . . κατέστρεψεν
John 2:16 τοῖς τὰς περιστερὰς πωλοῦσιν	Matt 21:12/Mark 11:15 τῶν πωλούντων τὰς περιστεράς

Words:

John 2:14 ἐν τῷ ἱερῷ	Matt 21:12/Mark 11:15 ἐν τῷ ἱερῷ
John 2:14 περιστεράς	Matt 21:12/Mark 11:15 τὰς περιστεράς
John 2:15 τῶν κολλυβιστῶν	Matt 21:12/Mark 11:15 τῶν κολλυβιστῶν

C) Agreement with Matt:
Parts of sentences:

John 2:15 πάντας ἐξέβαλεν	Matt 21:12 ἐξέβαλεν πάντας

II. 2:18, etc

Parts of sentences:

John 2:18 ταῦτα ποιεῖς

Matt 21:23/Mark 11:28/Luke 20:2 ταῦτα ποιεῖς

Words:

John 2:13 εἰς Ἱεροσόλυμα
John 2:14 ἐν τῷ ἱερῷ

John 2:18 σημεῖον (question)

Mark 11:27 εἰς Ἱεροσόλυμα
Mark 11:27/Luke 20:1 ἐν τῷ ἱερῷ (Matt 21:23 εἰς τὸ ἱερόν)
Matt 12:38–39/Mark 8:12; 16:2/Luke 11:29 σημεῖον (question)

Subject matter, not words:

John 2:18 τί σημεῖον
δεικνύεις ἡμῖν

Matt 21:23/Mark 11:28/Luke 20:2 ἐν ποίᾳ ἐξουσίᾳ

III. 2:19–20

Parts of sentences:

John 2:19 λύσατε τὸν ναὸν τοῦτον

John 2:19–20 ἐν τρισὶν ἡμέραις
John 2:19 λύσατε τὸν ναὸν τοῦτον
John 2:19 ἐν τρισὶν ἡμέραις

John 2:19 λύσατε τὸν ναὸν τοῦτον

Mark 14:58 καταλύσω τὸν ναὸν τοῦτον (Matt 26:61 καταλῦσαι τὸν ναόν)
Matt 26:61/Mark 14:58 διὰ τριῶν ἡμερῶν
Matt 27:40/Mark 15:29 ὁ καταλύων τὸν ναόν
Matt 27:40/Mark 15:29 ἐν τρισὶν ἡμέραις
Acts 6:14 καταλύσει τὸν τόπον τοῦτον

Words:

John 2:20 οἰκοδομήθη

John 2:20 ὁ ναὸς οὗτος

Matt 26:61 οἰκοδομῆσαι
Mark 14:58 οἰκοδομήσω
Mark 14:58 τὸν ναὸν τοῦτον

John 2:21 τοῦ ναοῦ   Mark 14:58/15:29/Matt
                                      26:61/27:40 τὸν ναόν

Variant words:
John 2:19 ἐγερῶ 20 ἐγερεῖς   Matt 26:61 οἰκοδομῆσαι
                                      Mark 14:58 οἰκοδομήσω

Boismard[45] distinguishes between three stages: C, John II-A and II-B. The first stage, C reads: (14) "and he found in the temple those who were selling oxen and sheep and pigeons, and the moneychangers (15) and . . . he drove all out of the temple (16b) and he said (:) . . . 'Take these things away. Do not make my Father's house a house of trade'".

Then John II-A adds verse 18: "The Jews then said to him, 'What sign have you to show us for doing this?'" Finally, the remaining parts of John 2:13–22 are expansions attributed to John II-B. In John II-B much comes from the Synoptics and at this stage the story of cleansing finds its present place in the Gospel.

Neirynck[46] agrees with Boismard about the dependence on the Synoptics but disagrees with him when a distinction is made between John II-A and II-B. Neirynck objects against the classification of the request for a sign (v. 18) to John II-A. He rightly refers to the parallel request for a sign in John 6:30 which Boismard refers to John II-B, not to John II-A.

Neirynck also points to weaknesses and inconsistencies in Boismard's distinction between different levels in II-B and II-A: Since Boismard thinks that 2:13–15 (parts) 16a, 17, 18, 19–22 resulted from the redactional activity of the Evangelist (John II-B), a very strong justification must be given by him for separating vv. 14, 15 (parts) and 16b into a source of its own. Neirynck does not find that Boismard has proven the case sufficiently. For example, Boismard states that the expression "my Father's house" (v. 16b) is typical for level C. The phrase, however, only occurs once elsewhere in the Gospel of John, (in John 14:2), and there "house" is the rendering of οἰκία, whereas the form οἶκος is used in 2:16b. Two occurrences of a phrase, even in variant forms, are not sufficient basis for calling the phrase

---

[45] Boismard (1977) 107ff.
[46] Neirynck (1979) 86–90.

"typical". Furthermore, it is hardly defensible to refer the words πρόβατον, βοῦς (sheep, oxen) to John II-B in v. 15, while the same words are referred to source C in v. 14.

Neirynck points to the fact that the cleansing of the temple in Mark 11:15–19 is followed by the controversy concerning the authority of Jesus in Mark 11:28. He maintains that the similarity here with John 2:13–18 (the cleansing and the request for a sign) cannot be denied. This observation is important, and we have also noted some verbal agreements between John 2:13–18 and Mark 11:27–28 par. Thus it seems that Neirynck's view finds good support here. In addition to verbal agreement between John's account of the cleansing of the temple and the account in Mark, there is significant agreement in the sequence of the cleansing, the request for a sign (John), and the question about authority (Mark).

Nevertheless, these similarities speak rather in favour of the views of Dodd, Brown, and others that the material in John 2:13–22 is not taken from the Synoptic Gospels, but represent an independent tradition running parallel to the synoptic tradition:

1. With regard to the verbal agreements between John 2:13–22 and one or more of the Synoptic Gospels, it must be said that they are not stronger than between the Pauline version of the institution of the Lord's Supper, 1 Cor 11:23–26, and the Markan version in Mark 14:22–25. (There are, for example, 60 words in John 2:14–16. Of these, 19 words are also used in Mark and Matt together. The corresponding figures for 1 Cor 11:23b–26 and Mark 14:22–25 are 68/25. Moreover, besides phrases and words, there is agreement between one complete sentence in 1 Cor 11:23–26 and Mark 14:22–25, while only agreements of phrase and word are present between John 2:13–16 and the synoptic parallels.)

2. There is similarity of sequence. The challenge to Jesus in Mark 11:27–28 is separated from the cleansing in Mark 11:15–17; yet the challenge seems to refer to the cleansing of the temple. As suggested by Dodd, Brown and others, it is probable that Mark has split up what belonged together in the pre-Markan stage of the tradition, a tradition testified to by John's independent witness.[47]

3. The employment of the word of Jesus about the destruction and rebuilding of the temple in John 2:19ff., does not weaken the

---

[47] Dodd (1953) 300–03; 450–51; Dodd (1963) 89–91; Brown (1966) 118–21.

theory of mutual independence between John and the Synoptics in John 2:13–22, although the saying found in John 2:19ff. has close verbal agreements with the Synoptics. One important difference, however, is that John is the only one to use ἐγείρειν (to raise up) (syn: οἰκοδομεῖν).

John's term is a proper word for construction, but may also refer to the resurrection of the body. Another difference is John's use of the imperative, λύσατε, which puts the burden of the destruction on "the Jews" (John 2:17).

These distinctive features fit well with the theological tendencies in John. They might seem, therefore, to be due to modifications of the Markan or Matthean texts. This is hardly the case, however. John 2:19ff. does not reflect any specific points from the contexts of the saying in Matt and Mark. The forms of the saying in Mark and Matthew themselves show that interpretative adaptations also have been at work in those Gospels. This is most clearly seen in Mark 14:58 where there is a contrast found between the temple that is made with hands and another that is not made with hands. The saying functions here as prophecy of a new temple, being of an entirely different nature than that in connection with the Jerusalem temple. Moreover, the use of this saying in the story of Stephen in Acts 6:14[48] indicates that it was used in the debates and controversies between the early church and the Jewish authorities. This was also probably the *Sitz im Leben* of John 2:13–22. The passage reflects a situation where the church, from a christological basis, was attempting to emancipate herself from the Jerusalem temple and its worship.

Although there is not extensive use of words from the story of the cleansing (2:13–16) in the subsequent section of vv. 17–22, several features suggest that John 2:17–22 is an expository commentary on the temple incident in vv. 13–16:

1. The terms τὸ ἱερόν (vv. 14–15) and ὁ οἶκος (v. 16) are interpreted in vv. 17–22. In the Old Testament quotation from Ps 69:9 in John 2:17 the term ὁ οἶκος from v. 16 is repeated, and in vv. 18–21 the synonym ὁ ναός is used in the word of Jesus about the destruction of the temple and in the elaboration which follows.

---

[48] The saying does not occur in Luke, although it is used in Acts, the second volume of the same work.

2. The concluding remark in v. 22 ". . . and they believed the Scripture and the word which Jesus had spoken," ties the quotation of Ps 69:9 in v. 17 and the subsequent word of Jesus together.[49] They indicate the meaning of the cleansing of the temple.

3. It is clear that verse 17 introduces the interpretation of the cleansing, since it is said that the disciples, against the background of the temple incident, remembered the Old Testament word from Ps 69:9.

4. The request for a sign in v. 18 refers back to the cleansing with the words "these things" (ταῦτα).

From this analysis it is seen that in John 2:13–22 the Evangelist has brought into his Gospel a unit from the expository activity of the Johannine community, a unit corresponding to Paul's expository interpretation of the institution of the Lord's Supper in 1 Cor 11:23–34 and the exposition of the healing story in John 5:1–18. Already in the Johannine community the story of the cleansing of the temple had been used separately from the Passion narrative to throw light upon the community's attitude towards the temple.[50]

Conclusion

The aim of this chapter has been twofold:

1. to discuss the agreements between John 2:13–22; 5:1–18; 6:51–58 and the Synoptics against the background of the two mutually independent traditions recorded in 1 Cor 10:3–4, 16, 17, 21; 11:23–34 and Mark 14:22–25.

The conclusion of the study is that the agreements between John 2:13–22; 6:51–58 and the Synoptics are neither closer, nor more striking, than those between the above mentioned Pauline passages and Mark, and in the case of John 5:1–18 there are less agreements with the Synoptics. To this extent the analysis of these three Johannine

---

[49] See Lindars (1972) 144: Scripture in v. 22 refers back to Ps 69:9 cited in v. 17: ". . . it is a fragment of a whole psalm which is known to be a Passion proof text in the primitive Church"; cf. Schnackenburg (1966) 367; Haenchen (1980) 203. Barrett (1978) 201, thinks that v. 22 probably means that the Old Testament predicts in a general way the vindication of the Messiah.

[50] Cf. Dodd (1963) 91; Dodd (1953) 300–02; Haenchen (1980) 201–03; Borgen (1983A) 136–38; Brown (1979) 49.

passages supports the hypothesis that John and the Synoptics are mutually independent.

2. to throw light upon the transmission of tradition and expository and paraphrasal usage of it in the Gospel. Here the transmission and expository use of the eucharistic tradition in 1 Cor 10 and 11 have proved to be relevantly parallel.

Although written documents have been examined, the oral tradition seems to be the primary source behind the documents. Also here the parallels between the passages discussed in John and those in 1 Cor 10 and 11 give support to this interpretation. Both in 1 Cor 10 and 11 and in John 2:13–22; 5:1–18 and 6:51–58 the traditions are interpreted to meet the challenges which existed in the Christian communities.

Added Note

In 1992 D. Moody Smith published a survey of research on John and the Synoptics, *John among the Gospels. The Relationship in Twentieth-Century Research.*[51] Moody Smith reaches the following conclusion: "At the beginning of the century, the exegete or commentator could safely assume John's knowledge of the Synoptics. We then passed through a period of a quarter of a century or more (1955–80) in which the opposite assumption was the safer one: John was perhaps ignorant of the Synoptics, certainly independent of them. We have now reached the point at which neither assumption is safe, that is, neither can be taken for granted. Any exegete must argue the case afresh on its merits . . ." (p. 189). After Moody Smith's book was in the hands of the publishers he was able to read the articles by F. Neirynck and myself reprinted in the present book. In a footnote Smith refers briefly to points in our debate and states: "Their interchange represents quite well the present divided state of opinion, in which the once-reigning consensus of John's independence has been challenged on the basis of putative points of contact with the texts, while its defenders object that John's redactional use of Mark (or other synoptics) cannot be explained adequately, and other possibilities for understanding the relationship are not explored . . ." (p. 186, n. 5).

---

[51] Smith (1992).

R. E. Brown's magisterial two volumes commentary on the passion narratives in the four gospels, *The Death of the Messiah. From Gethsemane to the Grave*, appeared in 1994.[52] In § 2, volume 1 pages 36–93, Brown deals with general gospel issues pertinent to the passion narratives, including the question of John and the Synoptics. His conclusion is: "John did not use any of the Synoptic PNs in writing his own account, even though some of the preGospel tradition on which he drew resembled material on which Mark and Luke drew" (p. 92). Brown expresses general agreement with the observations and views presented by the present author in the interchange with Neirynck: ". . . an important debate between P. Borgen and F. Neirynck on 'John and the Synoptics' . . . In his defence of Johannine independence of Mark, Borgen offers a theory of development of John and Mark from oral tradition very close to the one I espouse in this section" (p. 78, n. 96).

---

[52] Brown (1994).

Appendix:

Interchange with F. Neirynck[*]

A. Response to P. Borgen

In *Bread from Heaven* (1965) Peder Borgen compares John 6:51b–58 with 1 Cor 11:23–26, 27–29: "Paul shows the way a tradition about the eucharist can be reduced to fragments and used in a paraphrasing exposition. Paul's eucharistic comments suggest that fragments from the eucharistic traditions may have been paraphrased in a similar way in John 6:51–58". "The corresponding points between John and the haggadah of 1 Cor 10:1–4 indicate that fragments from a haggadic story about the manna and the well are also used in this section of John".[1]

In a more recent contribution on "The Use of Tradition in John 12:44–50" (1979) the hypothesis is reformulated and further developed in an application to other discourse material. The Pauline passages of 1 Cor 10 and 11 are presented as an example of the use of a tradition in the form of a quote followed by an exposition, in 1 Cor 11:23b–25(26) and 27–34, and in the form of an expository paraphrase of fragments from the eucharistic tradition itself, in 1 Cor 10:16–17, 21, comp. John 6:51–58. In John 12:44–45 a traditional Jesus-logion is quoted in a way which corresponds to Paul's quotation of the eucharistic tradition in 1 Cor 11:23ff., and John 12:46–50 is an expository

---

[*] The preceding paper was read at the Jerusalem Symposium 1984 on the theme "The Interrelations of the Gospels," and it was followed by this interchange between F. Neirynck and myself.

[1] Borgen (1965) 91–92.

159

elaboration of the Jesus-logion corresponding to Paul's paraphrase of eucharistic words in 1 Cor 11:27ff. and 10:16–17, 21.[2]

In his paper on "John and the Synoptics" (1984) P. Borgen takes a new step by extending this approach to the "narrative" material in John 2:13–22 and 5:1–18. The initial hypothesis concerning John 6:51–58 tends to become now a general method for the study of tradition in John. In John 2 and 5 a unit of tradition is followed by an expository commentary and this larger structure of "text" and commentary has its background in oral tradition, in the expository activity of the Johannine community. Borgen's conclusion is quite clear: "the analysis of these three Johannine passages (John 2:13–22; 5:1–18; 6:51–58) supports the hypothesis of John and the Synoptics being mutually independent".[3]

I. The Borgen-Dauer Thesis

The name of Peder Borgen has been connected with the study of John and the Synoptics for more than thirty years. I found the first reference to his name in *NTS*, September 1955.[4] His dissertation, mentioned there by his teacher N. A. Dahl, was published, at least in part, four years later in an article entitled "John and the Synoptics in the Passion Narrative", in *NTS* 1959.[5] He proposes the following thesis: "A direct literary relationship between John and the Synoptics cannot be considered, but, on the other hand, units of synoptic material have been added to the Johannine tradition."[6] This last conclusion is repeated in 1983: "at points influence from the Synoptics is probable",

---

[2] Borgen (1979).

[3] A slightly revised version of P. Borgen's 1984 paper (without the section on John 2:13–22) has appeared in 1987 under the title, "John and the Synoptics: Can Paul Offer Help?," Borgen (1987B) (cf. 87: "In this paper, John 5:1–18 will be in the center of the discussion"). In the introduction he refers to my "John and the Synoptics" (1977) to illustrate the "new impetus" given to the view of John's dependence. In the quotation of my conclusion ("not traditions . . . but the Synoptic Gospels themselves") the words "regarding John 20" are omitted and a generalizing comment is added: "F. Neirynck rejects theories of 'unknown' and 'hypothetical' sources behind John, whether they are supposed to be written or oral" (80).

[4] Dahl (1955–56), 17–32 (32).

[5] *NTS* 5 (1958–59).

[6] *ibid.*, 80.

with a reference to his earlier article and to A. Dauer's monograph on the passion narrative in John (1972) where "the same hypothesis (is) developed".[7]

The Borgen-Dauer thesis accepts a mediate contact of John with the Synoptics, some elements of the written Synoptic Gospels being fused together with the pre-Johannine oral tradition.[8] However, some significant variations can be observed in Dauer's defence of the common thesis. Dauer does not avoid calling it a pre-Johannine *source* and he reckons with the possibility of a *written* source: "ein zusammenhängende – schriftliche(?) – Quelle".[9] Both Borgen and Dauer take notice of the specific agreements between John and the individual Synoptic Gospels. I quote one of Dauer's partial conclusions: "Die Erzählung der joh Quelle (John 18:12–27) ist wieder nur verständlich, wenn die Synoptiker als existent und bekannt angenommen werden; nur so lassen sich die Parallelen zu den von Matthäus und Lukas am Mk-Stoff vorgenommenen Änderungen verstehen".[10] In Borgen's article the emphasis is much more on "parallel tendency" common tradition" and "mutually independent traditions".[11] Yet, the presence of synoptic material "added to the Johannine tradition" was noted in John 18:10–11, 26; 19:1–3 and 19:31, 38, 40–42, and he has reprinted this article in 1983 without withdrawing that conclusion: "John is based essentially on independent tradition, even though it had been influenced by the synoptic accounts".[12]

II. 1 Cor 11:23–25(26) and 27–34

The point of departure of Borgen's paper is a comparison between 1 Cor 11:23–25(26) and Mark 14:22–25, the two versions of the eucharistic tradition. This comparison should show what kind of

---

[7] Borgen (1983) 87 (cf. 91, n. 27). Another reference to Dauer is found in the Preface to Borgen (1983): "A. Dauer uses this thesis and builds further on my studies" (6).

[8] See my survey Neirynck (1977) 93–95; = Neirynck (1982) 385–87.

[9] Dauer (1972) 335 (see also 227). On Dauer's later study, Dauer (1984), compare Neirynck (1985) 655–80 (esp. 657–65: "John 20, 19–20").

[10] Dauer (1972) 99.

[11] Cf. Dauer's critical remarks: Dauer (1972) 131, n. 200; 170, n. 33; 171, n. 38.

[12] Borgen (1983) 6.

agreements may exist between two mutually independent versions of the same unit of tradition. And in view of the fact that the agreements between John and the Synoptics are not closer, nor more striking, and, in the case of John 5:1–18, even fewer, he concludes that in the passages considered John and the Synoptics are mutually independent.

Borgen proceeds to this "generalization" without even asking the question whether the example of the eucharistic tradition is indeed generalizable. The case of 1 Cor 11:23–25 is in some sense unique. More than in any other portion of the gospels liturgical practice is involved here, and it is far from evident that the degree of agreement that exists between 1 Cor 11:23b–25 and Mark 14:22–25 can be used as criterion in the study of John and the Synoptics. In this connection the counting of the words in 1 Cor 11:23b–25 is quite irrelevant.

A comparative study of 1 Cor 11:23b–25 and Mark 14:22–25 raises much more critical problems than Borgen seems to suggest in his paper. The possibility of Markan redaction and of Pauline interpretation within the traditional unit of verses 23b–25 is not even mentioned, although it is not at all improbable that the two traditions in their pre-Pauline and pre-Markan form would show an even higher degree of similarity.

Many scholars will agree, I think, with Borgen's description of 1 Cor 11:23–24 as "tradition received and handed on" and "paraphrasing commentary attached". "He (Paul) utilizes fragments – words and phrases – from the quote and builds them into a paraphrasing exposition together with legal terms, etc.". "Paul writes the exposition himself and applies the eucharistic tradition to a specific case".

Borgen is much less convincing in the commentary he adds to his own analysis. Paul uses traditional ethical/legal forms, but what is meant by "fused into traditional forms" (see "the guiding rule")? The tradition of 1 Cor 11:23b–25 "was brought orally to the church in Corinth", but Borgen tends to disregard the distinction between tradition and exposition when he maintains that "the oral form is primary", although the written form of the exposition in 1 Cor 11:27ff. is evident.

In fact, Borgen's use of 1 Cor 11:23–34 as a model in his analysis of John 2:13–22 and 5:1–18 is almost contradictory. In 1 Cor 11 the quote of a pre-Pauline tradition is followed by Paul's own exposition. A comparable situation in the Gospel seems to be the transmission of a traditional story (2:13–16; 5:1–9) followed by the evangelist's own expository commentary (2:17–22; 5:10–20).

III. "Text" and "Commentary"

In the section on John 6 Borgen reformulates his position regarding John 6:51b–58, with a few observations on the midrashic character of John 6:31–58 (cf. *Bread*). More innovating is the section on *"Text" and Commentary* where he uses the "model" of 1 Cor 11:23–34 in an analysis of John 5:1–18 and 2:13–22.

Of course, the notions of repetition, paraphrase and commentary are not new in the interpretation of John. In Borgen's hypothesis, however, the paraphrasing commentary is rather pre-Johannine: "text" and "commentary" (5:1–9, 10–18; 2, 13–16, 17–22) form a traditional unit from the transmitting and expository activity of the Johannine community.[13]

John 5:1–18

Borgen compares John 5:1–18 with the Sabbath controversies in Matt 12:1–8 and Luke 13:10–17 and concludes that the three passages follow a traditional structure for a controversial case being discussed by means of a subsequent judicial dialogue. Although Matt 12:5–7 is probably Matthew's interpretative expansion of Mark 2:23–28,[14] he rejects such an interpretative use of Markan material in John 5:1–18 because of some distinctive features in John 5:10–18. The verbatim agreement between John 5:8 and Mark 2:9 is waved aside as a stereotyped phrase,[15] and with regard to possible connections of John 5:18 with Mark 2:7 (blasphemy) and of John 5:16, 18 with Mark 3:6 (the persecution and the attempt to kill Jesus) he uses

---

[13] My response will concentrate on his analysis of John 5:1–18 and 2:13–22, of direct relevance to the theme of our discussion, "John and the Synoptics". On the problem of Paul and the Synoptics, see Neirynck (1986).

[14] Cf. *supra*, 145.

[15] Cf. 146.

the word "arbitrary":[16] there are no verbal agreements and, contrary to the expository commentary in John 5:10–18, the corresponding discussion in Mark 3:1–6 precedes the healing.

My first observation concerns the synoptic passages of Matt 12:1–8 and Luke 13:10–17. Unfortunately, the presentation of the "text" (with the separation of "the case" and the "expository dialogue": Matt 12:1, 2–8 and Luke 13:10–13, 14–17) is not followed by a real "commentary". The brief remark that the pericope of Luke 13:10–17 "is peculiar to Luke, and does not come from the other gospels" seems to suggest, although not unambiguously, that "at least the pericope as such" is traditional.[17] It could be mentioned that the style of the story is Lukan and that some commentators have "the impression that we have here to do with a more sophisticated type of writing than we find in Mark" and therefore suppose the evangelist himself to be responsible for the actual composition".[18] In his monograph on the miracle stories in Luke (1977), U. Busse has made the suggestion that "Die Auseinandersetzung mit dem Synagogenvorsteher sei kompositionell nachträglich in eine vorgegebene Wundererzählung aus dem Sondergut eingefügt, die Lukas dementsprechend uberarbeitet habe".[19] Anyway the problem of John and the Synoptics cannot be discussed without a more thoroughgoing examination of the synoptic parallels. The repetition of phrases, a "distinctive feature" in John 5:1–18,[20] is not wholly absent in Luke 13:10–17:

---

[16] Cf. 147.

[17] In the 1984 paper: "a pericope which is peculiar to Luke, and does not come from the other gospels (at least not the pericope as such)" Borgen (1984B) 34.

[18] Creed (1930) 182.

[19] Busse (1977) 293. For a tentative reconstruction of the traditional healing story in vv. 11–13, cf. 297. The debate in vv. 14–16 is secondarily added, "eine luk. Komposition, wobei er offensichtlich nur ein freies Wanderlogion zur Auffüllung der Argumentation benutzt hat" (*ibid.*). Vv. 10 and 17 are attributed to Lukan redaction (294, 297) Compare also Trautmann (1980) 191–92; Fiorenza (1983) 125: "it is possible that the healing story Luke 13:10–13 was originally independent and was expanded to a dialogue at a later stage".

[20] The phrase on "distinctive features" Borgen (1984B) 33 has been revised in the published text Borgen (1987B) 89: "a distinctive use of this common form").

11 ἰδοὺ . . . πνεῦμα ἔχουσα ἀσθενείας ἔτη δεκαοκτώ
16 ἣν ἔδησεν ὁ σατανᾶς ἰδοὺ δέκα καὶ ὀκτὼ ἔτη
16b ἔδησεν 16c ἀπὸ τοῦ δεσμοῦ τούτου
12 ἀπολέλυσαι 15 λύει 16 λυθῆναι
10 ἐν τοῖς σάββασιν 14 τῷ σαββάτῳ 14b τῇ ἡμέρᾳ τοῦ
σαββάτου
15 τῷ σαββάτῳ 16c τῇ ἡμέρᾳ τοῦ σαββάτου
14 τῷ ὄχλῳ 17 πᾶς ὁ ὄχλος

Another "distinctive feature" and one of the "stronger arguments against John's dependence on the Synoptics" is the elaborate form of changing the stage in John 5:10–18.[21] In fact, this feature is "distinctively Johannine", and not "distinctively traditional". It has been described by C. H. Dodd as "a kind of dramatic technique", "the device of two stages upon which the action is exhibited".[22] In John 5, the healed person is with:

    1–9   Jesus (at the Sheep Pool)
        10–13 the Jews
    14   Jesus (in the temple)
        15–18 the Jews and Jesus

Compare the healing of the blind man on the Sabbath (9:14, cf. 5:9b) in John 9:1–7 | the people: 8–12 | the Pharisees: 13–17 (the man), 18–23 (the parents), 24–34 (the man) | Jesus: 35–41. There is nothing similar in Matt 12:1–8. But no attention is given to the parallel text of Mark 2:23–28. This is most curious since it is normally not Matt 12:1–8 but Mark 2:1 – 3:6, and especially 2:1–12 and 2:23–28; 3:1–6, which is cited as the synoptic parallel. In Mark the two Sabbath pericopes are closely connected. Together they form the conclusion of the section of controversies (2:1 – 3:6). In Matthew they are separated from Matt 9:1–17 = Mark 2:1–22 and, as a result of the Matthean expansions in 12:5–7 and 11–12a and the transitional formula μεταβὰς ἐκεῖθεν in 12:9a, the two pericopes are more clearly distinguished than they are in Mark. I can agree with R. Pesch's form-critical

---

[21] Cf. *supra*, 147.

[22] Dodd (1953) 315 (John 4); 347–348 (John 7–8); Dodd (1963) 96–97 (John 18, 28–19, 16). See also Dauer (1972) 102–103; *et al.*

description of the connection of 3:1–6 with 2:23–28, at least with this reservation: the connection is not necessarily pre-Markan. I quote:[23]

a) in V 2 sind die Pharisäer von 2, 24 (vgl. V 6) als Subjekt vorausgesetzt, d.h., die vorangehende Erzählung ist vorausgesetzt, und durch sie sind Auflauern und Anklageabsicht motiviert;
b) Jesus Frage von V 4 (hier keine Gegenfrage) ist auf die Pharisäerfrage 2, 24 polemisch bezogen: Stichwortverbindungen: ἔξεστιν, τοῖς σάββασιν;
c) in V 1 (wie in den Formulierungen von VV 2.4) ist die Angabe von 2, 23, das das erzählte Geschehen *am Sabbat* spielt, vorausgesetzt; in einer selbständigen Erzählung wäre eine ausführlichere Exposition notwendig;
d) auch der Vergleich mit anderen Perikopenanfängen (z.B. 2, 13; 6, 1; 8, 27; 11, 11) kann den nicht-selbständigen Charakter unserer Erzählung bestätigen.

When we take Mark 2:23 – 3:6 as one section in Mark there is no ground for the objection that the discussion precedes the healing since the second pericope is a continuation of the debate following the plucking of grain on the Sabbath. And the Johannine change of the stage has a synoptic analogy in Mark 3:1.

A most typical sentence in Borgen's paper is found on p. 34:[24] "The agreement between John 5:10 . . . οὐκ ἔξεστιν . . . and Matt 12:2 is due to the circumstances that a traditional form is used in John's paraphrase, corresponding to Paul's use of traditional (gospel) forms in 1 Cor 10:21 and 11:27ff." (sic). Οὐκ ἔξεστιν is treated as an isolated phrase and the striking parallelism between the structure of John 5:1–18 and Mark 2:1–12; 2:23 – 3:6 receives no consideration.[25]

---

[23] Pesch (1976) 188.

[24] Borgen (1984) 34. Cf. *supra*, 147.

[25] My suggestion is, of course, not that "John has changed the term 'disciples' into the term 'man'", or that the man became a disciple, but the contrast Jews – Jesus (and the healed man) in John can be compared with that of the Pharisees – Jesus (and the disciples, the healed man) and its role in the narrative of Mark 2:23–28; 3:1–6.

John	Mark
5:1–9a the healing	2:1–12 the healing
5:8 . . . ἆρον τὸν κράβαττόν σου	2:11 . . . ἆρον τὸν κράβαττόν σου
5:9 . . . ἦρεν τὸν κράβαττον αὐτοῦ	2:12 . . . ἄρας τὸν κράβαττον
5:9 <u>ἦν δὲ σάββατον</u> ἐν . . .	2:23 <u>ἐν τοῖς σάββασιν</u>
5:10 ἔλεγον οὖν οἱ Ἰουδαῖο . . .	2:24 καὶ οἱ Φαρισαῖοι ἔλεγον . . .
<u>σάββατόν ἐστιν</u>, καὶ <u>οὐκ ἔξεστίν</u> σοι ἆραι τὸν κράβαττόν σου.	. . . ποιοῦσιν <u>τοῖς σάββασιν</u> ὃ <u>οὐκ ἔξεστιν</u>.
the *man* carrying his bed	the *disciples* plucking grain
5:11–16 *Jesus* ὁ ποιήσας αὐτὸν ὑγιῆ	3:1–6 *Jesus* εἰ . . . θεραπεύσει αὐτόν
. . . ἐν σαββάτῳ (cf. 7:23)	3:2 τοῖς σάββασιν
	3:4 ἔξεστιν τοῖς σάββασιν
5:17 . . . ἐργάζομαι.	ἀγαθὸν ποιῆσαι . . . ἢ <u>ἀποκτεῖναι;</u>
5:18 ἐζήτουν	3:6 συμβούλιον ἐδίδουν κατ' αὐτοῦ
αὐτὸν . . . <u>ἀποκτεῖναι</u>	ὅπως αὐτὸν <u>ἀπολέσωσιν</u>.

Compare Mark 3:6 (and John 5:18) with:

Mark	11:18	ἐζήτουν	πῶς αὐτὸν ἀπολέσωσιν
	12:12	ἐζήτουν	αὐτὸν κρατῆσαι
	14:1	ἐζήτουν	. . . πῶς αὐτὸν . . . κρατήσαντες ἀποκτείνωσιν.

The seeking to kill Jesus is indeed "central in John" (5:18; 7:1, 19, 20, 25; 8:37, 40; 11:53; cf. persecution: 5:16; 15:20), but in John and Mark the motif appears here for the first time (John 5:18; Mark 3:6) and in both gospels it is connected with the violation of the Sabbath and in both gospels too it is found at the conclusion of the same pattern: first the healing, then a controversial Sabbath case in the action of people who are related to Jesus: the healed man and the disciples, and finally Jesus' healing activity as a violation of the Sabbath. No modern interpreter of the gospel of Mark can blame the Fourth Evangelist for having made the connection between Mark 2:1–12 and Mark (2:23–28) – 3:1–6.

Three other features in John 5:10–18 can be explained in the light of Mark 2:1–12.

1. In the healing stories of John 5 and Mark 2 special emphasis is given to the order of Jesus: "rise, take up your bed, and walk" (John 5:8; Mark 2:11). In both gospels the phrase is repeated in the description of the healing as an immediate execution of Jesus' order (John 5:9; Mark 2:12) and, more significantly, the phrase is also used in the debate, in John 5:12 (cf. 11) in the Sabbath discussion (τίς ἐστιν . . . ὁ εἰπών σοι), and in Mark 2:9 in the debate about forgiveness of sin (τί ἐστιν εὐκοπώτερον . . . ἢ εἰπεῖν).

<table>
<tr><td>John 5</td><td>Mark 2</td></tr>
<tr><td></td><td>11 σοὶ λέγω,</td></tr>
<tr><td>8 ἔγειρε ἆρον τὸν κράβαττόν
σου καὶ περιπάτει</td><td>ἔγειρε ἆρον τὸν
κράβαττόν σου καὶ ὕπαγε
. . .</td></tr>
<tr><td>9 καὶ εὐθέως ἐγένετο ὑγιὴς
. . .</td><td>12 καὶ ἠγέρθη
καὶ εὐθὺς ἄρας τὸν</td></tr>
<tr><td>καὶ ἦρεν τὸν κράβαττον
αὐτοῦ καὶ περιεπάτει
(10) ἆραι τὸν κράβαττόν σου
(11) . . . μοι εἶπεν·
ἆρον τὸν κράβαττόν σου
καὶ περιπάτει</td><td>κράβαττον ἐξῆλθεν . . .</td></tr>
<tr><td>12 τίς ἐστιν ὁ ἄνθρωπος ὁ
εἰπών σοι·
ἆρον καὶ περιπάτει.</td><td>9 τί ἐστιν . . . ἢ εἰπεῖν·
ἔγειρε
καὶ ἆρον τὸν κράβαττόν
σου καὶ περιπάτει;</td></tr>
</table>

2. John 5:14 ἴδε ὑγιὴς γέγονας, μηκέτι ἁμάρτανε . . . The healing and the forgiveness of sin are closely connected in the story of Mark 2:1–12. Compare 2:9 and 5b, 10b–11. In light of the parallel in Mark, the healed paralytic is a man to whom Jesus has said: your sins are forgiven. As far as I see, this distinctive feature, the association of forgiveness and healing, is wholly absent in the case of the *adultera*!

3. The motif for the Jews seeking to kill Jesus is not only the violation of the Sabbath (John 5:18). One can compare once more with Mark 3:6: "Die Tötungsabsicht der Gegner erscheint am Ende der Perikope nicht besonders angemessen, wohl nach 2,1–3,5!", and: "Der Vorwurf der Lästerung (2:7) muss . . . mit 3,6 in Verbindung gesehen werden".[26] John 5:18: ὅτι οὐ μόνον ἔλυεν τὸ σάββατον, ἀλλὰ καὶ πατέρα ἴδιον ἔλεγεν τὸν θεὸν ἴσον ἑαυτὸν ποιῶν τῷ θεῷ. Cf. v. 17, "My Father is working still and I am working," and Schnackenburg's commentary: "Dem Mann ist mit der Heilung zugleich seine Sünde von Gott vergeben worden; das ist es, was Jesus mit dem Satz meint: 'Mein Vater arbeitet bis jetzt' (V 17)".[27] Compare Mark 2:7 βλασφημεῖ· τίςδύναται ἀφιέναι ἁμαρτίας εἰ μὴ εἷς ὁ θεός; In this connection John 10:33 should be quoted: . . . περὶ βλασφημίας, καὶ ὅτι σὺ ἄνθρωπος ὢν ποιεῖς σεαυτὸν θεόν (cf. v. 36).

In a final objection, Borgen opposes to the (traditional) Sabbath question in John 5:10–18 the evangelist's own discourse in 5:19ff. in which "the Christological idea in John 5:17 is developed more independently".[28] The evangelist's interest in the christological

---

[26] Gnilka (1978) 126, 102 (See also 100).

[27] Schnackenburg (1971) 123.

[28] Borgen departs from almost all commentators by withdrawing 5:17–18 from the evangelist's redaction. Cf. Kotila (1988) 19: "die communis opinio der Exegeten, dass die V. 17–18 in ihrer heutigen Fassung von E stammen. (n. 1:) Dies bestreitet heutzutage kaum jemand".

Borgen's distinction between the "case" in vv. 1–9 and the "expository dialogue" in vv. 10–18, both pre-Johannine, can be compared with the separation of tradition (vv. 2–9b) and redaction (vv. 9c–16) in J. Becker's (and Bultmann's) pre-Johannine SQ. The communis opinio is well represented in Fortna's new reconstruction of the Source: 5:2–9b (with a tacit correction of his earlier hypothesis: v. 14 is no longer mentioned).

But this scholarly consensus is not without fault. The miraculous knowledge of Jesus in v. 6b may be due to the evangelist, "der einzige Einschub des Evangelisten" for R. Schnackenburg and more recently for U. Schnelle. M.-É. Boismard attributes to the evangelist not only v. 6b but also v. 7 and finally the entire vv. 6b, c, 7, and he reduces the traditional healing story to vv. 5–6a, 8–9b. My objections to this understanding of vv. 6b–7 as an insertion into a pre-existent story have received a positive response in L. T. Witkamp's study. Starting from B. Lindars's description of 5:2b–9 as a fusion of two distinct stories, an amalgamation possibly due to John himself, Witkamp reckons with "intentional composition" of the evangelist redacting his traditional material. He accepts "a tradition-historical connection" between the formulation of Jesus' words in John 5:8 and Mark 2:9, 11. Cf. Witkamp (1986)

aspect is rightly emphasized, but it is precisely the weakness of Borgen's analysis, it seems to me, that he has not been able to grasp the christological (!) orientation in the progression from the healing in 5:1–9 to 5:18.

John 2:13–22

Borgen's reaction to the hypothesis of John's dependence on the Synoptics is less negative with regard to John 2:13–22. He also recognizes that in this case "there is not extensive use of words from the story of the cleansing (2:13–16) in the subsequent section of vv. 17–22".[29] Nevertheless his conclusion will be that "in John 2:13–22 the Evangelist has brought into his Gospel a unit from the expository activity of the Johannine community".[30]

Borgen presents three observations in favour of the theory of mutual independence between John and the Synoptics in John 2:13–22.

1. The verbal agreements are not stronger than between 1 Cor 11:23–26 and Mark 14:22–25. – As I noted above, this liturgical tradition is not an acceptable standard in the study of the gospels. The "agreement of one complete sentence in 1 Cor 11:23–26 and Mark 14:22–25" is that of τοῦτό μου ἐστιν τὸ σῶμα / τοῦτό ἐστιν τὸ σῶμά μου!

2. The agreement of sequence: Mark 11:15–17 and 11:27–28 probably "belonged together in a pre-Markan stage of the tradition, a tradition for which John testifies as an independent witness".[31]

It can be noted that Borgen fully recognizes the agreement between John 2:18 (τί σημεῖον δεικνύεις ἡμῖν ὅτι) ταῦτα ποιεῖς and Mark 11:28a (ἐν ποίᾳ ἐξουσίᾳ) ταῦτα ποιεῖς; (cf. 28b ἢ τίς σοι ἔδωκεν τὴν ἐξουσίαν ταύτην ἵνα ταῦτα ποιῇς). The possibility of a pre-Markan sequence can be considered (e.g., Mark 11:15, 28a, 29a, 30)[32] and

---

114–38.

[29] Cf. *supra*, 154.

[30] *ibid.*

[31] "As suggested by Dodd, Brown and others it is *probable* that Mark has split up . . ." (Borgen). Cf. Brown (1966) 119: "As Buse and Dodd suggest, it is quite *possible* that the intervening material has split up what was originally one scene" (italics mine).

[32] See, e.g., Farla (1978) 142.

John's immediate association of the cleansing and the question can be based on a pre-Johannine tradition. But, at a closer examination, this appears to be an unnecessary hypothesis.

In Mark the account of the cleansing is "sandwiched" between the two parts of the story about the fig tree, but there can be no doubt that ταῦτα ποιεῖς in 11:28 refers back to the temple cleansing. In both Matthew and Luke the complexity of the Markan composition (and its chronology of three days: cf. 11a, 15a, 27a) has been reduced by putting together the two parts of the story about the fig tree (Matthew) or by eliminating it (Luke):

Matt	Mark	Luke
(I) 21:(1–9), 10–11	(I) 11:(1–10), 11	19:(29–40), (41–44)
21:12–13		
21:14–17		
(II) 21:18–19	(II) 11:12–14	——
	11:15–17	—— 19:45–46
	11:18–19	—— 19:47–48 Summary
21:20–22	(III) 11:20–25	——
21:23–27	11:27–33	—— 20:1–7

A more radical simplification of the story is found in John 2:13ff. But, much better than Matthew and Luke, John has preserved the Markan meaning of the question about authority (ταῦτα ποιεῖς). John shows here a correct understanding of the Markan intercalation (or alternation):

Mark 11: 1–11	——
——	12–14
15–19	——
——	20–25
27–33	——

As noted above, the sequence (and combination) of the healing and the Sabbath debate in John 5:1–18 is another example of John's understanding of the Markan composition (the concentric structure of Mark 2:1 – 3:6).

3. Although the saying about the destruction and rebuilding of the temple in John 2:19 "has close verbal agreement with the

Synoptics", there is "one important difference" (John uses ἐγείρειν). Another difference is John's use of the imperative, λύσατε. The answer is given by Borgen: "These distinctive features fit well into the theological tendencies in John."

Two more specific observations are added. First, John 2:19 does not reflect "any specific points" from the saying in Matthew and Mark. Borgen correctly notes that the imperative λύσατε "puts the burden of the destruction on 'the Jews'", but he does not say more about his interpretation of λύσατε. Is it a conditional sentence (Dodd: "If you destroy this temple, I will raise it up"), or rather a prophetic imperative (cf. Bultmann, et al.)? In this last solution λύσατε (and ἐγερῶ) refer to the future and John's form of the saying comes close to Mark 14:58 καταλύσω – οἰκοδομήσω (ctr. Matt 26:61 δύναμαι καταλῦσαι – οἰκοδομῆσαι).

Secondly, "Acts 6:14 indicates that the saying was used in debates and controversies between the early church and the Jewish authorities". Before drawing any conclusion about "the Sitz im Leben of John 2:13–22" a correct understanding of the saying in Acts 6:14 should be given. I quote G. Schneider's commentary on Acts: "Mit Sicherheit verwendet hier Lukas das Tempelwort Jesu aus der markinischen Prozeßszene (Mark 14, 57f) und ändert es zu diesem Zweck um".[33]

Borgen's final observations concerning John 2:17 (ὁ οἶκος), 18 (ταῦτα), 19–21 (ὁ ναός), 22 (Scripture and the word of Jesus) are, of course, quite acceptable in the hypothesis of John's dependence on the Synoptics.

IV. Conclusion

The "form" of expository interpretation and paraphrasing commentary can be employed in the interpretation of the Fourth Gospel, although the vague description of this "form" will have to be specified in each peculiar section of the Gospel. But it has no relevance in a discussion about John's dependence on the Synoptics. And if any conclusion can be drawn from the "model" of 1 Cor 11:23–25(26) and 27–34, it would be that a "tradition" (saying or narrative) can be used by John as a starting point for a further elaboration. However, the presence of this structure, "text" and "commentary", allows

---

[33] Schneider (1980) 438.

of no conclusion about pre-Johannine or synoptic origin of this tradition.[34]

---

[34] This text was delivered at the Jerusalem meeting, April 16, 1984. Only a few updating notes were added to the original Response (notes 3, 9, 13, 25, 28).

B. Reply from P. Borgen

Tradition Received and Handed on. A Paraphrasing Commentary Attached

Let me start with Neirynck's conclusion which indicates some common ground between us:

> And if any conclusion can be drawn from the "model" of 1 Cor 11:23–25(26) and 27–34, it would be that a "tradition" (saying or narrative) can be used by John as a starting point for a further elaboration (p. 172).

In like manner Neirynck states:

> Many scholars will agree, I think, with Borgen's description of 1 Cor 11:23–34 as "tradition received and handed on" and "paraphrasing commentary attached". "He (Paul) utilizes fragments – words and phrases – from the quote and builds them into a paraphrasing exposition together with legal terms, etc.". "Paul writes the exposition himself and applies the eucharistic tradition to a specific case" (p. 162).

Some points should be presented here already at the outset:

1. Paul gives evidence for the existence of this model already in the fifties, that is, in the pre-synoptic and pre-Johannine period.

2. Paul shows that such paraphrasing commentary could have a unit of oral tradition as "text". Since the commentary addresses itself to a specific issue in the Corinthian Church and is part of a

letter to that Church, it replaces the orally delivered instruction which Paul would have given if he had been present in person.

3. Paul gives evidence for the fact that a unit of tradition and the subsequent commentary could be presented together, separate from a comprehensive Gospel Document.

In this way we receive a glimpse into pre-synoptic and pre-Johannine handling of tradition.

Neirynck and I seem to be in general agreement that this use of tradition is not limited to the pre-synoptic and pre-Johannine stage. There are three main possibilities:

a) The quotation of a tradition followed by a subsequent paraphrasing commentary may belong to the pre-synoptic and pre-Johannine stages;

b) it may result from an evangelist's own interpretation of oral tradition or

c) it may take place when a section of a Gospel was used as the text to be commented upon and paraphrased.

One difference between Neirynck and myself seems to be that he is more hesitant to consider possibilities 1. and 2. I must add here that when I discuss possibilities 1. and 2., I base the discussion on analysis of documents. The question asked is: How far can such settings (1. pre-synoptic and pre-Johannine and 2. the evangelist's own interpretation of oral tradition) explain, in a plausible way, the features of the document concerned?

The Eucharistic Tradition

Neirynck writes:

> The case of 1 Cor 11:23–25 is in some sense unique. More than in any other portion of the gospels liturgical practice is involved here and it is far from evident that the degree of agreement that exists between 1 Cor 11:23b–25 and Mark 14:22–25 can be used as a criterion in the study of John and the Synoptics (p. 162).

A reference to this occurs later in his response: "As I noted above, this liturgical tradition is not an acceptable standard in the study of the gospels" (p. 170).

Neirynck seems to hold the view that the wording of the eucharistic tradition was more stable and fixed in its versions than was the wording in other gospel traditions.

Neirynck relies here on a view which seem to have become a kind of stereotype. He does not present documentation in support of this interpretation. There is a remark in his response, however, which seems to imply that the eucharistic traditions in 1 Cor 11:23b–25 and Mark 14:22–25 are not so unique, as thought to be the case, since Neirynck maintains that here, just at other places, one should question whether or not possible editorial modifications of the tradition are probable.

Several observations show that the eucharistic tradition should be discussed together with the gospel material in general.

a) In Matt, Mark and Luke the eucharistic tradition is part of the Gospels. It is placed together with the other traditions about Jesus' words and actions. Consequently, the story of the institution of the eucharist is an integral part of the general run of each one of these gospels.

b) As Neirynck seems to indicate, if one holds the view that the wording of the eucharistic tradition is stable and fixed in a unique way, does it mean that the text of the gospel traditions had no stability at all at the oral stage?

c) The existence of different versions of the eucharistic tradition shows that it was not unique, but functioned in a way similar to that of the rest of the gospel tradition. The most obvious documentation of this is the Markan version, the longer and shorter version of Luke, and 1 Cor 11:23–25(26) seen within this context.

d) The eucharistic tradition can be used as basis for paraphrasing commentary, just as the other gospel traditions can, for example in applying the tradition to a specific issue.

e) Paul says explicitly in 1 Cor 11:23 that he has received the eucharistic text as tradition, and that he has transmitted it to the church in Corinth. The usual technical terms for the transmission of tradition are used by him (παρέλαβον, παρέδωκα).

Conclusion: Evidence from the texts does not support the view that the eucharistic tradition is unique. (See now further: P. Borgen, "Nattverdstradisjonen i I Kor 10 og 11 som evangelietradisjon," *Svensk Exegetisk Årsbok*, 51, (1986) 32–39.) It can be seen as other tradition can. As for the different versions, and Mark's independence of Paul, I refer to G. Bornkamm and H. Schürmann. An extensive list of scholars could here be added.

It may also be added that I compare texts of Paul and Mark in their present form because these are the texts we know. They also have their place in the transmission process of the tradition: They therefore illustrate what kind of agreement can exist between two independent versions of the same unit of tradition.

John 6:51b–58

As for John 6:51b–58, the conclusion of my analysis is that the agreement in wording, style and content between John 6:51–58 and 1 Cor 10:3–4, 10, 16–17, 21 and 11:23–29 show that John draws on eucharistic and manna traditions in a way similar to Paul: These similarities show that John is here closer to Paul than to the Synoptics. Since John elsewhere is not dependent upon 1 Cor, however, he is not dependent on Paul in John 6:51b–58 either. Thus, John utilizes an independent tradition on the institution of the Lord's Supper, and presupposes that the eucharistic tradition was already associated with the biblical stories of the manna and the well. It is in accordance with this conclusion of John's independence that he uses the term ἡ σάρξ and not τὸ σῶμα which is found in the synoptic and Pauline version. The Johannine version of the institution is also documented by Ignatius' use of the term ἡ σάρξ in *Ign. Rom.* 7:3; *Phld.* 4:1; *Ign. Smyrn.* 7:1 and also by Justin in *Apol.* 1:66:2, 29.

Our conclusion puts us in general agreement with Boismard's interpretation, when he suggests that John here reflects a liturgical tradition which is also represented by Paul. Boismard fails to draw the line from this conclusion to his analysis of other parts of the Gospel of John, where he prefers to employ literary source criticism. Against the background of John 6:51–58 this question is pertinent: Are there other passages in John which have their setting in the life of the Johannine community and its transmission and exposition of tradition?

In his response, Neirynck mentions my discussion of John 6:51b–58 in passing, without thereby making any comments on it. Since I here find myself in general agreement with Boismard, I expected to find Neirynck's treatment of this passage in his extensive discussion of Boismard's view in his book *Jean et les Synoptiques. Examen critique de l'exégèse de M.-E. Boismard* (= Neirynck (1979)). He refers to verses in 6:51ff. in his discussion of Boismard's analysis on textual criticism (pp. 25, 32–34, 37) and stylistic characteristics (pp. 46, 55, 68, 69, 210, 211, 214, 225, 228, 229, 232, 260, 295).

There is no discussion, however, of Boismard's treatment of John 6:51b–58 as a whole. Boismard (1977) 204–05 stressed the agreement between John 6:51b and 1 Cor 11:24, while in Neirynck's book 1 Cor 11:24 does not appear in the index. Thus, in both cases Neirynck has neither analysed nor made any comments on John 6:51b–58. I regret this, since in John 6:51b–58 and in 1 Cor 10 and 11 both eucharistic traditions and manna traditions are used. Consequently, John 6:51b–58 is a good starting point for our discussion of John.

John 5:1–18

Neirynck discusses at some length my analysis of John 5:1–18. As I read his response, he does not object to my understanding of the form of the passage, viz. that it follows a traditional structure for a controversial case being discussed by means of a subsequent halakhic dialogue.

I do not see any need for presupposing either Mark, Matt, or Luke as a source for this passage. The features of the passage, both in form and content, can be satisfactorily explained in the following two partly alternative ways:

1. The Evangelist utilized an instance of healing on the Sabbath as case story on the basis of which he developed a halakhic debate thereby relating Christology to the Sabbath question.

This understanding parallels nicely the combined Busse-Neirynck interpretation of Luke 13:10–17 where Luke utilizes a story of Sabbath healing as a case story. He then repeats phrases from the story in a subsequent halakhic dialogue. Neirynck is not precise in his citation of me when he states my view in this was: "The repetition of phrases, a 'distinctive feature' in John 5:1–18 . . ." (p. 164). My point is that only in John 5:10–18 phrases from the story (the case) are repeated quite *mechanically* (p. 148).

2. The Evangelist records a Sabbath healing which had already served in the Johannine community as a case story together with a subsequent halakhic debate.

Since the application of Christology to the Sabbath question does not seem to be of central importance in the Evangelist's own situation, I am inclined to find this alternative to be the more probable one. There are scholars, however, who hold the view that the Sabbath question and the question of the temple, and so forth, were central issues also at the time when the Gospel was written.

The choice between these two alternatives does not affect my thesis as such that John here is independent of the Synoptics and that the features of the passage receive a plausible and sufficient explanation in this way.

Moreover, several observations speak against the theory that John uses elements from Mark 2:1 – 3:6. Some of these are:

a) the healing in Mark 2:1–12 takes place in Capernaum, whereas in John 5:1ff. it takes place in Jerusalem at the Beth-zatha pool. This difference cannot be explained by John's interest in Jerusalem, since the healing in John 4:46 is located in Capernaum and the feeding of the five thousand in John 6 took place at the lake of Galilee.

b) Nothing is said in Mark 2:1 – 3:6 about "the carrying of the mat" being a violation of the Sabbath. The reason is, of course, that the healing in 2:1–12 did not take place on the Sabbath. Moreover, it seems improbable that such an interpretation in John 5:1–18 is based upon the healing of the man with a withered hand in Mark 3:1–6. In addition, the story in Mark 3:1–6 is located in Galilee.

c) In Mark 2:1 – 3:6 only Mark 2:23–28 has the same form as the one found in John 5:1–18: a controversial case is discussed by means of a subsequent judicial dialogue. In Mark 2:23–28 there is also an appeal to Scripture corresponding to the allusion to Gen 2:1ff. in John 5:1–18. The Scripture references are so different, however, that there can be no question of dependence. Mark 2:23–28 is not a story of healing and can therefore not be the basis for John 5:1–18.

3. Neirynck lists the word "man" John 5:9, and the word "disciples" Mark 2:24, among the agreements which to him show that John is dependent on Mark. His view that John has a literary dependence on Mark then means that John has changed the term "disciples" in Mark into the term "man". This point seems to lack plausibility.

4. Neirynck suggests that John's change of the scene in John 5:10–18 derives from Mark 3:1ff. This cannot be the case, since Mark 3:1ff. introduces a new case (Mark 2:23ff., the plucking of the grain; 3:1ff., the healing of a person with a withered hand). Moreover, John changes

the stage three times (vv. 10–13; the Jews and the person healed; v. 14: Jesus and the healed person; vv. 15–18: the healed person, the Jews and Jesus).

5. Neirynck stresses that in John 5:18 and Mark 3:6 the motif "of the seeking to kill Jesus" appears for the first time in both gospels. The motif occurs, however, in two different healing stories, the healing of the person with the withered hand (Mark 3:1ff.) and the healing of the paralytic (John 5:1ff.). And if John was dependent on Mark for this common motif, he should then have already mentioned it in John 2:13–18 as part of the cleansing of the temple, from its use in Mark's story of the cleansing of the temple in Mark 11:15–18.

6. The interpretation of John 5:1–18 suggested in my paper explains the form of the passage and the method used in the expository dialogue. It also explains why this elaboration of the healing story would be acceptable to the readers. The person who developed the paraphrasing dialogue in John 5:10–18 had as point of departure the givenness of the healing story, just as Paul has, as point of departure for his paraphrasing exposition (1 Cor 11:27ff.), the givenness of the tradition in 1 Cor 11:23–25(26). Accordingly, John 5:1–9 renders a unit of tradition which has been handed down and received, and which for that reason has authority and serves as basis for paraphrasing exposition.

As far as I can see, Neirynck has not clarified the Fourth Evangelist's method, the form used in his treatment of Mark, his understanding of Mark (and tradition), or how and why his readers would find his treatment of Mark acceptable and authoritative.

Conclusion: A plausible explanation of the features found in the text (John 5:1–18) is that a healing story (5:1–9) is taken up from oral tradition, and used as an authoritative case story for the halakhic debate (vv. 10–19). It is consistent with this view that the healing story (5:1–9) has the same form as some of the other healing stories in the gospels.

In the above analysis several objections have been raised against the view that John 5:1–18 is dependent upon Mark 2:1 – 3:6. It should be added that if John's readers knew Mark, and the Evangelist had treated Mark 2:1 – 3:6 in a violent manner, it would be hard to understand how they could accept both the method used and the outcome as authoritative.

Agreement, Disagreement, Desiderata

From the deliberations at the symposium some points of agreements and disagreements emerged:

There was broad agreement that John 6:51b–58 draws on a tradition that was abroad in the community. This tradition shows closer agreements with 1 Cor 10 and 11 than with the Synoptics. Similarily, there was broad agreement that a traditional healing story lies behind John 5:1–18.

Generally, one agreed that the Gospel of John should not be studied in isolation from the study of the Synoptic Gospels. Studies along these lines will not only throw light upon the Gospel of John, but will also prove fruitful for the study of the Synoptic Gospels.

Among the points of disagreement the following might be listed.

Borgen regards the sentence "take up your mat and walk" (John 5:8, etc. and Mark 2:9, etc.) as a stereotype phrase which would occur in various contexts, with no dependence among the stories. Neirynck and others think that the phrase comes from Mark 2:9 and cannot be isolated from its context. Borgen evaluates other similarities between John 5:1–18 and Mark 2:1 – 3:6 too distant and vague to indicate John's dependence of Mark. Moreover, the differences also speak against such dependence.

Neirynck and others think that the verbatim agreement between John 5:8 and Mark 2:9, the similarity of sequence between John 5:1–18 and Mark 2:1 – 3:6 (first the healing and then controversial Sabbath cases) prove, as part of a larger theory of Johannine dependence, that John is dependent on Mark.

These different views reflect different evaluations of what kinds of similarities prove dependence and what kinds of agreements are normal in mutually independent written or oral stories. Correspondingly, dissimilarities are also evaluated in different ways.

Another type of disagreement was also voiced at the symposium. Some (as did Neirynck and Borgen) look primarily to the Synoptic Gospels, the rest of the New Testament and the Jewish surroundings (not excluding Hellenistic influence) for analogies to the transmission and interpretation of the Johannine tradition and/or written gospel.

Others (such as David Dungan) raised the question whether one should look for analogies elsewhere, as for example in some of the Nag Hammadi documents.

In order not to make the "Desiderata" too comprehensive, the list is limited to three points:

1. Further studies should be undertaken on the agreements between John and each of the other gospels, Matt, Mark and Luke respectively.

2. The gospel material elsewhere, especially in the Pauline corpus, should be studied with regard to content, transmission and interpretative methods used, to see if more light might be thrown on John's use of oral and/or written sources.

3. In general the question of method and form used by the Johannine Community/the Evangelist in the handling of the gospel material should receive more emphasis. Analogous phenomena, not only in Paul but also elsewhere, should be examined and be brought more fully into the discussion.

6

The Independence of the Gospel of John:
Some Observations

Methodological Considerations

It has been my privilege to enter into a dialogue on John and the Synoptics with the scholar to whom this essay was dedicated when it was first printed in the *Festschrift* published to honour F. Neirynck in 1992. In the present study I wish to honour him by continuing this dialogue at some points. The dialogue which we have had so far, has been published in D. Dungan (ed.), *The Interrelations of the Gospels*, Leuven, 1990, pp. 408–58. My contribution, *John and the Synoptics*, covers pages 408–37. Neirynck's *John and the Synoptics. Response to P. Borgen* follows on pages 438–50, and finally my *John and the Synoptics. A Reply* is found on pages 451–58.* F. Neirynck has also published his response in his collection of essays, *Evangelica II*, Leuven, 1991, pp. 699–711, together with an additional note on pages 711–12.

There is some common ground between Neirynck and me, although the conclusions drawn by each of us differ. Neirynck formulates his agreement with me in this way: "The 'form' of expository interpretation and paraphrasing commentary can be employed in the interpretation of the Fourth Gospel ... And if any conclusion can be drawn from the 'model' of 1 Cor 11:23–25(26) and 27–34, it would be that a 'tradition' (saying or narrative) can be used by John as a starting point for further elaboration ..."[1]

---

* Reprinted at pp. 159–73 in the present book.
[1] Neirynck (1990) 450. (In the present book p. 172.)

Neirynck maintains that my analysis of the form of expository interpretation nevertheless has no relevance in a discussion about John's dependence on the Synoptics. And according to him the presence of the structure "text and commentary" allows of no conclusion about pre-Johannine or synoptic origin of this tradition.[2]

In his additional note in his *Evangelica II*, 711–12, however, Neirynck presents two viewpoints which are of importance for further dialogue: a) He does not "exclude John's use of oral-tradition or source material; . . . direct dependence on the Synoptic Gospels does not preclude the possibility of supplementary information". b) "If the fourth evangelist was a teacher and preacher in his community who knew the earlier gospels, conflation and harmonization may have been quite natural to him". Neirynck also quotes E. Simons, *Hat der dritte Evangelist den kanonischen Matthäus benutzt?* (Bonn, 1880), pp. 107–08: ". . . man hat sich eine gedächtnissmässige Aneignung vieler Partieen der Quellen zu denken, welche bei häufiger, koncentrirter und aus wenige Schriften beschränkter Lektüre, bei öffentlicher Verlesung derselben und Benutzung zum Unterricht fast von selbst zu Stande kommt, eine solche, wie wir theilweise für das Verhältniss neutestamentlicher Schriftsteller zu LXX, patristischer zum N.T., speciell zu den Evangelien, wegen der Freiheit der Citate, voraussetzen müssen".

These points made by Neirynck and Simons call for further analysis of methods and forms used by teachers or preachers in the transmission and interpretation of the oral/written sources. They also point to the relevance of examining the degree of agreements and differences which may exist between mutually independent versions of the same units of tradition. Moreover, since the teacher's or preacher's activities take place within the context of a community, then influence from the needs and functions of the community should be brought into the discussion.

When the teaching activity in this way takes place in the community, then various stages and layers in the community's use of the gospel traditions may be reflected. There seem to be three main possibilites: 1) the exposition of an oral or written tradition may have received its form in the pre-synoptic and pre-Johannine stages; the Evangelist has brought this layer of the tradition into his gospel; 2) it may result

---

[2] *ibid.*

from the Evangelist's own interpretation of some oral or written traditions which do not come from the present Synoptic Gospels; 3) the exposition may take place when one or more sections of one, two or all three Synoptic Gospels were received by the Evangelist or were subject to expository use by him. The Evangelist may have had direct access to one or more of the Synoptic Gospels, or the unit(s) of tradition may have been brought him by travelling Christians.

One difference between Neirynck and myself seems to be that he is more hesitant to consider the relevance of the points 1) and 2). Since Neirynck in the "Additional Note" mentioned above makes clear that he is open for the possibility that the Evangelist is a teacher in a community setting, and he does not exclude the possibility of the Evangelist's use of oral-tradition or source material, there seems to be a possibility for having a dialogue between us about all three stages. The challenge is then to identify features which may indicate that a certain stage or certain stages can be identified in the text. The present examination will concentrate on the analysis of specific passages assuming that the transmission/exposition was an ongoing process in the teaching activity within the Johannine community.[3] The study will not be based on any theory of one or more comprehensive written source(s) behind the Fourth Gospel, such as the theory of a *Grundschrift, Offenbarungsreden*, "Gospel of Signs", etc.[4]

Neirynck's citation from the book by Simons also makes evident that one should search for comparative material which may be of help in the analysis of John. By identifying method, form, historical situations and so forth with the assistance of observations made in sources from outside of John, the analysis can be more controllable and less subject to the danger of arbitrariness in objectifying one's own standards of consistency, and one's own opinion on the nature and degree of editorial freedom, quotations and allusions from memory, and so forth.[5] Simons suggests that such comparative examples might be found in the use which the New Testament writers

---

[3] Cf. the developed theories of the history of the community and its traditions suggested by Martyn (1979) and Brown (1979). Cf. also Dodd (1963); Lindars (1971); Ashton (1991).

[4] See the surveys in Smith (1984) 37–93.

[5] Cf. Smith (1984) 14–15.

make of the LXX, and in the Patristic use of the New Testament in general, and the gospels in particular.

The transmission and interpretation of tradition and of Scripture in Judaism should also be included, however. The glimpses which Paul gives on the kind of transmission and interpretation which existed in the middle of the first century A.D., are of special importance since he wrote his letters before the four gospels had come into existence. Accordingly this essay will concentrate on examining some passages in the Fourth Gospel and parallel material in the Synoptic Gospels. In this investigation material from Paul's First Letter to the Corinthians will be drawn on for comparison. I have already to some extent used this approach in comparing Paul's transmission and exposition of the eucharistic traditions in 1 Cor 10 and 11 with the transmission and exposition of traditions in John 12:44–50; 6:51–58; 5:1–18, and 2:13–22.

In this essay I shall attempt to bring such comparison with 1 Corinthians one step further by bringing into the analysis the sayings of Jesus in 1 Cor 7:10ff. and in 1 Cor 9:14. At points insights from Jewish sources will also utilized. The thesis is as follows: 1) The similarities between Paul's way of transmitting and interpreting Jesus-logia in the fifties A.D. and the transmission and exposition of tradition in John, strengthen the probability that this Fourth Gospel draws on a stream of traditions which was transmitted and elaborated upon in the history of the Johannine community, independently of the gospels of Matthew, Mark and Luke. 2) Insofar as some of the passages of John reflect their setting in the life of the Community, the probability is strenthened that these sections are independent of the Synoptic Gospels. 3) The investigation may also reveal other indications which support the thesis of John's independence, at least in the passages concerned.

1 Cor 7:10–16: Paul's Use of the Logion on Divorce

Scholars such as D. L. Dungan, B. Fjärstedt, D. C. Allison, and N. Walter have in recent years examined Paul and the sayings of Jesus.[6] These scholars concentrate on matters of content and compare Paul

---

[6] Dungan (1971); Fjärstedt (1974); Allison (1982) 1–32; Walter (1985) 498–522.

and the synoptics. In his essay "Paul and the Sayings of Jesus",[7] F. Neirynck gives a critical survey of these and other works and reaches the following conclusion: "In the Pauline Epistles there are two instances of an explicit reference to a command of the Lord, in 1 Cor 7:10–11 and 9:4, but there is no 'quotation' of the saying".[8] These two sayings, as rendered in 1 Cor 7:10–11 and 9:4, are then to be examined, to see if they might in turn illuminate aspects of the sayings of Jesus as rendered by John.

In 1 Cor 7:10–11 Paul refers to a saying of Jesus on divorce and adds in vv. 12ff. his own situational commentary:

The logion:
10 τοῖς δὲ γεγαμηκόσιν παραγγέλλω, οὐκ ἐγὼ ἀλλὰ ὁ κύριος, γυναῖκα ἀπὸ ἀνδρὸς μὴ χωρισθῆναι,
11 – ἐὰν δὲ καὶ χωρισθῇ, μενέτω ἄγαμος ἢ τῷ ἀνδρὶ καταλλαγήτω – καὶ ἄνδρα γυναῖκα μὴ ἀφιέναι.

The commentary:
12 τοῖς δὲ λοιποῖς λέγω ἐγώ, οὐχ ὁ κύριος·
   εἴ τις ἀδελφὸς γυναῖκα ἔχει ἄπιστον·
   καὶ αὕτη συνευδοκεῖ οἰκεῖν μετ' αὐτοῦ, μὴ ἀφιέτω αὐτήν·
13 καὶ γυνὴ ἥτις ἔχει ἄνδρα ἄπιστον,
   καὶ οὗτος συνευδοκεῖ οἰκεῖν μετ' αὐτῆς, μὴ ἀφιέτω τὸν ἄνδρα.
14 ἡγίασται γὰρ ὁ ἀνὴρ ὁ ἄπιστος ἐν τῇ γυναικί,
   καὶ ἡγίασται ἡ γυνὴ ἡ ἄπιστος ἐν τῷ ἀδελφῷ·
   ἐπεὶ ἄρα τὰ τέκνα ὑμῶν ἀκάθαρτά ἐστιν,
   νῦν δὲ ἅγιά ἐστιν.
15 εἰ δὲ ὁ ἄπιστος χωρίζεται, χωριζέσθω·
   οὐ δεδούλωται ὁ ἀδελφὸς ἢ ἡ ἀδελφὴ ἐν τοῖς τοιούτοις·
   ἐν δὲ εἰρήνῃ κέκληκεν ὑμᾶς ὁ θεός.
16 τί γὰρ οἶδας, γύναι, εἰ τὸν ἄνδρα σώσεις;
   ἢ τί οἶδας, ἄνερ, εἰ τὴν γυναῖκα σώσεις;

The words of the saying of Jesus as rendered in vv. 10–11, and Paul's use of these words in his formulations in vv. 11–16, are underscored.

---

[7] Neirynck (1991) 511–68.
[8] *ibid.*, 566.

The logion and its elaboration form part of Paul's advice regarding marriage and related matters. In 1 Cor 7:1–7 Paul deals with behaviour within marriage, in verses 8–9 with questions concerning the unmarried and widows, in verses 10–16 with divorce and mixed marriages, and in verses 17–24 with various advices based on the perspective of eschatological freedom.

The Jesus-logion in 1 Cor 7:10–11 is to be compared with the parallels in Mark 10:11–12, Matt 19:9, Matt 5:32 and Luke 16:18. The saying occurs in Mark 10:11/Matt 19:9 at the conclusion of the account of Jesus' debate with the Pharisees regarding divorce, Mark 10:1–12 and Matt 19:1–12. Matt 5:32 is one of the Antitheses, Matt 5:21–48, which in turn is part of the Sermon on the Mount. Finally, in Luke 16:18 the saying on divorce is placed between Jesus' word about the law and the prophets relative to John the Baptist and the kingdom of God, Luke 16:16–17, and the parable about the rich man and Lazarus, Luke 16:19–31.

There are several agreements and differences among the various versions found in the synoptic gospels, but for our purpose it suffices to quote two of them:

Matt 5:32   πᾶς ὁ ἀπολύον τὴν γυναῖκα αὐτοῦ παρεκτὸς λόγου
πορνείας, ποιεῖ αὐτὴν μοιχευθῆναι, καὶ ὃς ἐὰν
ἀπολελυμένην γαμήσῃ, μοιχᾶται.

ὃς ἂν ἀπολύσῃ τὴν γυναῖκα αὐτοῦ καὶ γαμήσῃ

Mark 10:11   ἄλλην, μοιχᾶται ἐπ' αὐτήν.

καὶ ἐὰν αὐτὴ ἀπολύσασα τὸν ἄνδρα αὐτῆς γαμήσῃ

12   ἄλλον, μοιχᾶται.

Paul's formulation differs from the synoptic parallels. He uses common Greek terms for divorcing a person, the verbs χωρισθῆναι (1 Cor 7:10; cf. Mark 10:9) and ἀφιέναι (1 Cor 7:11),[9] while another common term, ἀπολύειν, is used in the synoptic parallels.[10] Thus Paul and the synoptic gospels here illustrate how a saying of Jesus could

---

[9] There are no convincing reasons for regarding the verbs χωρισθῆναι and ἀφιέναι as a Pauline rewording, such as indicated by Neirynck (1991) 561.

[10] See references in Liddell and Scott (1940) on the respective verbs in 1 Cor and the synoptic gospels, and Lietzmann and Kümmel (1949) 31.

receive varied wordings. It is of interest to notice that Paul, like Mark, applies the logion in a non-Jewish way to both sexes.[11]

For the present investigation the question of content as such is not of interest. The aspect of importance is how 1 Cor 7:10ff. can give us insight into the way a saying of Jesus might be referred to and be interpreted, both with regard to method and form. As to form, the synoptic logion is preserved as a traditional casuistic rule: πᾶς ὁ... and ὃς ἐὰν... in Matt 5:32, and ὃς ἂν... ἐὰν..., Mark 10:11–12. Paul has a corresponding casuistic form in the paranthetical clause which is formulated as a condition, ἐὰν δὲ ... (v. 11), and in the subsequent commentary, εἴ τις ... (v. 12) and εἰ δὲ ... (v. 15). In v. 13 the case is expressed in a relative clause, ἥτις ... As for the Jesus-logion itself, Paul just renders it in indirect speech as a halakhic rule, without using conditional or relative clauses or participial formulations. The parallelism in the rendering reflects, however, that Paul draws on a tradition which had a relatively fixed form.[12]

In the parenthesis inserted into v. 11a, and in his commentary, vv. 12ff., Paul repeats and paraphrases the words from the saying of Jesus as cited in vv. 10 and 11. As indicated by the underscoring of words in the Greek text, Paul draws on words from the logion in his own commentary. Thus, he develops an expository application (and modification) of the Jesus-logion.

John 13:20 and Other Occurrences of a Jesus-Logion on Agency

Paul's quote and exposition of the Jesus-logion on divorce, and its synoptic parallels, can give us a better understanding of the use of tradition in John, and also throw some light on the question of John and the Synoptics. These parallels might give us insight into some of the ways in which a saying might be transmitted.

---

[11] Dungan (1971) 133, Taylor (1953) 419–20.

[12] See Schneider (1992) 194–95. Cf. that also the synoptic versions have parallelism. As for Matt 5:32, see Luz (1989) 299–300.

In my study *The Use of Tradition in John 12:46–50*, I made a survey of the varied use in the gospels of a Jesus-logion on agency.[13] The versions contained some or all of the following points: a) he who receives, etc., the agent of a sender b) receives, etc., the sender; c) he who receives, etc., the sender, who in turn himself is an agent d) does not receive the sender/agent e) he receives the sender. The logion in John 13:20 covers the following points:[14] a) ὁ λαμβάνων ἄν τινα πέμψω b) ἐμὲ λαμβάνει, c) ὁ δὲ ἐμὲ λαμβάνων d) – e) λαμβάνει τὸν πέμψαντά με. The same points are found in the parallels in Matt 10:40 and Luke 10:16, and in the different parallels in Mark 9:37 and Luke 9:48. In Mark 9:37 all the listed points from a) to e) are covered. Matt 10:40 is a close parallell to John 13:20. Matt 10:40 reads: a) ὁ δεχόμενος ὑμᾶς b) ἐμὲ δέχεται c) καὶ ὁ ἐμὲ δεχόμενος d) – e) δέχεται τὸν ἀποστείλαντά με.

The context of the saying as quoted in John 13:20 is the Last Supper and the Footwashing, John 13:1–20. The context of Matt 10:40 is the Missionary Discourse, Matt 9:36 – 11:1, and the context of Luke 10:16 is the Mission of the Seventy-Two, Luke 10:1–16. Mark 9:37 and Luke 9:37 conclude the Dispute about Greatness, Mark 9:33–37 and Luke 9:46–48.

By comparing the Jesus-logion on divorce in 1 Cor 7:10–11 and parallels in the Synoptic Gospels with the the Jesus-logion on agency in John 13:20 and parallels in the Synoptic Gospels the following observation is apparent: The circumstance that the verb used in the synoptic versions of the logion on divorce (ἀπολύειν) differs from Paul's terms (χωρισθῆναι and ἀφιέναι) is a phenomenon which is parallel to what can be observed when comparing the various versions of the Jesus-logion on agency. The basic form of the logion given in John 13:20 has the verb λαμβάνειν (cf. 12:48) and πέμπειν, while Matt 10:40, and also Mark 9:37 and Luke 9:48, have the synonymous words δέχεσθαι and ἀποστέλλειν.

From Paul's rendering of the Jesus-logion on divorce, 1 Cor 7:10–11, another observation can be made. A comparison with the more extensive forms of the parallels in the Synoptic Gospels makes it probable that Paul in 1 Cor 7:10–11 only cites parts of the Jesus-logion

---

[13] Borgen (1979) 18–35. On agency in John, see Borgen (1968) 137–48.

[14] See also *Ign. Eph.* 6:1 and *Didache* 11:4, and 1 *Clement* 42:1–2.

on divorce.[15] Correspondingly, in Luke 10:16a only two points of the logion on agency are used: a) ὁ ἀκούων ὑμῶν b) ἐμοῦ ἀκούει. c) – d) – e) – . Similarily, in John 5:23, 8:19, 12:44–45, 14:9, and 15:23 only some points of the logion are presented (cf. *Mek. Exod.* 14:31). As example, John 14:9 may be cited: a) – b) – c) ὁ ἑωρακὼς ἐμέ d) – e) ἑώρακεν τὸν πατέρα.

The conclusion is: In his varied use of the Jesus-logion on agency, John continues a method of transmission and interpretation which is demonstrated already by Paul in the fifties A.D. in his rendering of the Jesus-logion on divorce, 1 Cor 7:10–11. In mutually independent versions of the same logion different synonymous words can be used, and only parts of a logion may be cited. Thus, John's varied renderings of the logion on agency is the result of an independent process of transmission and interpretation in which the same methods are used as those demonstrated in 1 Cor 7:10–11 and Luke 10:16.

In the study *The Use of Tradition in John 12:44–50* I also substantiated the hypothesis that John 12:44–45 quotes a traditional Jesus-logion in a way which corresponds to Paul's quotation of the eucharistic tradition in 1 Cor 11:23ff.,[16] and just as in 1 Cor 11:27ff. the quote is in John 12:46–50 followed by an expository elaboration.[17] Correspondingly, as shown above, the logion on divorce is cited by Paul in 1 Cor 7:10–11, and it is followed in vv. 12–16 by a subsequent expository paraphrase of words from the logion. In v. 11 a parenthetical expository comment is inserted into the quotation of the logion. In parts of the exposition traditional (casuistic) forms are used.[18] As for Paul's use of casuistic forms in 1 Cor 7:10–16, by which the cases are formulated in conditional or relative clauses or participial phrase, John has participial phrases of the logion, ὁ πιστεύων εἰς ἐμέ in 12:44 and 46, ὁ θεωρῶν in v. 45, and from other versions of the logion, ὁ ἀθετῶν and μὴ λαμβάνων in v. 48. In v. 47 there is the casuistic form in which the case is described in a conditional clause, ἐὰν . . .

---

[15] Gerharsson (1961) 312: "Paul does not quote the saying in its entirety, but draws from it a short halakhic statement (with interpretation inserted)."

[16] Borgen (1979) 18–35.

[17] Dodd (1963) 355; Borgen (1979) 30–31. As for such sayings as typical for terminology used by commissioned agent, see Bühner (1977) 138–52.

[18] See also Ashton (1991) 541–45.

While the whole pericope in John 12:44–50 is formulated as words of Jesus, Paul distinguishes between the cited Jesus-logion and his own expository applications, as he himself writes in 1 Cor 7: "... but to the others I say, not the Lord: ..." P. Stuhlmacher stresses the importance of this distinction: "Erstens läßt sich aus einem Vergleich von 1 Kor 7:10 und 2 Kor 12:8f. leicht ersehen, wie genau Paulus zwischen seiner eigenen Anweisung und Herrenworten unterscheidet ...".[19] At other points Paul does not draw such a distinction, however. Thus in 1 Cor 7:10–11 he inserts a parenthetical specification into the Jesus-logion ("but if she is divorced, let her remain single or else be reconciled to her husband"), as if it was part of the logion. And when he cites the story of the institution of the Lord's Supper in 1 Cor 11:23–25, he elaborates on the words of Jesus in v. 26, referring to Jesus in the third person as the Lord, without drawing a distinction between the words of Jesus proper and his elaboration. Thus, C. K. Barrett rightly sees that Paul in 1 Cor 7:12 makes clear that the halakhic *application* of the Jesus-logion about divorce (vv. 10–11) to the case of mixed marriages (vv. 12–16) was his own, the reason being that Jesus had not dealt with this specific case.

The passage in John 12:44–50 is presented as words of Jesus because the traditional sayings and their exposition are woven together through revelatory inspiration.[20] It should be added, however, that John nevertheless deals with halakhic interpretation, corresponding to Paul's halakhic discussion. The themes discussed are very different, however. While Paul develops halakhic rules for marriage and divorce, John elaborates on halakhic rules of agency to describe the role of Jesus as the commissioned agent of the Father.[21]

The question should be raised if John in his extensive and varied use of the Jesus-logion on agency reflects the contexts of the logion in the Synoptic Gospels. The answer is on the whole to the negative. Nevertheless, certain observations related to John 13:20 should be made. The context of the Last Supper and the Footwashing for the logion has no parallels in the Synoptic Gospels. Nevertheless,

---

[19] Stuhlmacher (1983A) 243.

[20] See Ashton (1991) 541–45.

[21] Concerning the halakhic rules of agency, see the references in notes 13 and 17.

the saying in John 13:16, "a servant is not greater than his master; nor is an *apostolos* greater than he who sent him", has a parallel in Matt 10:24–25 (cf. Luke 6:40). Since the logion in John 13:20 has a parallel in the same Matthean chapter, in Matt 10:40, the two gospels probably drew on sayings of Jesus which were clustered together in the handing on of tradition. In terminology the two Johannine sayings and the synoptic parallels differ. Since they both deal with rules about agency, it was natural that they should be brought together in the transmission.[22]

Conclusion: Neither John 13:20 nor the extensive use of parts of this Jesus-logion throughout the Gospel reflects the contexts where it occurs in the Synoptic Gospels, Matt 10:40; Luke 10:16; Mark 9:37; Luke. 9:48. This observation and the formal parallel usage of another Jesus-logion by Paul, the one on divorce, support the view that John draws on a Jesus-logion which was transmitted and interpreted in the community, independently of the Synoptic Gospels.

John 3:3–8: An Exposition of a Logion in the Form of Question and Answer

In John 3:3–8 another logion is rendered and interpreted, this time in the form of question and answer:

The logion:
3 ἀμὴν ἀμὴν λέγω σοι,
    ἐὰν μή τις γεννηθῇ ἄνωθεν,
    οὐ δύναται ἰδεῖν τὴν βασιλείαν τοῦ θεοῦ.

Exposition:
Question (=objection):
4 λέγει πρὸς αὐτὸν ὁ Νικόδημος·
    πῶς δύναται ἄνθρωπος γεννηθῆναι γέρων ὤν;
    μὴ δύναται εἰς τὴν κοιλίαν τῆς μητρὸς αὐτοῦ δεύτερον εἰσελθεῖν
    καὶ γεννηθῆναι

---

[22] See especially Dodd (1963) 335–38. Dood argues convincingly that if John was copying Matthew, there is no logical explanation for John's omissions of parts of Matt 10:24–25, nor for the changes of the wording. See also Brown (1970) 569–70.

Answer:

5 ἀπεκρίθη Ἰησοῦς·
   ἀμὴν ἀμὴν λέγω σοι,
   ἐὰν μή τις γεννηθῇ ἐξ ὕδατος καὶ πνεύματος,
   οὐ δύναται εἰσελθεῖν εἰς τὴν βασιλείαν τοῦ θεοῦ.
6 τὸ γεγεννημένον ἐκ τῆς σαρκὸς σάρξ ἐστιν,
   καὶ τὸ γεγεννημένον ἐκ τοῦ πνεύματος πνεῦμά ἐστιν.
7 μὴ θαυμάσῃς ὅτι εἶπόν σοι, δεῖ ὑμᾶς γεννηθῆναι ἄνωθεν,
8 τὸ πνεῦμα ὅπου θέλει πνεῖ, καὶ τὴν φωνὴν αὐτοῦ ἀκούεις,
   ἀλλ' οὐκ οἶδας πόθεν ἔρχεται καὶ ποῦ ὑπάγει·
   οὕτως ἐστὶν πᾶς ὁ γεγεννημένος ἐκ τοῦ πνεύματος.

As seen by the underscoring, words from the logion in John 3:3 are being paraphrased and interpreted in vv. 4–8. Thus the logion receives an exposition similar to the expository elaboration of the logion on divorce in 1 Cor 7:10–18. The exposition in John 3:4–8 has the form of a dialogue, however. At this point the suggestion made by E. Simons in 1880 is of help when he says that the way in which the LXX is used in the New Testament may illuminate John's use of gospel material. In the case of John 3:3–8 relevant insights can even be gained from a comparison with the midrashic interpretation of the Old Testament quotation in John 6:31–58 on "bread from heaven".

More specifically, a comparison with John 6:31, 51ff. demonstrates that John here interprets the Jesus-logion in 3:3 in the same way as he interprets the Old Testament quotation in John 6:31. The Old Testament quotation is given in 6:31, and its interpretation in v. 51. Then the objection in 6:52, just as in John 3:4, is raised with the words πῶς δύναται:[23]

John 6:31, 51ff. Old Testament quotation and the interpretation:
31 . . . as it is written,
   "He gave them bread from heaven to eat"

---

[23] See Borgen (1965) 89–90; on pages 80–83 a slightly more developed form of exposition by means of question and answer (John 6:41–48) is analysed. *Mek. Exod.* 12:2 and Philo, *Mut.* 141a, 142b–44 are referred to as comparative material. It is to be noticed that the words πῶς δύναται in John 3:4 and 6:52 corresponds to the exegetical term כיצד in *Mek. Exod.* 12:2. See Bacher (1899) 77.

51 . . . and the bread . . . is my flesh.
Question (= objection):
52 The Jews then disputed among themselves, saying, "How can
(πῶς δύναται) this man give us his flesh to eat?"
Answer:
53 So Jesus said to them, "Truly, truly, I say to you, unless you eat
the flesh of the Son of Man and drink his blood, you have no
life in you . . .
55 for my flesh is truly food, and my blood is truly drink . . .".

A parallel use of question and answer is found in Philo's
interpretation of Gen 17:16 in *Mut.* 141, 142b–44:

The Old Testament quotation together with the interpretation reads:
141 . . . we must now explain "from her" (Gen 17:16).
142b . . . virtue is "the mother" of any good thing that has come
into being . . .

Question (= objection):
143 Some ask, however, whether the barren can bear children, since
the oracles earlier described Sarah as barren, and now admit
that she will become "a mother".
Answer:
It is to be said to this that it is not in the nature of a barren woman
to bear, any more than of the blind to see or of the deaf to hear.
The soul which is sterilized to wickedness and unfruitful of the
endless host of passions and vices, scarce any prosper in childbirth
as she . . .

Both in John 3:3–8, 6:31, 51–58 and in *Mut.* 141, 142–44 the same
kind of objections are raised, that of contradiction between a Jesus-
logion or a scriptural interpretation and empirical experience. In
John 3:3–8 and *Mut.* 141, 142–44 the problems have been formulated
within the context of biological and spiritual births. In John 6:31,
51–58 the problem is the distinction between eucharistic and
"cannibalistic" eating of the flesh of Jesus. The similarities in John
3:3–8, 6:31, 51–58 and Philo *Mut.* 141a, 142b–44 with regard to
expository methods and forms, and also the kinship as to the problems

discussed, show that the Johannine material has been subject to traditional exegetical approaches.

Parallels to the Jesus-logion in John 3:3 (and 5) are found in:

Matt 18:3 Ἀμὴν λέγω ὑμῖν, ἐὰν μὴ στραφῆτε καὶ γένεσθε ὡς τὰ παιδία,
οὐ μὴ εἰσέλθητε εἰς τὴν βασιλείαν τῶν οὐρανῶν.
Mark 10:15 = Luke 18:17 ἀμὴν λέγω ὑμῖν, ὃς ἂν μὴ δέξηται τὴν βασιλείαν τοῦ θεοῦ ὡς παιδίον,
οὐ μὴ εἰσέλθῃ εἰς αὐτήν.

The context of Matt 18:3 is the Dispute about Greatness, Matt 18:1–5. The logion is not found in the parallel sections in Mark 9:33–37 and Luke 9:46–48. The context of Mark 10:15 and Luke 18:17 is the story of the Blessing of the Children, Mark 10:13–16 and Luke 18:15–17. The logion is omitted from the parallel section in Matt 19:13–15.

The agreements between John and Matt/Mark/Luke are: John 3:3 and 5/Matt/Mark/Luke: ἀμὴν λέγω. John 3:5 εἰσελθεῖν (Matt εἰσέλθητε, Mark/Luke εἰσέλθῃ) εἰς τὴν βασιλείαν. The agreement between John and Mark/Luke is: John 3:3 and 5/Mark/Luke: τὴν βασιλείαν τοῦ θεοῦ, Mark/Luke in the protasis, John in apodosis. Agreement between John and Matthew: John 3:3, 5/Matt: ἐὰν μή (Mark/Luke: ὃς ἄν). Differences: Only John has a double ἀμήν. John has σοι, Matt/Mark/Luke ὑμῖν. John 3:3 reads τις γεννηθῇ ἄνωθεν and John 3:5 τις γεννηθῇ ἐξ ὕδατος καὶ πνεύματος while Matthew has στραφῆτε καὶ γένησθε ὡς τὰ παιδία, and Mark/Luke δέξηται τ. β. τ. θ. ὡς παιδίον. Only John 3:3 has ἰδεῖν τ. β. Only Mark and Luke have αὐτήν (referring to the kingdom of God). Only Matthew has τ. β. τῶν οὐρανῶν. John 3:3, 5 have οὐ δύναται while Matt/Mark/Luke have οὐ μὴ. The agreements between John and the synoptic gospels, and the fact that John here does not use his regular term "eternal life" but the "synoptic" term "kingdom of God", show that John renders a traditional logion.

B. Lindars regards the phrase γεννηθῇ ἄνωθεν, John 3:3, to be the more original and the phrase "by water and spirit" in v. 5 to be an explication of it. He then refers to the observation made by J. Jeremias that στραφῆτε καὶ γένησθε in Matt 18:3 is a Semitism = "become again". Since ἄνωθεν may mean "again", Lindars suggests that the Greek form of the logion as it came to John independently of the Synoptic Gospels was formulated with ... γένηται ἄνωθεν ὡς παιδίον ... According to Lindars John's γεννηθῇ is a deliberate change, and the Evangelist probably understood ἄνωθεν to mean "from above".[24] The problem with Lindars' interpretation is that the reconstruction seems somewhat forced, especially the change from γένηται to γεννηθῇ.

Thus, the problem as formulated by R. Schnackenburg still remains. He compares the Johannine and the Matthean versions and rightly states that they express two different principles: "Die Annahme, daß es aus Matt 18:3 bzw. Mark 10:15 umgeformt sei, bleibt schwierig, da der 4. Evangelist den Gedanken stark umgebogen hätte: Aus dem 'werden (wieder) wie die Kinder bzw wie ein Kind' hätte er ein direktes 'Kind-Werden' gemacht, daß er sehr real als Neugeburt, Neuschöpfung oder 'Zeugung von oben' verstand. Jenes ὡς gehört unlösbar zu beiden Gestalten des syn. Logions, wie umgekehrt das joh. Logion nicht auf die Umkehr des Menschen, sondern auf die Tat Gottes am Menschen abzielt".[25]

Although Schnackenburg's remark is true, still the Johannine and synoptic formulations probably had their origin in the same logion. The two aspects of man's conversion and the act of God suggest that the various formulations have developed from the same life-setting, that of the practice of baptism, cf. Acts 2:38, 1 Cor 6:9–11, and Titus 3:3–7. It is commonly held by exegetes that John 3:5 refers to baptism. For example C. K. Barrett interprets the meaning in this way: "Christian baptism so far as it was a washing with water was no more significant than John's [the Baptist's] ... Only if washing with water signified and was accompanied by the action of the Spirit could Christian baptism introduce one into the kingdom of God".[26] Thus, the logion had its *Sitz im Leben* in the performance of baptism in the Johannine community. Also in Mark and Luke the *Sitz im Leben* of the story on the blessing of the children, Mark 10:13–16 and Luke 18:15–17, probably was baptism.[27]

It has been noted that Matthew has the logion in a different pericope, the Dispute on Greatness, 18:1–5 and not like Mark and Luke in

---

[24] Lindars (1981) 289–92.

[25] Schnackenburg (1965) 381.

[26] Barrett (1978) 209.

[27] See Cullmann (1948), in particular "Anhang".

the story of the Blessing of the Children. Matthew has in Matt 18:1–5 inserted the logion, since it does not occur in the parallel sections in Mark 9:33–37 and Luke 9:46–48. Although Matthew has the logion in this dispute about greatness, the verb στραφῆτε in Matt 18:3 refers to conversion since it occurs in an "admission-logion": "unless you turn (στραφῆτε) and become like children, you will never enter the kingdom of heaven". A similar meaning of the verb is found in John 12:40 and in *Sib. Or.* 3:625. Since conversion and baptism belong together both in the work of John the Baptist, Mark 1:4 and Luke 3:3, and in early Christianity, Acts 2:38, etc., the wording of the Matthean version of the logion is easily also associated with baptism.

There are observations which suggest that the formulation of the logion in John 3:5 is primary rather than the version in 3:3. The phrase εἰσελθεῖν εἰς τὴν βασιλείαν τοῦ θεοῦ, John 3:5 and parallel phrases in Matt 18:3 and Mark 10:15 / Luke 18:17 supports this view. The use in John 3:3 of ἰδεῖν instead of εἰσελθεῖν in v. 5 seems to be a Johannine interpretation.[28] Moreover, the circumstance that the misunderstanding of ἄνωθεν, "again" or "from above" is possible only in Greek also indicates that the version of the logion in John 3:3 is secondary to the one in v. 5. Thus, the logion had its primary setting in the baptismal activity of the Johannine community, and the Evangelist has placed the main version of the logion in the answer given by Jesus to Nicodemus' objection.

As was the case in 1 Cor 7:10–11 relative to the synoptic parallels, so also is the case in John 3:3–8 relative to the synoptic parallels: in mutually independent versions of the same logion different, but corresponding wordings can be used.

1 Cor 9:14: The Logion on the Support of Apostles

In 1 Cor 9:14 Paul renders another Jesus-logion: ". . . the Lord commanded that 'those who proclaim the gospel should get their living by the gospel'". The basis for Paul's argument in 1 Cor 9 is his experience of seeing the risen Lord and being commissioned

---

[28] Lindars (1981) 289. Although the idea of "seeing" is Johannine, the background is probably Jewish mystical traditions about seeing God's kingdom, cf. Wis 10:10. See Dahl (1962) 124–42. Cf. also Luke 9:27.

by him as an apostle, that is, as the Lord's commissioned agent: "Am I not an apostle? Have I not seen Jesus our Lord?" (1 Cor 9:1; cf. 15:6–10; Gal 1:15–16; Acts 1:22). The presupposition is the understanding that it was constitutive for the apostles that they had seen the risen Lord.[29]

In order to defend his claim to apostleship Paul makes emphatically clear that he has the same right to receive support, just as the other apostles, although he has not made use of this right. In 1 Cor 9:13–14 he argues by drawing an analogy between the temple staff and those who proclaim the gospel. As the rule for those who proclaim the gospel, the Jesus-logion is cited in v. 14: τοῖς τὸ εὐαγγέλιον καταγγέλλουσιν ἐκ τοῦ εὐαγγελίου ζῆν. The same meaning is expressed in Luke 10:7 and Matt 10:10: ἄξιος γὰρ ὁ ἐργάτης τοῦ μισθοῦ αὐτοῦ (Matt τῆς τροφῆς αὐτοῦ).

There is no agreement at all between 1 Cor 9:14 and Luke 10:7 as far as vocabulary goes, but both sayings formulate the same principle. Since Paul refers to a specific function, that of proclaiming the gospel, his formulation may be a halakhic application and specification of a more general Jesus-logion like the one in Luke 10:7 and Matt 10:10.[30] It is worth noticing that Paul applies this Jesus logion to his own commission as apostle, a commission given him through the appearance of the risen Lord.[31]

A corresponding phenomenon is seen when comparing the saying of Jesus rendered in John 20:23 with the parallels in Matt 18:18 and 16:19.

John 20:23   ἄν τινων ἀφῆτε τὰς ἁμαρτίας, ἀφέωνται αὐτοῖς.
              ἄν τινων κρατῆτε, κεκράτηνται.
Matt 16:19   καὶ ὃ ἐὰν δήσῃς ἐπὶ τῆς γῆς ἔσται δεδεμένον
              ἐν τοῖς οὐρανοῖς,

---

[29] Tomson (1990) 146–47; Barrett (1971) 200–01.

[30] Gerhardsson (1961) 318. Cf. Dungan (1971) 78–80.

[31] There is much discussion among scholars on the question whether Paul knew some version of the missionary discourse. The following scholars are inclined to answer to the affirmative: Dungan (1971) 140; Fjärstedt (1974) 99: Allison (1982) 12–13. Allison has refined his position in Allison (1985) 369–75; Tuckett (1983) 612, and with more reservation in Tuckett (1984) 376–81.

καὶ ὃ ἐὰν λύσῃς ἐπὶ τῆς γῆς ἔσται λελυμένον
ἐν τοῖς οὐρανοῖς.

Matt 18:18   ὅσα ἐὰν δήσητε ἐπὶ τῆς γῆς ἔσται δεδεμένα ἐν
οὐρανῷ,
καὶ ὅσα ἐὰν λύσητε ἐπὶ τῆς γῆς ἔσται λελυμένα
ἐν οὐρανῷ.

The contexts in which the sayings occur differ. The saying in John 20:23 concludes the story of one of the appearances of the risen Jesus, at which he commissions his disciples on the basis of the halakhic rule of agency, here more precisely the rule of substitution, John 20:19–23. In Matt 16:19 Jesus commissions Peter after Peter has confessed Jesus as the Christ, the Son of God, Matt 16:13–20. Matt 18:18 is part of the pericope on Reproving One's Brother, Matt 18:15–19. It is then evident that the setting in John 20:19–23 is quite different from the settings of the parallels in Matthew.

When comparing John 20:23 with 1 Cor 9:14, the following observations are of interest for the present discussion: Both John 20:19–23 and 1 Cor 9:1ff. deal with the commissioning by the risen Jesus, of the disciples in John, of Paul and the other apostles in 1 Cor. In 1 Cor 9:1 the commissioning is referred to in the form of rhetorical questions: "Am I not an apostle? Have I not seen Jesus the Lord?" Correspondingly, John 20:20 reads ". . . the disciples were glad when they saw the Lord. Jesus said . . . 'As the Father has sent me, even so I send you' . . .".[32]

Within these parallel contexts Paul has in 1 Cor 9:14 a logion concerning the support of the agents (apostles) commissioned by Jesus, while John in John 20:23 reports on the commission itself. As already mentioned, there is no agreement at all between the Jesus-logion 1 Cor 9:14 and the parallel in Luke 10:7 as far as vocabulary goes, but both sayings formulate the same principle on support of Jesus' commissioned agents. Correspondingly, there is no agreement between the Jesus-logion in John 20:23 and the parallels in Matt 16:19 and 18:18 as far as vocabulary goes, but the sayings formulate the same principle about the charge given to Jesus' commissioned agents. Thus Paul in 1 Cor 9:14 and Matthew in 10:10 and Luke

---

[32] The words "As the Father sent me, even so I send you" is a commissioning formula based on the logion on agency, John 13:20. See Bühner (1977) 252.

in 10:7 demonstrate how a Jesus-logion about support may be given entirely different wordings in the process of transmission, just as also is the case with regard to the logion on the commission, as rendered in John 20:23 and Matt 16:19 and 18:18.

Still another correspondence might be mentioned: Just as the logion on support as rendered by Paul in 1 Cor 9:14 seems to be a halakhic specification of a more generally formulated rule as exemplified by the parallels in Matthew and Luke, so also John in 20:23 renders a more specified form than the parallels in Matthew, since only here the commission is defined as the authority to forgive or retain sins. This specification is not made by the Evangelist himself, however, since the expressions ἀφιέναι ἁμαρτίας and κρατεῖν are never found in John, apart from this one place.[33] In his discussion of John 20:23 Dodd's conclusion is: "We seem driven to postulate an alternative form of tradition regarding the authority committed to the apostles by the Lord, akin to, though not identical with, the tradition followed by Matthew, an alternative form which the Fourth Evangelist has independently followed".[34]

John 2:13–22; 5:1–18 and 6:51–58

It remains to connect the present study to some points in my previous research on John relative to the Synoptic Gospels.[35] In my book *Bread from Heaven* the institution of the Lord's Supper in 1 Cor 11:23–25 was brought into the investigation of John 6:51–58. Parts of this eucharistic tradition is also used by Paul in 1 Cor 10:3–4, 16, 17, 21 and 11:26–29(39). In the study *The Use of Tradition in John 12:44–50*, and in *John and the Synoptics* this approach was further developed. The insights gained were the following:[36]

---

[33] Dodd (1963) 348. See also Vögtle (1971) 251: Vögtle understands John 20:23 to be "vorjohanneische spezifierende Überlieferungsvariante zu der Matt 18:18 bezeugten Urform".

[34] Dodd (1963) 349. See also Barrett (1978) 571, and Brown (1970) 1023–24 and 1030–31.

[35] It would go beyond the limits of this essay to include my study in Borgen (1959) 246–59.

[36] Borgen (1990) 410–11. (In the present book p. 124.)

1. A comparison between 1 Cor 10:3–4, 16, 17, 21; 11:23–29 and Mark 14:22–25 makes possible the following generalizations: Between mutually independent versions (units of oral/written tradition) there may be close verbal agreements in the form of sentences, word pairs and set-phrases, single words and/or corresponding variant terms.

The agreements between John 2:13–22; 6:51–58 and the Synoptics are not closer, nor more striking, than those between the above mentioned Pauline passages and Mark, and, in the case of John 5:1–18, the agreements are even fewer.

Thus, our analysis of these three Johannine passages supports the hypothesis that John and the Synoptics here are mutually independent.

2. What is the nature of the tradition behind the gospels? The passages examined in 1 Cor 10 and 11 show that units of tradition were received and handed on and that they were used and activated in the Christian communities (1 Cor 11:23–25(26)). Some modifications took place in the process, but the formulations were quite stable even during decades of transmission (cf. 1 Cor 11:23–26 with Mark 14:22–25). Interpretative activity is also evident. The exposition could have the form of a commentary attached to a cited unit of tradition. In this way 1 Cor 11:(26)27–34 is attached to the quoted institution of the Lord's Supper in vv. 23–25(26), and John 5:10–18 is attached to the story in vv. 1–9. In the same manner John 2:17–22 is attached as an exposition of the cleansing of the temple in vv. 13–16. The unit of tradition may also be presupposed, and not quoted, as is the case in the discussion of the Lord's Supper in 1 Cor 10:3–4, 16, 17, 21 and in John 6:51–58.

3. The expositions have largely the form of paraphrases of sentences, phrases, word sets, and words from the given tradition. Synonyms may be used, and expressions may be rephrased. In the expository paraphrase, words and fragments from the tradition may be moulded into traditional form.

As for the placement of the passages in the various stages in the process of transmission, some observations were made: a) There is a similarity of sequence between John 2:13–18, where the cleansing of the temple is followed by the request for a sign, and Mark 11:15–19, the cleansing, which in 11:26 is followed by the controversy concerning the authority of Jesus. As suggested by Dodd, Brown and others, it is probable that Mark has split up what belonged together in the pre-Markan stage of the tradition. This observation speaks in favour of placing John 2:13–18 in stage 1 mentioned above, the pre-synoptic and pre-Johannine stage.[37] b) As for John 5:1–18 and its subsequent context, it is seen that the Evangelist has more interest in the christological aspect as such than in the Sabbath question. Accordingly, in the discussion which follows in John 5:19ff. phrases and terms about the Sabbath and the Sabbath controversy are not repeated any more, whereas the christological idea in John 5:17 ("My Father is at work even till now, and so I am at work too") is developed. The life setting of John 5:1–18 thus concerns the controversy between the church and the Synagogue, in which Christology, the Sabbath and the Law of Moses were woven together as central issues. That stage of the controversy seems to belong to the past, and John 5:1–18 therefore probably are to be placed in the pre-Johannine stage.[38]

Some further observations were also made with regard to John 6:51–58. The agreements in wording, style and content between John 6:51–58 and 1 Cor 10:3–4, 16, 17, 21 and 11:23–29 show that John draws on eucharistic and manna traditions in a way similar to Paul: These similarities show that John is here closer to Paul than to the Synoptics, without being dependent on 1 Cor, however. Thus, John utilizes an independent tradition on the institution of the Lord's Supper, and presupposes that the eucharistic tradition already was associated with the biblical stories on the manna and the well. The Johannine version of the institution, in which the term ἡ σάρξ and not τὸ σῶμα was used, is also documented by Ignatius' and Justin's eucharistic use of the term ἡ σάρξ.[39] The conclusion is that John 6:51–58 belongs to the stage 2 as outlined above: the passage results from the Evangelist's own interpretation of oral or written traditions which do not come from the present Synoptic Gospels. These observations and this conclusion show that Neirynck's view is inadequate when he only allows for supplementary use of oral-tradition or source material in addition to John's direct dependence on the Synoptic Gospels. John 6:51–58 together with its context demonstrates

---

[37] ibid., pp. 434–35 (In the present book pp. 153-55.)

[38] ibid., p. 431. (In the present book p. 149.)

[39] ibid., pp. 422 and 454. (In the present book pp. 138 and 177.)

that in John traditions not taken from the Synoptic Gospels play
a central role.

Conclusion

a) It is probable that John 2:13–18 basically comes from stage 1
mentioned at the outset, the pre-synoptic and pre-Johannine stage.
The controversies of John 5:1–18 seem to belong to the past, and
the pericope therefore is to be placed in the pre-Johannine stage.

b) All the other Johannine texts examined in this essay, including
John 6:51–58, belong in their present form to layer 2: The Evangelist
has by means of conventional expository methods and forms interpreted
some oral (or written) traditions which do not come from the present
Synoptic Gospels. In substance they are based on pre-synoptic gospel
tradition (stage 1), and reflect the process of transmission and
exposition in the Johannine community. This understanding receives
undergirding from the circumstance that John 3:5 has its setting
in the practice of baptism in the community, and John 6:51–58 draw
on traditions from its eucharistic celebration, and finally, John 20:19–23
express the self-understanding of the community as to its mission.

c) In the transmission and exposition of sections studied in this
essay, the relationship between the Johannine tradition and the
parallell synoptic tradition is of similar nature to the relationship
between 1 Cor 7:10–16; 9:14; 10:3–4, 16, 17, 20, 21, and 11:23–29
and the pre-synoptic tradition.

7

John 6: Tradition,
Interpretation and Composition

In 1975 I had the privilege of reading a paper at the twenty-sixth Biblical Conference of Louvain, Belgium, under the chairmanship of Professor M. de Jonge. Ten years later I served as the local host of the 40th General Meeting of *Studiorum Novi Testamenti Societas* at the University of Trondheim, Norway, and the President in charge was Professor de Jonge. On many other occasions I have had the privilege of learning greatly from his scholarship and of being enriched by his friendship. It was therefore with pleasure and gratitude that this essay was first published as a contribution to his Festschrift in 1993. In the essay I shall add some insights on a question which has engaged me for many years, the intriguing ch. 6 in the Gospel of John.

There are many puzzling problems in chapter 6. First, the collective designations of people vary. In 6:1–40 one reads about the disciples (vv. 1–21), the crowd, ὁ ὄχλος, the men, ὁ ἄνθρωποι, and then, in 6:41–58 the term "the Jews", οἱ Ιουδαῖοι, is used. Finally, when the general reaction to Jesus' discourse is told in 6:60–71, only the reaction of many among the disciples, οἱ μαθηταί, etc. are mentioned. Second, the term "sign", σημεῖον (σημεῖα) seems to have different meanings in vv. 2 and 14, and in v. 26, and v. 30. Although the crowd, according to v. 14 has seen a sign, they still ask for one in v. 30, and Jesus says in v. 26 that the crowd does not seek him because they saw a sign, although according to vv. 14–15 they saw the sign and therefore thought he was a prophet and wanted to make him king. Third, there is the long-debated question of relating the eucharistic formulations in vv. 51ff. to the preceding section of Jesus' discourse.[1]

In *Bread from Heaven*[2] I concentrated on the analysis of John 6:31–58, understood as an exposition of the scriptural quotation in v. 31b, "bread from heaven he gave them to eat". There is a need for looking more closely at chapter 6 as a whole and its thematic ties to the end of chapter 5, however. More recent scholarly analysis both by others and myself should also be brought into the investigation.

Jesus is not just the Prophet-like-Moses, John 6:1–21

The persons mentioned in this section are: Jesus, the disciples (with name-specifications in vv. 5–8), a lad (v. 9), and a large crowd (vv. 2 and 5: ὁ ὄχλος πολύς) and the people (vv. 10 and 14 ὁι ἄνθρωποι, numbering 5000, v. 10). In v. 4 there is a reference to "the Jews". The two stories narrate the actions and reactions among Jesus, the disciples and the crowd. Oral dialogue takes place between Jesus and Philip/Andrew in vv. 5–10a, and words said by Jesus as a greeting to the disciples are recorded in v. 20. There is no dialogue between Jesus and the large crowd/the people, but a report on what the people said (among themselves) is given in v. 14: ". . . they said, ' This is indeed the prophet who is to come into the world'".

This section begins with a general statement about "the signs which Jesus did on those who were diseased" (v. 2) and then one particular sign follows, the feeding of the 5000 (vv. 3–13). In vv. 14–21 the effects of the event are described – on the one hand the effect on the people and subsequently on Jesus (vv. 14–15), and on the other hand on the disciples and Jesus (vv. 16–21).

The story of the feeding of the 5000 in John 6:1–13 renders one version of a tradition which is narrated in all the four gospels, Matt 14:13–21; Mark 6:32–44, and Luke 9:10–17. The brief subsequent section, John 6:14–15, has no parallel in the synoptic gospels. These verses show the effect which the event had on the crowd, and how Jesus reacted to the crowd's understanding and action. The crowd understood the feeding miracle to have a meaning beyond itself. They thought the event showed Jesus to be prophet and king (like

---

[1] See commentaries and the survey given by Schenke (1985) 68–75.

[2] Borgen (1965).

Moses[3]), "When the people saw the sign which he had done, they said, 'This is indeed the prophet who is to come into the world!' (v. 14); 'Perceiving then that they were about to come and take him by force to make him king, Jesus withdrew again to the hills by himself'" (v. 15).

In John 6:16–21 the crowd is not in the picture, but "his disciples" who are seen as a distinct group. They got into a boat and crossed the sea. While a strong wind was blowing and the sea was becoming rough, Jesus came to them "walking on the sea and drawing near to the boat" (v. 19).

The two stories primarily tell about how Jesus acted in feeding the crowd and how they reacted – they wanted to make him king. This led to a responding action on Jesus' part – he withdrew to the hills. The reaction of the disciples was also in the form of an action – they went away across the sea.

While maintaining that the evangelist interpreted the feeding miracle meaningfully, J. Painter thinks that the same evangelist reported the story of the sea-crossing because it was already attached to the feeding story in the received tradition. But, according to Painter, the evangelist has used the story to good effect as it dramatically separates Jesus from the crowd which had followed him into the desert.[4]

When Painter interprets the sea-crossing (6:16–21) as an extension of the story of the miraculous feeding (6:1–15), he does not take seriously the fact that the disciples and Jesus are the persons mentioned in the sea-crossing, and not the crowd. The story of the crossing of the sea, therefore, has quite a central function. It makes clear that although Jesus withdrew from the crowd, the opposite happened to the disciples: he acted by miraculously coming to them.[5] Here, as elsewhere, John has made the traditional story express an idea which was central to him. The crowd misjudged the meaning of

---

[3] See especially Meeks (1967).

[4] Painter (1991) 226–27. The same view was already expressed in Painter (1989) 430–31.

[5] See Borgen (1965) 180, n. 1: "According to v. 15, the feeding miracle brought the people to the non-spiritual and external wish to make Jesus king. For the disciples, on the other hand, it resulted in a theophanic encounter with the Son of God, vv. 16–21. Barrett (1978) 279–80, finds this interpretation to be plausible.

the feeding miracle, while the disciples had an authentic and epiphanic encounter with Jesus.

The works done by Jesus are called signs. What is the definition of the term "sign", σημεῖον, in this context? John describes the miracles of Jesus both by the term "works", ἔργα, as in 5:36, and by the term "signs", σημεῖα, as in 6:2. The term "sign" suggests that the miracle has a function beyond itself in the form of carrying a certain meaning or creating a certain effect. The meanings or effects may vary somewhat, and the precise and detailed description of the term must therefore be made within the context in which it is used. In 6:14–15 the designation "sign" implies that the feeding miracle was understood to have a function beyond itself and to activate the people's expectations of a coming prophet/king. By withdrawing from the people at that point Jesus made clear that they had misunderstood the significance of his actions.

The Son of Man – the Father's Accredited Envoy, John 6:22–27

Verses 6:22–24 seem at first to be very confused, and the apparent obscurity has caused several variant readings to appear in the manuscripts.[6] The structure of the verses takes on meaning, however, when one realizes that John here repeats phrases from and makes references to the preceding stories and adds interpreting words.[7] In this way it is seen that in v. 22 he refers to the story of the crossing of the sea by the disciples (vv. 16–21). In vv. 23–24a he refers to the story about the feeding, while in vv. 24b–25a the crowd is brought to the destination of the disciples' crossing, Capernaum. Some of the repeated words are common to both stories, of course. In the following the words from the two stories are underscored.

From the crossing of the sea:
v. 22   ὁ <u>ὄχλος</u> ὁ ἑστηκὼς <u>πέραν</u> <u>τῆς θαλάσσης</u> εἶδον
ὅτι <u>πλοιάριον</u> ἄλλο οὐκ ἦν ἐκεῖ εἰ μὴ ἕν, καὶ

---

[6] See Barrett (1978) 285.

[7] Cf. Schnackenburg (1971) 44–47. Schnackenburg attempts to reconstruct a picture of the details in the movements of the crowd(s) as to timing and geography. His analysis demonstrates, however, that the text as it stand is not consistent.

ὅτι οὐ συνεισῆλθεν τοῖς μαθηταῖς αὐτοῦ ὁ Ἰησοῦς εἰς
  τὸ πλοῖον
ἀλλὰ μόνοι οἱ μαθηταὶ αὐτοῦ ἀπῆλθον.

From the feeding of the 5000:
v. 23 ἄλλα ἦλθεν πλοιάρια ἐκ Τιβεριάδος ἐγγὺς τοῦ τόπου
         ὅπου ἔφαγον ἄρτον [εὐχαριστήσαντος τοῦ κυρίου].[8]
v. 24 ὅτε οὖν εἶδεν ὁ ὄχλος ὅτι Ἰησοῦς οὐκ ἔστιν ἐκεῖ οὐδὲ οἱ
         μαθηταὶ αὐτοῦa

To Capernaum:
         ἐνέβησαν αὐτοὶ εἰς τὰ πλοιάρια καὶ ἦλθον εἰς
         Καφαρναοὺμ ζητοῦντες Ἰησοῦν.
v. 25 καὶ εὑρόντες αὐτὸν πέραν τῆς θαλάσσης εἶπον αὐτῷ

The elaborations emphasize that Jesus was not found with his disciples
when they crossed the sea. Neither was he present at the place where
the feeding miracle took place. After searching in vain in these two
places, the crowd looked for Jesus in Capernaum where they found
him. They asked where he had been:

v. 25: And having found him . . . they said to him:
  'Rabbi, when did you come here?'
v. 26: Jesus answered them,
  'Truly, truly, I say to you,
  You seek (ζητεῖτε) me, not because you saw signs, but because
  you ate your fill from the loaves.
v. 27: Do not labour for the food which perishes,
  but for the food which endures to eternal life,
  which the Son of Man will give to you;
  for this is the one whom God the Father has sealed'.

Jesus criticizes the crowd for having searched for him for the wrong
reason (v. 26) and then challenges them not to labour for perishable
food, but for food which endures to eternal life, which the Son of
Man will give, for on him God the Father put his seal.

---

[8] See Schnackenburg (1971) about the words in brackets which are lacking in
some mss and may be an added gloss.

It is important to notice that the main point in v. 27 is not the search by the crowd nor the choice as such with which Jesus confronts them but the seal which God the Father put on the Son of man. In order to understand this saying the term σφραγίζω, "to seal", must be examined. The use of the word here is debated by the exegetes.[9] B. F. Westcott has suggested that the sealing refers to Jesus' consecration unto death by the Father.[10] A similar argument is entertained by J. Marsh, who sees the aorist as a "prophetic perfect", which refers to the future glory of the cross and resurrection.[11] For B. Lindars the sealing tells that Jesus is chosen or marked out.[12] M.-J. Lagrange and G. H. C. Macgregor think that it is the authority of Jesus' miracle-working power that is referred to, including the miracle of the incarnation itself.[13] R. E. Brown emphasizes the idea that God sets his seal on the Son, not so much by way of approval, but more by way of consecration.[14] C. K. Barrett understands 'the sealing' to mean that it is "God the Father who attests to the authority and truth of Jesus".[15]

Moloney follows Barrett and defines the meaning in this way: "What is being said here is: 'You must work for the bread which endures for eternity; that bread will be given to you in the revelation of the Son of man. It is to the Son of man, and to him alone, that God has given such authority; what he reveals is the authentic revelation of God'".[16] This understanding by Barrett and Moloney is appropriate to the use of the term σφραγίζω here. An even more precise meaning can be given, however. In Liddell and Scott's Greek-English Lexicon the meaning of the word in John 6:27 and 2 Cor 1:22 is defined as "accredit as an envoy".[17] This interpretation is confirmed by the equivalent Hebrew and Aramaic word חם, to

---

[9] For the following, see Moloney (1978) 113–14.

[10] Westcott (1892) 100.

[11] Marsh (1968) 295.

[12] Lindars (1972) 255.

[13] Lagrange (1927) 173; MacGregor (1928) 138–39.

[14] Brown (1966) 261.

[15] Barrett (1978) 287.

[16] Moloney (1978) 114.

[17] Liddell and Scott (1940) 1742.

seal, which, as seen from M. Jastrow's Dictionary, is the technical term for sealing and signing as a witness.[18] An understanding along this line has been suggested by R. Schnackenburg: "Just as the One Sent by God (3.34) brings the testimony about the Father (cf. 3.35) from the heavenly world, so also the Father gives testimony about the Son (5:32, 37; 8:18)".[19]

The verb in John 6:27 has aorist form and refers to the sealing as a past event. This event is probably the commissioning of the Son of Man as the Father's emissary, as the Son of Man who descended from heaven (John 3:13).[20] This commissioning is indicated in several places in John, as in John 12:49: "For I have not spoken of myself, but the Father who sent me has himself given me commandment what to say and what to speak".[21]

The Manna-bread from Heaven, the Sign of the Son of Man, John 6:28–59

This section, John 6:28–59, consists of a dialogue between "they", that is, the crowd (vv. 28, 30, 34) and Jesus (vv. 29, 32, 35) which results in reactions and objections among the Jews (vv. 41, 52) followed by comments and answers given by Jesus (vv. 43, 53).

In John 6:59 it is written that Jesus said this in a Synagogue, as he taught at Capernaum. C. K. Barrett comments: "At v. 24 we learned that the scene was Capernaum, but the discourse with its interruptions suggests a less formal occasion than a Synagogue sermon".[22] Against Barrett, it must be said that questions and answers, direct exegesis and problem-solving exegesis were part of the discourses in the

---

[18] Jastrow (no date) 513–14.

[19] Schnackenburg (1971) 50.

[20] See Borgen (1983B) 138–42. As for the concept of agency in John, see Borgen (1983) 121–32. See further Bühner (1977).

As Jewish background material for God's, the Father's, sealing of the Son of Man, one might refer to the figures of Logos, Metatron and Yahoel, upon whom the name of God was, as understood from exegesis of Exod 23:20: ". . . for My name is on him"; Philo, *Migr*. 173–75; *b. Sanh*. 38b; 3 *Enoch* 12:5; *Ap. Ab*. 10. See Borgen (1993) 246–68.

[21] See Borgen (1979) 18–35.

[22] Barrett (1978) 300.

212 EARLY CHRISTIANITY AND HELLENISTIC JUDAISM

Synagogue. All of these elements are found in rabbinic midrashim, as for example in *Mekilta on Exodus*, as well as in Philo's commentaries. A glimpse into such practice is given by Philo in his description of the Therapeutai. When they assemble the leader "examines (ζητεῖ) some points in the sacred writings, or also solves (ἐπιλύεται) that which is propounded by another" (*Contempl.* 75). The term ζητέω and the composite verb ἐπιζητέω are used elsewhere in Philo's writings when an exegetical question is raised, such as in *Opif.* 77, "One might examine (ἐπιζητήσειε) the reason because of which . . .", cf. *Spec.* 1:214; *Leg. all.* 1:33; 1:48; 1:91; 2:103, and *Quaest. in Gen.* 1:62 (Greek fragment). Answers and solutions are given, and in *Leg. all.* 3:60 the verb λύω is used, corresponding to the use of the composite verb ἐπιλύω used in *Contempl.* 75. In *Contempl.* 79 the leader is said to have discoursed, διαλέγομαι, and since questions and answers were part of the discourse, the verb means "discuss". In Philo's commentary *Questions and Answers on Genesis and Exodus*, a question or a specific view is introduced by simple formulas, for example by phrases such as "some say" (*Quaest. in Gen.* 1:8; 2:64, and 3:13, cf. *Opif.* 77); or just "why" (*Quaest. in Gen.* 1:1; 2:13, 64, etc.) or "what" (*Quaest. in Gen.* 2:15, 59).

Thus in Philo's expositions, such as those seen in the *Allegorical Commentary* and elsewhere, direct exposition of a scriptural quotation is often interrupted by a question or an objection, and in *Quaest. in Gen.* a question is raised at the very outset, and direct exegesis and objections may then be given, as for example in *Quaest. in Gen.* 2:28.

The question:
  "What is the meaning of the words
  'He brought the spirit over the earth and the water ceased'?"
Interpretation:
  "Some would say that by 'spirit' is meant the wind through which the flood ceased."
Objection and alternative interpretation:
  "But I myself do not know of water being diminished by wind
  . . .
  Accordingly, (Scripture) now seems to speak of the spirit of the Deity . . ."

Against this background the following conclusion can be drawn: in John 6:30ff. John draws from the gospel tradition the claims that Jesus was asked to give a sign and that he gave his answer.[23] When John elaborates upon this tradition in 6:30–58, he develops the exegesis of an Old Testament quotation into learned midrashic expositions. Thus, the reference to a Synagogue as the setting (John 6:59) is appropriate.

The analysis from John 6:28 should be continued against the background of these observations. John 6:28 is a further discussion of the word ἐργάζεσθε in v. 27. The crowd asks Jesus: "What must we do, then, to 'work' the works of God (ἐργαζώμεθα τὰ ἐργα τοῦ θεοῦ)?" Although the term in v. 28 means "perform a work" and not as in v. 27 "to work for food" it has vv. 22–27 as background – the crowd acted wrongly and misunderstood the multiplication of the loaves to mean that the eschatological manna miracle was of earthly nature. Jesus corrects them and tells them to work for the food which endures to eternal life. In vv. 28ff. the crowd then logically asks what they shall do to receive the proper food.

In John 6:28 the crowd asks Jesus to define his understanding of the notion "the works of God", that is, the works willed by God. In v. 29 Jesus defines the term, but in the singular, "this is the work (τὸ ἐργόν) of God, that you believe in him whom he sent". On this basis they ask Jesus to provide the legitimation so as to demonstrate that he is to be identified as "him whom he (God) sent".[24] The question about the works/work which the crowd was to perform, has in this way been related to what Jesus could do to demonstrate his own identity as the Father's commissioned envoy (v. 30). "So they said to him, 'then what sign do you do (ποιεῖς), that we may see, and believe you? What work do you perform (ἐργάζη)?'" The dialogue form is appropriate to such a change of meaning given to ἐργάζομαι and ἐργα/ἐργον in vv. 28ff.

In v. 31 they refer to the manna miracle: "Our fathers ate the manna in the wilderness; as it is written, 'He gave them bread from heaven to eat'". This reference is strange, since according to vv. 14–15, as a reaction to the multiplication of the loaves, they understood

---

[23] See John 2:18; Matt 16:1ff./Mark 8:11ff.; cf. Matt 21:23ff./Mark 11:27ff./Luke 20:1ff.

[24] On agency in John, see references in n. 20.

Jesus to be a prophet, that is, the prophet like Moses (Deut 18:15, 18). If so, they already regarded the feeding miracle to be an eschatological event corresponding to the manna miracle in the desert (Exod 16). Against this background the repeated reference to the manna miracle in John 6:30–31 is puzzling, since they seemingly once more ask for the same sign that they already had experienced.

Exegetes have suggested various solutions to this problem. R. E. Brown states that it is difficult to reconcile the request for bread (vv. 30–31) with the indication that this is the same crowd that saw the multiplication of the loaves the day before. In his comments on v. 14 he writes: "Most likely this is a reference to the expectation of the prophet-like-Moses . . . for in v. 31 these people draw a connection between the food supplied by Jesus and the manna given by Moses".[25] As a response to Brown's interpretation, one must say that in v. 14 the crowd already seems to have understood the feeding miracle as an event corresponding to the manna miracle, since they thought that Jesus was the prophet-like-Moses. If so, Brown does not explain why the crowd in vv. 30ff. again ask Jesus to perform the manna miracle as a sign.

R. Schnackenburg thinks that vv. 2 (signs = healing miracles) and 15 (they wanted to make him king) express the misinterpretation of the signs by the crowd, while v. 14 formulates the understanding as intended by the Evangelist – Jesus was to be confessed as the prophet-like-Moses who actually exceeded Moses. When according to v. 31 the crowd asked for a sign similar to the manna given in the desert, it is to be seen as a literary device used by the Evangelist: "Wenn man diese Überleitung als literarisches Vorgehen des Evangelisten betrachtet, fällt die mehrfach erwähnte Schwierigkeit weg (oder wird begreiflich), dass die Teilnehmer an der Speisung ein Verlangen äussern, da sie nach dem von Jesus gewirkten Zeichen und ihrem eigenen Bekenntnis (V 14) als erfüllt ansehen sollten."[26] M. J. J. Menken rightly objects to Schnackenburg's interpretation, that it is the same crowd who pronounces both the confession of

---

[25] Brown (1966) 234.

[26] Schnackenburg (1971) 53; see also pages 31–32. Painter (1991) 230–31 seems mainly to see John 6:31 as a verse which introduces the theme of manna as a crucial issue in the subsequent conflict with the Jews, 6:49–58.

6:14 and the question of 6:30–31, and John does not indicate in his text a shift from one level of meaning to another.[27]

According to E. Haenchen the contradiction between the request for a sign in John 6:30–31 and the sign mentioned in v. 14 should not be taken seriously: "... der Evangelist will hier keine psychologisch durchsichtige Darstellung der Reaktionen bei den Hörern bringen. Die Zeichenforderung der Juden zeigt freilig einmal, wie unfähig die Menschen sind, die erlebten Zeichen als solche zu erfassen. Zum andern schafft der Evangelist sich damit den Übergang zum eigentlichen Thema, dem er zustrebt: das Himmelbrot."[28]

The contradiction disappears, however, if one understands vv. 30–31 along the lines suggested by Menken.[29] Then these verses are to be seen precisely as a restatement of the crowd's view that the feeding miracle corresponded to the manna miracle and thus legitimated Jesus as the prophet-like-Moses (vv. 14–15). In their view, since Jesus already had legitimated himself as a prophet by the feeding miracle, they now needed another sign which would demonstrate that he was the one sent by the Father, that is, the Son of Man who was sealed by the Father, God (vv. 27–29). The correct meaning of vv. 14–15 and vv. 30–31 is then: since the feeding miracle was the eschatological manna miracle, Jesus had legitimated himself as the prophet-like-Moses. Now in vv. 27–29 he seemed to imply that he was the Son of Man, the Father's (heavenly) commissioned envoy. Therefore there was the need for (another) sign which would demonstrate that this was the case.[30]

John 6:30ff. can be paraphrased in this way: The crowd said, "What sign do you do so that we may see, and believe that you

---

[27] Menken (1987) 141.

[28] Haenchen (1980) 321.

[29] Menken (1987) 145–46.

[30] This distinction between two levels of Christology is formulated by De Jonge (1977): "... it is evident that this identification of Jesus with the Mosaic Prophet, though perhaps pointing in the right direction, does not really explain the secret of Jesus' coming. Jesus' reaction towards the ideas of the crowd in the following discourse is entirely negative. In that chapter not the similarities but the dissimilarities receive all emphasis ... it is clear, however, that the unique relationship between Jesus and God is underlined by means of the expression 'my Father' (vv. 32, 37, 40, 44, and especially v. 46) and the notion of 'descent from heaven' (v. 33, 41, 42, 50, 51)."

are God's heavenly-sent envoy, the Son of Man, who is sealed by the Father? The manna sign which we experienced in the feeding miracle was a sign which, in our mind, showed that you were the prophet-like-Moses, but it did not legitimate you as God's heavenly-sent envoy, the Son of Man". Jesus answered, "You have misunderstood the manna miracle. It was not given by Moses, nor now by the prophet-like-Moses, but it was the gift from heaven, given by the Father, and I am (myself) the manna/bread".

Thus in vv. 32ff. Jesus, by means of his exegesis of v. 31b "bread from heaven he gave them to eat", demonstrated that the Scriptures bore witness to him (5:39) and that Moses wrote about him (5:46). The giving of the manna, rightly understood, was a sign about Jesus (not just as a prophet-king, but) as the one who came down from heaven.

From 6:30–40 there is an exegetical dialogue between Jesus and "they", that is the crowd, and from vv. 41–58 there are exegetical objections voiced among the Jews, followed by statements given by Jesus.

John 6:31–58 has many midrashic features. As shown in my book *Bread from Heaven* there are such features in vv. 32–33. Jesus develops philological exegesis and states in v. 32 that his Father and not Moses is the subject of the verb "to give" (ἔδωκεν, Hebrew נתן) in the Old Testament text. Moreover, the verb is not to be read as past tense, δέδωκεν (ἔδωκεν), but in the present tense, δίδωσιν. By means of midrashic exegesis, Jesus corrects the crowd when they refer to the manna/bread from heaven (v. 31) as a sign of the prophet-like-Moses.

Jesus' understanding of the Old Testament quotation follows in v. 33, introduced by γάρ[31]: "For *the bread* of God is that which (or he who) comes down *from heaven*, and gives life to the world". (The words from the Old Testament quotation are italicized). According to Jewish traditions the Torah, given at Sinai, gave life to Israel or the world (*Tanh. Shem.* 25; *Mek. Exod.* 15:26; *Exod. Rab.* 29:9). Thus, "the bread of God" in John 6:33 has the role of the Torah. This understanding presupposes the identification of the manna/bread from heaven with the Torah, as exemplified in Philo, *Mut.* 253–63

---

[31] Cf. Philo, *Deter.* 47–48, with exegesis of Gen 4:8: "it must be read in this way: 'Cain rose up and slew himself', not someone else. For (γάρ) . . ."

and *Mek. Exod.* 13:17. Moreover, in the expository application in John 6:32 the third person plural pronoun "them" (αὐτοῖς) has been interpreted as "you" (ὑμῖν).

In John 6:34 "they" (the crowd) ask for this Torah-bread from Jesus: "Lord, give us this bread always".[32] The exposition in vv. 32–33 made clear that God the Father gives the bread, but does not make explicit what kind of bread it is. The formulations seem to indicate that the bread means the wisdom of the life-giving Torah, and the crowd asks Jesus to give them this bread always, presumably as a teacher who gives the people the wisdom of the God-given Torah. Thus they had not recognized Jesus' identity, that he himself was the one who came down from heaven.[33] Then Jesus makes explicit his exegetical application of the Old Testament quotation (v. 31b) to himself in v: 35: "I am *the bread* of life; he who comes to me shall not hunger, and he who believes in me shall never thirst".

J. Painter regards John 6:35 as the pronouncement to which the dialogues of 6:25–36 lead. According to him, this verse is the text upon which the discourse as a whole is based. Thus the Old Testament quotation in 6:31b does not serve as the text, but v. 31 as a whole is used to leading up to the pronouncement of 6:35.[34] It must be said that Painter does not define the relationship between vv. 31 and 35 in an adequate way. The Old Testament quotation in v. 31b and the pronouncement in v. 35a are tied together in the way formulated in 5:39: "it is they (the Scriptures) that bear witness to me". Thus, on the basis of this hermeneutical key the pronouncement in John 6:35a, "I am *the bread* of life", renders the precise meaning of the central term in the Old Testament quotation in v. 31b "*bread*

---

[32] Painter (1991) 233, asks why the crowd according to John 6:34 should think of Jesus as the giver if he has said that it is his Father who gives this bread? Painter's answer is that the crowd, provisionally at least, has accepted Jesus as the emissary of God (6:29), that is, the Son of Man. It is not necessary to go quite as far as Painter does, however. Against the background of 6:31–33 the crowd might understand Jesus to be a teacher who through his teaching brings the Torah-manna which gives life. They would then understand Jesus to be a teacher who follows the principle formulated in 5:39: "You search the Scriptures, because you think that in them you have eternal life."

[33] Against Painter (1991) 233, who thinks that "the crowd, provisionally at least, has accepted Jesus as the emissary of God 6:29".

[34] Painter (1991) 229 and 232.

from heaven he gave them to eat". The scriptural text in v. 31b bears witness to Jesus.

Moreover, although v. 35 gives the precise meaning of the Old Testament quotation, it does not function as the text since it does not form the basis for a subsequent expository structure. The Old Testament quotation in v. 31b serves as such a text, however. In a systematic way the words from the Old Testament quotation are repeated and paraphrased. Only words from the first part of the quotation, "he gave them bread from heaven", are repeated and paraphrased and discussed in vv. 32–48. The last word, "to eat" is then added, so that the whole quotation is interpreted in vv. 49–58. Moreover, themes from the Old Testament quotation are developed in a systematic way.

1. vv. 32–49. In vv. 32–34 it is made clear that it is the Father who "gives the bread". Then in vv. 35–49 the theme is Jesus as the "bread".

2. vv. 49–58: In vv. 49–51a the focus is on the effect of the "eating of the bread" – it gives eternal life. This theme is continued in vv. 51b–58, but here with the emphasis on the idea that the bread is the flesh of Jesus as the "Son of Man" (referring back to the Son of Man in v. 27) which he "shall give for the life of the world".

The conclusion is that the Old Testament quotation in v. 31b serves as a text, while Jesus' word in v. 35 gives the precise expository meaning of the word "bread" in the quotation.

Painter's hypothesis of a distinction between quest stories as John's first edition and rejection stories as his second edition breaks down in 6:36–40. According to him the quest is made by the crowd, and the "Jews" (vv. 41 and 52) are the ones who reject. Verse 36 tells that the crowd rejected, however: they "do not believe". To Painter this causes embarrassment: "surprisingly, in the end we are told that the crowd's quest ended in failure, 6:36. But 6:36–40 is made up of a collection of isolated sayings forming a transition to the rejection story of 6:41ff."[35] According to Painter "*the* Jews" are the group associated with rejection. He does not give a plausible reason why John, who, according to Painter, is himself responsible

---

[35] *ibid.*, 229. See also pp. 236–37.

for both editions, here pointedly states that *"they"*, that is, *the crowd* (cf. v. 24) rejected Jesus. Painter indicates that the crowd's unbelief in v. 36 shows that the quest story ended in failure. If so, there is no real distinction between the quest story and the rejection story.

In John 6:35b–40 the identification of the manna/bread with Jesus (v. 35a) is related to the main point in the dialogue of vv. 29–30, believing in him whom the Father, God, has sent. Verse 35b refers to "coming" and "believing". In v. 36 Jesus accuses the crowd, saying that they "do not believe". Then vv. 37–40 combine the idea of "coming" and "believing" with the idea of Jesus as "the one sent by the Father". The section is an elaboration of the words "from heaven" in the Old Testament quotation in v. 31b, a phrase which is repeated in v. 38, and is an integral part of the dialogue about "the Son of man" and "the one whom God sent".

In the study "God's agent in the Fourth Gospel",[36] I have shown that in vv. 38–40 halakhic principles of a commissioned envoy are applied to Jesus, the one whom the Father sent. One such principle was that it was a legal presumption that an agent, that is, one who is sent, would carry out his mission in obedience to his sender. In accordance with this principle, Jesus was an obedient agent who did as the Father had commanded. He said, "I have 'come down *from heaven*' (see v. 31b 'from heaven') not to do my own will, but the will of him who sent me". The will of the sender is then defined in vv. 39–40.

Another halakhic principle of agency is also used, that in the context of a lawsuit the sender transferred his own rights and the property concerned to the agent. The will of the sender, the Father, in John 6:39 is based on this transfer: "This is the will of him who sent me, that all he has given me . . ." The transfer is even more pointedly stated in John 17:6: "thine they were, and thou gavest them to me . . ." The same idea is also formulated in 6:37: "All that the Father gives me . . ."

The Jews' objection to Jesus' exegesis in 6:41–42 is formulated with a term from the story about the manna, Exod 16:2, 7, 8: they "murmured" (ἐγόγγυζον), John 6:41, cf. v. 43. The objection has the form of an exegetical problem formulation followed by a solution,

---

[36] See reference in n. 20.

parallels to which are found in the midrash and in Philo. The exposition consists of the following points:

1. The Old Testament quotation: John 6:31, "Bread from heaven he gave them to eat".

2. The interpretation of the quotation: 6:41, "he (Jesus) said, 'I am the bread which came down from heaven'" (words taken from vv. 35 and 38).

3. The basis for the questioning of Jesus' exegesis: 6:42, "They said, 'Is not this Jesus, the son of Joseph, whose father and mother we know?'"

4. The questioning of the interpretation: 6:42, "how does he now say 'I have come down from heaven?'"

5. The answer to the objection and the solution of the problem: 6:43ff., "Jesus answered and said to them, 'Do not "murmur" among yourselves . . .'"

In Jesus' answer the word "he who believes . . ." in v. 47 refers back to vv. 35 and 29–30, and the words, "I am the bread of life" in v. 48 repeats v. 35a, which in turn is the interpretation of the word "bread" in the scriptural quotation in v. 31b.

In *Bread from Heaven*, I have referred to the corresponding points of exegetical exchange which are found in *Mek. Exod.* 12:1 and 12:2 and in Philo, *Mut.* 141a, 142b–44.[37]

It is noticable that the objection in John 6:41ff. is not raised by the crowd, but by "the Jews", οἱ Ἰουδαῖοι. Painter draws extensive conclusions from this introduction of the term "the Jews" in John 6:41: "It is argued here that the change of terminology from the crowd to the Jews indicates a change of audience and a change of time, and that the note concerning the Synagogue in 6:59 indicates a change of location. John 6:41–59 reflects the struggle between the Johannine Christians and the Synagogue. For this text 'the Jews' is the appropriate term of reference. They do not represent the Galilean crowd which had followed and subsequently come seeking Jesus".[38] Against Painter it must be said that the reason for this change of terminology cannot be that "the Jews" rejected Jesus, while the crowd did not. On the basis of the text, it might even be said that "the Jews" who "murmured" expressed scepticism about Jesus'

---

[37] Borgen (1965) 80–83.

[38] Painter (1991) 237.

exegesis,[39] while "they", that is the crowd, rejected Jesus outright, as stated in v. 37,[40] and nothing in v. 41 indicates a different time and location from the setting of the preceding verses.

Several scholars think that "the Jews" in John 6:41 refers to "the crowd" (6:22, 24) and thus does not carry the usual meaning of the Jewish authorities.[41] There is one observation which indicates that the term "Jews" also here refers to the Jewish authorities, but in the role as midrash scholars. In John 6 the "crowd" wants to make Jesus a king, they seek him and address him as rabbi, and make requests to him. They do not perform scholarly midrashic exegesis, however, as rabbi Jesus and "the Jews" do. Thus "the Jews" in John 6:41 and 52 are the midrashic experts, as distinct from the common people, "the crowd". As Jesus and "the Jews" in John 5:10–18 had a halakhic and midrashic exchange on the commandments about the Sabbath in the Law of Moses, so rabbi Jesus and "the Jews" in 6:41ff. and 51ff. had a scholarly midrashic exchange. The difference is that the Jewish authorities in 5:10–18 persecuted Jesus and sought to kill him, while the Jewish scholars in 6:41 and 52 expressed objection to Jesus' application of the scriptural quotation about the bread from heaven (v. 31b). Thus the attitude of "the Jews" in John 6:41 and 52 are similar to the attitude associated with the term in 1:19; 2:18, 22, where the designation expresses scepticism and unbelief, but not hostility. In 6:41, 52 "the Jews" represent those who, as stated in 5:39, execute (professional) midrashic exegesis of the Scriptures, but refuse to accept that the Scriptures bear witness to Jesus.

Jesus' answer leads in 6:49ff. into further elaboration of the application to himself of the scripture quotation in v. 31b to himself. Now the word "to eat" (φαγεῖν) from v. 31 is introduced and is

---

[39] Ashton (1991) 200: ". . . called οἱ Ἰουδαῖοι (6:4, 41, 52), but their 'murmuring' (γόγγυσμός, v. 41) is prompted more by bewilderment than by real antagonism".

[40] Painter (1991) 238, ignores Jesus' word to the crowd that they do not believe, v. 36, and writes: "The crowd, though it has misunderstood Jesus, requests that Jesus should always give them the bread of which he has been speaking, 6:34. On the other hand the Jews do nothing but raise *objections* to what Jesus has said. They represent a hardening attitude of the Synagogue . . .". Against Painter it must be said that objections do not represent a hardening attitude when compared with the attitude of unbelief of the crowd.

[41] See the survey in Wahlde (1982) 33–60.

placed in the centre of the exposition to the end, v. 58.[42] As Jesus did in v. 32, he also here criticizes the misunderstanding expressed by the crowd in vv. 14–15, 26 and 31.

In John 6:51b the "bread" of the scripture quotation in v. 31b is interpreted as Jesus' "flesh". This application of the scriptures to Jesus is again met with exegetical objection in dispute among "the Jews" (v. 52). Also the objection here has the form of an exegetical problem formulation followed by a solution, parallels to which are found in the midrash and in Philo. The same five points as found in vv. 41–48 are also found here, except point 3, which in an explicit way stated the basis for the questioning of Jesus' exegesis in vv. 41–48.

1. The Old Testament quotation: John 6:31, "Bread from heaven he gave (ἔδωκεν) them to eat (φαγεῖν)".

2. The interpretation of the quotation: 6:51, ". . . the *bread* (ὁ ἄρτος) which I *shall give* (δώσω) for the life of the world is my 'flesh' (ἡ σάρξ)".

3. The basis for the questioning of Jesus' exegesis (the basis is implied in point 4).

4. The questioning of the interpretation: 6:52, "The Jews then disputed among themselves, saying, 'How can this man *give* (δοῦναι) us his "flesh" (τὴν σάρκα) *to eat* (φαγεῖν)?'"

5. The answer to the objection and the solution to the problem: 6:53ff, "So Jesus said to them, 'Truly, truly I say to you . . .'".

In 6:53–58 there is an expository elaboration on the theme of eating in v. 31, tied together with the theme of the Son of Man in vv. 53 and 27, and the theme of the one whom the Father sent in vv. 57 and 29. It should be added that the formula used when raising the question in John 6:52, πῶς δύναται, corresponds to the technical midrashic term כיצד.[43]

Although the exposition in John 6:31–58 consists of dialogue and scholarly exchanges, there are several unifying threads which demonstrate that the passage is composed as a whole – throughout the words "Bread from heaven he gave them" (v. 31b) are built into the formulations, and from 6:49 and onwards the word "to eat" from v. 31 is added. Moreover, the statement "our fathers ate

---

[42] Concerning the use of τρωγεῖν in vv. 54–58, see Borgen (1965) 92–93.

[43] Borgen (1965) 89–90; Bacher (1899) 77.

manna in the wilderness" (v. 31) is repeated with some changes in v. 49 and in v. 58. These threads which run through 6:31–58 demonstrate that the passage as a whole is composed to serve as a scriptural debate in response to the question raised in v. 30: "Then what sign do you do, that we may see, and believe you? What work do you perform?"

The Reaction among the Disciples, John 6:60–71

It is surprising that the subsequent section of John 6:60–71 reports the reaction among the disciples. They have not been mentioned in 6:25–59, although their presence must then be presupposed. The section refers at several points back to the earlier parts of the chapter. The disciples are mentioned several times in 6:3–21 and also in 6:22–24. The disciples "murmured" (γογγύζουσιν), 6:61, just as "the Jews" did (6:41). This "murmur" has its background in Exod 16:2 and shows that the scriptural story about the manna still serves as frame of reference. The words in 6:62 ("If then you see the Son of Man ascending to where he was before?") presuppose the words about the Son of Man in 6:27, 53 and the words about (his) descent from heaven (6:38, 41, 51).[44] The term "flesh" occurs in 6:63 and back in 6:51–56.[45] Some of the disciples "do not believe" (6:64) just as with the crowd (6:36). John 6:65 cites a previous saying of Jesus, actually a composite of words from 6:37 and 6:44. In contrast to the unbelief of the crowd (6:36) and of some of the disciples (6:64) Peter, representing "the Twelve", says that they have believed (6:69). Thus Peter gives a positive response to Jesus' word in 6:29: "This is the work of God, that you believe in him whom he has sent".

These observations demonstrate that the section 6:60–71 is an integral part of the chapter. How is its function to be defined in a more precise way? At the outset it is to be noticed that the subsequent result of the feeding miracle for the disciples is the walking on the sea in 6:16–21 – Jesus miraculously came to the disciples (6:16–21)

---

[44] It is difficult to define the exact meaning of John 6:62 because it has the protasis, but lacks the apodosis. See commentaries, and Borgen (1965) 187, Moloney (1978) 120–23; and Schenke (1992) 113ff.

[45] Concerning the meaning of John 6:63 in relation to 6:51–56, see commentaries, and Borgen (1965) 181–83; Schenke (1992) 109; 114–17.

after he had withdrawn from the crowd who mistakenly wanted to make him king (6:14–15). The works of Jesus, that is, the healing miracles, the feeding miracle and the walking on the sea, bore witness to him and the disciples experienced an epiphanic encounter with him.

Jesus' words about perishable and life-giving food and about the Father bearing witness about the Son of Man were addressed to the crowd (6:27). His words about believing in him whom God sent, and his application to himself of the scriptural word about the manna-bread from heaven, resulted in unbelief by the crowd and in exegetical objections stated by the Jewish scholars (6:28–58). Thus it remains to learn how the disciples reacted to the witness to the Son of Man, given by the Father (6:27–28), who sealed and sent him (6:27–28), and by the Scriptures (6:31–58).

Then from 6:60–71 we learn that the reaction among the disciples was divided – many said that Jesus' discourse was a hard saying, and they subsequently left him. Peter, representing the Twelve, accepted Jesus' words. Thus they accepted that God bore witness about him and so also did the Scriptures: "You have the words of eternal life; and we have believed, and have come to know, that you are the Holy One of God" (6:68–69). As for Jesus' "words (ῥήματα) of eternal life" it is to be noticed that according to 5:47 the writings of Moses and the words of Jesus coincide: "but if you do not believe his (Moses') writings, how shall you believe my words (ῥήματα)?" Moreover, John 10:36 makes evident that "the Holy One of God" means consecrated by God and sent by Him into the world: ". . . him, whom the Father consecrated (made holy) and sent into the world".[46] Thus, the christological designation used by Peter has the same meaning as that expressed by the designations used in 6:27, "on him the Father has set his seal", and in 6:29, "him whom he has sent".[47]

---

[46] Cf. Brown (1966) 298; Schnackenburg (1971) 110–11; Barrett (1978) 307.

[47] There is no need in this essay to discuss whether John 6 implies an antidocetic polemic. See commentaries, and Borgen (1965) 183–92; Schenke (1992) 105–21.

The Transition from John 5 to John 6

The transition from John 5 to John 6 represents one of the most striking aporias of the Fourth Gospel. In ch. 5 Jesus was in Jerusalem, and in ch. 6 he is in Galilee and goes to the other side of the Sea of Galilee (6:1ff.). Then he comes to Capernaum (6:24, 59). Moreover, there is in John 7:23 a reference back to the healing story in 5:1–18, and both 5:16–18 and 7:1ff. report that "the Jews" persecuted Jesus and wished to kill him. Scholars such as Bultmann and Schnackenburg thus reverse the order of chs. 5 and 6, and Lindars and Ashton regard ch. 6 as an addition made by the evangelist himself.[48]

The present study is an analysis of ch. 6. Thus it would go beyond the limits of this paper to deal with its relationship to ch. 5, especially since such an undertaking would necessitate a thorough examination of this latter chapter. Some observations might be listed, however, as a point of departure for further research on the subject.

It might prove fruitful to investigate whether points in John 5:31–47, the final part of the discourse of Jesus in 5:19–47, serve as the thematic background of ch. 6. If so, such a thematic connection would indicate that ch. 6 is in its right and original place in the Gospel. These points from ch. 5 may also give an important insight into the composition of ch. 6.

Such an approach was indicated in an embryonic form in my book *Bread from Heaven*. I suggested that John 6:31–58 might be an elaboration upon and an illustration of points discussed in 5:37–47. The conclusion was: "The close connection between John 5:37–47 and 6:31–58 speaks against any rearrangement of the sequence of chs. 5 and 6 in spite of the obvious geographical discrepancies (ch. 5 in Jerusalem; ch. 6 at the sea of Galilee, etc.)".[49]

The most obvious point deals with the interpretation of Scriptures (5:39–40) for which 6:31–58 is an illustration. References back to 5:39 have already been made in the present study. The connection is then as follows: in John 5:39–40 a hermeneutical principle is formulated – (v. 39) "You search the Scriptures, because you think that in them you have eternal life; and it is they that bear witness

---

[48] Bultmann (1941) 154–77; Schnackenburg (1971) 6–114; Lindars (1972) 50, 206–09 and 234; Ashton (1991) 200–01.

[49] Borgen (1965) 152, with the quotation taken from n. 2.

to me (v. 40); yet you refuse to come to me that you may have life." The same principle is also found in 5:46–47: "If you believed Moses, you would believe me, for he wrote of me. But if you do not believe his writings, how will you believe my words?" Then in ch. 6 a quotation from the Scriptures is given in v. 31, "as it is written, 'He gave them bread from heaven to eat'", and midrashic interpretations and diverse responses are seen in vv. 32–59, and various attitudes are also pictured in vv. 60–71. Thus John 6:31–58 serves as an illustration of the searching of the Scriptures mentioned in John 5:39–40. The phrase ἐρευνᾶτε (τὰς γραφάς) in John 5:39 is even a Greek equivalent for the technical term for performing midrashic exegesis.

This link between chs. 5 and 6 provides a basis for investigating whether other connections might be found. John 5:36 might give us a lead. According to this verse Jesus' works bear witness to him: ". . . the works which the Father has granted me to accomplish, these very works which I am doing, bear me witness that the Father has sent me". The line here may be drawn to 6:1–13. If so, light might be thrown on the puzzling verse 6:2 – why should the evangelist here report that the crowd followed Jesus because they saw the signs which he performed on those who were diseased? Actually only one healing is reported by him to have taken place in Galilee (4:46–54). Seemingly, E. Haenchen is right when he states that the context does not explain why it is said that a large crowd followed Jesus. The verb ἠκολούθει even has imperfect form to show that the crowd's following of Jesus was a lasting phenomenon![50] The preceding context, that is, John 5:36, may provide a clue. This verse says that Jesus' works, τὰ ἔργα, bear witness to him, and 6:1–13 may be meant to illustrate this witnessing function of the works, first by giving a summary statement about Jesus' healing activity in v. 2[51] and then reporting in vv. 3ff. more specifically on how Jesus' feeding miracle bore witness to him.

---

[50] Haenchen (1980) 300: "Das eine grosse Menge Jesus folgt (Imperfekt der Dauer!), wird hier aus dem Kontekst freilich nicht verständlich." Cf. Schnackenburg (1971) 17: "Woher die grosse Volksmenge stammt, die hier unvermittelt auftaucht, wird nicht gesagt. Von einem 'Nachfolgen' so vieler Menschen ist sonst nirgends im Joh-Ev die Rede . . ."

[51] Summarizing statements about Jesus' healing activity are found in Matt 4:23–25; 9:35; Acts 2:22; 10:38. See also John 20:30.

Also John 5:37, "And the Father who sent me has himself borne witness to me", might prove to be of interest. Does the evangelist here think of a particular occasion or a particular kind of witness? Scholars have made several different suggestions. It has already been mentioned above that Schnackenburg has joined the idea about the testimony of the Father, in John 5:37 with John 6:27b where it is said that it is the Father, God, who sealed the Son of Man and bore witness to him as His envoy.[52]

If further analysis offers support for these suggestions, then there are three witnesses. First, Jesus' works (v. 36), secondly, the Father who sent him (v. 37), and thirdly, the Scriptures (vv. 39–40 and 46–47). It is interesting to note that three corresponding sections seem to be found in ch. 6 since the main focus in vv. 1–21 is on Jesus' works as signs,[53] in vv. 22–27 on the Father and in vv. 28–71 on the Scriptures.

Summary

Jesus is not just the Prophet-like-Moses, John 6:1–21

The two traditional stories about the feeding of the multitude and the crossing of the sea in John 6:1–21 primarily report how Jesus acted in feeding the crowd and how they reacted: they thought the feeding was a new manna miracle and that Jesus was the prophet-like-Moses, and they wanted to make him king. This reaction, in turn, led to a further action on Jesus' part – he withdrew to the hills. The reaction of the disciples as a distinct group was also in the form of an action – they went away across the sea and Jesus miraculously came to them.

The Son of Man – the Father's Accredited Envoy, John 6:22–27

In 6:22–24 John repeats phrases from and makes references to the preceding stories and inserts additional interpretation. In this way it is seen that in v. 22 he refers to the story of the crossing of the

---

[52] Schnackenburg (1971) 50.

[53] See Borgen (1965) 180: "... the feeding miracle offers an example of the works mentioned in 5:36".

sea by the disciples (vv. 16–21). In vv. 23–24a the story about the feeding is referred to, while in vv. 24b–25a he brings the crowd to the destination of the disciples' crossing, Capernaum. In this way it is shown that the crowd was searching for Jesus.

The concluding point in v. 27 is not the search of the crowd nor the choice as such with which they are confronted by Jesus, but the seal which God the Father put on the Son of Man. The word σφραγίζω and its Hebrew and Aramaic equivalents are technical terms for sealing and signing as a witness. Thus, the Son of Man (and not the prophet-like-Moses) gives the bread which endures for eternal life.

The Manna-bread from Heaven, the Sign of the Son of Man, John 6:28–59

The structure of John 6:28–59 is as follows: Against the background of the general statements about "the Son of Man" and "the one who is sent" by God (6:27, 29) the question is raised whether Jesus is "the Son of Man" and "the one who is sent" by God (6:30). Exchanges on the scriptural story about the giving of the manna follow in 6:31–58, with particular focus on the interpretation of the quotation "bread from heaven he gave them to eat" (6:31b). In this way it is made clear that Jesus himself is the manna-miracle, as the bread/the Son of Man who came down from heaven (6:31–58).

The common people, "the crowd", addresses Jesus as "rabbi" (6.25) and asks questions (6:25, 28, 30, 34), while Jesus and "the Jews" practise scholarly midrashic exegesis. Jesus accuses "the crowd" of unbelief (6:36), and he criticizes "the Jews" because they object to his application of the scriptural quotation to himself (6:43ff. and 54ff.).

The Reaction among the Disciples, John 6:60–71

From 6:60–71 we learn that the reaction among the disciples was also divided – many disciples left him. Peter, representing the Twelve, accepted Jesus' words. Thus they acknowledged that both God and the Scriptures bore witness about him, "You have the words of eternal life; and we have believed, and have come to know, that you are the Holy One of God" (6:68–69). John 10:36 makes evident that "the Holy One of God" means consecrated by God and sent by him into the world. Thus, the christological designation used by Peter has the same meaning as that expressed by the designations used in 6:27 and in 6:29.

III

ACTS OF THE APOSTLES AND PAUL'S LETTERS

8

Catalogues of Vices, the Apostolic Decree, and the Jerusalem Meeting

In several studies the present author has discussed aspects of Paul's Letter to the Galatians.[1] The analyses have been focused on the claim made by Paul's opponents that he preached circumcision (5:11) and pleased men (1:10). These points have also been related to the role played by the Jerusalem meeting (2:1–10) within the context of the letter and the conflict in Galatia.

Galatians 5:11

In Gal 5:11, Paul says, "And I, brethren, if I am still preaching circumcision, why am I, despite this fact, persecuted? In that case the stumbling block of the cross is done away with."[2] The conditional clause has the form of a real case. Thus, Paul's opponents had evidently been saying that he himself was still preaching circumcision. Commentators have had difficulties deciding on what basis the opponents made this claim.[3]

There is a good reason for raising anew the question whether the context of Gal 5:11 can yield more information about Paul's preaching of circumcision. The question may be formulated in this way: Does Paul in this context reiterate ideas from his missionary

---

[1] See Borgen (1983A) 15–42, 75–97; Borgen (1985) 225–49.

[2] See De Witt Burton (1921) 287.

[3] Schlier (1971) 238–39; Haenchen (1971) 480–81 and elsewhere.

233

preaching in Galatia, ideas that the opponents have misunderstood and misused in support of their circumcision campaign? In Gal 5:19–21 Paul states explicitly that he repeats points from his previous preaching to the Galatians: "Now the works of the flesh are manifest, such as fornication, etc., respecting which I tell you beforehand, as I have already previously told you, that they who do such things will not inherit the Kingdom of God." In his preaching to the pagan Galatians, Paul spoke against the works of the flesh. With some variation in wording Paul repeatedly stresses this point in his preaching:

Gal 5:13 εἰς ἀφορμὴν τῇ σαρκί
5:16 ἐπιθυμίαν σαρκός
5:17 ἡ ... σὰρξ ἐπιθυμεῖ ...
κατὰ τῆς σαρκός
5:24 τὴν σάρκα ...
σὺν τοῖς παθήμασιν καὶ ταῖς ἐπιθυμίαις

Against this background the following hypothesis can be formulated: Paul refers pointedly to this topic taken from his previous preaching, because his opponents have claimed that in this way he preached circumcision to be the same as the removal of passions and desires. On what basis could they make this claim? The reason was that, among the Jews of that time, circumcision was understood to portray the removal of passions, desires, and evil inclination. In the works of Philo of Alexandria this interpretation of circumcision is very common, and he uses terminology similar to that which Paul uses in Gal 5:13, 16, 17, 19, 24:

De migratione Abrahami 92: τὸ περιτέμνεσθαι ἡδονῆς καὶ παθῶν πάντων ἐκτομὴν ... ἐμφαίνει (receiving circumcision portrays the excision of pleasure and all passions).

De specialibus legibus 1:305: περιτέμνεσθε τὴν σκληροκαρδίαν (Lev 26:41; cf. Deut 10:16), τὸ δέ ἐστι, τὰς περιττευούσας φύσεις τοῦ ἡγεμονικοῦ, ἃς αἱ ἄμετροι τῶν παθῶν ἔσπειράν τε καὶ συνηύξησαν ὁρμαί ("Circumcise the hardness of your hearts," that is, the superfluous overgrowths of the mind, which the immoderate appetites of the passions have sown and raised).

Of special interest is *Quaest. in Gen*. 3:52, since here the term "flesh" – central to Paul – symbolizes the passions: "the flesh of the foreskin, symbolizing those sensual pleasures and impulses (= ἡδονὰς καὶ ὁρμάς) which afterwards come to the body."[4] Although Philo has a dichotomic view of man, in these passages he does not make a sharp dualism between body and soul. He applies circumcision to both entities, so that both the body and the soul/mind/heart are to be circumcised.

In a similar way, we read in the Qumran writings, in 1QpHab 2:13, that the foreskin of the heart is to be circumcised in addition to the circumcision of the body, which seems to be taken for granted. A parallel to the thoughts of Paul and Philo occurs also in 1QS 5:5–6, where it says that the foreskin of the evil inclination is to be circumcised.[5] It is of importance that in 1QpHab 2:13–14 this inclination leads to drunkenness, a vice that Paul includes among the works of the flesh in Gal 5:21 (μέθαι κῶμοι).

In *Migr*. 92, Philo shows that such ethical interpretations of circumcision might lead to different attitudes and practices. Philo criticizes some Jews who, although they have the right understanding of the ethical meaning of circumcision, ignore the external observance of it. Philo himself stresses that the ethical ideas are of necessity tied to the external observance of bodily circumcision. Although Philo, according to *Quaestiones in Exodum* 2:2, gives heathens the status of proselytes on the basis of ethical circumcision of the pagan pleasures, he means that the observance of bodily circumcision is to follow.[6] In a similar way Paul's opponents have linked Paul's preaching against fleshly pagan desires closely to bodily circumcision: ethical circumcision is to be followed by obedience to the commandment to carry out bodily circumcision. The idea that the observance of circumcision should follow and complete ethical circumcision is supported by Gal 3:3, where Paul writes, "Having begun with the Spirit, will you now complete with the flesh?" A. Oepke suggests that Paul's opponents in Galatia argued that the Galatians needed a supplement, needed a completion by obeying the law of Moses.[7]

---

[4] Marcus (1953) 253, n. l.

[5] See Lohse (1971).

[6] See Borgen (1983A) 17–18.

[7] Oepke and Rohde (1973) 101.

Circumcision played a basic role in this complete submission to the law. Thus, Paul's opponents – who appeared as his followers – said that he preached circumcision (Gal 5:11).

Galatians 1:10b

The Judaizers, who worked among the Galatians, claimed that Paul preached circumcision, as they did themselves. This claim implied that Paul, like them, wanted the Christian congregations to conform to the Jewish community. In Gal 1:10, Paul seems to deal with this matter: εἰ ἔτι ἀνθρώποις ἤρεσκον, Χριστοῦ δοῦλος οὐκ ἂν ἤμην ("If I still tried to please men, I would not be the slave of Christ"). H. Schlier, F. Mussner, and others rightly understand the sentence to be "biographical": ἔτι, "still," is then understood to refer to the time after Paul's call (1:13ff.)[8] When Schlier and Mussner specify what Paul refers to when he talks about pleasing men, their interpretations become more problematic. They maintain that Paul's opponents criticized him for pleasing men when he proclaimed a gospel free from circumcision and the other requirements of the law.[9] This interpretation of the opponents' criticism cannot be correct, however, since according to Gal 5:11 they maintained that Paul still preached circumcision.

It must be remembered that Paul and the Judaizers formulate the same point in different ways. Hence, what Paul in a derogatory sense would call pleasing men, they would evaluate in a positive way: Paul wished to be accepted by the Jewish community after he had received the call to be an apostle.

When Gal 5:11 and 1:10 are seen together, they give clues to the way the Judaizers claimed that Paul represented their own cause. They claimed that Paul continued (cf. ἔτι) to preach and practise circumcision after he received his call. In this respect, there was continuity between his teaching before and after he became an apostle. As has been shown in our analysis of Gal 5:11, the conformists had reason for their claim: Paul continued to draw on traditions about circumcision and related Jewish traditions. Accordingly, the conformists drew the conclusion that Paul wanted to be accepted

---

[8] Schlier (1971) and Mussner (1974).

[9] Schlier (1971) 42 and Mussner (1974) 63.

by the Jewish community and please men by still advocating circumcision. Some of the conclusions preached are:

1. When Paul preached that the heathen Galatians should depart from the desires of the flesh and enter the society of those who serve and love each other, the Judaizers claimed that this was the ethical meaning of circumcision. Thus, Paul, in their view, still preached circumcision, and the task of these Judaizers was to persuade the Galatians to make bodily circumcision follow upon their ethical circumcision. By obedience to the commandment of circumcision the Galatian converts would make evident that they lived under the law of Moses. Thus, in the opinion of the Judaizers, Paul wanted to be accepted by the Jewish community and to please men by continuing to advocate circumcision.

2. But Paul objected to this misunderstanding and misuse of his preaching to the Galatians. For him their transition from the pagan desires of the flesh to a communal life in love was in an exclusive way tied to their being crucified with Christ, not to bodily circumcision and the jurisdiction of the law of Moses. Thus, Paul's service of Christ meant conflict with the Jewish communities: "If I still tried to please men, I would not be the slave of Christ" (Gal 1:10). Christianity was not a nationally bound religious movement but cross–national in its nature.

In the present study, this understanding will be related to some of the more debated questions relative to the Jerusalem meeting. A further analysis of Paul's Letter to the Galatians may throw new light on the Jerusalem meeting and on the so–called apostolic decree in Acts 15:20, 29 and 21:25.

Paul's Report on his Preaching at the Jerusalem Meeting

In our observations we shall not raise the historical questions about the Jerusalem meeting itself. Our concern here is with the role Gal 2:1–10 plays in Paul's letter. This approach is akin to that of H. D. Betz in his commentary. He interprets the letter using a legal defence plea as a model in accordance with the recommended practice of various standard authorities on rhetoric.[10] We are, however, focusing

---

[10] Betz (1979).

on the actual issues in the controversy between Paul and his opponents and not on the formal rules of rhetoric.

The issue of circumcision is explicitly mentioned in Gal 2:3: "Not even Titus who was with me and who was a Greek was compelled to be circumcised." Let us try to characterize in a precise way Paul's view and the view the opponents held on this issue. Paul's reference to his preaching in Gal 2:2 will serve as a point of departure. In Gal 2:2, Paul writes, "And I laid before them the gospel which I preach among the gentiles." A corresponding reference to Paul's preaching is found in Gal 5:11: "If I still preach circumcision . . ." Several observations indicate that these two formulations refer to the same preaching by Paul.

1. The same technical term for preaching is used in both places: κηρύσσειν. Betz makes the following comment on Gal 5:11:[11] "The language suggests that κηρύσσειν περιτομήν ("preach circumcision") is Paul's language, formulated in contrast to κηρύσσειν Χριστόν ("preach Christ"), his usual concept." This is probable, but a sharper distinction should be made between Paul's view and that of his opponents. The opponents represent the view that both phrases mean the same: to preach the gospel of Christ means to preach physical circumcision. Paul does not make this identification, however, but contrasts the two formulations.

2. In both Gal 2:2 and 5:11 the Gentiles are the addressees of the preaching. In Gal 2:2 there is an explicit reference to the Gentiles, and in 5:11 the preaching refers in particular to Paul's missionary activity among the Galatian Gentiles, although the attention here is focused on Paul's preaching since the time of his call.

3. Paul does not make a distinction between his preaching in Galatia and his preaching prior to the meeting in Jerusalem. His report from the Jerusalem meeting in Gal 2:1–10 is rather meant to give support to his preaching in Galatia – that is, to counter the opponents' misunderstanding of it. Two observations in Gal 2:1–10 demonstrate this:

a) In 2:5 Paul states that his action in Jerusalem was taken for the benefit of the Galatians – "in order that the truth of the gospel might remain with you."

---

[11] *ibid.*, 268–69.

b) The present tense used in Gal 2:2 presupposes that Paul preached the same gospel before the Jerusalem meeting and since that time up to the writing of the letter: "Und schliesslich geht aus dem 'zeitlosen' Präsens κηρύσσω hervor, dass er dieses spezifike Heiden–Evangelium auch jetzt noch unter den Heiden verkündet und auch bei den Galatern verkündet (vgl. auch 1:11)."[12]

How can Gal 2:2 and 5:11 refer to the same preaching by Paul? Both in Gal 5:11ff. and in Gal 2:2ff. Paul objected to the misunderstanding and misuse of his preaching to the heathen Galatians. Although he preached Christ within the context of Jewish proselyte traditions, such as the catalogue of pagan vices (Gal 5:19–21), he did not imply that the gentile Christians should undergo physical circumcision and become citizens of the Jewish nation. In this polemic against the opponents and the Galatian churches, Paul tells them that he at the Jerusalem meeting presented the same gospel, exclusive of physical circumcision. The pillar apostles agreed with him.

Our conclusion is then the following: The problem Paul faced in Galatia was that he, in his preaching of the gospel of Christ, drew on the Jewish teaching about proselytes in which catalogues of pagan vices and physical circumcision were an integral part. Correspondingly, when Paul reported on his preaching of the gospel in Jerusalem, the following question was raised: When Paul preached Christ to the Gentiles within the context of Jewish proselyte traditions, did this mean that the Gentiles had to undergo physical circumcision and join the Jewish nation? Paul's opponents in Galatia, just like the opponents at the Jerusalem meeting, maintained that physical circumcision was basic. They claimed that Paul held this view as well. Paul, on the other hand, although drawing on the Jewish traditions about proselytes in his preaching, that is, that they were to turn away from pagan vices, did not intend for them physical circumcision and Jewish citizenship.

Some Catalogues of Vices and Virtues

Some of the proselyte traditions employed by Paul should be discussed in more detail. In this context, lists of vices and virtues illustrate

---

[12] Mussner (1974) 102.

the contrast between the pagan way of life and the Jewish and Christian way of life.[13]

In Gal 5:19–21, Paul explicitly states that he repeats points from his previous preaching to the Galatians. These points are in the form of a list of vices. "Now the works of the flesh are manifest, such as fornication, etc., respecting which I tell you beforehand, as I have already previously told you, that they who do such things will not inherit the Kingdom of God." In his initial preaching, Paul spoke against the works of the flesh and exemplified such works by means of a catalogue of vices. Also elsewhere in his letters Paul uses catalogues of vices to illustrate the pagan way of life, which for the converts belonged to the past. For example, Paul addresses himself in 1 Cor 6:9–11 to the readers who were cleansed and purged of the pagan vices:[14] "Do you not know that the unrighteous will not inherit the kingdom of God? Do not be deceived; neither the immoral, nor idolaters, nor adulterers, nor homosexuals, nor thieves, nor the greedy, nor drunkards, nor revilers, nor robbers will inherit the kingdom of God. And such were some of you. But you were washed, you were sanctified, you were justified in the name of the Lord Jesus Christ and the Spirit of our God" (RSV).

In the two lists of Gal 5:19–21 and 1 Cor 6:9–11 there is agreement in the wording at two points, namely, in the reference to idolatry (Gal 5:20, εἰδωλολατρία; 1 Cor 6:9, εἰδωλολάτραι) and to adultery (Gal 5:19, πορνεία; 1 Cor 6:9, πόρνοι). Apart from these two terms, there are a variety of words used, although some overlap in their meanings.

In the Jewish traditions, idolatry and sexual misdeeds are closely associated. Idolatry is, moreover, seen as the root of all vices. Thus, in the context of a catalogue of vices in Wis 14:12–26, we read, "The devising of idols was the beginning of fornication, and the invention of them the corruption of life."[15] From Gal 5:19–21 and 1 Cor 6:9–11 it is evident that Paul in his preaching to the Gentiles made use of catalogues of vices to characterize the life from which they ought to depart, and which they as converts already had left behind. The themes of idolatry and fornication were central, and together with

---

[13] Borgen (1983A) 28, 81–82.

[14] Kamlah (1964) 11–14, 178; Vögtle (1936) 224–25; and Easton (1932) 4–5.

[15] Easton (1932) 1–3.

these, a variety of other vices were mentioned by him. Considering this variety, it is obvious that it is unwarranted to think in terms of a more fixed proselyte catechism. Proselyte traditions had much more flexibility and variation.[16]

As a contrast to the catalogue of vices in Gal 5:19–21, Paul in 5:22–23 offers a list of virtues to portray Christian life: "But the fruit of the Spirit is love, joy, peace, patience, kindness, goodness, faithfulness, gentleness, selfcontrol." No corresponding characterizations of the new life are given in 1 Cor 6:9–11, but in both places it is said that new life is based on the reception of the Spirit. From this it is evident that the virtues given in Gal 5:22–23 exemplify the life in the Spirit which the pagan Corinthians were sanctified to partake in according to 1 Cor 6:9–11. A further characterization of the new life is found in Gal 5:13–14: the "freedom" to which the Galatians were called meant that they should serve as slaves to one another, "for the whole law is fulfilled in this one word, you shall love your neighbour as yourself" (Gal 5:14, quoting Lev 19:18).

The objection might be raised against the above analysis that in Jewish sources the use of catalogues of vices and virtues was not confined to traditions connected with proselytism. Neither does such a limitation apply to the love commandment of Lev 19:18. There is truth in this objection, but it is sufficient for the purpose of the present study simply to document the fact that this material, besides having other uses, also served to describe to the proselytes the pagan background for their entry into the life of a proselyte.[17] Documentation of this is found in *Virt.* 180–82, where Philo says that the conversion of the pagans to monotheism serves as a basis for the new life exemplified by a catalogue of virtues:

> For it is excellent and profitable to depart without backward glance to the ranks of virtue and abandon vice that malignant mistress; and where honour is rendered to the God who is, the whole company of the other virtues must follow in its train as surely as in the sunshine the shadow follows the body. The proselytes become at once temperate, continent, modest, gentle,

---

[16] See Vögtle (1936) 3–4; and Wibbing (1959) 4–7.

[17] Borgen (1983A) 28, 81–84.

kind, humane, serious, just, high-minded, truth-lovers, superior to the desire for money and pleasure . . .

The parallelism between Gal 5:22–23 and *Virt.* 182 is obvious. Some of the virtues are even direct parallels: Paul, ἀγάπη; Philo, φιλάνθρωποι. Paul, χρηστότης; Philo, χρηστοί. Paul, ἐγκράτεια; Philo, ἐγκρατεῖς.

The first virtue listed in Gal 5:22 is "love," ἀγάπη. As background for this virtue, Paul quoted the love commandment of Lev 19:18 in Gal 5:14. This indicates that the summary of the law in the love commandment had a place in the instruction of proselytes. The *Babylonian Talmud Sabb.* 31a supports this view. Here it is said that Hillel summed up the law of Moses in the Golden Rule. Hillel made this summary for a heathen whom he accepted as a proselyte. The Golden Rule was in turn so closely associated with the love commandment of Lev 19:18 that in the Jerusalem Targum both are paraphrased together to render Lev 19:18. Consequently, this use of the Golden Rule within the context of proselytism makes probable that the love commandment also was used within the same setting.

It remains to relate these observations made on catalogues of vices and virtues to the preceding discussion of Paul's report on the Jerusalem meeting in Gal 2:1–10.[18] When Paul in Jerusalem reported on his preaching of the gospel to the Gentiles (2:2), his gospel comprised the Jewish proselyte tradition. His preaching included catalogues of vices which served to illustrate the pagan way of life and catalogues of virtues which exemplified the new life in the Spirit (Gal 5:19–23). The similar lists given by Paul in other letters show that various catalogues were used by him, and not only one form. The question debated in Jerusalem was, then, whether such proselyte traditions could be separated from physical circumcision and Jewish citizenship. According to Paul, "Those . . . who were of repute added nothing to me." This meant that they did not add the requirement of physical circumcision to Paul's preaching of Christ within the context of Jewish proselyte traditions.

---

[18] Cf. Borgen (1985) 235–43.

Jewish Proselyte Tradition – Not Apostolic Decree

This analysis of Paul's presentation of the Jerusalem meeting within the context of the Galatian controversy, and his use of catalogues of vices and virtues in this connection, throws light on the use of a catalogue of vices in Acts 15:20, 29, and 21:25, often called the apostolic decree.

The apostolic decree is in various manuscripts presented in two different main versions, the Alexandrian and the Western.[19] The Alexandrian version of Acts 15:20 reads, "to abstain from the pollutions of idols, and unchastity and from what is strangled and from blood." The Western version omits "what is strangled" and adds the Golden Rule in Acts 15:20 and 15:29. Thus, in 15:20 the Western text reads, "to abstain from the pollution of idols, and unchastity and blood; and all things they do not want happening to them, do not do towards others."

This "decree" has been much debated among New Testament scholars. In general it is understood as a decree that, according to the author of the Acts, was impressed upon the gentile Christians to make possible full social intercourse between Gentiles and Jews in the churches. Consequently, scholars find that this decree contradicts Paul's report from the Jerusalem meeting in Gal 2:6: "Those . . . who were of repute added nothing to me." Our hypothesis is that no such contradiction exists.

At the beginning of this century, A. Resch brought the apostolic decree into the discussion of the catalogues of vices in the New Testament.[20] According to him, the basis of the catalogues was the three vices of idolatry, adultery, and murder. The original form of the apostolic decree consisted of these three points, according to Resch, and the many catalogues of vices in the New Testament were elaborations of this apostolic decree. But Resch's hypothesis has several weaknesses. The textual support for Resch's suggested original form of the decree is weak. His derivation of the many catalogues of vices in the New Testament from this decree is too mechanical and seems to be too much of a historical simplification.

---

[19] See Metzger (1975) 429–34; Haenchen (1971) 468–72; Conzelmann (1963) 84–85; Roloff (1981), 225–28; and Schneider (1982) 189–92.

[20] Resch (1905),19–127. Cf. Vögtle (1936) 5–6.

After Resch the apostolic decree has been largely ignored in the discussion of the catalogues of vices in the New Testament.[21] Instead, the decree has largely been understood against the background of Leviticus 17 and 18 and the Noahittic commandments, or in the light of rabbinic teachings about the deadly sins, idolatry, adultery, and murder.[22] Although Resch's hypothesis as such cannot be maintained, it is pertinent to ask again if the apostolic decree should not be included among the New Testament catalogues of vices and be interpreted on that basis.

In comparison with the catalogues in Gal 5:19–21 and 1 Cor 6:9–11, the catalogue in Acts 15:20, 29, and 21:25 is quite short. The Alexandrian version in Acts 15:20 has four parts:

a. Pollutions of idols
b. Unchastity
c. What is strangled
d. Blood

The Western version consists of three parts:

a. Pollution of idols
b. Unchastity
c. Blood

Furthermore, the Golden Rule is added.

Such short catalogues of vices are not uncommon, however. Eph 5:5 has three (or four) parts:

a. Fornicator
b. Impure person
c. One who is covetous, i.e., (d) an idolator

Five (six) parts are found in Col 3:5:

a. Unchastity
b. Impurity
c. Passion
d. Evil desire
e. Covetousness, which is (f) idolatry

Rev 22:15 lists six parts:

a. Dogs
b. Sorcerers
c. Fornicators

---

[21] See Vögtle (1936) ; Wibbing (1959); and Kamlah (1964).

[22] See surveys in the works listed in n. 19 above.

   d. Murderers
   e. Idolators
   f. Everyone who practices falsehood
In 2 Cor 12:21, three parts are listed:
   a. Impurity
   b. Unchastity
   c. Licentiousness
Acts 15:20, 29, and 21:25, with a list of four – or three – parts, fits very well into the pattern of short catalogues. Moreover, there are parallels, and even close agreements, between the catalogue in Acts and several of the other short lists: Idolatry and unchastity occur in Acts 15:20, 29; 21:25; and in Rev 22:15, as well as in Col 3:5 and Eph 5:5. Murderers in Rev 22:15 (οἱ φονεῖς; cf. Rom 1:29) parallel blood(shed) (τὸ αἷμα) in the Western version of the catalogue in Acts. The Alexandrian version has the same term "blood," τὸ αἷμα, but here it may refer to the eating of blood.[23] It is significant that the longer catalogues in Gal 5:19–21 and 1 Cor 6:9–11 also list idolatry and unchastity in close agreement with Acts 15:20, 29; 21:25. These two vices are central in Jewish characterizations of the pagan way of life.

Thus, both the numbers of vices and the kind of vices listed support the hypothesis that Acts 15:20, 29 and 21:25 do not render a specific apostolic decree, but the list of vices in these verses is to be ranked together with the many other catalogues of vices, especially those which characterize the pagan way of life.

The function of the catalogue of vices in Gal 5:19–21 and of the one in Acts 15:20, 29 will be analysed further, since both passages are connected with the Jerusalem meeting. The analysis above of Gal 2:1–10 showed that Paul's preaching in Galatia was the same as his preaching of the gospel prior to the Jerusalem meeting, about which he reported at the meeting. This means that he preached Christ all the time within the context of Jewish proselyte traditions. Included in such traditions were catalogues of pagan vices, such as the one in Gal 5:19–21. The Gentiles were to turn away from such vices when they became Christians. Correspondingly, the catalogue of vices in Acts 15:20, 29, and 21:25 does not constitute an apostolic decree but exemplifies the kind of Jewish proselyte instruction that

---

[23] See, among others, Conzelmann (1963) 85.

was part of the Christian preaching. The issue both in Acts 15 and in Gal 2:1–10 and 5:11–26 can be formulated in this way: Should and could the Christians, when using Jewish proselyte teachings (exemplified by a catalogue of pagan vices from which the gentile converts were to turn away), neglect the requirement of physical circumcision and the integration of gentile converts into the Jewish nation? From Gal 2:6 we learn that "those who were of repute" in Jerusalem did not add the requirement of physical circumcision to Paul's preaching of Christ within the context of Jewish proselyte traditions. He had excluded physical circumcision from this teaching, and "those who were of repute" agreed with him. The conclusion is that neither the catalogue of pagan vices in Acts 15:20, 29, and 21:25 nor the catalogue of vices in Gal 5:19–21 is in contradiction with Gal 2:6.[24] Both list pagan vices from which the Gentiles were to turn away according to Jewish and Christian proselyte instruction. Such catalogues therefore were part of the missionary preaching and teaching that were taken for granted before, during, and after the Jerusalem meeting. Thus, at the meeting it was decided that this preaching, including such catalogues of vices, should continue without physical circumcision being required.

Several observations support the view that the catalogue of vices (the apostolic decree) in Acts 15:20, 29, and 21:25 has its place in traditions related to the institution of proselytism in Judaism:

1. The catalogue of vices from which the gentile Christians were to abstain spells out the implications inherent in the conversion of the Gentiles. The term ἐπιστρέφειν (Acts 15:19) is a term commonly used to denote the conversion of a Gentile.[25]

2. The catalogue of vices from which they were to abstain is not presented as a burden to be laid upon the gentile Christians.[26] The burden (παρενοχλεῖν, Acts 15:19) is to be interpreted as the requirement of physical circumcision. Thus, the joyful message (Acts 15:31) sent to the churches in Antioch, Syria, and Cilicia was that the "Christian proselyte" preaching of abstention from pagan vices did not imply physical circumcision (Acts 15:23–29). The phrase ἡμῖν πλέον μηδὲν ἐπιτίθεσθαι ὑμῖν βάρος πλὴν τούτων τῶν ἐπάναγκες in Acts

---

[24] See the survey in Haenchen (1971) 468.

[25] See Acts 9:35; 26:18; 1 Thess 1:9.

[26] See Dibelius (1956) 97 and Haenchen (1971) 449 n.3.

15:28 is to be understood accordingly. The meaning is not that some burden (though not so great as circumcision) is to be laid on the Gentiles but that no burden at all is to be imposed.[27] In the teaching of the Christian proselytes, the abstention from pagan vices was to be kept while the requirement of physical circumcision was to be abandoned.

3. The various versions of the catalogue of vices in Acts 15:20, 29, and 21:25 have features that clearly tie them to Jewish proselyte traditions. In the various versions it is said that the Gentiles are to abstain from idolatry and adultery, two points that, as we have seen, are also central in the proselyte catalogues in Gal 5:19–21 and 1 Cor 6:9–11. Moreover, the version in the Alexandrian text (counseling abstention from the pollution of idols and from fornication, and from things strangled, and from blood) draws on points from Lev 17:8, 10ff., 13; 18:6ff.,[28] which refer to the proselytes, according to Jewish exegesis.[29]

4. Finally, the inclusion of the Golden Rule in the Western text is in agreement with the way in which Hillel, according to b. Sabb. 31a, summed up the law of Moses in the Golden Rule. On that basis Hillel accepted him as a proselyte. As shown above, the Golden Rule was associated with the love commandment in Jewish tradition.[30] Therefore it is relevant to observe that Hillel's use of the Golden Rule is parallel to Paul's application of the love command (Lev 19:18) to the Christian "proselytes" in Galatia (Gal 5:13–14).

How can it be explained that there are two versions and several variant readings of the catalogue of vices in Acts 15:20, 29, and 21:25? The reason is that the catalogue is no apostolic decree made at the Jerusalem meeting but a representative example of Jewish proselyte traditions already used in the Christian preaching and teaching of "Christian proselytes." Thus, the decision taken at the Jerusalem meeting did not have the definite wording of a decree but said that such proselyte teachings should be taught and practised independently of physical circumcision. Thus, in later reports from

---

[27] See Haenchen (1971) 453 n.2.

[28] See Conzelmann (1963) 84–85; and Haenchen (1971) 469.

[29] Siegert (1973) 135. The LXX trans. makes Leviticus 17–18 refer to proselytes.

[30] Borgen (1983A) 82–84.

the meeting, such as the ones in Acts 15:20, 29; 21:25; and Gal 2:1–10 – seen together with Gal 5:11–26 – the actual wording of such catalogues of pagan vices varied, but the points against pagan worship and unchastity were stable elements.

One major problem remains to be solved: How can one explain the point against "what is strangled" in the Alexandrian version, and that the author includes Paul among those who stood behind it? The apostles and the elders, together with the whole church at Jerusalem, sent Judas and Silas with Paul and Barnabas to Antioch to deliver to the church there the message that was agreed upon at the meeting (Acts 15:22–35). According to his letters, Paul was quite liberal as to the Jewish dietary laws and even limited the prohibition against eating pagan sacrificial meat to the actual participation in the cultic sacrificial acts themselves. Different interpretations of these letters have been suggested by scholars. C. K. Barrett thinks that Paul's liberal views about eating articles of food that had been offered in pagan sacrifice contradict the requirements of the apostolic decree (see 1 Cor 8; 10). He claims that it is difficult to believe that Paul was present when the decree was drawn. According to Barrett, the Cephas group in Corinth attempted to introduce into the church at Corinth the Jewish Christian orthopraxy of the decree.[31] Correspondingly, some scholars think that the men who came from James to Antioch (Gal 2:11ff.) brought the decree and demanded that it be put into effect.[32]

These suggestions do not explain how a *decree* agreed upon at the Jerusalem meeting could lead to such completely opposite views and practices. The answer is that the catalogue against pagan vices in Acts 15:20, 29, and 21:25 was not a decree. The meeting in Jerusalem took up only the issue of "Christian proselytes" and circumcision. The decision was that Jewish proselyte tradition should be taught without the inclusion of physical circumcision. The numerous other problems involved in the complex and varied Jewish teachings addressed to proselytes were not taken up. The conflict about table fellowship in Antioch (Gal 2:11ff.) and the controversies about dietary matters in Corinth (1 Cor 8 and 10) show that dietary matters had not been decided upon at the Jerusalem meeting. The application

---

[31] Barrett (1965): 142–50.

[32] Catchpole (1977): 428–44.

of Jewish dietary regulations to the Christian proselytes became an issue both at Antioch and in Corinth, and probably also elsewhere.[33]

Our analysis indicates that the explanation of the two versions and the variant readings in Acts 15:20, 29, and 21:25 should be based on two observations:

1. In Acts 15 and in 21:25 the Jerusalem meeting and the present teaching of the author are seen together, just as Paul includes what was said at the Jerusalem meeting in his argument with his opponents in Galatia.

2. The Jerusalem meeting separated the requirement of physical circumcision from the Christian use of Jewish proselyte traditions, such as the catalogues against pagan vices. Thus, the many other problems which were present in these traditions were not taken up.

Thus, Jewish proselyte traditions were used continuously before, during, and after the Jerusalem meeting, and this meeting dealt with one specific point in this connection. These circumstances explain why we actually find in Acts 15 two main versions of a Jewish catalogue against pagan vices that was associated with the meeting: the Alexandrian version of Acts 15:20, etc., and the Western version of Acts 15:20, etc. Within these two main versions there are also several variant readings in manuscripts, patristic literature, and the like. The sample catalogue used at the Jerusalem meeting and brought into the letter sent to Antioch, Syria, and Cilicia (Acts 15:20–35) was then in some circles actualized along the lines of Leviticus 17–18 so as to specify dietary matters as in the Alexandrian version.[34] Both the men from James (Gal 2:11ff.) and the persons in Corinth who advocated strict observance (1 Cor 8) were among those who after the Jerusalem meeting in particular activated the elements of dietary observances in the Jewish proselyte traditions. They even might have thought that Paul accepted such dietary observances, since at the Jerusalem meeting physical circumcision was the issue

---

[33] Conzelmann (1963) 85: "Gal 2:11 zeigen, dass das Problem der Tischgemeinschaft von Juden und Heidenchristen auf dem Konzil noch nicht besprochen wurde."

[34] Cf. Siegert (1973): "Das Aposteldekret galt eben nicht christlichen Gottesfürchtigen, sondern aus den Heiden kommenden getauften Gemeindegliedern – wenn man so will, christlichen Proselyten." Siegert bases his argument on the LXX interpretation of Leviticus 17–18, in which the regulations for "strangers" have explicitly been applied to "proselytes".

and this requirement was the only one removed from the Jewish proselyte traditions. Other circles interpreted the Jerusalem sample catalogue by emphasizing the pagan ethical vices, together with idolatry. The Western version of Acts 15:20, etc., listing three vices and the Golden Rule, is akin to the Pauline version built into Gal 5:13–21 which consists of an extensive list of vices and the love command and also includes a proselyte catalogue of virtues (5:22–23).

Conclusion

The present analysis has sought to demonstrate that there was no apostolic decree decided upon at the Jerusalem meeting. In the Christian employment of Jewish proselyte traditions exemplified at the meeting by a catalogue against pagan vices (Acts 15:20, 29; 21:25; cf. Gal 5:19–21; 1 Cor 6:9–11), the requirement of physical circumcision was taken out, and thus the gentile converts were not required to become Jews and citizens of the Jewish nation. The exact wording of the sample catalogue used at the Jerusalem meeting is not preserved, but the renderings are found in later reports and documents. Thus, two versions can be identified: the Alexandrian version, with emphasis on ritual observance, and the Western version, which focuses upon ethical vices and virtues. The catalogues against pagan vices found in Gal 5:(13f.,) 19–21, and 1 Cor 6:9–11 give further documentation of the kind of (Jewish) proselyte traditions of which the catalogue in Acts 15:20, 29, and 21:25 is an example.

Added note: τὰ δόγματα in Acts 16:4

Acts 16:4 reads: "As they went on their way through the cities, they delivered to them for observation the decisions (τὰ δόγματα) which had been made by the apostles and elders who were at Jerusalem."

In Acts 15 the decisions made by the apostles and the elders are introduced by the verb ἔδοξε:

V. 22: Τότε ἔδοξε
τοῖς ἀποστόλοις καὶ τοῖς πρεσβυτέροις σύν ὅλῃ τῇ ἐκκλησίᾳ ἐκλεξαμένους ἄνδρας ἐξ αὐτῶν πέμψαι εἰς . . .

V. 25: ἔδοξεν
ἡμῖν γενομένοις ὁμοθυμαδόν, ἐκλεξαμένους ἄνδρας πέμψαι
πρὸς ὑμᾶς . . .

V. 28: ἔδοξεν
γὰρ τῷ πνεύματι τῷ ἁγίῳ καὶ ἡμῖν μηδὲν πλέον ἐπιτίθεσθαι
ὑμῖν βάρος, πλὴν τούτων τῶν ἐπάναγκες, . . .

Thus the decisions were: (1) The gentile Christians were not to be circumcised, and (2) messengers were appointed and sent to communicate that the apostles and the elders stood behind this view and did not comply with the alternative view of the troublemakers whom the apostles and the elders had not authorized, Acts 15:24.

9

Jesus Christ, the Reception of the Spirit and a Cross-National Community

1. Introduction

Two passages will provide the main focus in this paper, Gal 3:1–5 and Acts 15:5–9.

> You foolish Galatians! Who has bewitched you, before whose eyes 'Jesus Christ (the) crucified' was so vividly portrayed? This only do I want to learn from you: did you 'receive the Spirit' by 'works of (the) Law' or by 'hearing of (the) faith'? Are you so foolish? Having begun 'in (the) Spirit' are you now completing 'in (the) flesh'? Have you experienced such things in vain? If so, it really was in vain! Does he, therefore, who supplies the Spirit to you and who works power-manifestations among you (do so) by 'works of (the) Law' or by 'hearing of (the) faith'? (Gal 3:1–5)

> But some believers who belonged to the party of the Pharisees rose up and said, "It is necessary to circumcise them, and to charge them to keep the Law of Moses." The apostles and the elders were gathered together to consider the matter. And after there had been much debate, Peter rose and said to them, "Brethren, you know that from the earliest days God made choice among you, that by my mouth the Gentiles should 'hear the word of the gospel and believe'. And God the knower of hearts bore witness to them 'giving them the Holy Spirit' just as he did to us; and he made no distinction between us and them, but cleansed their hearts 'by faith'." (Acts 15:5–9)

253

When the Christian message was brought to the non-Jews and early Christianity became a movement which comprised both Jews and Christians, then the church which emerged had to face several difficult problems. It needed to make basic decisions as to what course to follow on questions such as circumcision and Jewish proselytism, cultic calendar, intermarriage between Jews and non-Jews, table fellowship, dietary observances, attitudes and practices towards polytheistic society and cults, different ethical standards and ways of life, and so on. In both passages cited above, cases from the experience of hearing the Gospel, of believing, and of receiving the Spirit are used as a decisive argument against the need for Gentile Christians to undergo circumcision. This observation invites further analysis of these passages.

In order to understand better the general historical setting of these two stories about the reception of the Spirit some aspects of the letter to the Galatians should perhaps be outlined. According to this letter, the Jerusalem meeting (Gal 2:1–10) had the function of being a guidepost for Paul and for the leaders of the Jerusalem church in the ongoing struggle about the status of the Gentile Christians. This understanding is confirmed by the fact that Paul connects the dispute at the Jerusalem meeting with the conflict in Galatia. In the preceding chapter on catalogues of vices some of the ways in which Paul makes this connection have been analysed. Here two points should be emphasized:[1]

First, the question of whether or not Gentile Christians should undergo circumcision is common to both. Circumcision was the central issue at the Jerusalem meeting, as is explicitly stated by Paul in Gal 2:3: "Not even Titus who was with me and who was a Greek was compelled to be circumcised." The same problem was at the centre of the Galatian conflict, as seen from Gal 5:2 where Paul writes: ". . . if you receive circumcision, Christ will be of no value to you at all." Paul's concern was caused by the circumstance that some people had come to the newly converted Galatians and wanted to compel them to be circumcised, Gal 6:12. The gravity of this issue as Paul perceives it is also expressed in 5:4, 6, 11 and 6:13, 15.

---

[1] Cf. Borgen (1987C) 262–64.

Second, at the Jerusalem meeting Paul reported on his preaching (Gal 2:2). Paul does not distinguish between his own preaching in Galatia and his preaching prior to the meeting in Jerusalem. His report from Jerusalem in Gal 2:1–10 is rather meant to reinforce his preaching in Galatia – that is, to counter the opponents' misunderstanding of it.[2]

Given this, it is possible to draw conclusions from Paul's preaching in Galatia concerning the main points of his preaching at an earlier time, even back to his missionary activity before the Jerusalem meeting. For example, in Gal 5:19–21 Paul explicitly states that he repeats points from his previous preaching to the Galatians.[3] These points are in the form of a list of vices: "Now the works of the flesh are manifest, such as fornication . . ., respecting which I warn you, as I have already previously told you, that those who do such things will not inherit the Kingdom of God." Thus Paul's gospel before, during and after the Jerusalem meeting included catalogues of vices which served to illustrate the pagan way of life from which the Gentile Christians had turned. See further discussion of this subject in the preceding chapter on catalogues of vices.

With this background in mind, the question arises whether Paul's argumentation from the experience of the Galatians as related in Gal 3:1–5 represents a new development in his thinking or if this line of argument also goes back to an earlier time, even to the meeting in Jerusalem and possibly before.

The close parallels between Paul's case-history taken from Galatia and Peter's account from Caesarea support the view that both together exemplify one type of argument in the ongoing struggle about the status of the Gentile Christians. Although the reference to the Cornelius story in Acts 15:6–9 clearly shows Luke's interpretative and literary creativity, it is probable that instances such as this one and the Galatian episode were referred to at the meeting. Luke, then, had historical and theological basis for using such traditional material as the story about Cornelius, and he built it into his overall scheme of the Acts of the Apostles.

---

[2] Mussner (1974) 102.

[3] See Borgen (1987C) 246–47; Borgen (1988) 130–33; 137; 139. (The latter essay is reprinted in the preceding chapter, see esp. pp. 238–42; 247; 250.)

2. Paul's Argument From a Case: The Reception of the Spirit by the Galatian Converts (Gal 3:1–5)

Gal 3:1–5 reports what had happened in the (recent) past when Paul stayed as a missionary among the Galatians. The case concerns the experience of the addressees of the letter, namely their reception of the Spirit. Paul writes to them in the second person plural:

v. 2: τὸ πνεῦμα ἐλάβετε
v. 5: ὁ οὖν ἐπιχορηγῶν ὑμῖν τὸ πνεῦμα
καὶ ἐνεργῶν δυνάμεις ἐν ὑμῖν

In v. 2 Paul uses the traditional formula-like phrase τὸ πνεῦμα ἐλάβετε (cf. Rom 8:15; 1 Cor 2:12; 2 Cor 11:4; Acts 2:38; 8:15, 17, 19; 10:47; 19:2). In Gal 3:5 Paul speaks of the continued presence of the Spirit and specifies that God is the source and that he works "power manifestations" (δυνάμεις). This reception of the Spirit by the Galatian converts was brought about by Paul's missionary preaching of "Jesus Christ crucified" (Gal 3:1), and thus resulted from "a hearing of faith" (ἐξ ἀκοῆς πίστεως 3:2).

Paul is pointedly critical of the Galatians: "You foolish Galatians! Who has bewitched you . . .?" (Gal 3:1). "Are you so foolish?" (3:3). "Have you experienced such things in vain? If so, it really was in vain!" (3:4). The phrase "Who has bewitched you" probably alludes to the intruders who had come to the Galatian converts and troubled them (Gal 1:7).[4]

In Gal 3:5 the danger of their possible deviation is stated more specifically: "Having begun with the Spirit, are you now completing with the flesh?" A. Oepke suggests that Paul's opponents have argued that the Galatians needed a supplement, a completion by "flesh" – that is, circumcision.[5] Since the term "flesh" here alludes to circumcision, the question arises how exactly one should understand the related contrast between "by works of the law" (ἐξ ἐργων νόμου, Gal 3:2, 5) and "by the hearing of faith" (ἐξ ἀκοῆς πίστεως, 3:2).

---

[4] De Witt Burton (1921) 143; Schlier (1971) 120–21; Betz (1979) 131.
[5] Oepke and Rohde (1973) 101.

The two phrases are much debated in New Testament research. There is a strong exegetical tradition in which the contrast is seen as that of God's gift of grace over and against man's self-achievement. In his interpretation of Gal 3:2, H. Schlier formulates this understanding in the following way: "Der Christ lebt sein spezifisches Leben, sein Leben im Geiste oder auch sein 'übernaturliches' Leben nicht aus dem Prinzip (νόμος) und der Kraft (ἔργα) der eigenmächtigen Existenz, sondern aus dem Grund (ἀκοή) und Macht (πίστις) göttlicher Tat."[6]

E. P. Sanders understands the phrases differently. He takes his point of departure in what he regards as Paul's dogmatic conviction that if ". . . the death and resurrection of Christ provide salvation and receiving the Spirit is the guarantee of salvation, *all other means are excluded by definition.*" "What the Galatians hope to achieve by the law *can* come *only* another way, by the death of Christ and by believing."[7] J. D. G. Dunn maintains that Sanders has thereby drawn ". . . the false conclusion that in disparaging the 'works of the law' Paul is disparaging law as such, has broken with Judaism as a whole."[8] In a later study Sanders places heavier emphasis on Stendahl's hypothesis that Paul dealt with the concrete relationship between Jews and Gentiles.[9] Two quotations from his book *Paul, the Law, and the Jewish People* indicate his main thrust:

The Subject of Galatians is not whether or not humans, abstractly conceived, can by good deeds earn enough merit to be declared righteous at the judgment; it is the condition on which Gentiles enter the people of God.[10] The debate in Galatians is a debate about 'entry' in the sense of what is essential in order to be considered a member *at all*. Paul holds that faith is the sole membership requirement; his opponents would require also circumcision and acceptance of the Mosaic law . . . it is not doing

---

[6] Schlier (1971) 122. This view was pointedly formulated in the Reformation, and is today followed by scholars such as Bultmann (1951) 254; Hübner (1978) 102, where he also cites Bultmann (1977) 102: ". . . schon die Absicht, durch Gesetzerfüllung vor Gott gerecht zu werden, sein καύχημα zu haben, ist Sünde".

[7] Sanders (1977) 484.

[8] Dunn (1983) 120.

[9] Stendahl (1977).

[10] Sanders (1983) 18.

the law in and of itself which, in Paul's view, is wrong. Circumcision is, from one perspective, a matter of indifference (Gal 6:15). It is completely wrong, however, when it is made an essential requirement for membership.[11]

Paul's phrase the "works of the Law" does not refer to how many good deeds an individual must present before God to be declared righteous at the judgment, but to whether or not Paul's Gentile converts must accept the Jewish law in order to enter the people of God or to be counted truly members.[12]

In his essay "The New Perspective on Paul" Dunn restricts the definition of the "works of the Law" to Jewish identity markers: "... by 'works of the law' Paul intended his readers to think of *particular observances of the law like circumcision and the food laws.*"[13] Thus, he thinks that Paul is not arguing against works, nor even against the Mosaic Law as such, but against works which express Jewish nationalistic limitations and prerogatives. God's covenant should no longer be conceived in such nationalistic or racial terms.[14] In his later publications Dunn does not advocate this restrictive sense of the phrase "works of the law", however. It is Paul's characterization of what the law requires, focused in particular test cases, in particular the undertaking of circumcision and the practice of food laws.[15] In Galatians, "Paul objects to covenantal nomism understood as it then was consistently throughout Judaism – that is, covenantal nomism as restricting the covenant to those within the boundaries marked by the law, to Jews and proselytes."[16] He now criticizes E. P. Sanders for making *"too sharp a distinction between entry* (into the covenant) *and continuance* or maintenance of status within the

---

[11] *ibid.,* 20.

[12] *ibid.*

[13] Dunn (1983) 107. A similar understanding of the "works of the law" is hold by Heiligenthal (1984) 38–53.

[14] *ibid.,* 114–15.

[15] Dunn (1990) 206–64, and Dunn (1992) 99–117.

[16] Dunn (1990) 249.

covenant . . . Consequently *the issue of the continuum between faith and its outworking/corollary was obscured.*"[17]

Entry into the People of God or Remaining in It?

In general the approach of Stendahl, Sanders and Dunn is supported by the fact that Paul draws on a widespread formula which was often used when Gentiles, for various reasons, were compelled to become Jews. As demonstrated in the preceding study on militant and peaceful proselytism, the formula occurs in Paul's letter to the Galatians and in Josephus' writings, and also in a fragment from a non-Jew, Ptolemy the Historian (end of first century B.C.?).

The formula is: ἀναγκάζειν τινὰ περιτέμνεσθαι.

Gal 6:12: "they compel (ἀναγκάζουσιν) you to be circumcised"

Josephus, *Life* 113: "When the Jews would have compelled (ἀναγκαζόντων) them to be circumcised if they wanted to be with them, I did not allow any compulsion to be put upon them . . ."

Gal 2:3: ". . . not even Titus who was with me and who was a Greek was compelled (ἠναγκάσθη) to be circumcised."

Ant. 13:318: ". . . he . . . compelled (ἀναγκάσας) the inhabitants . . . to be circumcised, and to live according to the Jewish laws."

Ptolemy:[18] "The Idumaeans . . . having been subjugated by the Jews and having been compelled (ἀναγκασθέντες) to undergo circumcision . . ."

Although these parallels occur in different contexts, all demonstrate that it was common to regard circumcision as such as a basic identity

---

[17] *ibid.*, 246.
[18] Quoted from Stern (1976) 356, n. 146.

marker for a Jew and that, when needed, Gentiles were forcefully circumcised. By this act they were made citizens of the Jewish nation.

These parallels have lent support to the views of Stendahl, Dunn and Sanders that Galatians deals with the concrete relationship between Jews and Gentiles. They also seem to support the view of Sanders that the theme of Galatians is the controversy surrounding the condition on which Gentiles enter the people of God.

There were several aspects other than circumcision involved in becoming a Jewish proselyte, however. For example, Philo of Alexandria generally concentrates on three aspects:[19] First, the religious conversion. Here the central theme is the change from worshipping many gods to the worship of the One True God. See for example *Virt.* 102–04, and in Paul, Gal 4:8, etc. Second, the ethical conversion. The change here is from pagan vices to the Jewish virtues. See for example *Virt.* 181–82, and in Paul, Gal 5:19–23, etc. Third, the social or national conversion. The proselytes have left their family, their country and their customs and entered the Jewish nation, "a new and godly commonwealth", *Spec.* 1:51.

From the Jewish side there were subtle discussions about exactly when a Gentile convert received the status of being a Jew. Although the *Babylonian Talmud* was written at a much later time, *Yebamot* 46a exemplifies how such distinctions could be made: "If he is baptized and not circumcised such a person is a proselyte, for this we find regarding our (fore-)mothers, who were baptized and not circumcised."

More important for the understanding of the Galatian situation is a corresponding but entirely different distinction drawn by Philo in *Quaes. Exod.* 2:2. He differentiates between ethical circumcision and bodily circumcision:

> προσήλυτος is not the one who has circumcised his uncircumcision but the one who (has circumcised) his desires and sensual pleasures and the other passions of the soul. For in Egypt the Hebrew nation
> . . .

Philo gives an answer here to the question: When does a person receive status as a proselyte in the Jewish community and cease

---

[19] For the following, see Borgen (1987C) 61–71, 207–32. See also pp. 62–64 in the present book.

to be a heathen? In this saying ethical circumcision, and not bodily circumcision was the basic requirement for entering the Jewish community. Bodily circumcision was one of the commandments which the proselytes had to obey upon having received the status of a Jew.[20]

Against this background of discussion it can be seen that Sanders' understanding of Galatians is not sufficiently precise. The Galatian converts had turned away from polytheism and from pagan immorality (Gal 4:8 and 5:13–25). They had received the Spirit both with its power manifestations and with its ethical fruits (3:2–5; 5:22–26).[21] Thus the issue in Galatians is: How shall the Galatian Christians *remain* in the people of God? Accordingly, for Paul the Galatians are in danger of falling away from being members of the people of God, of "... turning back again to the weak and beggarly elemental spirits ..." (Gal 4:9). And they are encouraged to stand firm: "For freedom Christ has set us free; stand fast therefore, and do not submit again to a yoke of slavery" (5:1).

The opponents who had come to the Galatian Christians understood the situation differently from Paul. They wanted to persuade the Galatian Christians to adopt bodily circumcision as a necessary complement to their ethical circumcision. For them this was the requirement for retaining membership of the people of God.

So far it has been seen that some Jews would regard ethical circumcision as the point at which a Gentile convert received the status of "Jew". Bodily circumcision and the other commandments

---

[20] Borgen (1980) 88, and Borgen (1987C) 220: "Philo's and Hillel's understanding has thus been that bodily circumcision was not the requirement for entering the Jewish community, but was one of the commandments which they had to obey upon receiving status as a Jew". Dunn (1990) 246 and 260, uses this quotation as support for his interpretation of Galatians.

[21] There is kinship between Paul's understanding and the understanding of some Jews who stressed the ethical circumcision, but ignored the observance of bodily circumcision itself, as related by Philo in *Migr.* 92. They and Paul rejected the observance of bodily circumcision. There was at the same time a basic difference, since Paul alone gave the ethical life new and eschatological foundation in the death and resurrection of Jesus Christ. See Borgen (1980) 86–87 and 91–92, and Borgen (1987C) 220; 223; 235; 238–39; 257–58.

were then to follow in order for them to remain within the Jewish people of God.[22]

When A. Oepke (on the basis of Gal 3:3) suggests that Paul's opponents have argued that the Galatians needed a supplement and a completion by "flesh", that is, by being circumcised, an important question needs to be asked: Could the opponents also have integrated the Galatians' reception of the Spirit into *their* argument? Is there evidence that reception and possession of the Spirit could characterize a Gentile who had become a Jewish proselyte? One passage in Philo shows that it was possible to regard the reception and the indwelling of the Spirit as a phenomenon in the life of the Jewish community as the people of God. The passage is *Virt*. 212–19, where Abraham, as the prototype of the proselytes, receives the Spirit. Philo tells how Abraham turned from astrology and polytheism to the One God, the Creator. "And therefore, he is the first person spoken of as 'believing God', since he first grasped a firm and unswerving conception of the truth that there is one Cause above all, and that it provides for the world and all that there is therein" (216). As a result of this conversion and as a prototype of proselytes Abraham received the Spirit:

> . . . the divine Spirit,
> which, having been breathed upon him from on high, made its lodging in his soul,
> invested his body with singular beauty,
> > his words with persuasiveness,
> > and his hearers with understanding.

---

[22] Basically the same objection to Sander's understanding was formulated from a different angle by Gundry (1985) 8–9: ". . . the question of staying in *is* the issue, at least the primary one, in Galatians. There, contrary to Sanders' statement that 'the subject of Galatians is . . . the condition on which Gentiles enter the people of God', Paul does not deal with a question whether believing Gentiles had *gotten* in; rather, he deals with the question whether believing Gentiles could *stay* in without submitting to circumcision and keeping other parts of the law." Gundry only refers in a general way to the Jewish bakground and is thus quite vague in his discussion of the possible view of the Judaizers, *ibid.*, 9. Laato (1991) 217–21 takes my studies as the starting point in his discussion of Galatians, and stresses that the question in the letter is not entry into the people of God, but remaining in it.

τοῦ θείου πνεύματος,
ὅπερ ἄνωθεν καταπνευσθὲν εἰσῳκίσατο τῇ ψυχῇ,
περιτιθέντος τῷ μὲν σώματι κάλλος ἐξαίρετον,
τοῖς δὲ λόγοις πειθώ,
τοῖς δ' ἀκούουσι σύνεσιν (217)

Abraham thus ranked among the prophets (218).

Philo concludes:

He (Abraham) is the standard (κανών) of nobility for all proselytes, who abandoning the ignobility of strange laws and monstrous customs which assign divine honours to sticks and stones and lifeless (ἀψύχοις) things in general, have come to settle in a better land, in a truly vital (ἔμψυχον) and living (ζῶσαν) commonwealth (πολιτείαν), with truth as director and president (219).

The model for this new life as member of the Jewish people was then the reception and indwelling of the Spirit as seen from the picture given of the experience of the proto-proselyte, Abraham.[23]

This passage in Philo's writings shows that Paul's opponents could have integrated the reception of the Spirit by the Galatian (as they saw it: Jewish) proselytes into their strategy for keeping them as members of the Jewish people of God by having them undergo bodily circumcision. They may have taught the Galatians that they confirm their status as Jews by fulfilling the commandment of circumcision. Paul then emphatically counters that the Galatian converts received the Spirit by accepting (through faith) the preaching of Jesus Christ crucified. Accordingly, they would *remain* members of the people of God without submitting to circumcision, and thereby become members of the Jewish people under the Law of Moses.

---

[23] It may be added here that in the book *Joseph and Asenath* Asenath is transformed as she became a Jewish proselyte. Asenath ate the honeycomb which was full of the spirit of life and she was renewed as a person, 15:14–16. She was transformed to heavenly beauty (18:6–11), and she also received the Spirit of life, wisdom and truth: "And Joseph kissed Asenath and gave her spirit of life, and he kissed her a second time and gave her spirit of wisdom, and he kissed her the third time and gave her spirit of truth" (19:11).

4. The Argument from a Corresponding Case: The Reception of the Spirit by the Gentiles Gathered in Cornelius' House (Acts 10:44–47; 11:1–2, 15–18; 15:6–11)

According to Acts 15:1–2 some men from Judea (v. 24 from the Church in Jerusalem, but without authorization) went to Antioch and insisted that the Gentile Christians had to become Jewish proselytes in order to be saved: "Unless you are circumcised after the custom of Moses, you cannot be saved" (ἐὰν μὴ περιτμηθῆτε τῷ ἔθει τῷ Μωϋσέως, οὐ δύνασθε σωθῆναι). Conzelmann finds this verse reminiscent of Gal 2:12, where it is related that certain men came from James to Antioch and intervened in the issue of table fellowship between Jewish and Gentile Christians.[24] The situation described by Luke is nearer the situation in the Galatian churches, however.[25] Both in Antioch and in Galatia persons came from the outside as "intruders" and insisted that the Gentile Christians had to undergo circumcision. In Antioch Paul was present, while he had to involve himself in the situation in Galatia by means of a letter. In both places Paul actively took part in the dissent and debate, in Antioch together with Barnabas. Luke tells how this conflict in Antioch was brought to the Jerusalem Church, while Paul in the letter to Galatians ties the Galatian conflict closely to the Jerusalem meeting which had taken place in the past.

At the meeting in Jerusalem the argument was not based on the reception of the Spirit by the Gentile Christians in Antioch (corresponding to Paul's reference to the experience of the Galatian Christians in Gal 3:1–5). Instead, Peter referred to the Cornelius episode (Acts 10:1 – 11:18) and said: ". . . from the earliest days God made choice among you that by my mouth the Gentiles should hear the word of the Gospel and believe. And God the knower of hearts, bore witness to them giving them the Holy Spirit just as he did to us . . ." (Acts 15:7–8). Dibelius comments on this point: ". . . this . . . allusion to Acts 10:1ff. cannot be understood by Peter's

---

[24] Conzelmann (1987) 115.

[25] Concerning the differences between Acts 15:1–29 and Galatians 2:1–10, see Haenchen (1971) 462–72, and the books and essays referred to by him on pages 441–42.

hearers, though it can by readers of the book. For the latter the Cornelius story has a normative significance . . . and this is the work of the writer Luke . . ."[26] Many scholars hold a view similar to that of Dibelius.[27] But light may be thrown on Peter's argument from Cornelius' case at the Jerusalem meeting by comparing it with a report on the reception of the Spirit by the Galatians given by Paul in Gal 3:1-5.

There are similarities between Acts 15:6-9 and Gal 3:1-5. Both refer to an incident in the past. Both refer to the reception of the Spirit by converts, the description in Acts 15:6-9 also clearly referring back to Acts 10:44-47 and 11:15. Some of the parallel phrases are:

Acts 15:8: αὐτοῖς δοὺς τὸ πνεῦμα τὸ ἅγιον

Acts 10:44 and 11:15: ἐπέπεσεν τὸ πνεῦμα τὸ ἅγιον

Acts 10:45 ἐπὶ τὰ ἔθνη ἡ δωρεὰ τοῦ ἁγίου πνεύματος ἐκκέχυται

Acts 10:47 τὸ πνεῦμα τὸ ἅγιον ἔλαβον

Gal 3:2: τὸ πνεῦμα ἐλάβετε

Gal 3:5: ὁ οὖν ἐπιχορηγῶν ὑμῖν τὸ πνεῦμα

From these parallels we notice that just as Paul in Gal 3:2 uses a standard phrase to describe the reception of the Spirit, τὸ πνεῦμα ἐλάβετε, so also Luke uses a corresponding standard phrase in Acts 15:8, δοὺς τὸ πνεῦμα τὸ ἅγιον (cf. John 3:34; Luke 11:13; Acts 8:17-18 (cf. 10:45); Rom 5:5; 1 Thess 4:8; 1 John 3:24; 4:13). Just as Paul sees God as the source (". . . he who supplies the Spirit to you . . ." Gal 3:5), so also Luke says that God is the one who gives the Spirit (Acts 15:8). And the wording in Acts 10:47 particularly resembles that in Gal 3:2. Rather varied formulations are then found in the parallels in Gal 3:5; Acts 10:44-45 and 11:15.

---

[26] Dibelius (1956) 94-95, an English translation of Dibelius (1951) 85.

[27] Haenchen (1971) 445; Schille (1983) 319-20; Conzelmann (1987) 116-17.

From Gal 3:1–2 we learn that this reception of the Spirit was brought about by Paul's missionary preaching of "Jesus Christ crucified", and specifically by "a hearing of faith" (ἐξ ἀκοῆς πίστεως). Similarly, in Acts 15:7 it was induced by the Gentiles' hearing of the gospel preached by Peter and their believing on that basis, διὰ τοῦ στόματός μου ἀκοῦσαι τὰ ἔθνη τὸν λόγον τοῦ εὐαγγελίου καὶ πιστεῦσαι. The idea of faith recurs in 15:9. The connection between preaching and the reception of the Spirit is also clear in Acts 10:44 and 11:15.

Paul concludes from the premise of their reception of the Spirit that the Galatian converts should not yield to the circumcision campaign of the intruders. As the conflict in Antioch was brought to Jerusalem, the same dissent also emerged there and Peter argues likewise against "some believers who belonged to the party of the Pharisees" in Jerusalem who "said, 'It is necessary to circumcise them, and to charge them to keep the law of Moses'", Acts 15:5. Peter contests their view by reporting how the centurion Cornelius and other Gentiles received the Spirit (Acts 10:17 – 11:19). Further points of agreements between Paul and Luke include the fact that both call circumcision a "yoke" (ζυγός, Gal 5:1 and Acts 15:10) and while Paul speaks of "power manifestations" (δυνάμεις) of the Spirit (Gal 3:5), Luke informs us that Cornelius and the others spoke in glossolalia (Acts 10:46).[28]

Although Luke thus draws on tradition when he tells the story about Peter and the centurion Cornelius,[29] Dibelius and others are right insofar as they maintain that Peter's speech at the Jerusalem meeting (Acts 15:7ff.), reveals the literary embellishment of Luke himself. Luke's creative activity can be seen from the fact that he draws a line from Peter's speech at the Jerusalem meeting not merely back to the Cornelius episode, but beyond it to the outpouring of

---

[28] For an interpretation of δυνάμεις as ecstatic phenomena, see Schmithals (1972) 47 and Lull (1978) 69–71; Mussner (1974) 211, interprets the term to mean charismatic gifts; Betz (1979) 135 translates the word as "miracles", and states that it remains unclear what kind of miracles Paul has in mind.

[29] Concerning the debate on the question of traditions behind the Cornelius episode in Acts, see the survey in Haenchen (1971) 355–57 and 360–63; and especially Haacker (1980), 234–51. The unevenness and variations among the various sections of Acts 10:1–11:18 and 15:6–9 are discussed in commentaries, and dealt with in a more concise form in studies like the above mentioned essays by Dibelius and Haacker.

the Spirit at Pentecost too. In his perception, the Cornelius episode was a "Pentecost" for the Gentiles; thus Peter's remark in 11:15, "And as I began to speak, the Holy Spirit fell on them, even as on us in the beginning." Moreover, Luke makes Peter's reference to chapters 10:1–11:18 at the Jerusalem meeting in such an allusive way that only the *readers* of Acts would understand the connection. Given, too, that Acts was probably written between A.D. 80 and 90 – that is, decades after the Jerusalem meeting took place – one might doubt the historical reliability of Luke's report of the meeting.[30]

However, when the Jerusalem meeting is understood as part of an ongoing debate, struggle, and conflict in Early Christianity, Luke's use and interpretation of the tradition receives a plausible historical basis. Paul's report and his way of arguing in Gal 3:1–5 offer help at this point. He gives evidence for the fact that an incident of the same nature as the Cornelius episode took place in the Early Church and played an important role in the dispute about the status of the Gentile converts. Consequently, the traditions about the reception of the Spirit by Cornelius and other Gentiles have a historical basis. Moreover, as shown above, Galatians ties together the Jerusalem meeting, Paul's preaching activity before the meeting and his "present" struggle in Galatia. It is therefore probable that his position on the Galatians' reception of the Spirit is an example of one kind of argument already more widely employed against those who insisted Gentile believers should become Jewish proselytes. The similarities between Paul's conversion account from Galatia and Peter's account of Caesarea support the view that Luke's use of the Cornelius story in Acts 15:7–11 exemplifies a type of argument which was used not merely at the Jerusalem meeting but also more widely both before and after. And by the same token it is probable that cases like the Cornelius incident or the Galatian episode, were referred to at the Jerusalem meeting, regardless of whether or not the Cornelius episode was itself specifically included. Luke, it would appear, had good historical and theological basis for using one such tradition (as it happened, the story about Cornelius), and for building it into his overall scheme of the Acts of the Apostles, for this way of arguing had played an

---

[30] Concerning the date of composition of Acts, see for example Conzelmann (1987) xxxiii, and for the date of the Jerusalem meeting, *ibid.*, 121.

important role in the debates on matters related to the Gentile converts in Early Christianity.

5. Jesus Christ, Jews and Gentiles

Paul links the Galatians' reception of the Spirit specifically to the proclamation of the crucified Jesus Christ (Gal 3:1ff.). The phrase "Jesus Christ the crucified" is one point taken from the christological kerygma (Acts 2:36: 4:10; cf. Matt 20:19: Luke 24:7). This abbreviated form of the kerygma is found also in 1 Cor 1:23 and 2:2, and drawn on in Gal 5:11 and 24. Thus the reception of the Spirit by the Galatians was brought about by their "hearing (the proclamation) of faith"[31] when the kerygma about Jesus Christ was proclaimed to them.

In Gal 3:2 the "hearing of the faith" is contrasted with the "works of the law." How can the proclamation of Christ crucified and the hearing of faith be an alternative to the works of the law? Paul's answer is twofold. First, "Jesus Christ crucified" is the foundation for a new kind of community, as said in Gal 5:6: "For in Christ Jesus neither circumcision nor uncircumcision means anything . . ." (See further 6:15 and 3:27–28). On this basis a new "paradigm" emerged, distinct on the one hand from the Jewish people as the people of the Law of Moses and on the other hand from the polytheistic cults and pagan way of life. Second, since it was *the preaching of Christ crucified* that led to the reception of the Spirit, it was demonstrated that this experience happened to the Gentile Christian converts even though they were not Jewish proselytes committed to the Law of Moses and obliged to undergo circumcision. Thus, according to Paul, they belonged to the people of God without having become citizens of the Jewish nation.

"Jesus Christ crucified" therefore meant transition away from the *Jewish* "paradigm" as well as away from the pagan one. It would go beyond the limits of this essay to examine further how Paul develops these two themes in his letter. Only a few observations can be mentioned. Paul centres his understanding of the transition around this very point from the kerygma, Christ crucified. This movement away from the Jewish "paradigm" is stated by Paul in Gal 3:13–14:

---

[31] For further discussion of the missionary concept of ἐξ ἀκοῆς πίστεως, see Betz (1979) 133, n. 50, and Lull (1978) 55, and ns. 17–20.

Christ has redeemed us from the curse of the Law by becoming a curse for us – for it is written, "Cursed is everyone who hangs on a tree" – in order that the blessing of Abraham might come upon the Gentiles through Jesus Christ, that we might receive the promise of the Spirit through faith.

The precise meaning of these verses in their context is problematic and much debated.[32] Only two remarks should be made. First, Paul tells here how it has been made possible for the Gentiles to receive the Spirit through faith, the very same experience which had happened to the Galatian converts (Gal 3:1–5). Second, Paul says that this new "paradigm" based on "Jesus Christ crucified" was not new, since it was actually the "paradigm" of the "will" and "promise" given to Abraham, ". . . in order that the blessing of Abraham might come upon the Gentiles through Jesus Christ . . ."[33] As for the movement away from the pagan "paradigm", Gal 5:24 gives a clue: "And those who belong to Christ Jesus have crucified the flesh with its passions and desires." The term "flesh" refers here back to the catalogue in Gal 5:19–21, which lists idolatry and other pagan vices. Thus the kerygmatic element of Christ's crucifixion is seen as the foundation for the turning away from the pagan way of life.

Turning again to the Acts of the Apostles an important point of similarity between Paul and Luke can be added: just as the reception of the Spirit by the Galatians resulted from their hearing of Paul's proclamation of the kerygma about Jesus Christ, so also the reception of the Spirit by Cornelius and the other Gentiles came when Peter proclaimed the kerygma (Acts 10:34–42). Again, as Paul did in Gal 3:1, 13, Luke also refers to the crucifixion of Jesus: ". . . him they killed, hanging him on a tree . . ." (ὃν καὶ ἀνεῖλαν κρεμάσαντες

---

[32] Cf. Betz (1979) 148–53; Wilcox (1977) 85–99; Bruce (1982) 27–36; Dunn (1990) 225–32.

[33] The sharp distinction drawn by E. P. Sander between the Jewish "covenental nomism" and Paul's "participation theology" is criticized by Hooker (1982) 47–56. She points to the fact that Paul in Gal 3 implies the concept of covenant when he speaks about the will, meaning the promises given to Abraham and his offspring, promises which were fulfilled in Jesus Christ. Thus the idea of covenant also belongs to Paul's "participation theology" and the contrast between Judaism and Paul should not be so sharply drawn as Sanders does.
As for the idea of covenant, see Marshall (1987) 126–28.

ἐπὶ ξύλου), Acts 10:39. It is important that Luke here, as in 5:30, alludes to Deut 21:22, the very Old Testament verse which is quoted by Paul in Gal 3:13. The application of this Old Testament verse to the crucifixion therefore belonged to an early Christian exegetical tradition utilized by both Paul and Luke. Moreover, the combination of the reception of the Spirit and the proclamation of the kerygma about Christ both in Gal 3:1–5, 13–14 and in Acts 10:34–44, as also in 11:15 and 15:7–8, demonstrates that Luke's employment of the christological kerygma in the Cornelius story in Acts 10 is not as such due to his own literary creativity, but comes from the tradition which he had inherited.[34] This observation does not mean that Luke has not used his skill as a writer integrating the tradition into his book and interpreting it within his own view of history, as we have seen.

In spite of this important parallel between Paul and Luke, however, there is also a difference in the way in which they develop the argument further and apply it. Luke does not concentrate on the crucifixion as Paul does, but has a broader range of christological and soteriological points which are relevant to the cross-national perspective of the context:[35] Jesus "is Lord of all" (Acts 10:36), ". . . he is the one ordained by God to be judge of the living and the dead" (10:42), and "everyone who believes in him receives forgiveness of sins through his name" (10:43). In addition the picture of Jesus' ministry would be relevant to the situation: ". . . how God anointed him with the Holy Spirit and with power, who went about doing good, and healing all who were oppressed by the devil, for God was with him . . ." (10:38). Luke's most pointed argument, however, is the remark which follows the reception of the Spirit: The Gentiles received the Spirit just as the Jewish Christians have, even with particular reference to the Pentecost experience of the Spirit (Acts 2; cf. Acts 10:47; 11:15–17; 15:8–9). Paul does not use this argument, although he makes clear by his employment of the first person plural that both Jewish and Gentile Christians have the Spirit. In Gal 3:14 he

---

[34] Contra Dibelius (1956) 165; Haenchen (1971) 351. For further criticism of Dibelius' analysis and for careful examination of the connection between Peter's speech and the context, see Haacker (1980) 244–46; Pesch (1986) 33–34, and Dauer (1990) 82–83, 86–87.

[35] For the following points, see Haacker (1980) 245.

writes: ". . . that *we* might receive the promise of the Spirit", and in Gal 5:25: "If we live by the Spirit, let us also walk by the Spirit."

Although Luke may himself have influenced these specific points, in general they probably render various emphases which already existed in the kerygmatic tradition. For example, Luke's combination of the point about Jesus' resurrection with his future function as a judge has not only a parallel in the Areopagos speech (Acts 17:31) but also in the part from the missionary kerygma given by Paul in 1 Thess 1:10: ". . . whom he (God) raised from the dead, Jesus who delivers us from the wrath to come." Moreover, the fact that Luke mentions these relevant christological and soteriological points listed above without elaborating upon them theologically, also supports the understanding that he reports on motifs which he had received.

A final question is to be asked: How can it be explained historically that the Jew Jesus, and the churches' Christology, came to create a cross-national community-paradigm *different* from the national community-paradigm of the Law of Moses? No elaborate answer can be given here, but some thoughts can be offered for further consideration.

First, this development took place within the context of a process in which different views and lines of action were present. Thus, although it is impossible to give a precise definition of the Christology of Paul's opponents in Galatia, it is clear that they regarded the Galatian converts as Jewish proselytes and as members of the Jewish nation. They did not see Christology as a foundation for a cross-national community-paradigm as Paul did. Second, the historical fact that Jesus was executed by means of crucifixion within the context of the legal system had the potential to provide an alternative paradigm to the existing model.[36] Such a background would not explain, however, why Christology led to a paradigm of *cross-national* nature rather than merely to a Jewish sect. A possible historical explanation for such a development would be that the historical ministry of Jesus, and thus also his death and subsequent resurrection, was understood to initiate the eschatological era which also should comprise the non-Jewish nations.[37] Thus the crucifixion of Jesus and his association with the inauguration of the eschatological era for both Jews and

---

[36] Cf. Hooker (1982) 55.

[37] Cf. the perspective in the essay of Dahl (1974) 10–36.

Gentiles could possibly lead to a new community paradigm, one not based on the division between those circumcised according to the law and those uncircumcised. From its starting point with the historical Jesus, the new paradigm was worked out in the struggle between conflicting viewpoints and conflicting community models.

IV

THE REVELATION TO JOHN

10

Polemic in the Book of Revelation

Introduction

In the messages to the church (*ekklesia*) in Smyrna and the church in Philadelphia, the phrase "Synagogue of Satan" is used, Rev 2:9 and 3:9. Rev 2:9 reads: ". . . the slander of those who say that they are Jews and are not, but are a Synagogue of Satan." In Rev 3:9 the corresponding sentence reads: "Behold, I will make those of the Synagogue of Satan who say that they are Jews and are not, but lie . . ." In his book *The Devil and the Jews*, J. Trachtenberg refers to these and other New Testament passages as documentation for the animosity of the Early Church toward the Jews.[1] He draws the line from the New Testament to the fourth and fifth centuries, when the Church had established itself, using Chrysostom of Antioch as a main source. Chrysostom maintained that the Synagogues of the Jews are the homes of idolatry and devils, and that the Jews did not worship God but devils.[2] Since Trachtenberg concentrates on the impact which such New Testament concepts made on people throughout the centuries, he does not enter into an analysis of Rev 2:9 and 3:9 in their own historical context.

Correspondingly, in *The American Family Bible*, published by "The American Institute for the Study of Racial and Religious Cooperation", Philadelphia 1986, Rev 2:9 and 3:9 are among the verses which are reformulated because of their assumed anti-Semitic

---

[1] Trachtenberg (1943) 20–21.
[2] *ibid.*

275

connotations. The reformulation of Rev 2:9 reads: ". . . I know the blasphemy of them which say they are religious, and are not, but are the assembly of Satan." Similarily, Rev 3:9 is rephrased in this way: "Behold, I will make them of the assembly of Satan, which say they are religious, and are not, but do lie . . ." In another publication sponsored by "The American Institute", the anthology *Jews and Christians. Exploring the Past, Present, and Future,* edited by J. H. Charlesworth, a more precise understanding of these passages is presented. In his contribution to this volume, D. Moody Smith makes the observation that the term *Ioudaioi* only appears twice in Rev (2:9; 3:9), in both cases in an indirectly positive sense. That is, members of the "Synagogue of Satan" are said to claim to be Jews although in reality they are not. "Jew" is still used in a positive sense even if the "Synagogue of Satan" means Jews in Smyrna, or Philadelphia, or even contemporary Jews generally. In that case, they have defected from proper Judaism.[3] A. Yarbro Collins entertains a similar view. The name "Jews" is denied the Jews of the local Synagogues, because the followers of Jesus are held to be the true Jews. Thus the term "Jew" is not here derogatory in and of itself.[4]

It is debated whether those who call themselves Jews in Rev 2:9 and 3:9 are actually Jews or whether they are Christians. In the latter case, the tension reflected is an inner Christian conflict. M. Newman, H. Koester, H. Kraft and S. Sandmel assume this background for the controversy. Newman and Koester assume that those who call themselves Jews are Christians belonging to the group of Nicolaitans.[5] E. Schüssler Fiorenza takes issue with this interpretation, and maintains that those who call themselves Jews are actually Jewish citizens in Smyrna and Philadelphia. John says that the *ekklesiai* might suffer persecution from the so-called Jews, no such persecution is mentioned in the statements about the Nicolaitans. Thus, some Jews endanger the churches by persecution from the outside, while the Nicolaitans endanger the churches from the inside by advocating

---

[3] Smith (1990) 88–89.

[4] Yarbro Collins (1984) 85–87.

[5] Koester (1971) 114–57; Newman (1968) 30; Kraft (1974) 60–61; Sandmel (1978) 122–23.

that Christians had freedom to become part of the syncretistic pagan society.[6]

The question of polemic in Revelation is much broader than the debate on the meaning of the polemic statements in Rev 2:9 and 3:9. All scholars recognize this fact. The view that guides the present study is that John builds on traditions, thought-categories and outlooks held by segments of the Jewish people, and that he transforms them on the basis of belief in Jesus Christ. The book reflects a situation where Christians understood themselves to be a distinct group within a Jewish context, and even thought themselves to be the true Jews.

Jewish Tradition and Perspective

The Jewish character of the Book of Revelation is obvious and commonly recognized. Although the book was written in Asia Minor on the island of Patmos and seven Asian towns are mentioned by name, it draws on and interprets a Biblical and traditional Jewish geographical outlook. This is the case whether or not the geographical references are to be interpreted as symbols of a spiritual reality only or they also are thought of as geographical locations in the external and concrete world.[7]

Accordingly, Jerusalem plays the central role in the thought-world of the book. The vision of the future centres around the new Jerusalem, the Holy City which is coming down out of heaven from God (Rev 21:2; see also 3:12). It is pictured as an imperial capital: "By its light shall the nations walk; and the kings of the earth shall bring their glory into it . . .". (21:24–25).[8] The hill of Jerusalem's temple, Mount Zion is also mentioned, Rev 14:1: "Then I looked, and lo, on Mount Zion stood . . . a hundred and forty-four thousand . . ." As indicated by the number 144,000, that is 12 x 12,000, the city is the centre for

---

[6] Fiorenza (1985) 117–20. For a more detailed discussion of the Nicolaitans, see Kraft (1974) 72–74; Beck (1962) 547–48.

[7] Concerning the problem of spiritual and/or concrete and spatial, see commentaries, such as Beasley-Murray (1974) 23; 305ff., etc.; Mounce (1977) 39–45; 368ff., etc.

[8] The new Jerusalem, see T. Dan 5:12; 2 Bar 32:2–4; 4 Ezra 7:26. As for the thought that the kings of the earth shall bring their glory into the new Jerusalem, cf. Isa 60.

the people of God, Israel, with its twelve tribes. Correspondingly, on the gates of Jerusalem the names of the twelve tribes of the sons of Israel are inscribed (Rev 21:12). At this point, the question will not be raised whether John here refers to the Jews, Jewish Christians or the Church as the new Israel.[9] For our present purpose, it is sufficient to say that the author bases his presentation on Jewish geographical and ideological outlook.

In agreement with parts of the Old Testament (see for example Isa 13; 47, etc.: Jer 50; 51; 52; Dan 4; 5; Mic 4:10; Zech 2:7ff.) Babylon is the main city of the enemy, Rev 14:8; 16:19; 17:5; 18:2, 10, 21. Babylon is associated with "impure passions" (14:8; 18:3), "harlots and earth's abominations" (17:5); "dwelling place of demons", "fornication ... wealth" (18:2–3, 9, 21ff.). The polemic is harsh, and the city suffers devastating destruction.

The Book of Revelation remains within the context of Jewish views when this biblical conflict between Israel and Babylon is applied to the new historical situation in which Rome is seen as the evil enemy. Babylon serves then as a symbolic name for Rome, as also is the case in *Sib. Or.* 5:143, 4 *Ezra* 15:43ff. and 16:1ff. The analogy between Babylon and Rome underlies the setting of 4 *Ezra* and 2 *Bar.*[10] In the Book of Revelation it is related how Babylon/Rome were destroyed: "Then a mighty angel took up a stone like a great millstone and threw it into the sea, saying, 'So shall Babylon the great city be thrown down with violence, and shall be found no more ...'", and correspondingly in 4 *Ezra* 15:43ff. it says: "They shall go on steadily to Babylon, and shall destroy her".

Thus, the Book of Revelation draws on Jewish traditions and perspectives in its geographical and political outlook.

The same is seen within the more specifically religious realm. The polemic against participation in pagan polytheistic cults in Revelation follows Jewish traditions. According to the Torah, it was a crime for the Israelites to take part in pagan idolatry. The passage in Num 25:1–9 exemplifies this attitude: Here it is said that the Israelites "began to play the harlot with the daughters of Moab. These invited the people to the sacrifices of their gods, and

---

[9] See commentaries, such as Charles (1920) 1:188–99; 2:4, 162. Beasley-Murray (1974) 139–41; 222; 320.

[10] See Charlesworth (1983) 396; 520; 557; 615–17.

the people ate, and bowed down to their gods." It is then related how Phinehas took a spear in his hand and pierced it through an Israelite man and a pagan woman who committed the crime together. Balaam and Balak are not mentioned in Num 25:1ff., but a widespread Jewish exegetical tradition makes the inference from the advice given by Balaam in Num 31:16 that Balak should use Moabite women to seduce Israelites to commit adultery and idolatry: "Behold, these caused the people of Israel, by the counsel of Balaam, to act treacherously against the Lord in the matter of Peor . . ."

Philo, in *The Special Laws* 1:54–57 illustrates the function of the Phinehas episode in the first century A.D.:[11]

> But if any members of the nation betray the honour due to the One, they should suffer the utmost penalties . . . And it is well that all who have a zeal for virtue should be permitted to exact the penalties offhand and with no delay . . . There is recorded in the Laws the example of one who acted with this admirable courage. He had seen some persons consorting with foreign women and through the attraction of their love-charms spurning their ancestral customs and seeking admission to the rites of a fabulous religion. One in particular he saw, the chief ringleader of the backsliding, who had the audacity to exhibit his unholy conduct in public and was openly offering sacrifices, a travesty of the name, to images of wood and stones in the presence of the whole people. So seized with inspired fury, keeping back the throng of spectators on either side, he slew without a qualm him and her, the man because he listened to lessons which it were a gain to unlearn, the woman because she had been the instructor in wickedness.

In his rendering of Num 25:1–9 Josephus applies the passage to the pressures felt by Jews in his own days. In his advice to king Balak Balaam concluded:[12]

> . . . when they shall see these youths overmastered by their passions, let them quit them and, on their entreating them to stay, let them

---

[11] See Seland (1995) 103–81.
[12] See Unnik (1974) 241–61.

not consent till they have induced their lovers to renounce the laws of their fathers and the God to whom they owe them, and to worship the gods of the Midianites and Moabites. (*Ant.* 4:(126–)130)

Viewpoints expressed by the pagans against the Jews in Josephus' own times are reflected in the words of the Midianite women:

Seeing then . . . that you . . . have customs and a mode of life wholly alien to all mankind, insomuch that your food is of a peculiar sort and your drink is distinct from that of other men, it behoves you, if you would live with us, also to revere our gods . . . Nor can any man reproach you for venerating the special gods of the country whereto you are come, above all when our gods are common to all mankind, while yours has no other worshippers. (*Ant.* 4:137–38)

The non-conforming Israelites defended themselves in the speech of Zambrias (Num 25:14: Zimri) addressed to Moses:

. . . I have married, as thou sayest, a foreign wife . . ., and I sacrifice to gods to whom I hold sacrifice to be due, deeming it right to get at the truth for myself from many persons, and not to live as under a tyranny, hanging all my hopes for my whole life upon one . . . (*Ant.* 4:(145–)149. This speech has no warrant in the biblical account.)

Elements from such traditions are drawn on by John in the edict[13] to the *ekklesia* in Pergamum: "But I have a few things against you: you have some there who hold the teachings of Balaam, who taught Balak to put a stumbling block before the sons of Israel, that they might eat food sacrificed to idols and practice immorality", Rev 2:14.

The sharp polemic against participation in polytheistic cults is also found in the edict to the *ekklesia* in Thyatira: "But I have this against you that you tolerate the woman Jezebel, who calls herself

---

[13] Concerning the letters to the seven churches as edicts, see Aune (1990) 182–204.

a prophetess and is teaching and beguiling my servants to practise immorality and to eat food sacrificed to idols" (Rev 2:20).

The problem of prophets encouraging the Israelites to join the pagans in worshipping idols is stated in Deut 13:1ff. In the first century A.D. Philo paraphrases this passage:

> Further, if anyone cloaking himself under the name and guise of a prophet and claiming to be possessed by inspiration lead us on to the worship of the gods recognized in the different cities, we ought not to listen to him and be deceived by the name of prophet. (*Spec.* 1:315)

The conclusion is that John's Revelation 2:14 and 20 formulate Jewish polemic against participation in pagan polytheistic cults, such as found in Philo and Josephus. Moreover, John's statements, just as the ones by Philo and Josephus, give evidence for the existence of a tension within the people of God between different approaches to the surrounding world. In Pergamum, Thyatira and Alexandria and other places there were Jews and Christians who wanted to function within society at large, and respond positively to the conditions set by the pagans, like the one rendered by Josephus in *Ant.* 12:125–26: ". . . the Ionians agitated against them (the Jews) . . . and claimed that, if the Jews were to be their fellows, they should worship the Ionians' gods . . ." (Cf. the words of the Midianite women, *Ant.* 4:137–38, cited above). Others would follow the line of John in Rev 2:14–16 and 20–23, and Philo in *The Special Laws* 1:54–57 and 315ff.: such participation in pagan cult was forbidden and resulted in punishment.

Both in Jewish and Christian polemic pagan polytheistic worship can be associated with demonic forces.[14] Such a characterization of pagans is found in the Septuagint translation of Psalm 96 (95):4ff.: "For all the gods of the peoples are demons." Similarily, Paul says that what pagans sacrifice they offer to demons and not to God (1 Cor 10:20). The meaning of such labelling of pagan worship is not to say that they worship gods carrying the names of demonic powers, such as the Devil, Satan, etc., but such terms are labels to distinguish "us" from "them" in a dualistic manner.

---

[14] See Smith (1978) 425–39.

Against this background one might think that the phrase "Synagogue of Satan" in Rev 2:9 and 3:9 indicates that there existed a dualistic relationship between the Christian *ekklesia* and the Jewish Synagogue like the one between Christianity/Judaism and the Gentiles with their pagan worship. If so the conflict is extra-mural in nature.The survey of research given at the beginning of the present study showed that the two passages picture an intra-mural Jewish conflict. The question behind the phrase the "Synagogue of Satan" is: Where are the true Jews to be found, in the *ekklesia* or in the Synagogue?

With this in mind it is important to note that demonic concepts are used as characterizations of the opponents in intra-mural controversies, within Christianity as well as within Judaism.[15] As background for Rev 2:9 and 3:9 we therefore must look into conflicts between groups among the Jews. The Dead Sea Scrolls have given us first hand information about a covenantal community, often called the Qumran community, that harshly criticized other Jews.[16] Israel in general is caught in "the nets of Belial", the lord of the evil forces (4QpPsa 1–10 II 10–11). These are the traps mentioned in CD 4:14–18 as consisting of fornication, riches and the defilement of the Temple. The Qumran community is saved from these nets and will "inherit the earth" (1–10 II 9–11). It is waiting for the destruction of the wicked and for the moment when it will rule Jerusalem.

Although the formulations in the Thanksgiving Hymns, the Hodayot, might be poetic and general and therefore might not in the same way give concrete references to specific persons and groups, it is of interest to note that the phrase "Synagogue of Satan", Rev 2:9 and 3:9, has a striking parallel in the phrase "the congregation of Belial," 1QH 2:22. The Hebrew word which here is translated as "congregation", עדה, might even be translated as "Synagogue", since in the Septuagint the Greek word συναγωγή, Synagogue, is used most frequently to render this Hebrew term, (see, e.g., Num 26:9 (LXX)).

Other writings also tell about the dualistic relationship between the Qumran community and other persons and communities within Judaism. "The Spouter of Lies" was the leader of a rival congregation.

---

[15] *ibid.*

[16] For the following, see Dimant (1984) 483–550, esp. 508–10 and 542–43.

He is accused for "building through bloodshed his city of vanity and erecting through falsehood a congregation" (1QpHab 10:10). The "Teacher of Rightousness", in contrast, leads "the congregation of His elect" (4QpPsa 1–10 II 5; 1–10 III 5), symbolized by the eschatological Jerusalem. Another adversary is "the Wicked Priest". He profaned Jerusalem and the Sanctuary, persecuted "the Teacher of Righteousness", a priest, and his followers (1QpHab 8:8–13; 8:16 – 9:2; 11:4–8, 12–15; 12:2–6, 7–10).

Thus, the Qumran writings exemplify how a community within Judaism understood its relationship to other Jews in dualistic terms. Within the context of Judaism, the Qumran community associated "the others" with demonic forces such as the figure of Belial. Similarily, "the others" in Rev 2:9 and 3:9 are called the Synagogue of Satan.

While the opponents in Rev 2:9 and 3:9 are Jews in Smyrna and Philadelphia in Asia Minor, the polemic in the Qumran writings is primarily against persons and groups in Jerusalem, more specifically priestly circles in the Jerusalem Temple. John's polemic includes also a polemic against Jerusalem, however, as can be seen in Rev 11:1–13. The "two witnesses" will be killed after they have finished their testimony "and their dead bodies will lie in the street of the great city which is allegorically called Sodom and Egypt, where their Lord was crucified" (Rev 11:8). The reference to the crucifixion of Jesus shows that Jerusalem is meant. Thus, in Revelation there is a dual interpretation of Jerusalem. On the one hand it is associated with salvation and the heavenly bliss (Rev 3:12; 21:2, etc.), and on the other hand she is subject to severe criticism. The historical city is under judgment and is in Rev 11:8 symbolically characterized as "Sodom" and "Egypt". Corresponding statements of criticism and judgments against Jerusalem are found in Isa 1:9–10 where those who live in Jerusalem are called "rulers of Sodom" and "people of Gomorrah".[17] The persecution of the two witnesses and of their "Lord", Jesus, corresponds to the persecution suffered in Jerusalem by the founder of the Qumran community and his followers. The conclusion is that in spite of all differences between the Dead Sea

---

[17] See Yarbro Collins (1984) 86–87. Another interpretation is suggested by Mounce (1977) 226–27: "The great city" in Rev 11:8 means the power of Rome. "The inclusion of a reference to the crucifixion is not to identify a geographical location but to illustrate the response of paganism to righteousness."

Scrolls and the Book of Revelation, both reflect intra-mural conflicts in Jewish communities in which the adversaries are associated with evil demonic forces.

As background for the reference to a "Synagogue of Satan" in the edict to the *ekklesia* in Smyrna, it is significant that there was a strong Jewish community in the city, as documented by inscriptions and literary works.[18] The Jewish community in Smyrna played an active role in the martyrdom of Polycarp, and later in the Decian persecution it took an active part in the martyrdom of Pionius.[19] These other evidences for Jews persecuting Christians support the understanding that John has such persecutions from (other) Jews in mind when he wrote: "Do not fear what you are about to suffer. Behold, the devil is about to throw some of you in prison, that you may be tested, and for ten days you will have tribulation. Be faithful unto death, and I will give you the crown of life", Rev 2:10. John also indicates that the superior status and power of the Synagogue in Philadelphia will be changed to the effect that they will have to render the *ekklesia* respect and homage:". . . I will make them come and bow down before your feet . . ." (Rev 3:9).

Thus we have substantiated the view that John builds on traditions, thought-categories, and outlooks held by segments of the Jewish people. Next the task is to examine the way in which John has transformed this background on the basis of belief in Jesus Christ.

The *Ekklesia* of Christ as the True Jews

As seen in other chapters of this book, several writings in the New Testament offer documentation for tension and conflict to exist between Christian Jews and other Jews, as an intra-mural controversy within the Jewish communities. As a small and growing movement, persons in the Early Church suffered persecution from their fellow-Jews (see e.g., Acts 4:1–31; 5:17–42; 6:8 – 8:3; 11:19 – 12:19; 17:1–10; 18:12–17; 21:27–36; 23:12–22; 2 Cor 11:23–26; cf. Gal 5:11; John 16:1–2). In a recent dissertation, Torrey Seland has placed such persecutions within the broader context of reactions by zealous persons within

---

[18] Schürer (1986) 20–21; Stern (1974) 151.
[19] See Charles (1920A) 56–57; Horst (1989) 116–17.

Jewish communities against nonconformists. Similar phenomena in other (non-Jewish) ethnic groups, nations and religious communities are also discussed. He further shows that passages in the Law of Moses, such as the Phinehas episode (Num 25:6–9) and the law against false prophets (e.g. Deut 13:1–11), demanded that deviators who committed serious crimes that were understood to be of anticonstitutional character should be persecuted and killed, if necessary by fellow Jews on the spot. These actions were intra-mural measures against persons who were felt seriously to threaten the identity of the community and its foundations. Such persecutions should be classified as vigilante actions – acts or threats of coercion in violation of the formal boundaries or laws of an established sociopolitical order; those acts or threats however, are intended by the violators to defend that order from some form of subversion.[20] Accordingly, the Jewish persecution of Christian fellow Jews and the polemic reactions by Christians are not to be seen as Jewish anti-paganism or Christian anti-Semitism, but as an intra-mural conflict, parallels to which are found in many other communities and groups in the world. When this intra-mural controversy was in the distant past and non-Jewish Christians attacked the Jewish nation as a collective from the outside, then the conflict turned extra-mural and in many cases became anti-Semitic.

So far it has been shown that the polemic in the Book of Revelation is to be understood within the context of Jewish traditions, thought-categories, and perspectives. Further discussion is needed in order to trace the distinctively Christian use and transformation of this Jewish heritage on the basis of which John interprets the situation of the *ekklesiai* of Christ in Asia Minor.

One might ask if the idea of Jewish proselytism is interpreted afresh and transformed from Christian notions. Rev 5:9–10 and 7:9ff. might be understood in this way. In Rev 5:9 we read about the Lamb who was slain and by his blood ransomed men for God "from every tribe and tongue and people and nation". Similarily 7:9 tells about "a great multitude which no man could number, from every nation, from all tribes and peoples and tongues". From 7:14 one learns that they have washed their robes and made them white in the blood of the Lamb. There are observations which speak

---

[20] Seland (1995) 10–11.

in favour of regarding this multitude as Christian proselytes. They came from many (pagan) nations; they needed redemption and cleansing. Philo and Josephus do not specify that cleansing was part of becoming proselytes, but Asenath, in the process of becoming proselyte, is told by the angel to wash her face and hands with living water and undress the black dress of mourning and dress in a new linen robe, *Joseph and Asenath* 14:12–17. Moreover, Paul states in 1 Cor 6:11 that the Corinthian Gentiles became Christian proselytes by being washed and sanctified. Thus, there is some support for suggesting that the washing of the robes in Rev 7:14 reflects ideas from Jewish proselytism. Accordingly, on the surface it seems natural to understand 7:9ff. as a reference to Gentile Christians from all nations, while 7:1–8 about the 144,000 from the twelve tribes of Israel seems to refer to the Jewish Christians. There are scholars who entertain such interpretations.[21]

Rev 5:9–10 speaks against drawing such a distinction between Jewish Christians and Gentile Christians, however, since those who are ransomed from every tribe and tongue and people and nation are characterized as Israel in accordance with Exod 19:6: "You shall be to me a kingdom of priests and a holy nation". The Jewish institution of proselytism might still be behind this idea, since there are several sources which testify to the view that the proselytes became full citizens of God's Israel.[22]

The redemptive death of Jesus Christ is not seen only as the means by which Gentiles become proselytes, however. His death is so fundamental that it constitutes the people of God (the true Jews) as such, as is seen from Rev 1:5–6: "To him who loves us and has freed us from our sins by his blood and made us a kingdom, priests to his God (... βασιλείαν, ἱερεῖς τῷ θεῷ) and Father ..." As in Rev 5:9–10 the basis for this characterization of Israel is Exod 19:6.[23] The idea of Israel as a priestly nation was widespread in Judaism, as can be seen from 2 Macc 2:17; *Mek. Exod.* 19:6; *Jub.* 16:18; Philo,

---

[21] See Bousset (1906) ad loc; Flusser (1988) 449, n. 191; Feuillet (1967) 197–98.

[22] Borgen (1987C) 207–54; Segal (1988) 336–69. The proselytes receive equal rank with all the privileges of the native-born Jews according to Philo, *Spec.* 1:52; *Virt.* 102–03. The same rule is stated in rabbinic writings, see Montefiore and Loewe (1938) 571–73.

[23] For further discussion of Rev 1:5–6 and 5:9–10, see Fiorenza (1985) 68–81.

Abr. 56;98; *Sobr.* 66; *Mos.* 1:149. The Jewish nation had received the gift of priesthood and prophecy on behalf of all mankind, *Abr.* 98, and this nation was destined to be consecrated above all others to offer prayers for ever on behalf of the human race, *Mos.* 1:149.[24] According to Rev 1:5–6 the redemptive death of Jesus Christ brought this priestly people of God into being. No distinction is made here between Jewish Christians and Gentile Christians. In the word "us" John includes himself and the seven Churches as representatives of the true Israel founded by Christ. Thus the priestly nation consists of all those who have been freed from their sins by the sacrificial death of Jesus Christ, Jews and Gentiles alike.[25] It should be remembered that there were rabbinic traditions which stated that the conditions for the admission of Gentiles were the same as the constitutive elements of the people of Israel: Just as one who is admitted to Judaism must submit to circumcision, ablution and sacrifice, so Israel during the Exodus did not receive the Torah until they had performed these three ceremonies, *Mekilta Rabbi Simon* 96–97.[26] Similarily, the washing of the robes in Rev 7:14 of the multitude from many nations may allude to the Israelites washing their clothes when approaching God at Sinai. Among the many varied and often conflicting Jewish eschatological ideas there were also expectations that people from other nations would convert and become proselytes, that the other nations would join Israel in worshipping the one true God and have Jerusalem as mother city and that they would throw away their own laws and accept the Torah.[27] Against such background ideas John has interpreted the Church as the inclusive eschatological Israel who comprises both Jews and Gentiles in the one people of God. Thus, the twelve tribes of the sons of Israel (Rev 7:4–8) and the great multitude from every nation, all tribes and peoples and tongues (7:9–14) do not refer to two different groups, the Jewish Christians and the Gentile Christians. The redemption through the death of Christ constitutes

---

[24] For a discussion of the wording, see Charles (1920A) 1:16, and other commentaries. Concerning Philo, see Borgen (1992) 342–51.

[25] For a discussion of Rev 1:5–6, see Fiorenza (1985) 78, n. 18.

[26] Ginzberg (1968) 88.

[27] See Philo, *Mos.* 2:44; *Tanchuma* (Buber), *Debarim* 2b fin; *Siphre Deut* §354 (on 33:18); *Midr. Ps.* on Ps 100:1. Montefiore and Loewe (1938) 564–65.

the true people of Israel who are drawn from the Jewish nation as well as other nations. As implied in Rev 2:9 and 3:9 they are then the true Jews, in contrast to those who say that they are Jews but are not.

Thus the thinking in the Book of Revelation indeed resembles the self-understanding of the Qumran community that they were the true Israel within Judaism. In this way the polemic in both cases comes from an internal polemic between the true Jews and those "who say that they are Jews and are not" (Rev 2:9; 3:9).[28] The Christian Israel in Revelation has a cross-national structure that is lacking in the Qumran community, even though the Qumran community, like John, looks forward to the victory of God and his people over the enemies, i.e. over demonic forces and evil people and nations, the Roman Empire in particular.[29]

Did the general populace in the various cities involved look upon this polemic between the Christian *ekklesia* and the Synagogue as an intra-mural conflict? Before we answer this question, the general observation should be made that at several places in Asia Minor the interaction between Jews and Christians was so extensive that the distinctions between both groups were blurred.[30] This situation was at times felt to be such a threat to leading circles in the Church that sharp polemic and conflict arose. In New Testament times Christianity grew up from within Judaism and struggled with the question of whether or not Gentile converts were to be understood as Jewish proselytes. The Judaizers came to the churches in Galatia and wanted to bring the newly won Christians fully into Jewish proselyte status, as can be learned from Paul's Letter to the Galatians.[31] The Letter to the Colossians contains a warning against Jewish ceremonial observances and dietary laws. Thus the members of the Church seemed to follow Jewish life style, mixed with a cult of angels, Col 2:16–19.

Early in the second century Ignatius of Antioch admonishes the Churches of Magnesia and Philadelphia not to yield to Judaizing

---

[28] See Flusser (1988) 79.

[29] See Mussner (1985) 209–27.

[30] For the following survey, see especially Sheppard (1979) 169–80; Horst (1989) 106–21.

[31] See Borgen (1987C) 206–72.

influence. Inscriptions that were found in the area around Acmonia and Eumenia that date to the third and fourth centuries A.D. display a blending of Jewish and Christian features. In Sardis, in early Byzantine times, a market street with Jewish and Christian shops side by side existed behind the Synagogue. After the cessation of imperial cult activities in the Sebasteion in Aphrodisias, premises seemed to have been used as shops. Here both menorahs and crosses have been incised on some of the doorjambs. The intense attack by John Chrysostom of Antioch in his eight homilies preached in A.D. 386–87 against the Jews and against Christians who frequented the Synagogue illustrates how vehement polemic could presuppose extensive interaction and some degree of practical integration between the Christians and the synagogual community. Chrysostom levels charges against Christians who go to the Synagogue on the Sabbath, who receive circumcision, celebrate the Jewish Pesach, and who keep the Jewish dietary laws and other observances, such as fasting. Moreover, in canon 29 of the Council of Laodicea, which was held in the second half of the fourth century, the following formulation occurs: "It is forbidden that Christians live like Jews and rest on Sabbath; they should work on that day. They should prefer the Lord's day to rest on, if possible, since they are Christians. If they turn out to be Judaizers, let them be accursed by Christ." Canon 38 deals also with the problem of Judaizing: "It is forbidden to take unleavened bread from the Jews or to participate in their godless acts." Canon 37 forbids Christians to participate in the festivals of the Jews, and canon 36 warns the clergy against making *phylacteries*, protective amulets, probably meaning Jewish *tefillin*, small boxes with leather straps, to be placed on the arm and the upper forehead, containing strips of parchment on which are written Deut 6:4–9; 11:13–21, and Exod 13:1–16.

How far does the Book of Revelation reflect common Jewish community features and social "markers" which could be recognized by people from the outside? One major common characteristric between the Synagogue and the *ekklesia* was the circumstance that they were organized groups that rejected the pagan polytheistic gods and worship. Insofar as there was tension within the groups with regard to separation from or integration into the pagan surroundings, they had this struggle in common. John and some (other) Jews had in common that they opposed the Roman ideology and government on the basis of Jewish traditions. Moreover, both groups based their self-understanding in general on Jewish traditions and ideas. They also had in common some of the ethical standards and life-styles. Since John understood the true Israel to be cross-national, the *ekklesia* comprised both Jewish Christians and Gentile Christians. Nevertheless, the strong Jewish character of the book and the Jewish community features mentioned above indicate that John and the Christian congregations referred to still had their base in Jewish milieus and had Jews as members. It is to be noticed, however, that questions of circumcision, Sabbath and Jewish dietary laws are not discussed in Revelation apart from the prohibition against eating pagan sacrificial food, Rev 2:14 and 2:20. Some of these omissions may be due to the emphasis on the polemic against pagan Rome. In any case, free attitudes towards observances existed in some segments of the Jewish communities, as documented by Philo in *Migr.* 89–93.

Why then, was there tension between the *ekklesia* and the Synagogue, which both claimed to be Israel, to the effect that they mutually denied the right of the other group to carry the name? On the level of theology and ideology the reason must have been that each group made an exclusive claim to be the legitimate owner of the Jewish traditions. When the redemptive death of Jesus Christ is understood to be the constitutive foundation of the true Israel and the true Jews, then from the viewpoint of John the other Jews say that they are Jews, but are not. One aspect of this Christian self-understanding was the conviction that the new eschatological era had dawned. Correspondingly, the Jews in the Synagogue would make an exclusive claim on the basis of their understanding of the constitutive elements of the people of Israel, and as a result they would be inclined to persecute members of the *ekklesia*. Implicitly, John's formulations mean then that the Synagogues in Smyrna and Philadelphia are the ones that are in the process of pursuing anti-Jewish persecutions against the members of the *ekklesia*, the true Jews.

Theology and ideology are interwoven with political aspects. Although some (many?) Jews in the Synagogues were sharply critical towards Rome and the local governments, still as Jews they were a recognized group who had been given several privileges by the governmental authorities.[32] Jewish Christians must have been excluded from the Synagogue and the Christians were moving into a situation were they had to face political and legal insecurity in the grey zone in between the synagogal community and society at large.[33] The *ekklesia* was cross-national and more inclusive than the Synagogue, but had to struggle with a community structure that cut across legal and social boundaries. In spite of this complex situation, the polemic between the Synagogue and the *ekklesia* was intra-mural, and the Christians were at this stage in history the ones who lived under the threat of persecution from the synagogal communities.

---

[32] See for example Thompson (1990) 133–45; Smallwood (1976) 120–43.

[33] See Yarbro Collins (1984) 85–87.

11

Illegitimate Invasion and Proper Ascent

A study of passages in Philo's writings and the Revelation to
John

The Ascent of the Jewish Nation

In the essay "Heavenly Ascent in Philo" the present author referred
to an article by D. J. Halperin in which he points to the dualistic
contrast between two ways of approaching the divine realm, invasion
in contrast to proper ascent.[1] Halperin writes:

> The belief in ascension exists in two main variants. In one, the
> ascending figure is a hero, the narrator of the story sympathizes
> with this quest, and the audience is expected to rejoice at his
> triumph. In the other, the ascending figure is sinister and demonic,
> the narrator regards his quest as a threat to the divine order,
> and the audience is expected to rejoice at his fall.[2]

In the present essay the study of passages of this kind in Philo's
writings will be brought one step further. Certain specific questions
are asked: 1. What is the relationship between spiritual ascent by
reason, the soul, and so on, and the ascent by persons and peoples
and political leaders? In this way light will be thrown on the
relationship between Philo's historical writings, *De Legatione ad
Gaium* and *In Flaccum*, and his other writings. 2. How far do these
passages and their contexts reflect the distinction between the Jewish
people and other peoples? 3. Are there parallels in large enough

---

[1] In Halperin (1988) 47–67. See Borgen (1993).

[2] Halperin (1988) 47.

number between Philo's writings and the Book of Revelation to suggest that a comparison between them might at points prove to be fruitful ?

Several other important questions might have been asked, such as how the weaving together of Jewish and Hellenistic (Greek) elements can be traced in the passages. This latter question was raised in my article mentioned above, and more work along this line is needed. In the present essay these problem areas are only touched on.

The introduction to the treatise *De Legatione ad Gaium* may serve as a fruitful starting point, since here the ascent of souls occurs in a book which reports on historical events. The inability of reason to ascend is given as a contrast. Some central questions receive illumination in the examination of this passage. These include: When Philo says that souls ascend, what is the relationship of such spiritual (and allegorical) ascent to the particular persons in biblical stories and in history? How far can the notion of ascent be associated not only with the experience of individuals, but also with collective groups?

Legat. 5 reads:

. . . souls (ψυχαῖς) which have soared above (ὑπερκύψασαι= put one's head over) all that is created and has been schooled to see (ὁρᾶν πεπαίδευνται) the uncreated and divine, the primal good,
more excellent than the excellent,
more blessed than blessedness,
more happy than happiness itself,
and any perfection there may be greater than these.

Here the motif of ascent is both formulated as a movement upwards, as in putting the head above, and as in seeing. It is to be noticed that the souls were schooled to see, probably meaning being trained in the laws of Moses.

When Philo tells about the visions of souls, then spiritualistic and universal terminology is used: visionary souls might exist among human beings in general.

The context of *De Legatione ad Gaium* makes this universal interpretation impossible, however. In *Legat.* 3–4 it is made clear that "the souls" refer to "the suppliants' race," which is the portion of the Father and King of the universe. This race is called in the Hebrew tongue "seeing God."[3]

Most important is the fact that the whole treatise deals with the persecution of the Alexandrian Jews, and the problem underlying the book is the question of God's providential care for His people in these tragic events.

Are there similar statements about the Jewish people in the other treatises? Yes, there are. In *Spec.* 2:164–66 Philo notes that both Greeks and barbarians recognize God the creator but combined this recognition with polytheism, and only *the Jews soar above all created objects and serve the Uncreated God:*

> When they went wrong in what was the most vital matter of all, it is the literal truth that the error which the rest committed was corrected by the nation of the Jews (τὸ ᾽Ιουδαίων ἔθνος), which soared above (ὑπερκύψαν= put one's head over) all created objects . . . and chose the service of the Uncreated and Eternal . . .

The concrete Jewish nation is mentioned in a direct way without drawing on spiritualizing concepts like "the souls", as in *Legat.* 5. The ascent motif is formulated in the same way both places, however, as putting one's head above all created things.

Against this background there is reason for identifying the olympic and heavenly soul (sing., ψυχή) in *Imm.* 151 with the Jewish nation:

> . . . an olympic and heavenly soul, which has left the region of earth (τὸν μὲν περίγειον χῶρον ἀπολελοιοίας), has been drawn up (ἀνειλκυσμένης), and dwells with divine natures.[4]

The identification of "a soul" with the Jewish nation is, moreover, supported by the reference to the disciples of Moses, a most populous nation, in *Imm.* 148. The ascent as a movement upwards to the divine

---

[3] Concerning "the suppliants' race" and the etymological interpretation of Israel to mean "seeing God," see Smallwood (1970) 152–54. Among other studies in which the etymology "seeing God" is discussed, are Borgen (1965) 115–18; Delling (1984); Birnbaum (1984).

[4] Divine natures are identified as angels in *Migr.* 115.

realm is clearly expressed and is understood to be a call, not an invasion.

At times Philo may give a positive evaluation up to a certain point of the search upwards by philosophers who may not be Jews. This is the case in *Spec.* 1:37–50. *On the Special Laws* 1 is an exposition of the first two of the Ten Commandments. In § 32 two questions are asked: "One is whether the Deity exists . . . , the other is what the Deity is in essence." The second question is answered in §§ 36–50. The outline of §§ 37–50 runs as follows:

A. The ascent.
Who are ascending: those who have not taken a mere sip of philosophy but have feasted more abundantly on its reasonings and conclusions. *The journey*: their reasoning power (ὁ λογισμός) soars through the ether and accompanies the revolutions of the sun and moon and the whole heaven.
The radiance: the soul's eye (τὸ τῆς ψυχῆς ὄμμα) is dizzied by the flashing of the rays of the sun and moon and the whole heaven.

B. Commentary.
The Analogy of the stars: we cannot know their essence, but persist in the search because of our love for learning.
Vision of God: the clear vision of God is denied us, but we ought not to relinquish the quest. Compare the fact that the eye cannot see the sun in itself, but sees the emanations of its rays.

C. The hierophant, Moses, Exod 33:13–23.
Prayer: "Reveal Yourself to me," Exod 33:13 (LXX). God's answer is a polemic against illegitimate invasion: "Know yourself, then, and do not be led away by impulses and desires beyond your capacity, nor let yearning for the unattainable uplift and carry you off your feet, for of the obtainable nothing shall be denied you," *Spec.* 1:44. *Prayer*: "I beseech You that I may at least see the glory that surrounds You . . ." (§ 45, cf. Exod 33:18 (LXX)). The answer is that neither God nor his Powers can be apprehended in their essence. The imprint of the Powers in the order of the universe may be seen, however.

The ascent is in *Spec.* 1:37 seen as a movement upwards away from earth to the sun and the moon (ἀπὸ γῆς ἄνω μετέωρος ἀρθείς).

This philosophical search upwards leads to observations which may serve as analogies to the understanding of God (*Spec.* 1:39–40), such as: it is impossible with certainty to know the essence of the stars, likewise it is impossible to have a vision of God as he really is, but one should not abandon the quest. Moses is the hierophant, the sacred guide, to the right search for God, as seen from his prayers for God to reveal himself to him, Exod 33:13–23, and God answers that he will give him a share in what is attainable, *Spec.* 1:41–50. Thus, the true search and the reception of revelation as far as it is possible, have Moses as guide. The ascent motif has in these paragraphs the form of a dialogue between Moses who addresses God in prayers, and God who replies.

Thus, in *Spec.* 1:37 ff. the general search upwards through philosophical reasoning receives a positive evaluation. Philo seems in this way also to look with favour on such search outside the Jewish nation. Nevertheless, the proper ascent is tied to the nation under the laws of Moses. This conclusion receives support from the subsequent context in § 51, where it is said that the ones who are of the same sort (τοὺς ὁμοιοτρόπους) as Moses are those who are faithful to the nobility of their birth (i.e. Jews) and proselytes, who have joined the new and godly *politeia*. And the specifications given in *Spec.* 1:51–53 relative to the proselytes, prove that the concrete Jewish nation is meant. The proselytes have left their fatherland, kinsfolk and friends and are to receive citizenship and equal rights with the native born.

General illegitimate invasions

Before examining some examples which directly deal with illegitimate ascent, it may be helpful to make some comments on *Legat.* 6 in the introduction to the treatise *De Legatione ad Gaium*. As a contrast to the ascent of "souls", i.e. the Jewish people, *Legat.* 3–5, the inability of reason to ascend is described in § 6.

> ... For reason (ὁ λόγος) cannot attain to ascend (προσαναβαίνειν) to the entirely sacred and impalpable God, but it sinks and falls back unable to find the proper words by which it may approach to describe – I do not say The Existent One – for even if the whole

heaven should become an articulate voice, it would lack the apt and appropriate terms needed for this – but for his Powers, which are his body-guard, the creative, the kingly, the providential and others as many as are both beneficial and punitive . . .

In this statement Philo makes the point that reason is unable to ascend to, and find proper words for, God and for his Powers. Although the formulation as such is general, within its context it has a special application: "The argument in 4–7 is that what the unaided human intellect (λόγος) fails to attain, the Jew with his special insight (4) can attain through a mystical experience."[5]

Those who attempt to ascend by means of reason or similar human means are then making an illegitimate invasion into the heavenly realm. The story about the tower of Babel is understood by Philo to be such an illegitimate ascent, as can be seen in *Somn.* 2:283ff. In *Somn.* 2:274–99 Philo lists three kinds of wrong speaking: 1. the speaking of the pleasure lovers, represented by Pharaoh (276–78); 2. of the sophists, represented by the people of Egypt (279–82); 3. and the third kind, which consists of those who deny the existence of God and providence, such as those who built the tower of Babel (Gen 11):

> . . . those who extended the activities of their word-cleverness to heaven itself . . . They declared that nothing exists beyond this world of our sight and senses, that it neither was created nor will perish, but is uncreated, imperishable, without guardian, helmsman or protector. Then piling enterprises one upon another they raised on high like a tower their edifice of unedifying doctrines . . . And therefore when they hoped to soar to heaven in mind and thought to overthrow the eternal kingship, the mighty indestructable hand cast them down and overturned their edifice and their doctrine. And the place is called 'confusion' . . . (*Somn.* 2:283–86).[6]

With regard to this somewhat sketchy reference to philosophical ideas, Philo would in his criticism primarily have in mind the denial

---

[5] Smallwood (1970) 155. Cf. Goodenough (1935) 12.

[6] See Wolfson (1948) 1:164–67; 299; 2:382; PLCL 5:610.

of providence by the Sceptics and the Epicureans and the uncertainty expressed by the Sceptics as to the existence of the gods. Philo understands such views to be an attack on God's eternal cosmic government. The passage calls the attempt an ascent, a running up, to heaven in the realm of thoughts (εἰς οὐρανὸν ταῖς ἐπινοιάις ἀναδραμεῖσθαι, cf. *Op.* 36; *Cher.* 41; *Plant.* 22; *Spec.* 2:6), and the invasion is described in drastic terms, as a running up "for the overthrow, ἐπὶ καθαιρέσει, of the eternal kingship." As punishment "the mighty indestructable hand cast them down, καταβάλλει."

This invasion takes place in the realm of thinking, and the reference to the eternal kingship leads in the subsequent context to ideas about the political realm of rulers and government, *Somn.* 2:286–91. This oscillation between philosophy and politics is seen in *Somn.* 2:290–91:

> But so long as they remain unpunished . . . they deal out destruction to the government of the universe with their unholy words, enrol themselves as rulers and kings (ἄρχοντας καὶ βασιλέας), and make over the indestructable sovereignty of God to creation which passes away and perishes . . . Thus it is their way to talk bombastic, boastful absurdities such as 'We are the rulers (ἡγεμόνες), we are those who reign; all things are based on us. Who can cause good or its opposite, save we? With whom does it really and truly rest to benefit or harm, save us? They are but idle babblers who say that things are linked to an invisible power, and think that this power presides over everything in the world whether human or divine.'

In a footnote in PLCL a comment is made at this point: "The description of the third class, though primarily an attack on philosophical creeds, passes in this and the subsequent sections into a general denunciation of human pride."[7] Although the political terms ἄρχων, βασιλεύς, ἡγεμών, οἱ δυναστεύοντες, may be used figuratively about human pride in general, it seems more probable to state that the description passes into a denunciation which has its main focus on the pride of political rulers who do not recognize God as the ruler of the universe. Thus, Philo has in this interpretation

---

[7] PLCL 5:573, n. b.

of the tower of Babel primarily in mind non-Jewish philosophies and godless governments.

Also in *Conf.* 111–14 the invasion of heaven by the building of the tower of Babel is interpreted by means of a language which fuses together (non-Jewish) philosophical ideas, terms about man-centred government and human vices:

> 'Let us build ourselves a city' (Gen 11:4), which is like . . . Let us enact laws which shall eject from our community the justice whose product is poverty and disrepute – laws which shall assure the emoluments of the stronger to the succession of those whose powers of acquisition are greater than others. And let a 'tower' (Gen 11:4) be built as an acropolis, as a royal and impregnable castle for the tyrannic evil, whose feet shall walk upon the earth, and whose head reaches to 'heaven' (Gen 11:4), carried by our arrogance to that vast height. For in fact that tower not only has human misdeeds for its base, but it seeks to rise to the region of celestial ('olympic') things, with the argument of impiety and godlessness in its van. Such are its pronouncements, either that the Deity does not exist, or that it exists but does not exert providence, or that the world has no beginning in which it was created, or that though created its course is under the sway of varying and random causation . . .[8]

In support of the view that the passage quoted above includes the claims of political rulers, the passage in *Plant.* 67–68 may be mentioned. In this passage Philo makes the distinction between on the one hand boasting persons who have acquired kingship and supremacy and made themselves masters, some even of all earth's regions, all nations, Greek and barbarian alike, all rivers, and seas, and also extended their rule to the high realm of unlimitless freedom, and on the other hand great kings who receive God as their portion.

The idea of ascent to the divine realm as an illegitimate invasion is formulated in a general way in Philo's exposition of Num 15:30 in *Virt.* 171–72: "'Whosoever sets his hand to do anything with

---

[8] Concerning tyrannic rule, etc. see Goodenough (1938) 86, 93, etc. Concerning Philo's rejection of views found in Greek philosophical traditions, see Wolfson (1948) 1:108ff.; 165ff.; 295ff., and PLCL 3:508, n. on §199.

presumptuousness provokes God. '. . . the arrogant man is always filled with the spirit of unreason, holding himself, as Pindar says, to be neither man nor demigod, but wholly divine, and claiming to overstep the limits of human nature." L. Cohn considers this description of the arrogant man to be an obvious allusion to the emperor Gaius Caligula, as seen from the parallel in *Legat.* 75: ". . . he claimed to remain no more within the limits of human nature, but soared above them desiring to be thought a god." See also *Legat.* 218. F. H. Colson disagrees with Cohn and remarks: "It seems to me rather unnecessary even if it can be verified chronologically."[9] In any case, the passage in *Virt.* 171–74 illustrates that the exegesis and the expositions in Philo's works outside of the treatises *In Flaccum* and *De Legatione ad Gaium* contain thoughts which may readily serve as an ideological framework for the interpretation of history in those two treatises.

The conclusion is that in these passages about proper ascent and illegitimate invasion Philo oscillates between spiritual ideas and concrete social and political phenomena. The distinction between the Jewish people and others seems to be predominant, and the passages have an ideological perspective which fits well together with the interpretation of history found in *In Flaccum* and *De Legatione ad Gaium*. Accordingly, these two treatises are to be understood within the context of Philo's other writings.

The illegitimate invasion by Gaius

Gaius Caligula was a historical manifestation of a ruler who illegitimately went beyond the limits of human beings and invaded the divine realm.[10] The notions of ascent and invasion are clearly present, while the point on punishment of the emperor Gaius is not stated by Philo, at least not in an explicit way in the preserved writings. He ascended in the sense that he claimed that he had passed from the realm of human beings to that of the gods, as stated in the phrase already cited above, *Legat.* 75: ". . . he no longer considered it worthy of him to abide within the bounds of human nature but overstepped (put one's head over: ὑπερέκυπτε) them in his eagerness

---

[9] Heinemann, Adler and Theiler (1962) 363, nn. 1 and 2. PLCL 8:269, n. b.

[10] Cf. Halperin (1988) 47–67.

to be thought a god."[11] It is to be noticed that the verb used here is the same as in *Legat*. 5, where it refers to the proper ascent of the souls of Israel. Gaius at first likened himself to the so-called demigods, Dionysos, Heracles and the Dioscuri, *Legat*. 78. He then worked up from them to the great gods, Hermes, Apollo and Ares, §§ 93 and 114. Gaius regarded himself as a god before whom men had to prostrate themselves, *Legat*. 116.[12]

According to Philo the Jews alone opposed Gaius in principle. They were trained by the sacred laws "to aknowledge one God who is the Father and Maker of the world," *Legat*. 115. In the case of Gaius, "the created and corruptible nature of man was made to appear uncreated and incorruptible by a deification which our nation judged to be the most grievous impiety," § 118. Considering that he was a law into himself, Gaius abrogated those laid down by legislators, § 119.[13] According to Philo, Gaius' viceroy in Syria, Petronius, characterized his superior in this way: ". . . a despot who is young and judges that whatever he wishes is beneficial and that what he has once decreed is as good as accomplished, be it ever so unprofitable and charged with contentiousness and arrogance. For having soared above (leapt over: ὑπερπηδάω) man, he is already enrolling (γράφει) himself among gods," § 218.

This description of Gaius has much in common with Philo's interpretation of the builders of the tower of Babel in *Somn*. 2:283–95, part of which has been cited above: ". . . they hoped to soar up (run up: ἀνατρέχω) to heaven in the realm of thoughts for the overthrow of the eternal kingship," § 285; ". . . they enroll (ἀναγράφουσι) themselves as rulers and kings (ἄρχοντας καὶ βασιλέας), and make over the indestructible sovereignty of God to creation which passes away and perishes . . . Thus it is their way to talk bombastic, boastful absurdities such as 'We are the rulers, we are those who reign; all things are based on us. Who can cause good or its opposite, save us? With whom does it really and truly rest to benefit or harm, save

---

[11] See Meeks (1976) 50–51. Concerning Gaius' claim to divinity, see Smallwood (1970) 191–92 and 209–11.

[12] See Smallwood (1970) 209–11.

[13] See Goodenough (1935) 186, n. 36, with reference to Cicero, *De legibus*, 3:1, 2. See further Suetonius, *Gaius Caligula* 29:1: "Remember that all things are permitted to me – and against all [men]."

us?" §§ 290–91. Thus criticism like that expressed in *Somn.* 2:283–95 could readily be applied to Gaius.

The Proper Ascent of Moses and Other Leaders

In Philo's expositions many biblical persons ascended to the divine realm. In some cases they represent general and/or spiritualizing concepts, in other cases it is just said that they ascended as persons.

Migr. 168–70 may serve as an example. The theme of *Migr.* 164–75 is good fellow-travelling, such as Isaac going with Abraham, meaning the union of self-taught nature and acquired skill. Then in §§ 168 and 169 the ascents of Abraham and of Moses are brought together.

Migr. 168 reads:

> The one high-soaring who has been lifted up so high (ὁ δὲ ἐπὶ τοσοῦτον ἄνω μετέωρος ἐξαρθείς) will no longer suffer any parts of the soul (τῆς ψυχῆς) to dwell on things mortal, but will draw them all up with him, just like hanging on a rope.

Abraham is interpreted as πατὴρ μετέωρος, *Abr.* 82, etc. In his ascent, *Migr.* 168, there are three elements: a) the ascent on high; b) the (blessed) experience on high: not dwelling on things mortal; and c) the action from on high: drawing all things up with him, as illustrated by Abraham bringing with him Eshcol (=fire) and Aunan (=eyes), *Migr.* 164–65, and Isaac (§§ 166–67). The ascent and dwelling on high are pictured in a vivid spatial way, so that the drawing up is likened to things hanging on a rope.

At Sinai Moses, "the wise man," (ὁ σόφος) was called up together with others as related in Exod 24:1:"'Come up to your Lord, You and Aaron and Nadab and Abihu and seventy of the Senate of Israel.' This means:

> 'Come up, O soul (ψυχή), to behold the Existent One, come being in harmony, with speech and reason, willingly, fearlessly, affectionately, come in the holy and perfect measures of seven multiplied tenfold.' . . . These are the powers that form the

bodyguard of the mind (νοῦς) that is worthy of royal sovereignty, and it is meet that they should accompany the king as his escort. (*Migr.* 167–68).

These ascents take place on the level of soul and mind, and are accordingly applied to the wise man, the sage, ὁ σόφος. The ascents of several persons, such as Aaron, Nadab and Abihu, are understood to mean the qualities and abilities the mind needs in the ascent. Moreover, the mind is pictured as a king who is accompanied by his bodyguard.[14]

In other passages the ascent is seen as being made by the person Moses, for example in some of the places where Philo interprets Exod 20:21 (LXX): ". . . Moses went into the darkness where God was." This verse is used by Philo in *Mos.* 1:158; *Post.* 14; *Gig.* 54; *Mut.* 7; and in *QE* 2:28. Both in *Post.*14 and *Mut.* 7. Exod 20:21 occurs together with Exod 33:13 where Moses prays that he might be allowed to see God. In both places the passages are understood to mean Moses' wish to see the true existence of God, by entering "into the darkness where God was." This wish of his is denied him, but he is granted to see what is below God. Compare the similar points made in *Spec.* 1:41–50, a section which was discussed above. The interpretation of Exod 20:21 in *Gig.* 54 is different. In the terminology of mysteries, Moses' entry "into the darkness where God was" is understood to mean that Moses learned the secrets of the most holy mysteries. There he becomes not only one initiated, but also the hierophant of secret rites and teacher of divine things, which he will impart to those whose ears are purified.

In these passages the ascent is done by the person Moses. However, a spiritualizing tendency is present in *QE* 2:28 where Philo sees Moses as "the prophetic mind" (Marcus: προφητικὸς νοῦς). Nevertheless, the picture of the divine realm into which Moses went when he entered "the darkness" (Exod 20:21) is concrete. Moses/the prophetic mind, dwelt in the forecourt of the palace (Marcus: αὐλῇ vel sim.) of the Father. The picture of God's heavenly court and palace was a well known idea in Judaism, especially in

---

[14] Concerning the danger of making a wrong kind of ascent, *Migr.* 170ff., see Borgen (1993) 261–63.

apocalyptic literature and in the later *hekhalot* literature.[15] Thus Philo's Platonizing descriptions in *Mos.* 1:158; *Post.* 14; *Gig.* 54; *Mut.* 7 of the darkness in Exod 20:21 as the invisible and incorporeal realm are further interpretations of the notion of God's royal premises.

Moses as king and as cosmic emperor is the context of Exod 20:21 in *Mos.* 1:158. Instead of being the heir to the throne of the Pharaoh of the Egyptian people, the royal 'prince' Moses became king of a priestly nation more populous and mightier, §§ 148–49. Moses was God's friend and shared in his possession (ἡ κτῆσις), and received the whole cosmos as his portion (κλῆρον), §§ 155–56. Moreover, he was named god and king like God himself, and entered into the darkness where God was, § 158. Being transformed he became a model for those who are willing to copy it, §§ 158–59. Being destined to be a legislator, he became ahead of time an impersonation of law, § 162. As shown by W. Meeks, Philo draws here on a Jewish tradition which is also preserved in rabbinic writings.[16]

Moses is seen as the legitimate emperor, a contrast to the counterfeit, Gaius. Like Gaius the whole earth and sea belonged to him, *Mos.* 1:155 and *Legat.* 8. Like Gaius he was called god and entered the divine realm, *Mos.* 1:158 and *Legat.* 75, 78, 94, 218. Like Gaius Moses was an impersonation of law, *Mos.* 1:162 and *Legat.* 119.

The imperial beasts, Gaius, Moses and Jesus

The purpose of the following brief survey of points from the Book of Revelation and Philo's writings is to demonstrate the relevance of a comparison between observations made in both. Further studies are necessary to explore these and other aspects in detail.

It is commonly recognized that the figures of the two beasts in Rev 13 refer to the Roman emperor and his government and to emperor worship. John the Seer pictures the dragon's descent from heaven, Rev 12:4–13, but he still retains the idea of ascent, but of a beast from the sea and another beast from the earth. The beast from the sea ascended to the divine realm, as shown by the blasphemous name it had upon its heads, 13:1. Such blasphemous names were

---

[15] Concerning heaven as a royal court and palace, see Himmelfarb (1993) 14.

[16] Meeks (1967) 156–59; 205–09.

the divine titles, such as *divus* or *deus* applied to the emperors.[17] It may also have been the application to the emperor of the name of a specific god. For example, Gaius had taken initiative to convert the Jerusalem Temple "into a temple of his own to bear the name of 'Gaius, the New Zeus Epiphanes' (Ζεύς ' Επιφανής Νέος Γάιος) by bringing in a statue as an image of himself "(*Legat.* 346, cf. 188).

According to both Philo and John the Seer, the image of the emperor and acts of *proskynesis* were elements in the worship of the emperor, *Legat.* 188 and 346, *Flac.* 41–42, and *Legat.* 134–36; Rev 13:14–15; 14:9–11. According to both, the whole world, but for the Jews and the Christians respectively, took part in worshipping the emperor, *Legat.* 115–17, 352 and Rev 13:8. According to both, the ascent took the form of conquest and victory. As stages leading up to the claim of being a god, the emperor Gaius won three contests, the one with the senatorial order, the second with the equestrian order, and the third with his whole family. At every step he gained victory by getting people killed, among the senators by the murder of Silanus, among the equestrians by the murder of Macro, and in his family by the murder of his cousin and co-heir; then, "he no longer considered it worthy of him to remain within the bounds of human nature but overstepped them in his eagerness to be thought of as a god," *Legat.* 74–75. Correspondingly, Jesus gained victory as part of the ascent to his heavenly role and charge, but, paradoxically, by himself being put to death, Rev 5:6, 12.

The biblical and mythological background of these figures is not of our concern in the present study. It will be sufficient to point out the contrasting parallelism between Jesus, the Lamb, and the beasts. This contrasting parallelism is commonly recognized by exegetes. The Lamb was slaughtered, Rev 5:6, 9, and the sea-beast had a mortal wound, 13:3. The Lamb received a charge from the One on the throne and received power, 5:7, 12, so does the beast receive power and a charge from the dragon, 13:2. As the Lamb ruled over human beings from everywhere, 5:9, so does the beast, 13:7. As the Lamb is worshipped by means of *proskynesis*, 5:12, so is also the beast, 13:4.[18]

---

[17] Charles (1920) 1:347–48; Roloff (1993) 156, and other commentaries.

[18] Concerning the beast in Rev 13:1–10 as a parody of Jesus as he was pictured in Rev 5, see Roloff (1993) 155, and other commentaries.

Similarily, at least three parallel observations can be made between John the Seer's picture of Jesus, the Lamb, and Philo's picture of Moses. First, by both the people is characterized as a priestly people, *Mos.* 1:149, Rev 5:9–10. Here also a difference is seen. To Philo the priestly people is the Jewish people, while John the Seer referred to a people drawn from all nations.[19] Second, as already stated above, God gave into Moses' hands the whole cosmos, *Mos.* 1:155–56. Correspondingly, Jesus, as the Lamb, had cosmic authority, which he carried jointly with Him who sits upon the throne, Rev 5:13. Third, both Moses and Jesus, the Lamb, were located next to God, *Mos.* 1:158; *QE* 2:28 and Rev 5:6–7 and 5:13.

This list of parallels is not complete, but the large number of similarities and contrasts shown demonstrate sufficiently the relevance of comparing further points from the Revelation to John and Philo's writings.

---

[19] See Fiorenza (1972) 91–92 and 282–90.

12

Autobiographical Ascent Reports: Philo and John the Seer

Introduction

The author of the Book of Revelation did not hide himself behind pseudonymity, as authors of apocalypses did. Thus he did not name an Old Testament person as the author, but wrote in his own name, John, Rev 1:1, 4, 9; 22:8, and gave an autobiographical report on his own visions. Scholars have explained this phenomenon by the understanding that the spirit of prophecy had descended afresh with the advent of Christianity, and thus the risen Christ and the Spirit gave John authority to write in his own name.[1]

It may seem irrelevant to bring Philo into this problem area, since his writings are seldom used to throw light upon apocalyptic literature. In an essay entitled "Apocalypse and Philo", Samuel Sandmel emphasized the difference between Philo and apocalyptic literature.[2] The main reason for this conclusion was his understanding that apocalypticism concentrated on predictions of future events, especially future eschatological events, while actual prophetic predictions played a marginal role for Philo.

There has in recent scholarship been an increasing awareness of the fact that apocalyptic literature was not necessarily centred on eschatology. Thus, the focus on the aspects of heavenly ascents and on journeys in the other-worldly regions have been given more

---

[1] See Charles (1920) 1:xxxviii–xxxix; Roloff (1993) 7; Russell (1964) 127ff.; Beasley-Murray (1978) 14–15; Lohse (1979) 3–4; Lohse (1988) 325; Müller (1984) 27.

[2] Sandmel (1979) 383–87.

weight.[3] It is then seen that apocalyptic and mystical texts overlap. Against this background it is relevant to use Philonic passages on heavenly ascents as comparative material to the Revelation to John.[4] Moreover, Sandmel overlooks the fact that Philo's picture of the future given in the treatise *On Rewards and Punishments* and in other places also makes possible comparisons between some of his expositions and apocalyptic and other forms of eschatology.[5]

Since Paul's report on heavenly ascent in 2 Cor 12:2–4 is probably autobiographical, one might then draw this passage into the discussion.[6] J. D. Tabor does not only maintain that this text is evidence of an actual *experience* of ascent to heaven from the early Roman period, but also that it is the only *firsthand* account of such a journey to heaven surviving from this period.[7] He then overlooks the fact that Philo gives a firsthand account of his own ascents in *Spec.* 3:1–6.

As for Philo and apocalyptic ascents in general, it was mentioned in the preceding chapter that in her book *Ascent to Heaven in Jewish and Christian Apocalypses*, Martha Himmelfarb states that the most extended treatment in Jewish or Christian literature of the divinization of a human being is Philo's treatment of Moses.[8] As an example she cites *Mos.* 1:158, and makes the following comment: "Philo's description of Moses uses a vocabulary and concepts drawn from the philosophical discussions of Alexandria. The position of Enoch in 2 *Enoch* is rather similar to the one Philo gives Moses, but the language of the two works differ dramatically".[9]

Philo's Ascent

As already stated, Philo did not only tell of the ascents of Biblical persons, he reports on his own ascents in *Spec.* 3:1–6. It is worth

---

[3] See Gruenwald (1980); Rowland (1982); Stone (1980) 29, 42, 113–14.

[4] On the theme of ascent in ancient sources, see Segal (1980) 1354–59; Meeks (1967); Borgen (1993) 246–68; Bousset (1901) 136–69; 229–73; Tabor (1986); Gundel (1966), 29–30; 180–81, etc.; Himmelfarb (1993); Himmelfarb (1988) 73–100.

[5] See Borgen (1992) 341–61.

[6] See Roloff (1993) 68.

[7] Tabor (1986) 1.

[8] Himmelfarb (1993).

[9] *ibid.*, 49.

looking into the possibility that this passage might illuminate John the Seer's autobiographical visions and ascents. First, Philo's report needs be examined.

On The Special Laws 3:1–6.[10]

A. Time for philosophy and contemplation of cosmos:

Time Reference:
1. There was a time when

Preliminary Description of the Experience:
a) having leisure for philosophy and for the contemplation of the cosmos and its content (θεωρίᾳ τοῦ κόσμου καὶ τῶν ἐν αὐτῷ)
b) I made its reason (νοῦς) my own in all its beauty and loveliness and true blessedness,
c) when my constant companions were divine themes and verities (θείοις ἀεὶ λόγοις συγγινόμενος καὶ δόγμασιν), wherein I rejoiced with a joy that never cloyed or sated.

Specification and Elaboration of the Experience:
That which I avoided:
I had no base or abject thoughts nor grovelled in search for reputation or for wealth or bodily comforts,

My heavenly journey:
but seemed always to be borne aloft into the heights with a soul possessed by some God-sent inspiration (ἄνω μετάρσιος ἐδόκουν

---

[10] A Jewish (and Christian) phenomenon which at the same time took place within a Hellenistic context. For example, it was reported that the astronomer Ptolemy told the following about his own experience: "Mortal as I am, I know that I am born for a day, but when I follow the serried multitude of the stars in their circular course, my feet no longer touch the earth; I ascend to Zeus himself to feast me on ambrosia, the food of the gods." Quoted from Cumont (1912) 81. In Lucian's *Icaromenippus* Menippus claims to have returned from a visit to heaven. He speaks of a three-stage flight, from moon, to sun, to heaven. The ascent is bodily, and he has heard and seen wonderful things. Menippus reports: "Here I am, I tell you, just come back today from the very presence of your great Zeus himself, and *I have seen and heard wonderful things* . . ."

ἀεὶ φέρεσθαι κατά τινα τῆς ψυχῆς ἐπιθειασμὸν) and to travel together with the sun and moon and the whole heaven and universe (καὶ συμπεριπολεῖν ἡλίῳ καὶ σελήνῃ καὶ σύμπαντι οὐρανῷ τε καὶ κόσμῳ)

The ethereal stand point:
2. Ah then I gazed down from the ether, and straining the mind's eye beheld, as from some commanding peak, the multitudinous world-wide spectacles of earthly things, and blessed my lot that I had escaped by main force from the plagues of mortal life.

B. The Descent and Occasional Ascents:

I Was Pulled Down:
3. But, as it proved, my steps were dogged by the deadliest of mischiefs, the hater of the good, envy (φθόνος), which suddenly set upon me and ceased not to pull me down with violence till it had plunged me in the ocean of civil cares (εἰς μέγα πέλαγος τῶν ἐν πολιτείᾳ φροντίδων), in which I am swept away, unable even to raise my head above the water.

Raising My Head Above the Waters:
My general attitude from my youth:
4. Yet amid my groans I hold my own, for, planted in my soul from my earliest days I keep the yearning for *paideia* which ever has pity and compassion for me, lifts me up and relieves my pain.

Situational applications:
To this I owe it that sometimes I raise my head and with the soul's eye – dimly indeed because the mist of extraneous affairs (ἡ τῶν ἀλλοκότων πραγμάτων ἀχλὺς) has clouded their clear vision – I yet make shift to look around me in my desire to inhale a breath of life pure and unmixed with evil.

That which I occasionally experience:
5. And if unexpectedly I obtain a spell of fine weather and a calm from civil (ἐν πολιτείᾳ) turmoils

Air travel:
I get me wings and ride the waves and almost tread the lower air, wafted by the breezes of knowledge (ἐπιστήμη) which often urge me to come to spend my days with her,

The escape:
A truant as it were from merciless masters in the shape not only of men but of affairs (πραγμάτων) which pour in upon me like a torrent from different sides.

Thanks to God:
6. Yet it is well for me to give thanks to God even for this, that, though submerged, I am not sucked down into the depths, but can also open the eyes, which, in my despair of comforting hope, I thought I had now lost their sight, and am irradiated by the light of wisdom (σοφία), and am not given to lifelong darkness.

C. My Hermeneutical Endeavour:

So behold me daring, not only to read the sacred messages of Moses, but also, in my love of knowledge, to peer into each of them and unfold and reveal what is not known to the many (τοῖς πολλοῖς).

In this opening section of *Spec.* 3 Philo tells about his own ascent to the heavenly bodies and his descent because of envy and cares connected with the (Jewish) *politeia* (*Spec.* 3:1–6). The section consists of three main parts: a) Philo's ascent up to an ethereal sphere, at a distance from the plagues of mortal life on earth, *Spec.* 3:1–2, having time for philosophy and contemplation, ascending to the ethereal sphere (*Spec.* 3:1), and looking down from heaven to the earthly things (*Spec.* 3:2). b) Philo descending to the cares of the *politeia*, and experiencing lower ascents while struggling with civil cares and turmoil. Pulled down by envy into the great sea of matters in the *politeia* he descends to earth (*Spec.* 3:3). At times he still can ascend and almost tread the aerial sphere (*Spec.* 3:4–6). c) This experience made it possible for him to unfold the meaning of the messages of Moses, i.e. the Laws of Moses (*Spec.* 3:6).

In this passage, *Spec.* 3:1–6, Philo has a report on his own ascents as he experienced them in two different situations. In one situation he felt himself to be at a distance from earthly troubles, *Spec.* 3:1–2. In the other, he was deeply involved in the cares and troubles of the Jewish *politeia*, 3:3–6a.

Among the many questions which may be raised, one is of primary interest for the present discussion, namely the nature of the civil cares and their historical context.[11]

It has been suggested that this descent, because of envy, refers to the pogrom against the Alexandrian Jews in A.D. 38, and Philo's role as head of the Jewish delegation which was sent to Rome. Some observations speak in favour of such an understanding. When Philo in *Spec.* 3:3 speaks of a great sea of cares in the *politeia*, this indicates that he had to face a serious and major problem. The pogrom in A.D. 38 and the subsequent encounter with the emperor in Rome certainly would fit such a description. Moreover, both in *On The Special Laws* 3:1–6 and in *On the Embassy to Gaius* Philo uses the metaphor of being pulled down into turbulent streams of water: "... the great sea ... in which I am swept away ... though submerged I am not sucked down into the depths ..." (*Spec.* 3:3 and 6); "... we were able to lift our head above water ... Waterlogged by such considerations we were dragged down and submerged into the depths ..." (*Legat.* 370 and 372). Furthermore, just as in *Spec.* 3:3ff. so also in the conflict in A.D. 38 envy was the cause of the troubles, *Flac.* 29.

Again, against the background of this "biographical" information given by Philo in *Spec.* 3:1–6 one might suppose that there may be allusions to this crisis in the other parts of *On The Special Laws*, Book 3 and also in the treatises which follow in Philo's *Exposition of the Laws of Moses*: *On the Special Laws*, Book 4, *On the Virtues* and *On Rewards and Punishments*.

Thus the Emperor Gaius' claim to be a god fits the interpretation of Num 15:30 ("... the person who does anything with a high hand ... reviles the Lord") in *Virt.* 171–74. Here it is said that the arrogant

---

[11] PAPM ad loc.

sinner who oversteps human nature by holding himself wholly divine (cf. *Legat.* 75) will have God as accuser and revenger.[12] Philo in *Legat.* 122 (cf. 363) tells of the Alexandrians pillaging the Jews; he says that they jeered and reviled (κατακερτομοῦντες καὶ ἐπιχλευάζοντες) them. The same Greek term is used by him in *Praem.* 169 to characterize the attitude and action by the enemies of the Jews, before the eschatological reversal will take place. The Jews suffered cruelty, *Flac.* 59–66, and *Praem.* 171. The enemies rejoiced in the misfortunes of the nation, *Legat.* 137 and 353f., and *Praem.* 169. The term lamentation (ὀλοφύρσις) is used in *Praem.* 171 and the verb lament (ὀλοφύρομαι) occurs in *Legat.* 197 and 225.

The principle of reversal is central in the eschatological outlook of *Praem.* 169–71: "Everything will suddenly be reversed, God will turn the curses against the enemies of these penitents . . ." (*Praem.* 169). Flaccus suffered punishment on the basis of this rule of reversal, *Flac.* 146–91.[13]

Finally, in *Flac.* 121–24 the Jews, when Flaccus was arrested, offered thanks to God because he had taken pity and compassion (οἶκτος καὶ ἔλεος) on them. They had deplored their desolate situation, deprived as they were of everything. Likewise, in *Spec.* 4:179–80, interpreting Deut 10:17–18 (". . . he executes justice for the fatherless . . ."), Philo says that the whole Jewish race is in the position of an orphan. When misfortunes fall upon them they have none to take their part. Nevertheless, the Jewish people are always an object of pity and compassion (ἔλεος καὶ οἶκτος) to the Ruler of the Universe whose portion it is.

Although these observations support the understanding that Philo refers to his role in or after the tragic events of A.D. 38–41, they are not strong enough to prove that this, without doubt, is the case.[14] Nevertheless, if he refers in *Spec.* 3:3, etc., to situations which took place at an earlier time, they probably were preludes to these critical events of A.D. 38–41. In spite of the privileges granted the Jews by Augustus and Tiberius, the Alexandrian Jewish community had a continuous struggle for full civil rights during the Roman

---

[12] The identification with Gaius is made by Cohn et alii (1910) 362–63. Cf. Borgen (1984) 251. Colson (1929–62) 8:269, n. b, finds Cohn's interpretation to be unecessary.

[13] See Fischer (1978) 203–04, and Borgen (1992) 341–61.

[14] Cohn (1899) 433ff. and Morris (1987) 844.

period, and it lived in tension in between the native Egyptians and the Greek full citizens of the city.[15]

As for Philo's hermeneutical endeavour, he states in *Spec.* 3:6 that this heavenly perspective enables him to unfold and reveal in the Laws of Moses what is not known to the many:

> So behold me daring, not only to read the sacred messages of Moses, but also in my love of knowledge, to peer (διακύπτω) into each of them and unfold (διαπτύσσω) and reveal (ἀναφαίνω) what is not known to the many.

Philo makes varied use of the term διακύπτω. In most cases it means to stoop or peer so as to get the view of the inside, *Migr.* 222; *Her.* 111, as through a curtain, *Ebr.* 167; look into the inner realities, heaven, *Jos.* 146, or look down from the realm of the stars, *Spec.* 3:2. Here in *Spec.* 3:6 the word means that Philo peers into the inside meaning of the Laws of Moses.

The verb διαπτύσσω is used rather infrequently by Philo. In two places it characterizes exegetical activity, however: 1) in *Somn.* 2:127 where the general exegetical activity of the Jews on the Sabbath is pictured: "Will you sit in your conventicles . . . and read in security your holy books, expounding (διαπτύσσω) any obscure point . . ." 2) In *Contempl.* 78 Philo characterizes the exegetical work of the Therapeutai. He says that they employ allegorical interpretation. The literal ordinances are the body of Scriptures and the soul is the invisible meaning ("mind") in its wording:

> It is in this mind especially that the rational soul begins to contemplate the things akin to itself and looking through the words as through a mirror beholds the marvellous beauty of the concepts . . . unfolds (διαπτύσσω) the symbols . . .

---

[15] See Tcherikover (1963) 1–32. This continuing tension and incidents related to it (cf. *Spec.* 3:159–62) would give sufficient cause for Philo to enter into the matters of the *politeia*. The circumstance that there was no direct persecution or oppression in respect of the Jews of Alexandria during the reign of Tiberius, is therefore no argument for not seeing that period as background for *Spec.* 3:1–6, as maintained by Morris (1987) 843–4.

Thus the word may bear allegorical interpretation, but can also have the more general meaning of unfolding what is not clear in the Laws of Moses.

The verb ἀναφαίνω, cause to give light, display, bring to light, shows that Philo's interpretations are not esoteric, but are displayed to others. This point is evident when Philo in *Mos.* 2:26 says that as long as the Laws of Moses only existed in the Chaldean(=Hebrew) language they had not yet displayed/revealed (ἀναφαίνω) their beauty to the rest of mankind. This display was then made when the Laws were translated into Greek.

Philo's use of these terms together with the context of *Spec.* 3:1–6 shows that his hermeneutical statement in §6 refers to the deeper insight, which his "stays" in the ethereal and aerial spheres gave into earthly matters and into the Sacred writings. This interpretation includes allegory, but is not limited to it, as is evident from Philo's Exposition of the Laws of Moses of which *Spec.* 3:1–6 is a part. In this comprehensive work of Philo allegorical interpretations are not prominent. The historical context reflected in the passage suggests that Philo's exegesis is meant to offer meaningful interpretations in a troublesome situation which includes the aspect of persecution and suffering.

Philo and John the Seer

The problem of a troublesome situation and (impending) persecution also characterizes the context of the Book of Revelation. As in Philo's *Flac.* and *Legat.* an important aspect of the troubles was the pressure felt from the Roman imperial cult. Against this background similarities and differences between Philo and John the Seer can be brought into the discussion.

Philo (*Spec.* 3:1) and John (Rev 4:1–2) ascend through inspiration. Philo writes: "I . . . seemed always to be borne aloft into the heights (ἄνω μετάρσιος ἐδόκουν ἀεὶ φέρεσθαι) with a soul possessed by some God-sent inspiration (κατά τινα τῆς ψυχῆς ἐπιθειασμὸν) a fellow-traveller with the sun, moon and the whole heaven and cosmos."[16]

Correspondingly, Rev 4:2–3 reads: "... in heaven an open door (θύρα ἠνεῳγμένη ἐν τῷ οὐρανῷ). And the first voice ... said: 'Come up hither, and I will show you what must take place after this'. At once I was in the Spirit, and lo, a throne stood in heaven ...", (καὶ ἡ φωνή ... λέγων, ᾿Ανάβα ὧδε, καὶ δείξω σοι ἃ δεῖ γενέσθαι μετὰ ταῦτα. εὐθέως ἐγενόμην ἐν πνεύματι. καὶ ἰδοὺ θρόνος ἔκειτο ἐν τῷ οὐρανῷ ...).

Although both Philo and John the Seer refer to inspiration, they picture the ascent itself differently. Philo experienced himself as beeing carried (φέρεσθαι), Spec. 3:1, and as getting wings, Spec. 3:5,[17] while the Seer saw an open door in heaven and was asked to come up, Rev 4:1.[18]

In Spec. 3:1–2 Philo has the region of moon and sun and in Spec. 3:5 the aerial sphere as a lookout-place for viewing earthly things. Both in apocalyptic and in Hellenistic sources there are examples given about ascents to the heavenly region from which the person gets a view of earthly matters.[19] Also John the Seer gains a heavenly perspective on earthly events, as is said by the angel in Rev 4:1: "Come up hither, and I will show you what must take place after this." A true insight into earthly matters is gained when one views things from the vantage point of heaven.

Philo experiences this view from above in two different situations: 1. His presence in heaven in Spec. 3:1–2 was experienced at a time when he had leisure for philosophy, could contemplate the universe, had divine themes and verities as companions and had a blessed escape from the plagues of mortal life.

---

[16] As for Philo's wordings in Spec. 3:1–2, see Opif. 70, where it is said that the mind "was borne even higher to the ether and the circuit of heaven, and is whirled around with (συμπεριπολέω) the dances of the planets and the fixed stars ...", and in Spec. 3:1 Philo says that he seemed "... to be borne aloft into the heights with a soul possessed by some God-sent inspiration, whirling around with (συμπεριπολέω) the sun and the moon and the whole heaven and cosmos ..." In Opif. 70–71 the mind goes still further to the intelligible world and to God himself. See Borgen (1993) concerning the Greek background of the terminology.

[17] See Aptowitzer (1925), 150–69.

[18] See 1 Enoch 14:15; T. Levi 5:1.

[19] See Dean-Otting (1984) 18–20, 143, 196–97.

Similarily, R. H. Charles suggested that John the Seer in Rev 4 pictured the serenity and calm of the heavenly throne-room as a contrast to the churches' troublesome situation as pictured in the letters in Rev 2–3: "The scene of John's vision is no longer earth with its failure, troubles, and outlook darkened with the apprehension of universal martyrdom, but heaven with its atmosphere of perfect assurance and peace and thanksgiving and joy."[20] This understanding is hardly correct. The heavenly scenes in Rev 4 and 5 set the stage and are the points of departure for all that follows in the book.

2. After Philo had been pulled down by envy which plunged him into the ocean and torrents of civil cares, then his ascents to the aerial sphere relieve his pain, make it possible for him to inhale a breath of life pure and unmixed with evil, to spend his days with knowledge and with the soul's eye open so that he was irradiated by the light of wisdom. On this basis Philo dares, not only to read the Laws of Moses, but to penetrate more deeply into them to gain a deeper insight than what is known to the many, *Spec.* 3:3–6. Here there is more kinship between Philo's experience and the experience of John the Seer.

Both to Philo and to John the Seer the ascent serves a hermeneutical function. Philo states explicitly that he in this way gained a deeper insight into the Laws of Moses (*Spec.* 3:6), and his treatises are accordingly expository commentaries on these Laws.

John the Seer does not in the same way refer to the Laws of Moses or to the other books of the Old Testament. He hears the words: "Come up hither, and I will show you what must take place after this" (Rev 4:1). The Book of Revelation makes evident, however, that this vision implies an extensive expository use of the Scriptures, largely by using the method of transference of Biblical ideas, themes and thought-patterns. For example, ideas about the people of Israel have been transferred onto the church as the people of God, as has been shown above in the essay "Polemic in the Book of Revelation". Also, in other areas, John the Seer draws extensively on scriptural material, such as in his presentation of the work of Christ, of the events of eschatological judgment and salvation, and of his own visionary experience.[21]

---

[20] Charles (1920) 1:xxvi.

[21] Fekkes (1994) 70–71.

For the comparison between Philo and the Book of Revelation it is important that some of the same tendencies and motifs are seen to be at work. As shown above, the larger work *The Exposition*, of which *Spec.* 3:1–6 is a part, concludes with the treatise *On Rewards and Punishments* which has an eschatological outlook, even including the theme of reversal. This is a central feature in several apocalyptic writings, the Book of Revelation included.[22] Moreover, as shown in the preceding essay, John the Seer's sharp protest against emperor worship, especially in chapters 13–19, is in basic agreement with Philo's criticism of the Emperor Gaius Caligula and his claim to divinity, as expressed in the treatises *Flac.* and *Legat.* as well as in Philo's interpretation of Num 15:30 in *Virt.* 171–74. Here it is said that the arrogant sinner who oversteps human nature by holding himself wholly divine (cf. *Legat.* 75) will have God as accuser and avenger. Correspondingly, according to John the Seer, God's wrath comes upon the idolatrous imperial power in Rev 6:9–11; 14:7–11; 16:5–6; 18:20; 19:20 and 20:4.

Thus Philo does not only have reports on the ascents of Biblical persons such as Abraham, Enoch, Moses and Elijah, but gives a report of his own ascent as exegete and author. This observation should be considered when discussing the fact that the author of the Book of Revelation, John, tells of his own ascent. Thus John is not unique when he refers to his own name and gives an autobiographical report on his own ascent.[23]

---

[22] Sanders (1989) 456–58, states that what is peculiar to the works which have traditionally been considered Palestinian Jewish apocalypses is the combination of revelation with the promise of restoration and reversal. Sanders notes that Philo in *Praem.* 94–97, 162–72 expresses the hope of restoration and reversal. According to Sanders Philo lacks the the notion of inspired revelation. As seen from our analysis of *Spec.* 3:1–6, there is an revelatory aspect of Philo's exposition of the Laws of Moses. See further Aune (1983) 147–52.

[23] The fragment 4Q491 11, 1.12–19 also probably describes the ascent of a human being, probably of the author himself since it is a report in autobiographical form: ". . . none shall be exalted but me . . . For I have taken my seat in the [congregation] in the heavens . . ." See Smith (1992A) 290–301; Evans (1994) 563–65.

Abbreviations

AASF	Annales academiae scientiarum Fennicae
AB	Anchor Bible
ABD	*Anchor Bible Dictionary*
ABRL	Anchor Bible Reference Library
ABSA	*Annual of the British School at Athens*
ANRW	*Aufstieg und Niedergang der römischen Welt*
AnSt	*Anatolian Studies*
ARW	*Archiv für Religionswissenschaft*
AW	*Antike Welt*
BETL	Bibliotheca ephemeridum theologicarum Lovaniensium
Bib.	*Biblica*
BJRL	*Bulletin of the John Rylands University Library of Manchester*
BZ	*Biblische Zeitschrift*
CBQ	*Catholic Biblical Quarterly*
CRINT	Compendia rerum iudaicarum ad Novum Testamentum
EKK	Evangelisch-katholischer Kommentar
ETL	*Ephemerides theologicae Lovanienses*
ExAu	*Ex Auditu*
FB	Forschung zur Bibel
HNT	Handbuch zum Neuen Testament
HTKNT	Herders theologischer Kommentar zum Neuen Testament
HTR	*Harvard Theological Review*
HUCA	*Hebrew Union College Annual*
ICC	International Critical Commentary

IDB	*Interpreter's Dictionary of the Bible*
Ist M	*Istanbul Mitteilungen*
JAC	*Jahrbuch für Antike und Christentum*
JBL	*Journal of Biblical Literature*
JJS	*Journal of Jewish Studies*
JQR	*Jewish Quarterly Review*
JSJ	*Journal for the Study of Judaism in the Persian, Hellenistic and Roman Period*
JSNT	*Journal for the Study of the New Testament*
JSS	*Jewish Social Studies*
LCL	Loeb Classical Library
MAMA	*Monumenta Asiae Minoris Antiqua*
MeyerK	H.A.W. Meyer, Kritisch-exegetischer Kommentar über das Neue Testament
MGWJ	*Monatsschrift für Geschichte und Wissenschaft des Judentums*
NovT	*Novum Testamentum*
NovTSup	Novum Testamentum, Supplements
NTD	Das Neue Testament Deutsch
NTS	*New Testament Studies*
PLCL	Philo, Loeb Classical Library
PAPM	Les œuvres de Philon d' Alexandrie
PW	Pauly-Wissowa, Real-Encyclopädie der classischen Altertumswissenschaft
QAL	Quaderni del archeologia della Libia
RVV	Religionsgeschichtliche Versuche und Vorarbeiten
SHAW.PH	*Sitzungsberichte der Heidelberger Akademie der Wissenschaften, Philologisch-Historisch Klasse*
Str-B	[H. Strack and] P. Billerbeck, Kommentar zum Neuen Testament
SVF	Stoicorum veterum fragmenta
Tem	*Temenos*
ThHNT	Theologischer Handkommentar zum Neuen Testament
TLZ	*Theologische Literaturzeitung*
TU	Texte und Untersuchungen zur Geschichte der altchristlichen Literatur
TWNT	*Theologisches Wörterbuch zum Neuen Testament*
WUNT	Wissenschaftliche Untersuchungen zum Neuen Testament
ZTK	*Zeitschrift für Theologie und Kirche*

Bibliography

Akurgal, E. 1978, *Ancient Civilizations and Ruins of Turkey*, 4th ed. (Istanbul: Haset Kitabevi).

Aland, K. and Cross, F. L. (eds.) 1957, *Studia Patristica*, 2 (Berlin: Akademie-Verlag).

Alexander, L. (ed.) 1991, *Images of Empire* (Sheffield: Sheffield Academic Press).

Alexander, P. S. 1991, "The Family of Caesar and the Family of God: The Image of the Emperor in the Heikhalot Literature," in Alexander, L. (ed.) 1991, 276–97.

Allison Jr., D. C. 1982, "The Pauline Epistles and the Synoptic Gospels: The Pattern of Parallels," *NTS* 28, 1–32.

Allison Jr., D. C. 1985, "Paul and the Missionary Discourse," *ETL* 61, 369–75.

Alon, G. 1977, *Jews, Judaism and the Classical World* (Jerusalem: Magnes).

Applebaum, S. 1979, *Jews and Greeks in Ancient Cyrene* (Leiden: Brill).

Applebaum, S. 1984, "The Organization of the Jewish Communities in the Diaspora," in Safrai and Stern (eds.) 1984, 464–503.

Aptowitzer, V. 1925, "Die Seele als Vogel," *MGWJ* 69, 150–69.

Arnaldez R. et al. (eds.) 1967, *Les Oeuvres de Philon d'Alexandrie*, 31 (Paris: Cerf).

Arnaldez R. et al. (eds.) 1972, *Les Oeuvres de Philon d'Alexandrie*, 32 (Paris: Cerf).

Arnim, H. F. A. von (coll.) 1921, *Stoicorum veterum fragmenta*, 1 (Leipzig: Teubner).

Ashton, J. (ed.) 1986, *The Interpretation of John* (London: SPCK).

Ashton, J. 1991, *Understanding the Fourth Gospel* (Oxford: Clarendon).

Attridge, H. W. 1984, "Historiography," in Stone (ed.) 1984, 157–84.

Aune, D. 1983, *Prophecy in Early Christianity and the Ancient Mediterranean World* (Grand Rapids: Eerdmans).

Aune, D. 1990, "The Form and Function of the Proclamations to the Seven Churches (Rev 2–3)," *NTS* 36, 182–204.

Avi-Jona, M. 1977, *The Holy Land from the Persian to the Arab Conquest (536 B.C.–A.D. 640. A Historical Geography* (Grand Rapids: Baker).

Aziza, C. 1987, "L'utilisation polémique du récit de l'Exode chez les écrivains alexandrins (Ivème siècle av. J.-C. – Ier siècle ap. J.-C.), " *ANRW* II:20, 2, 41–65.

Bacher, W. 1899, *Die exegetische Terminologie der jüdischen Traditionsliteratur* (Leipzig, repr. Darmstadt, 1965).

Baer, Y. 1961, "Israel, the Christian Church, and the Roman Empire," in Fuks and Halpern (eds.) 1961, 79–145.

Bammel, E. 1952, "Φίλος καὶ Καίσαρος," *TLZ* 77, cols. 205–10.

Barraclough, R. 1984, "Philo's Politics, Roman Rule and Hellenistic Judaism," *ANRW* II:21, 1, 417–53.

Barrett, C. K. 1965, "Things sacrificed to idols," *NTS* 11, 138–53.

Barrett, C. K. 1968, *The First Epistle to the Corinthians* (New York: Harper & Row).

Barrett, C. K. 1971, *A Commentary on The First Epistle to the Corinthians*, 2nd ed. (London: Black, repr. 1979).

Barrett, C. K. 1978, *The Gospel according to St John*, 2nd ed. (London: SPCK).

Barton, S. 1981, "A Hellenistic Cult Group and the New Testament Churches," *JAC* 24, 7–41.

Bauckham, R. 1993, *The Climax of Prophecy. Studies in the Book of Revelation* (Edinburgh: T.&T. Clark).

Beasley-Murray, G. R. 1974, *The Book of Revelation* (Grand Rapids: Eerdmans).

Beasley-Murray, G. R. 1978, *The Book of Revelation*, 2nd ed. (Grand Rapids: Eerdmans, repr. 1983).

Beck, D. M. 1962, "Nicolaitans," *IDB* 3, 547–48.

Bell, H. I. 1924, *Jews and Christians in Egypt* (Westport, Conn: Greenwood).

Bell, H. I. 1926, *Juden und Griechen im Römischen Alexandria* (Leipzig: Hinrich).

Benoit, P. and Boismard, M. -É. (eds.) 1977, *Synopse de quatre évangiles en francais* (Paris: Cerf).

Betz, H. D. 1979, *Galatians* (Philadelphia: Fortress).

Birnbaum, E. 1994, *The Place of Judaism in Philo's Thought: Israel, Jews, and Proselytes* (Atlanta: Scholars).

Blaufuss, H. 1909, *Roemische Fests und Feiertage nach den Traktaten ueber fremden Dienst (Abodah Zarah) in Mischnah, Tosefta, Jerusalemer und babylonischem Talmud* (Nürnberg: Stich).

Böckman, P. W. and Kristiansen, R. E. (eds.) 1987, *Context*. FS P. J. Borgen (Trondheim: Tapir).

Boismard, M. -É. 1977, *L'évangile de Jean*. In Benoit and Boismard (eds.) 1977.

Borgen, P. 1959, "John and the Synoptics in the Passion Narrative," *NTS* 5, 246-59 (repr. in Borgen 1983, 67-80).

Borgen, P. 1965, *Bread from Heaven*, NovTSup 10 (Leiden: Brill, repr. 1981).

Borgen, P. 1968, "God's Agent in the Fourth Gospel," in Neusner (ed.) 1968, 137-48 (repr. in Borgen 1983, 121-32, in Borgen 1987, 171-84, and in Ashton (ed.) 1986, 67-78).

Borgen, P. 1979, "The Use of Tradition in John 12:44-50," *NTS* 26, 18-35 (repr. in Borgen 1983, 49-66, and in Borgen 1987, 185-204).

Borgen, P. 1980, "Observations on the Theme 'Paul and Philo'," in Pedersen (ed.) 1980, 85-102.

Borgen, P. 1982, "Paul Preaches Circumcision and Pleases Men," in Hooker and Wilson (eds.) 1982, 37-46.

Borgen, P. 1983, *'Logos Was the True Light' and Other Essays on the Gospel of John* (Trondheim: Tapir).

Borgen, P. 1983A, *'Paul Preaches Circumcision and Pleases Men' and Other Essays on Christian Origins* (Trondheim: Tapir).

Borgen, P. 1983B, "The Son of Man Saying in John 3:13-14," in Borgen 1983, 133-48 (also in Borgen 1987, 103-20. Cf. de Jonge 1977, 243-58).

Borgen, P. 1984, "Philo of Alexandria," in Stone (ed.) 1984, 233-82.

Borgen, P. 1984A, "Philo of Alexandria. A Critical and Synthetical Survey of Research Since World War II," *ANRW* II:21, 1, 98-154.

Borgen, P. (ed.) 1985, *The Many and the One*. FS H. Ludin Jansen (Trondheim: Tapir).

Borgen, P. 1986, "Nattverdtradisjonen i 1 Kor 10 og 11 som evangelietradisjon," *Svensk Exegetisk Årsbok* 51, 32-39.

Borgen, P. 1987, "Aristobulus and Philo," in Borgen 1987C, 7–16.

Borgen, P. 1987A, "Creation, Logos and the Son: Observations on John 1:1–18 and 5:17–18," *ExAu* 3, 88–97.

Borgen, P. 1987B, "John and the Synoptics: Can Paul Offer Help?" in Hawthorne and Betz (eds.) 1987, 80–94.

Borgen, P. 1987C, *Philo, John and Paul* (Atlanta: Scholars).

Borgen, P. 1988, "Catalogues of Vices, The Apostolic Decree and the Jerusalem Meeting," in Neusner, Borgen, Frerichs and Horsley (eds.) 1988, 126–41.

Borgen, P. 1990, "John and the Synoptics," in Dungan (ed.) 1990, 408–37.

Borgen, P. 1992, "There Shall Come Forth a Man. Reflections on Messianic Ideas in Philo," in Charlesworth, J. H. (ed.) 1992, 341–61.

Borgen, P. 1993, "Heavenly Ascent in Philo: An Examination of Selected Passages", in Charlesworth and Evans (eds.) 1993, 246–68.

Borgen, P. 1993A, "Polemic in the Book of Revelation," in Evans and Hagner (eds.) 1993, 199–211.

Borgen, P. 1995, "Militant Proselyttisme og Misjon," in Hvalvik and Kvalbein (eds.) 1995, 9–26.

Bornkamm, G. 1959, *Studien zu Antike und Christentum*, Gesammelte Aufsätze, 2 (München: Kaiser).

Bousset, W. 1901, "Die Himmelreise der Seele," *ARW*, 4, 136–69 and 229–73.

Bousset, W. 1906, *Die Offenbarung Johannis*, 2nd ed. (Göttingen: Vandenhoek & Ruprecht).

Brown, R. E. 1961, "Incidents that are Units in the Synoptic Gospels but Dispersed in St. John," *CBQ* 23, 143–60.

Brown, R. E. 1966, *The Gospel according to John I–XII*, AB (Garden City, NY: Doubleday).

Brown, R. E. 1970, *The Gospel According to John XIII–XXI*, AB (Garden City, NY: Doubleday).

Brown, R. E. 1979, *The Community of the Beloved Disciple* (London: Chapman).

Brown, R. E. 1994, *The Death of the Messiah. From Gethsemane to the Grave*, 1, ABRL (New York: Doubleday).

Bruce, F. F. 1982, "The Curse of the Law," in Hooker and Wilson (eds.) 1982, 27–36.

Brunt, J. C. 1985, "Rejected, Ignored, or Misunderstood? The Fate of Paul's Approach to the Problem of Food Offered to Idols in Early Christianity," *NTS* 31, 113–24.

Buckler, W. H. and Calder, W. M. (eds.) 1939, *Monuments and Documents from Phrygia and Caria*, in Calder, W. M. (ed.) 1939, *MAMA*, 6 (Manchester: Manchester University Press).

Bühner, J. -A. 1977, *Der Gesandte und sein Weg im 4. Evangelium* (Tübingen: Mohr-Siebeck).

Bultmann, R. 1931, *Die Geschichte der Synoptichen Tradition*, 2nd ed. (Göttingen: Vandenhoek & Ruprecht).

Bultmann, R. 1941, *Das Evangelium des Johannes* (Göttingen: Vandenhoek & Ruprecht, 18th ed. 1964).

Bultmann, R. 1951, *Theology of the New Testament*, 1 (New York: Scribner's).

Bultmann, R. 1955, "Zur johanneischen Tradition," *TLZ* 80, 521–26.

Bultmann, R. 1971, *The Gospel of John* (Philadelphia: Fortress).

Bultmann, R. 1977, *Theologie des Neuen Testaments*, 7th ed. (Tübingen: Mohr-Siebeck).

Burton, E. de Witt 1921, *A Critical and Exegetical Commentary on the Epistle to the Galatians*, ICC (Edinburgh: T.&T. Clark).

Busse, U., 1979, *Die Wunder des Propheten Jesus*, FB 24, 2nd ed. (Stuttgart: Katolisches Bibelwerk).

Bussman, C. 1971, *Themen der paulinischen Missionspredigt auf dem Hintergrund der spätjüdisch-hellenistischen Missionsliteratur* (Bern: Peter Lang).

Calder, W. M. (ed.) 1939, *Monumenta Asiae Minoris Antiqua (MAMA)*, 6 (Manchester: Manchester University Press).

Catchpole, D. 1977, "Paul, James, and the Apostolic Decree," *NTS* 23, 428–44.

Chambers, R. R. 1980, *Greek Athletics and the Jews: 165 B.C.–A.D. 70*, Ph.D. diss. (Miami: Miami University).

Charles, R. H. 1920, *A Critical and Exegetical Commentary on the Revelation of John*, 2, ICC (Edinburgh: T.&T. Clark, repr. 1989).

Charles, R. H. 1920A, *A Critical and Exegetical Commentary on the Revelation of St. John* 1, ICC (Edinburgh: T.&T. Clark, repr. 1985).

Charlesworth, J. H. (ed.) 1983, *The Old Testament Pseudepigrapha*, 1 (Garden City: Doubleday).

Charlesworth, J. H. (ed.) 1985, *The Old Testament Pseudepigrapha*, 2 (Garden City: Doubleday).

Charlesworth, J. H. (ed.) 1990, *Jews and Christians. Exploring the Past, Present, and Future* (New York: Crossroad).

Charlesworth, J. H. (ed.) 1992, *Jesus and the Dead Sea Scrolls* (New York: Doubleday).

Charlesworth, J. H. (ed.) 1992A, *The Messiah* (Minneapolis: Fortress).

Charlesworth, J. H. and Evans, C. A. (eds.) 1993, *The Pseudepigrapha and Early Biblical Interpretation* (Sheffield: Sheffield Academic Press).

Chilton, B. and Evans, C. A. (eds.) 1994, *Studying the Historical Jesus* (Leiden: Brill).

Cohen, J. D. 1989, "Crossing the Boundary and Becoming a Jew," *HTR* 82, 13–33.

Cohn, L. 1899, "Einteilung und Chronologie der Schriften Philos," *Philologus Sup 7* (Berlin: Dieterich-Weicher).

Cohn, L., Heinemann, I., Adler, M. and Theiler, W. 1910, *Philo von Alexandria. Die Werke in Deutscher Übersetzung*, 2 (Breslau: Marcus, repr. Berlin: De Gruyter 1962).

Cohoon, J. W. 1961 (ed. & trans.), *Dio Chrysostom* with an English Translation, 1, LCL (London: Heinemann).

Collins, A. Yarbro 1976, *The Combat Myth in the Book of Revelation* (Missoula, Montana: Scholars).

Collins, A. Yarbro 1984, *Crisis and Catharsis. The Power of the Apocalypse* (Philadelphia: Westminster).

Collins, J. J. 1984, "The Sibylline Oracles," in Stone (ed.) 1984, 357–82.

Collins, J. J. 1987, "The Development of the Sibylline Tradition," *ANRW* II:20, 1, 421–59.

Colson, F. H. (ed. trans.) 1929–62, *Philo with an English Translation*, LCL (Cambridge, Mass.: Harvard University Press).

Conzelmann, H. 1963, *Die Apostelgeschichte* (Tübingen: Mohr-Siebeck).

Conzelmann, H. 1969, *Der erste Brief an die Korinther*, MeyerK (Göttingen: Vandenhoeck & Ruprecht).

Conzelmann, H. 1987, *Acts of the Apostles* (Philadelphia: Fortress).

Creed, J. M. 1930, *The gospel according to St. Luke* (London: Macmillan).

Cullmann, O. 1948, *Die Tauflehre des Neuen Testaments* (Zürich: Zwingli).

Cumont, F. 1912, *Astrology and Religion among the Greeks and Romans* (New York: Dover, repr. 1960).

Dahl, N. A. 1955–56, "Die Passionsgeschichte bei Matthäeus," *NTS* 2, 17–32.

Dahl, N. A. 1962, "The Johannine Church and History," in Klassen and Snyder (eds.), 124–42 (repr. in Ashton (ed.) 1991, 122–40).

Dahl, N. A. 1974, *The Crucified Messiah and Other Essays* (Minneapolis: Augsburg).

Dauer, A. 1972, *Die Passionsgeschichte im Johannesevangelium* (München: Kösel).

Dauer, A. 1984, *Johannes und Lukas. Untersuchungen zu den johanneisch-lukanischen Parallelperikopen Joh 4,46/Luke 7,1–10 – Joh 12,1–8/Luke 7,36–50; 10,38–42 – Joh 20,19–29/Luke 24,36–49*, FB 50 (Würzburg: Echter).

Dauer, A. 1990, *Beobachtungen zur literarischen Arbeitstechnik des Lukas* (Frankfurt am Main: Hain).

Davies, W. D. and Finkelstein, L. (eds.) 1986, *The Cambridge History of Judaism* 2 (Cambridge: Cambridge University Press).

De Jonge, M. 1977, *Jesus: Stranger from Heaven and Son of God* (Missoula Montana: Scholars).

De Jonge, M. (ed.) 1977, *L 'évangile de Jean*, BETL 44 (Leuven: Leuven University Press).

Dean-Otting, M. 1984, *Heavenly Journeys* (Frankfurt am Main: Lang).

Deichgäber, R. 1967, *Gotteshymnus und Christushymnus in der frühen Christenheit* (Göttingen: Vandenhoek & Ruprecht).

Deissmann, A. 1923, *Licht vom Osten*, 4th ed. (Tübingen: Mohr-Siebeck).

Delling, G. 1970, *Studien zum Neuen Testament und zum hellenistischen Judentum. Gesammelte Aufsätze 1950–1968* (Berlin: Evangelische Verlagsanstalt).

Delling, G. 1974, "Perspektiven der Erforschung des hellenistischen Judentums," *HUCA* 45, 133–76.

Delling, G. 1984, "The 'One Who Sees God' in Philo," in Greenspahn, Hilgert, and Mack (eds.) 1984, 27–41.

Delling, G. 1987, *Die Bewältigung der Diasporasituation durch das hellenistische Judentum* (Göttingen: Vandenhoeck & Ruprecht).

Descamps, Albert and de Halleux, R. P. André (eds.) 1970, *Mélanges Bibliques en hommage au R. P. Béda Rigaux* (Duculot: Gembloux).

Dibelius, M. 1951, *Aufsätze zur Apostelgeschichte* (Göttingen: Vandenhoeck & Ruprecht).

Dibelius, M. 1956, *Studies in the Acts of the Apostles* (New York: Scribner's).

Dimant, D. 1984 "Qumran Sectarian Literature," in Stone (ed.) 1984, 483–550.

Dodd, C. H. 1953, *The Interpretation of the Fourth Gospel* (Cambridge: Cambridge University Press).

Dodd, C. H. 1963, *Historical Tradition in the Fourth Gospel* (Cambridge: Cambridge University Press, repr. 1979).

Doran, R. 1987, "The Jewish Hellenistic Historians Before Josephus," *ANRW* II:20, 1, 246–97.

Dungan, D. L. 1971, *The Sayings of Jesus in the Churches of Paul. The Use of the Synoptic Tradition in the Regulation of Early Church Life* (Philadelphia: Fortress).

Dungan, D. L. (ed.) 1990, *The Interrelations of the Gospels*, BETL 95 (Leuven: Peeters).

Dunn, J. D. G. 1983, "The New Perspective on Paul," *BJRL* 65, 95–122.

Dunn, J. D. G. 1990, *Jesus, Paul and the Law* (Louisville: Westminster/Knox).

Dunn, J. D. G. 1992, "Yet Once More – 'the Works of the Law'," *JSNT* 46, 99–117.

Dunn, J. D. G. 1993, *The Epistle to the Galatians* (London: Black).

Dvornik, F. 1966, *Early Christian and Byzantine Political Philosophy*, 1 (Washington, DC: Dumbarton Oak Center for Byzantine Studies).

Easton, B. S. 1932, "New Testament Ethical Lists," *JBL* 51, 1–12.

Eckstein, H. -J. 1983, *Der Begriff Syneidesis bei Paulus* (Tübingen: Mohr-Siebeck).

Eichhorn, D. M. (ed.) 1965, *Conversion to Judaism. A History and Analysis* (New York: KTAV).

Eitrem, S. 1915, *Opferritus und Voropfer der Griechen und Römer.* (Kristiania: Dybwad).

Engberg-Pedersen, T. (ed.) 1994, *Paul in His Hellenistic Context* (Edinburg: T.&T. Clark).

Evans, C. A. and Hagner, D. A. (eds.) 1993, *Anti-Semitism and Early Christiany* (Minneapolis: Fortress).

Evans, C. A. 1994, "The Recent Published Dead Sea Scrolls and the Historical Jesus," in Chilton and Evans (eds.) 1994, 547–65.

Farla, P. J. 1978, *Jesus' oordeel over Israël* (Kampen: Kok).

Fekkes, J. 1994, *Isaiah and Prophetic Traditions in the Book of Revelation* (Sheffield: Sheffield Academic Press).

Feldman, L. H. 1968, "The Orthodoxy of the Jews in Hellenistic Egypt," *JSS* 22, 215–37.

Feldman, L. H. 1969, *Josephus with an English Translation*, 9, LCL (London: Heinemann).

Feldman, L. H. 1993, *Jew and Gentile in the Ancient World. Attitudes and Interactions from Alexander to Justinian* (Princeton: Princeton University Press).

Feuillet, A. 1967, "Les 144,000 Israélites Marqués d'un Sceau," *NovT* 9, 191–224.

Fiebig, P. 1925, *Der Erzählungsstil der Evangelien* (Leipzig: Hinrich).

Fiorenza, E. Schüssler 1972, *Priester für Gott* (Münster: Aschendorff).

Fiorenza, E. Schüssler (ed.) 1976, *Aspects of Religious Propaganda in Judaism and Early Christianity* (Notre Dame, Indiana: University of Notre Dame Press).

Fiorenza, E. Schüssler 1983, *In Memory of Her. A Feminist Reconstruction of Christian Origins* (New York: Crossroad).

Fiorenza, E. Schüssler 1985, *The Book of Revelation. Justice and Judgment* (Philadelphia: Fortress).

Fischer, U. 1978, *Eschatologie und Jenseitserwartung im hellenistischen Diasporajudentum* (Berlin: de Gruyter).

Fishman, P. (ed.) 1973, *Minor and Modern Festivals* (Jerusalem: Keter).

Fjärstedt, B. 1974, *Synoptic Tradition in 1 Corinthians 1–4 and 9* (Uppsala: Uppsala Divinity School).

Flusser, D. 1988, *Judaism and the Origins of Christianity* (Jerusalem: Magnes).

Fortna, R. 1970, *The Gospel of Signs* (Cambridge: Cambridge University Press).

Fraser, P. M. 1972, *Ptolemaic Alexandria*, 1 (Oxford: Clarendon).

Frey, P. Jean-Baptiste 1952, *Corpus Inscriptionum Iudaicarum*, 2 (Rome: Pontificio Istituto di Archeologia Cristiana).

Fuks, A. and Halpern, I. (eds.) 1961, *Scripta Hierosolymitana 7, Studies in History* (Jerusalem: Magnes).

Geiger, F. 1932, *Philon von Alexandreia als sozialer Denker* (Stuttgart: Kohlhammer).

Gerhardsson, B. 1961, *Memory and Manuscript* (Uppsala: Gleerup).

Gerhardsson, B. 1977, *Die Anfänge der Evangelientradition* (Wuppertal: Brockhaus).

Gesenius, W. 1949, *Hebräisches und Aramäisches Handwörterbuch über das Alte testament*, repr. of the 17th ed. (Berlin: Springer).

Ginzberg, L. 1968, *The Legends of the Jews*, 3 (Philadelphia: Jewish Publication Society).

Gnilka, J. 1978, *Das Evangelium nach Markus*, EKK 2:1 (Neukirchen-Vluyn: Neukirchener Verlag).

Goodenough, E. R. 1928, "The Political Philosophy of Hellenistic Kingship," in *Yale Classical Studies*, 1 (New Haven: Yale University Press) 55–102.

Goodenough, E. R. 1935, *By Light, Light. The Mystic Gospel of Hellenistic Judaism* (New Haven: Yale University Press, 1935; repr. Amsterdam, 1969).

Goodenough, E. R. 1938, *The Politics of Philo Judaeus* (New Haven: Yale University Press; repr. Hildesheim, 1967).

Goodenough, E. R. 1953–68, *Jewish Symbols in the Graeco-Roman Period*, 1–13 (New York: Pantheon Press).

Grässer, E. and Merk, O. (eds.) 1985, *Glaube und Eschatologie*, FS W. G. Kümmel (Tübingen: Mohr-Siebeck).

Green, W. S. (ed.) 1981, *Approaches to Ancient Judaism, 3: Text and Context in Early Rabbinic Literature* (Chico, CA: Scholars).

Green, W. S. (ed.) 1985, *Approaches to Ancient Judaism, 5: Studies in Judaism and its Graeco-Roman Context* (Atlanta: Scholars).

Greenspahn, F. E., Hilgert, E., and Mack, B. (eds.) 1984, *Nourished with Peace. Studies in Hellenistic Judaism in Memory of Samuel Sandmel* (Chico: Scholars).

Gruben, G. 1976, *Die Tempel der Griechen*, 2nd ed. (München: Hirmer).

Gruenwald, I. 1980, *Apocalyptic and Merkavah Mysticism* (Leiden: Brill).

Gundel, H. G. 1966, *Astrologumena: Die astrologische Literatur in der Antike und ihre Geschichte* (Wiesbaden: Steiner).

Gundry, R. H. 1985, "Grace, Works, and Staying Saved in Paul," *Bib.* 66, 1–38.

Haacker, K. 1980, "Dibelius und Cornelius. Ein Beispiel formgeschichtlicher Überlieferungskritik," *BZ*, N.F. 24, 234–51.

Haenchen, E. 1959, "Johanneische Probleme," *ZTK* 56, 19–54.

Haenchen, E. 1971, *The Acts of the Apostles* (Oxford: Blackwell, repr. 1982).

Haenchen, E. 1980, *Das Johannesevangelium: ein Kommentar* (Tübingen: Mohr-Siebeck).

Haenchen, E. 1984, *John*, 1 (Philadelphia: Fortress).

Halperin, D. J. 1988, "Ascension or Invasion: Implications of the Heavenly Journey in Ancient Judaism," *Religion* 18, 47–67.

Hansen, E. V. 1971, *The Attalids of Pergamum*, 2nd ed. (Ithaca: Cornell University Press).

Harris, H. A. 1976, *Greek Athletics and the Jews* (Cardiff: University of Wales Press).

Hawthorne, G. F. and Betz, O. (eds.) 1987, *Tradition and Interpretation in the New Testament*. FS E. Earle Ellis (Grand Rapids: Eerdmans).

Hayward, R. 1982, "The Jewish Temple at Leontopolis," *JJS* 33, 429–43.

Heiligenthal, R. 1984, "Soziologische Implikationen der Paulinischen Rechtferigungslehre im Galaterbrief am Beispiel der 'Werke des Gesetzes'," *Kairos* 26, 38–53.

Heinemann, I. 1962, *Philons griechische und jüdische Bildung*, repr. (Darmstadt: Wissenschaftliche Buchgesellschaft).

Hellholm D. (ed.) 1983, *Apocalypticism in the Mediterranean World and the Near East* (Tübingen: Mohr-Siebeck), 655–86.

Hengel, M. 1969, *Judentum und Hellenismus* (Tübingen: Mohr-Siebeck).

Hengel, M. 1974, *Judaism and Hellenism*, 1–2 (Philadelphia: Fortress).

Hengel, M. 1983, "Messianische Hoffnung und politischer 'Radikalismus' in der 'Jüdisch-hellenistischen Diaspora'," in Hellholm D. (ed.) 1983, 655–86.

Hengel, M. 1989, *The 'Hellenization' of Judaea in the First Century after Christ* (London: SCM).

Hicks, E. L. (ed.) 1890, *Priene, Iasos and Ephesos*, 2, in Newton (ed.) 1890, Part 3.

Himmelfarb, M. 1988, "Heavenly Ascent and the Relationship of the Apocalypses and the *Hekhalot* Literature," *HUCA* 59, 73–100.

Himmelfarb, M. 1993, *Ascent to Heaven in Jewish and Christian Apocalyses* (New York/Oxford: Oxford University Press).

Holtz, T. 1971, *Die Christologie der Apokalypse des Johannes*, 2nd ed. (Berlin: Akademie).

Hommel, H. 1975, "Juden und Christen im kaiserzeitlichen Milet. Überlegungen zur Theaterinschrift," *IstM* 25, 167–95.

Hooker M. D. and Wilson, S. G. (eds.) 1982, *Paul and Paulinism*, FS C. K. Barrett (London: SPCK).

Hooker, M. 1982, "Paul and 'Covenantal Nomism'," in Hooker and Wilson (eds.) 1982, 47–56.

Horst, P. W. van der 1989, "Jews and Christians in Aphrodisia in the Light of their Relations in Other Cities of Asia Minor," *Nederlands Theologisch Tijdsschrift*, 43, 106–21.

Hübner, H. 1978, *Das Gesetz bei Paulus* (Göttingen: Vandenhoeck & Ruprecht).

Hurd, J. C. 1965, *The Origin of I Corinthians* (London: SPCK).

Hvalvik, R. And Kvalbein, H. 1995, *AD ACTA. Studier til Apostlenes Gjerninger og urkristendommens historie.* FS E. Larsson (Oslo: Verbum).

Jastrow, M. no date, *A Dictionary of the Targumim, the Talmud Babli and Yerushalmi, and the Midrashic Literature* repr. (Israel).

Jeremias, J. 1955, *The Eucharistic Words of Jesus* (New York).

Jörns, K. P. 1971, *Das hymnische Evangelium* (Gütersloh: Mohn).

Kamlah, E. 1964, *Die Form der katalogischen Paränese im Neuen Testament* (Tübingen: Mohr-Siebeck).

Käppel, L. 1992, *Paian. Studien zur Geschichte einer Gattung* (Berlin: Gruyter).

Käsemann, E. 1954/55, "Sätze heiligen Rechtes im Neuen Testament," *NTS* 1, 248–260.

Käsemann, E. 1964, *Essays on New Testament Themes* (Naperville, Ill.: Allenson).

Kasher, A. 1985, *The Jews in Hellenistic and Roman Egypt* (Tübingen: Mohr-Siebeck).

Kasher, A. 1988, *Jews, Idumaeans, and Ancient Arabs: Relations of the Jews in Eretz-Israel with the Nations of the Frontier and the Desert during the Hellenistic and Roman Era (332 B.C.E.–70 C.E.)* (Tübingen: Mohr-Siebeck).

Kasher, A. 1990, *Jews and Hellenistic Cities in Eretz-Israel* (Tübingen: Mohr-Siebeck).

Kasher, A., Rappaport, U. and Fuks, G. (eds.) 1990, *Greece and Rome in Eretz Israel* (Jerusalem: Yad Izhak ben-Zvi).

Katsh, A. I. and Nemoy, L. (eds.) 1979, *Essays on the Occasion of the Seventieth Anniversary of the Dropsie University (1909–1979)* (Philadelphia: Dropsie University).

Kittel, G. 1944, "Das kleinasiatische Judentum in der hellenistisch-römischen Zeit," *TLZ* 69, cols. 9–20.

Klassen, W. and Snyder, G. F. (eds.) 1962, *Current Issues in New Testament Interpretation* (New York: Harper).

Koester, H. 1971, "GNOMAI DIAPHOROI: The origin and Nature of Diversification in Early Christianity," in Robinsen and Koester (eds.) 1971, 114–57.

Kotila, H. 1988, *Umstrittener Zeuge. Studien zur Stellung des Gesetzes in der johanneischen Theologiegeschichte*, AASF Diss. 48 (Helsinki: Suomalainen Tiedea-Katemia).

Kraft, H. 1974, *Die offenbarung des Johannes* (Tübingen: Mohr-Siebeck).

Kysar, R. 1975, *The Fourth Evangelist and His Gospel* (Minneapolis: Augsburg).

Laato, T. 1991, *Paulus und das Judentum* (Aabo: Aabo Akademi).

Lagrange, M. -J. 1927, *Évangile selon saint Jean*, 3rd ed. (Paris: Lecoffre).

Le Déaut, R. 1971, "A propos a Definition of Midrash," *Interpretation*, 25, 259–82.

Leivestad, R. 1954, *Christ the Conqueror* (London: SPCK).

Levine, L. I. 1975, *Caesarea under Roman Rule* (Leiden: Brill).

Lewis, N. 1985, *Life in Egypt under Roman Rule* (Oxford: Clarendon).

Liddell, H. G. and Scott, R. 1940, *Greek-English Lexicon*, A New Edition (Oxford: Clarendon, repr. 1958).

Lietzmann, H. and Kümmel, W. G. 1949, *An die Korinther I/II*, HNT 9: 4th ed. (Tübingen: Mohr-Siebeck).

Lindars, B. 1969/70, "Two Parables in John," *NTS* 16, 318–29.

Lindars, B. 1971, *Behind the Fourth Gospel* (London: SPCK).

Lindars, B. 1972, *The Gospel of John* (London: Oliphants).

Lindars, B. 1981, "John and the Synoptic Gospels: A Test Case," *NTS* 27, 287–94.

Lohmeyer, E. 1953, *Die Offenbarung des Johannes*, 2nd ed. (Tübingen: Mohr-Siebeck).

Lohse, E. 1971, *Die Texte von Qumran* (München, Kösel).

Lohse, E. 1979, *Die Offenbarung des Johannes*, NTD 11 (Göttingen: Vandenhoeck & Ruprecht).

Lohse, E. 1988, "Wie christlich ist die Offenbarung des Johannes?" *NTS*, 34, 321–38.

Lull, D. J. 1978, *The Spirit in Galatia* (Chico, CA: Scholars).

Lull, D. J. (ed) 1988, *Society of Biblical Literature 1988 Seminar Papers* (Atlanta, GA: Scholars).

Luz, U. 1989, *Matthew 1–7* (Minneapolis: Augsburg).

MacGregor, G. H. C. 1928, *The Gospel of John* (London: Hodder & Stoughton).

Mack, B. 1972, "Imitatio Mosis: Patterns of Cosmology and Soteriology in the Hellenistic Synagogue," *Studia Philonica* 1, 27–55.

MacMullen, R. 1967, *Enemies of the Roman Order* (Cambridge, Mass.: Harvard University Press).

MacMullen, R. 1981, *Paganism in the Roman Empire* (New Haven: Yale University Press).

Malherbe, A. J. 1994, "Determinism and Free Will in Paul: The Argument of 1 Cor 8 and 9," in Engberg-Pedersen, T. (ed.) 1994, 231–55.

Manson, T. W. 1962, *Studies in the Gospels and Epistles*, ed. by M. Black (Manchester: Manchester University Press) 190–224.

Marcus, R. (ed.trans.) 1953, *Philo. Supplements*, 1–2, LCL (Cambridge, Mass.: Harvard University Press).

Marsh, J. 1968, *Saint John* (Harmondsworth: Penguin).

Marshall, I. H. 1973, "Palestinian and Hellenistic Christianity: Some Critical Comments," *NTS* 19, 217–75.

Marshall, I. H. 1987, "Some Observations on the Covenant in the New Testament," in Böckman and Kristiansen (eds.) 1987, 121–36.

Martyn, J. L. 1977, "Glimpses into the History of the Johannine Community," in de Jonge (ed.) 1977, 149–76.

Martyn, J. L. 1979, *History and Theology in the Fourth Gospel*, 2nd rev. ed. (Nashville: Abingdon; 1st ed., New York, 1968).

Martyn, J. L. 1986, "Source Criticism and Religionsgeschichte in the Fourth Gospel," in Ashton (ed.) 1986, 99–121.

Maurer, C. 1964, "σύνοιδα κτλ.," in *TWNT*, 7, 897–918.

McEleney, N. J. 1974, "Conversion, Circumcision and the Law," *NTS* 20, 319–40.

McKnight, S. 1991, *A Light Among the Gentiles. Jewish Missionary Activity in the Second Temple Period* (Minneapolis: Fortress).

Meeks, W. A. 1967, *The Prophet-King*, NovTSup 11 (Leiden: Brill).

Meeks, W. A. 1976, "The Divine Agent and His Counterfeit in Philo and the Fourth Gospel," in Fiorenza (ed.) 1976, 43–67.

Mendels, D. 1992, *The Rise and Fall of Jewish Nationalism*, ABRL (New York: Doubleday).

Mendelson, A. 1982, *Secular Education in Philo of Alexandria* (Cincinnati: Hebrew Union College Press).

Menken, M. J. J. 1987, "Some Remarks on the Course of the Dialogue: John 6:25–34," *Bijdragen, tijdschrift voor filosofie en theologie*, 48, 139–49.

Metzger, B. M. (ed.) 1975, *A Textual Commentary on the Greek New Testament* (New York: United Bible Societies).

Meyer, R. 1937, *Hellenistisches in der rabbinischen Anthropologie* (Stuttgart: Kohlhammer).

Moloney, F. J. 1978, *The Johannine Son of Man* (Rome: Libreria Ateneo Salesiano).

Montefiore, C. G. and Loewe, H. (eds.) 1938, *A Rabbinic Anthology* (London: Macmillan).

Moore, C. A. 1992, "Esther, Additions to," in *ABD*, 2:626–33.

Moore, C. A., 1992A, "Esther, the Book of," in *ABD*, 2:633–43.

Moore, G. F. 1927–30, *Judaism*, 1–3 (Cambridge, Mass.: Harvard University Press).

Morris, J., "The Jewish Philosopher Philo," in Schürer 1987, 809–89.

Mosbeck, H. 1951, *Sproglig Fortolkning til Første Korinterbrev*, 2nd ed. (Copenhagen: Gyldendal).

Mounce, R. H. 1977, *The Book of Revelation* (Grand Rapids: Eerdmans).

Müller, U. B. 1984, *Die Offenbarung des Johannes* (Gütersloh: Mohn and Würzburg: Echter).

Mussner, F. 1974, *Der Galaterbrief*, HTKNT 9 (Freiberg: Herder).

Mussner, F. 1985, "'Weltherrschaft' als eschatologisches Thema der Johannesapokalypse," in Grässer and Merk (eds.) 1985, 209–27.

Nauck, W. 1957, *Die Tradition und der Charakter des ersten Johannesbriefes*, WUNT 3 (Tübingen: Mohr-Siebeck).

Neirynck, F. 1977, "John and the Synoptics," in de Jonge (ed.), 73–106.

Neirynck, F. 1979, *Jean et les Synoptiques. Examen critique de l'exégèse de M. -E. Boismard*, BETL 49 (Leuven: Peeters).

Neirynck, F. 1982, *Evangelica*, BETL 60 (Leuven: Peeters).

Neirynck, F. 1984, "John 4:46–54. Signs Source and/or Synoptic Gospels," *ETL* 60, 367–75.

Neirynck, F. 1985, "Lc 24:36–43: Un récit lucanien, in À *cause de l'évangile*. FS J. Dupont (Lectio Divina, 123), (Paris: Cerf) 655–80.

Neirynck, F. 1986, "Paul and the Sayings of Jesus," in Vanhoye (ed.) 1986, 265–321.

Neirynck, F. 1990, *John and the Synoptics, Response to P. Borgen*, in Dungan (ed.) 1990, 438–50.

Neirynck, F. 1991, *Evangelica*, 2, BETL 99 (Leuven: Peeters).

Neumann, "Amicus" 1894, in *PW*, 1 (Stuttgart: Metzlersche Verlag), cols. 1831–33.

Neusner, J. 1964, "The Conversion of Adiabene to Judaism," *JBL* 83, 60–66.

Neusner, J. (ed.) 1968, *Religions in Antiquity*, E. R. Goodenough Memorial Volume (Leiden: Brill).

Neusner, J., Borgen, P., Frerichs, E. and Horsley, R. (eds.) 1988, *The Social World of Formative Christianity and Judaism*, FS Howard C. Kee (Philadelphia: Fortress).

Newman Jr, B. M. 1968, *Rediscovering the Book of Revelation* (Valley Forge, Pa: Judson).

Newton, C. T. (ed.) 1890, *The Collection of Ancient Greek Inscriptions in the British Museum*, 3 (Oxford: Clarendon).

Nickelsburg, G. W. E. 1982, *Jewish Literature Between the Bible and the Mishnah* (Philadelphia: Fortress).

Nickelsburg, G. W. E. 1984, "The Bible Rewritten and Expanded," in Stone (ed.) 1984, 89–156.

Nolland, J. 1981, "Uncircumcised Proselytes?" *JSJ* 12, 173–79.

Oepke, A. and Rohde, J. 1973. *Der Brief an die Galater*, ThHNT 9, 3rd ed. (Berlin: Evangelische Verlagsanstalt).

Ohlemutz, E. 1940, *Die Kulte und Heiligtümer der Götter in Pergamum* (Würzburg; repr. Darmstadt: Wissenschaftliche Buchgesellschaft, 1968).

Oster, R. 1987, "Holy Days in honour of Artemis," *New Documents Illustrating Early Christianity* 4, 74–82.

Painter, J. 1989, "Tradition and Interpretation in John 6," *NTS* 35, 421–50.

Painter, J. 1991, *The Quest for the Messiah* (Edinburgh: T.&T. Clark).

Pancaro, S. 1975, *The Law in the Fourth Gospel* (Leiden: Brill).

Pearson, B. 1984, "Philo and Gnosticism," *ANRW* II:21, 1, 295–342.

Peck, A. 1981, "Cases and Principles in Mishna; A Study of Terumot Chapter Eight," in Green (ed.) 1981, 35–46.

Pedersen, S. (ed.) 1980, *Die Paulinische Literatur und Theologie* (Aarhus: Aros).

Pelletier, A. 1967, "In Flaccum," in Arnaldez et al. (eds. & trans.) 1967.

Pelletier, A. 1972, "Legatione ad Gaium," in Arnaldez et al. (eds. & trans.) 1972.

Pesch, R. 1976, *Das Markusevangelium*, 1, HTKNT (Freiburg: Herder).

Pesch, R. 1986, *Die Apostelgeschichte*, 1 (Neukirchen-Vluyn: Neukirchener).

Porten, B. 1968, *Archives from Elephantine* (Los Angeles: University of Calefornia Press).

Porton, G. G. 1988, *GOYIM. Gentiles and Israelites in Mishnah-Tosefta* (Atlanta, GA: Scholars).

Price, S. R. F. 1984, *Rituals and Power. The Roman Imperial Cult in Asia Minor* (Cambridge: Cambridge University Press).

Radt, W. 1978, *Pergamon. Archaeological Guide,* 2nd ed. (Istanbul: Türkiye Turing ve Otomobil Kurumu).

Radt, W. 1978A, "Pergamon – Vom Leben in der Antiken Stadt," *AW* 9, 3–20.

Radt, W. 1988, *Pergamon, Geschichte und Bauten, Funde und Erforschung einer antiken Metropole* (Köln: DuMont).

Rajak, T. 1985, "Jewish Rights in the Greek Cities under Roman Rule," in Green (ed.) 1985, 19–36.

Resch, G. 1905, *Das Aposteldekret nach seiner ausserkanonischen Textgestalt untersucht* TU N.F. 13:3 (Leipzig: Hinrich).

Resch, A. 1904, *Der Paulinismus und die Logia Jesu,* TU N.F. 12 (Leipzig: Hinrich).

Riesenfeld, H. 1970, *The Gospel Tradition* (Philadelphia: Fortress).

Robinsen, J. M. and Koester, H. (eds.) 1971, *Trajectories through Early Christianity* (Philadelphia: Fortress).

Roebuck, C. 1951, *Corinth XIV: The Asclepieion and Lerna* (Princeton: Princeton University Press).

Roloff, J. 1981, *Die Apostelgeschichte* (Göttingen: Vandenhoeck & Ruprecht).

Roloff, J. 1984, *Die Offenbarung des Johannes,* Zürcher Bibelkommentare (Zürich: Theologischer Verlag, repr. 1987).

Roloff, J. 1993, *The Revelation of John. A Continental Commentary* (Minneapolis: Fortress).

Rosenbloom, J. R. 1978, *Conversion to Judaism. From the Biblical Period to the Present* (Cincinnati, Ohio: Hebrew Union Press).

Rostovtzeff, M. 1941, *The Social and Economic History of the Hellenistic World,* 1 (Oxford: Clarendon).

Rowland, C. 1982, *The Open Heaven. A Study of Apocalyptic in Judaism and Christianity* (New York: Crossroad).

Russell, D. S. 1964, *The Method and Message of Jewish Apocalyptic* (London: SCM).

Sabbe, M. 1977, "The Arrest of Jesus in John 18,1–11 and its Relation to the Synoptic Gospels," in de Jonge (ed.) 1977, 203–34.

Sabbe, M. 1980, "John and the Synoptists: Neirynck vs. Boismard," *ETL* 56, 125–31.

Sachau, E. 1911, *Aramäische Papyrus und Ostraka aus einer jüdischen Miltitärkolonie zu Elephantine,* 1–2 (Leipzig: Hinrich).

Safrai, S. and Stern, M. (eds.) 1974, *The Jewish People in the First Century,* CRINT 1:1 (Assen: van Gorcum).

Sandelin, K. -G. 1991, "The Danger of Idolatry According to Philo of Alexandria," *Tem* 27, 109–50.

Sanders, E. P. 1977, *Paul and Palestinian Judaism* (London: SCM).

Sanders, E. P. 1983, *Paul, the Law, and the Jewish People* (Philadelphia: Fortress).

Sanders, E. P. 1989, "The Genre of Palestinian Jewish Apocalypses," in Hellholm (ed.) 1989, 447–60.

Sandmel, S. 1978, *Anti-Semitism in the New Testament* (Philadelphia: Fortress).

Sandmel, S. 1979, "Apocalypse and Philo," in Katsh and Nemoy (eds.) 1979, 383–87.

Schenke, L. 1985, "Die literarische Vorgeschichte von Joh 6,26–58," *BZ* 29, 68–89.

Schenke, L. 1992,"Das Johanneische Schisma und die 'Zwölf' (Johannes 6:60–71)," *NTS* 38, 105–21.

Schille, G. 1983, *Die Apostelgeschichte des Lukas* (Berlin: Evangelische Verlagsanstalt).

Schlier, H. 1960, "ἐλεύθερεος," *TWNT* 2, 484ff.

Schlier, H. 1971, *Der Brief an die Galater*, MeyerK (Göttingen: Vandenhoeck & Ruprecht).

Schmithals, W. 1972, *Paul and the Gnostics* (Nashville: Abingdon).

Schnackenburg, R. 1965, *Das Johannesevangelium, 1. Einleitung und Kommentar zu Kap. 1 – 4* (Freiburg: Herder).

Schnackenburg, R. 1971, *Das Johannesevangelium, 2. Kommentar zu Kap. 5 – 12* (Freiburg: Herder).

Schnackenburg, R. 1975, *Das Johannesevangelium, 3: Kommentar zu Kap. 13 – 21* (Freiburg: Herder).

Schneider, G. 1980, *Die Apostelgeschichte*, 1 (Freiburg: Herder).

Schneider, G. 1982, *Die Apostelgeschichte*, 2 (Freiburg: Herder).

Schneider, G. 1992, *Jesusüberlieferung und Christologie* (Leiden: Brill).

Schürer, E. 1973, *The History of the Jewish People in the Age of Jesus Christ (175 B.C. – A.D. 135.* A new English Version by Vermes, G. and Millar, F., 1 (Edinburgh: T.&T. Clark).

Schürer, E. 1979, *The History of the Jewish People in the Age of Jesus Christ (175 B.C. – A.D. 135.* A new English version by Vermes, G. and Millar, F., 2 (Edinburgh: T.&T. Clark).

Schürer, E. 1986, *The History of the Jewish People in the Age of Jesus Christ (175 B.C. – A.D. 135.* A new English version by Vermes, G. and Millar, F., 3:1 (Edinburgh: T.&T. Clark).

Schürer, E. 1987, *The History of the Jewish People in the Age of Jesus Christ (175 B.C.–A.D. 135*. A new English version by Vermes, G. and Millar, F., 3:2 (Edinburgh: T.&T. Clark).

Schürmann, H. 1955, *Der Einsetzungsbericht* Lk 22:19–20 (Münster: Aschendorff).

Schürmann, H. 1970, *Ursprung und Gestalt* (Düsseldorf: Partmos).

Segal, A. F. 1980, "Heavenly Ascent in Hellenistic Judaism, Early Christianity and their Environment," *ANRW* II:23, 2, 1333–94.

Segal, A. F. 1988, "The Costs of Proselytism and Conversion," in Lull (ed.) 1988, 336–79.

Segal, A. F. 1990, *Paul the Convert* (New Haven: Yale University Press).

Seland, T. 1995, *Establishment Violence in Philo & Luke: A Study of Non-Conformity to the Torah & Jewish Vigiliante Reactions* (Leiden: Brill).

Seligson, D. J., 1965, "In the Post-Talmudic Period," in Eichhorn, D. M. (ed.) 1965, 67–95.

Sheppard, A. R. R. 1979, "Jews, Christians and Heretics in Acmonia and Eumeneia," *AnSt* 29,169–80.

Sherwin-White, A. N. 1963, *Roman Society and Roman Law in the New Testament* (Oxford: Clarendon).

Siegert, F. 1973, "Gottesfrüchtige und Sympatisanten," JSJ 4, 109–64.

Simons, E. 1880, *Hat der dritte Evangelist den kanonischen Matthäus benutzt?* (Bonn).

Smallwood, E. M. 1970, *Philonis Alexandrini Legatio ad Gaium*, 2nd ed. (Leiden: Brill).

Smallwood, E. M. 1976, *The Jews under Roman Rule* (Leiden: Brill).

Smith, D. Moody 1963/64, "The Source of the Gospel of John: An Assessment of the Present State of the Problem," *NTS* 10, 336–51.

Smith, D. Moody 1980, "John and the Synoptics: Some Dimensions of the Problems," *NTS* 26, 425–44.

Smith, D. Moody 1982, "John and the Synoptics," *Bib.* 63, 102–13.

Smith, D. Moody 1984, *Johannine Christianity* (Columbia, SC).

Smith, D. Moody 1990, "Judaism and the Gospel of John," in Charlesworth (ed.) 1990, 76–96.

Smith, D. Moody 1992, *John among the Gospels. The Relationship in Twentieth-Century Research* (Minneapolis: Fortress).

Smith, J. Z. 1978, "Towards Interpreting Demonic Powers in Hellenstic and Roman Antiquity," in *ANRW* II:16, 1, 425–39.

Smith, M. 1992A, "Two Ascended to Heaven – Jesus and the Author of 4Q491,"in Charlesworth (ed.) 1992, 290–301.

Sperber, A. 1968, *The Bible in Aramaic Based on Old Manuscripts and Printed Texts.* 4 A: *The Hagiographa* (Leiden: Brill).

Stählin, G. 1973, "φίλος κτλ," *TWNT* 9, 112–69.

Stanton, G. N. 1983, "Matthew as a Creative Interpreter of the Sayings of Jesus," in Stuhlmacher (ed.) 1983, 273–88.

Stein, S. 1957, "The Dietary Laws in Rabbinic and Patristic Literature," in Aland and Cross (eds.) 1957, 141–54.

Stemberger, G. 1983, *Die Römische Herrschaft im Urteil der Juden.* *Erträge der Forschung* (Darmstadt: Wissenschaftliche Buchgesellschaft).

Stendahl, K. 1977, *Paul among Jews and Gentiles, and Other Essays* (Philadelphia: Fortress).

Stern, M. 1974, "The Jewish Diaspora," in Safrai and Stern (eds.) 1974, 117–83.

Stern, M. 1976, *Greek and Latin Authors on Jews and Judaism.* 1: *From Herodotus to Plutarch* (Jerusalem: Israel Academy of Sciences and Humanities).

Stone, M. 1980, *Scriptures, Sects, and Visions* (Philadelphia: Fortress).

Stone, M. (ed.) 1984, *Jewish Writings of the Second Temple Period,* CRINT 2:2 (Assen: van Gorcum).

Stuhlmacher, P. (ed.) 1983, *Das Evangelium und die Evangelien,* WUNT 28 (Tübingen: Mohr-Siebeck).

Stuhlmacher, P. 1983A, "Jesus-tradition im Römerbrief?," *Theologische Beiträge* 14, 240–50.

Tabor, J. D. 1986, *Things Unutterable: Paul's Ascent to Paradise in its Graeco-Roman, Judaic, and Early Christian Context* (Lanham, MD: University Press of America).

Taylor, L. Ross 1931, *The Divinity of the Roman Emperor* (Middletown, Conn.: American Philological Association, repr. Chico, CA: Scholars, no date).

Taylor, V. 1953, *The Gospel According to St Mark* (London: Macmillan).

Tcherikover, V. (ed.) 1957, *Corpus Papyrorum Judaicarum,* 1 (Cambridge, Mass.: Harvard University Press).

Tcherikover, V. 1963, "The Decline of the Jewish Diaspora in Egypt in the Roman Period," *JJS* 14, 1–32.

Tcherikover, V. 1966, *Hellenistic Civilisation and the Jews* (Philadelphia: The Jewish Publication Society of America).

Thompson, L. L. 1990, *The Book of Revelation. Apocalypse and Empire* (New York: Oxford University Press).

Tomlinson, R. A. 1969, "Perachora: the Remains outside the Two Sanctuaries," *ABSA* 64, 164–72.

Tomson, P. J. 1990, *Paul and the Jewish Law: Halakha in the Letters of the Apostle to the Gentiles* (Assen: Van Gorcum and Minneapolis: Fortress).

Trachtenberg, J. 1943, *The Devil and the Jews. The Medieval Conception of the Jew and its Relation to Modern Antisemitism* (New York: Harper & Row, repr. 1966).

Trautmann, M. 1980, *Zeichenhafte Handlungen Jesu. Ein Beitrag zur Frage nach dem geschichtliche Jesus*, FB 37 (Wurzburg: Echter).

Trebilco, P. 1991, *Jewish Communities in Asia Minor* (Cambridge: Cambridge University Press).

Tuckett, C. M. 1983, "1 Corinthians and Q," *JBL* 102, 607–19.

Tuckett, C. M. 1984, "Paul and the Synoptic Mission Discourse?" *ETL* 60, 376–81.

Unnik, W. C. van 1970, "'Worthy is the Lamb'. The Background of Apoc 5," in Descamps and de Halleux (eds.) 1970, 445–61.

Unnik, W. C. van 1974, "Josephus' Account of the Story of Israel's Sin with Alien Women in the Country of Midian (Num 25.1ff.)," in van Voss et al. (eds.) 1974, 241–61.

Vanhoye, A. (ed.) 1986, *L'Apôtre Paul Personnalité, style et conception du ministère*, BETL 73 (Leuven).

Vawter, B. 1960, "Apocalyptic: Its Relation to Prophecy," *CBQ* 22, 33–46.

Vermes, G. 1961, *Scripture and Tradition in Judaism* (Leiden: Brill).

Vicker, M. no date, *Greek Symposia* (Oxford: Joint Association of Classical Teachers).

Vögtle, A. 1936, *Die Tugend – und Lasterkataloge im Neuen Testament* (Münster: Aschendorff).

Vögtle, A. 1971, *Das Evangelium und die Evangelien* (Düsseldorf: Patmos).

Volz, P. 1934, *Die Eschatologie der jüdischen Gemeinde*, 2nd ed. (Tübingen: Mohr-Siebeck).

Voss, M. Heerma van et al. (eds.) 1974, *Travels in the World of the Old Testament*. FS M. A. Beek (Assen: van Gorcum).

Wächter, T. 1910, *Reinheits-vorschriften im griechischen Kult*, RVV 9:1 (Giessen: Töpelmann-Ricker).

Wahlde, U. C. von 1982, "The Johannine 'Jews': A Critical Survey," *NTS* 28, 33–60.

Walter, N. 1964, *Der Thoraausleger Aristobulus* (Berlin: Akademie).

Walter, N. 1985, "Paulus und die urchristliche Tradition," *NTS* 31, 498–522.

Walter, N. 1987, "Jüdisch-hellenistische Literatur vor Philon von Alexandrien," *ANRW* II:20, 1, 67–112.

Wanke, J. 1980, "Kommentarworte. Alteste Kommentierungen von Herrenworten," *BZ* 24, 208–33.

Weinreich, O. 1919, "Stiftung und Kultsatzungen eines Privatheiligtums in Philadelphia in Lydien," *SHAW.PH*, 16 (Heidelberg: Winter) 1–68.

Westcott, B. F. 1892, *The Gospel according to John* (London: Murray).

Wibbing, S. 1959, *Die Tugend – und Lasterkataloge im Neuen Testament* (Berlin: Töpelmann).

Wilcox, M. 1977, "'Upon the Tree' – Deut 21:22–23 in the New Testament," *JBL* 96, 85–99.

Wilson, J. A. 1962, "Egypt," *IDB* 2, 39–66.

Windisch, H. 1909, *Der messianische Krieg und das Urchristentum* (Tübingen: Mohr-Siebeck).

Windisch, H. 1924, *Der zweite Korintherbrief*, MeyerK (Göttingen: Vandenhoeck & Ruprecht, repr. 1970).

Witkamp, L. T. 1985, "The Use of Traditions in John 5:1–18," *JSNT* 25, 19–47.

Witkamp, L. T. 1986, *Jesus van Nazareth in de gemeente van Johannes. Over de interaktie van traditie en ervaring* (Kampen: Van den Berg).

Wolfson, H. A. 1948, *Philo*, 1–2 (Cambridge, Mass.: Harvard University Press).

Wright, A. G. 1966, "The Literary Genre Midrash," *CBQ* 28, 105–38 and 417–57.

Zeitlin, S. 1935–36, "The Jews, Race, Nation, or Religion," *JQR* 36, 313–47.

Zeitlin, S. 1965, "Proselytes and Proselytism during the Second Commonwealth and the Early Tannaitic Period," in *Harry Austryn Wolfson Jubilee Volume on the Occasion of His Seventy-fifth Birthday*, 2, English Section (Jerusalem: American Academy of Research) 871–81.

Index of References

345

Old Testament Apocrypha

Pseudepigrapha

Josephus

The Dead Sea Scrolls (Qumran)

Church Fathers et aliter

Rabbinic Literature

Greek and Latin Authors

Index of Modern Authors

Index of Subjects

Note: Only general references to books of the Bible and ancient authors appear in this index. Specific references are to be found in the Index of References.